MISSOURI LAW *and the* AMERICAN CONSCIENCE

MISSOURI LAW *and the* AMERICAN CONSCIENCE

HISTORICAL RIGHTS & WRONGS

Edited by Kenneth H. Winn

UNIVERSITY OF MISSOURI PRESS
Columbia

University of Missouri Press, Columbia, Missouri 65211
Printed and bound in the United States of America

First paperback printing, 2021.

ISBN: 978-0-8262-2251-0 (paperback : alk. paper)
Library of Congress Control Number: 2015960094

∞™ This paper meets the requirements of the
American National Standard for Permanence of Paper
for Printed Library Materials, Z39.48, 1984.

Typefaces: Caslon, Avenir

Contents

MISSOURI LAW *and the* AMERICAN CONSCIENCE

INTRODUCTION

Searching for Rights in Missouri History

Kenneth H. Winn

THE ESSAYS IN THIS volume examine and explain Missouri law, and in so doing, illumine the American past. Legal history is uniquely suited to helping us understand our history as people. When the territory of the Louisiana Purchase transferred from France to the United States, lawyers rushed in faster than farmers.[1] Ever since, practically every issue one can imagine—some of great importance—has become an issue of law, and so it continues, as this volume shows, to the present day.

As Missouri's new state archivist in the early 1990s, I looked at a small collection of circuit court records from Pemiscot County from the 1920s. Pemiscot is one of the most impoverished and sparsely settled counties located in Missouri's "Bootheel." There were neither famous names nor famous cases in the records, but I was bowled over by the picture of ordinary life that emerged from the routine discussions of prohibition, race relations, politics, and the important environmental change that was transforming the region at the time. That experience convinced me that such records were much underused by historians. They could provide insights into the past found nowhere else. That conviction was partially responsible for the eventual appearance of this book.[2]

While one could write very useful essays about everyday life, it is easier to see these ten essays as chapters in the story of Missourians' search for their rights. Although the essays were not chosen for this perspective, they nevertheless point in this direction. By "rights," a contentious term, I refer to a specific moral claim that transcends ordinary law and compels recognition of rights (entitlements), privileges (liberties), powers, and immunities for specific individuals or peoples.[3] These rights have proven historically adaptable: old rights lose their meaning, and new ones are "discovered" or asserted. Some chapters in this volume began as stories of political and human rights—those of women and slaves, for example. But most of the events recounted here arose from mundane, if sometimes tragic, circumstances—a car wreck, a failed marriage proposal, a murder, a juvenile's bad behavior, an insurance case, a property quarrel, an employment contract dispute. As the authors show, seemingly simple issues unexpectedly put much larger principles at stake, and the cases turned into serious power struggles that, in time, came to illustrate important issues in American society.

Several of these essays are based on information previously unknown to history. When I invited the authors to write for this volume, I asked each of them to develop a topic with scholarly rigor but write about it in an interesting way that would make it accessible to nonlawyers. The authors have attempted to explain or avoid legal phrases not familiar to educated laypersons. They, of course, have retained their own unique voices and points of view, but this basic guideline set the tone for what follows.

The chapters that resulted discuss significant topics—the uneasy incorporation of ethnic and cultural populations into the United States, political loyalty tests, the alleviation of cruelty to poor and criminally institutionalized children, the restriction on women's ability to sit on juries decades after they had won the right to vote. Some chapters tell of cases that caught the nation's attention—a slave's suit for his freedom, a woman's quest for female suffrage, a scandal that led to national judicial reform, and a fight over a tragically injured woman's "right to die." All of the controversies had lasting significance.

The book formally begins with William E. Foley's masterly essay, "Testing the Limits of American Justice: Indian Trials in Nineteenth-Century Missouri." Following the Louisiana Purchase, the territory soon to be known as Missouri became a testing ground for attempts by U.S. authorities to force native peoples before the American bar of justice. Foley shows how Missouri's nineteenth-century Indian cases ran the gamut from criminal proceedings involving charges of murder, assault, and stealing to civil suits alleging illegal enslavement and contesting inheritance rights. These cross-cultural judicial proceedings evoked strong feelings, raised complicated legal and policy questions, underscored the differences between Indian and white notions of justice, and revealed the declining fortunes of once-dominant Indian nations. Beyond that, the records they generated give voice to lesser-known native people whose compelling stories had been long since forgotten.

The cultural divide between Native Americans and whites during the territorial period was vast, but divisions within the white community were endemic, if far less deadly. For instance, an unusual frontier sexual arrangement started a bitter quarrel that casts light on the period's social and economic tension. In "The Frown of Fortune: George Sibley, Breach of Promise, and Anglo-Francophone Conflict on the Missouri Frontier," I tell the previously unknown story of the 1813 lawsuit against George Sibley for breach of promise. Well remembered by historians, Sibley began his career as a politically connected factor, or government Indian trader, at remote Fort Osage, a military post near present-day Kansas City. During his service, the thirty-year-old Sibley became involved with a fifteen-year-old French girl named Ellen Lorr. She later claimed that he wrote out a marriage contract; in his version, he contracted her to be his concubine. When Sibley failed to formally marry Lorr upon their return to St. Louis, she sued him for breaching his promise of marriage. Enter the wealthy and powerful Indian trader Pierre Chouteau, an economic rival and personal enemy of Sibley's. When Chouteau stepped in on the girl's behalf, the legal battle proved much less unequal than it had first seemed. What had begun years before as a personal quarrel between Sibley and Chouteau blossomed into a larger contest—with Lorr now as its pawn—between the ethnic French and the Yankee newcomers.

One thing that both the "Yankees" (that is Easterners, as even people from Virginia and Kentucky were once locally called), and the Francophones (like the Chouteaus) had in common in the period was a devotion to the institution of slavery. But as in all species of ownership, there were legal rules that slaveholders had to obey in handling their human property if they wanted to keep it. For example, people did not take their slaves to live in free states or territories and expect to retain them, even should they eventually return to a slave state. If they violated basic rules like these they lost their property—or at least that is the way Missouri slave laws worked during most of the antebellum years.

Then on April 6, 1846, an obscure St. Louis slave represented by an obscure lawyer petitioned the local circuit court to release him from his bondage. What made this case so unusual was neither the slave nor the grounds for his petition. It was that powerful white men began arguing about his freedom. When the United States Supreme Court finally decided the Dred Scott case eleven years later, it shook the country to its foundation, and edged it closer to civil war. Given the national implications of the federal decision historians have tended to skip over the state's legal proceedings, but they are interesting and important in their own right. In "The Politics of Slavery and Missouri's First Elected Supreme Court: *Dred Scott v. Emerson,*" Paul Finkelman argues that Missouri's shift from gubernatorial appointment to popular election of Supreme Court judges had tragic effect. The first judicial election occurred in

1851. The following year, overruling nearly thirty years of precedent as well as the St. Louis Circuit Court that freed Scott, the newly elected judges embraced the passion of their time and paved the way for a national catastrophe.

That catastrophe, the Civil War, created generations of bitterness. In its wake, military might and law were used to see that men like those who sat on the Dred Scott case would never make judicial decisions again. In 1865, delegates to a constitutional convention in St. Louis wrote the "Drake Constitution," named after its master spirit, Charles Drake. They ambitiously sought to remake Missouri socially and politically, beginning with the emancipation of the slaves. To make sure their work could never be undone, they instituted harsh loyalty oaths that disenfranchised those who had supported or even sympathized with the Confederacy, and they set out to remake the state's judiciary. In "The Judicial Ouster Ordinance of 1865 and Radical Reconstruction of Missouri," historian Dennis W. Belcher recounts how the Drake Convention enacted a controversial judicial ouster ordinance, potentially removing all judicial officers—from Supreme Court judges down to county sheriffs—to be replaced as "Radical" Governor Thomas Fletcher saw fit. In the end, not all of the six hundred judicial officials who fell under the ordinance lost their positions. But the geographical areas in which Radicals suspected judicial officials of harboring pro-Southern, or even simply anti-Radical, sentiments, felt the effect of the ordinance keenly. This was nowhere truer than in those counties along central Missouri's "Little Dixie" slave belt.

In "Disfranchised and Degraded: Virginia L. Minor and the Constitutional Case for Women's Suffrage," historian Bonnie Stepenoff asks whether voting is a fundamental human right. Voting was denied to black men before the war and pro-Southern white men afterward, but it was denied to Missouri women the whole of the nineteenth century. The era's political feminists saw the prohibition against women voters as demeaning and a rejection of their full rights of human autonomy. In 1872 St. Louisan Virginia Minor, in a politically calculated act, attempted to register to vote. When the registrar refused to let her do so she sued him. In 1874, denied relief by local and state courts, Minor took her case to the United States Supreme Court. There, her attorney husband, Francis, argued on her behalf that voting was one of the "privileges and immunities" of citizenship guaranteed by the new Fourteenth Amendment that the nation had adopted to guarantee the freedmen suffrage after the Civil War. In a unanimous vote the justices disagreed, saying that the power to enfranchise citizens still remained with the individual states. Though Minor was unsuccessful in suit, Stepenoff argues that the Minor case made activists and scholars reexamine the meaning of citizenship in a democratic republic—a concept that continues to raise questions today.

If women lacked full civil rights, children had almost no rights. They were the most dependent and dispossessed of all humans. For most of its history Missouri's treatment of juvenile criminals, delinquents, and the poor (the three were rarely distinguished) reads like a Charles Dickens novel. There is probably nothing surprising about that; indeed, juvenile justice fared little worse in Missouri than it did across the rest of the nation. What *is* surprising is that in the 1970s, Missouri, guided by innovative professionals and backed by prominent state politicians, changed its ways, becoming a "guiding light of reform" to others. Douglas E. Abrams's essay, "Missouri's Long Road to Juvenile Justice," offers a sweeping history of how Missouri's long-ineffectual and often disturbing history of juvenile justice underwent a surprising transformation largely as a result of successful government policies.

Missouri's juvenile justice system became a national model, but even before it did, the state's unique method of judicial selection, adopted in 1940, began spreading across the country. The "Missouri Court Plan" replaced the elective Supreme Court created prior to the Dred Scott case with a complex appointive system that covered all of the courts of appeal and the Kansas City and St. Louis circuit judges. This new method of judicial appointment emerged most immediately out of a bitter 1938 clash between Kansas City political boss Thomas Pendergast and the state's ambitious governor, Lloyd Stark. But the "non-partisan court plan" was actually the product of a long struggle over how democratic values and the desire for professional merit could be reconciled. In "The Living Example: Laurance M. Hyde and the Missouri Nonpartisan Court Plan," I explain how Missouri Supreme Court Judge Laurance Hyde, a Depression-era Republican, became not only the country's first "non-partisan" judge, but how he was recognized as the embodiment of a system whose exaltation of political disinterest brought it credit and Hyde fame.

No matter how judges were selected in 1940, those judges did not see women jurors. Women's suffrage became a reality in Missouri in 1920, but while women could vote, hold office, and even be judges, they could not serve on a jury. In "Constitutional Mollycoddling: How Women Won the Right to Serve as Jurors in Missouri (but only if they wanted to)," Karen Anderson Winn relates Missouri's part in a national movement, describing how women's organizations like the Missouri League of Women Voters had been fighting for the right of females to serve on juries since the early 1920s. Unlike the struggles of women in Kansas, Iowa, and Illinois, however, their efforts remained ineffectual until World War II, when the enormous demand for female labor subverted traditional gender stereotypes and finally paved the way for women's jury service during a wartime state constitutional convention. As Winn shows, the constitutional convention debates offer a particularly unique forum to understand how mid-century Missouri male politicians understood the proper role of women in American society.

Like women's jury service, many of these essays describe a quest for the right to break loose of legal constraints imposed by others. Under baseball's reserve clause players had no professional will of their own. During their short playing careers their bonds might have been gilded, but bound they were nonetheless, to rich baseball owners who treated their players as suited their fancy, trading them from one team to another across the continent, or effectively ending their careers with little notice. One can hardly imagine such a situation in a different profession. In "Shaking the Shackles: Curt Flood's Challenge to Baseball's Reserve Clause," law professor James R. Devine recounts the fabled career of Curt Flood. From 1958 to 1969, Flood played center field for the St. Louis Cardinals and batted at the top of the order. He won seven "Gold Glove" awards in a row and played on three all-star teams and in several World Series. In the wake of the 1969 National League Baseball strike, the team, which included a remarkable number of Hall of Fame members, was broken up. Without his knowledge Flood was traded to the Philadelphia Phillies. He decided to sue to break the reserve clause that allowed baseball owners a special antitrust status. In 1972, with former Supreme Court Justice Arthur Goldberg serving as his attorney, Flood's case went to the United States Supreme Court. While Flood lost his appeal in a split decision, the decision also sounded the death knell for the reserve clause, giving way to baseball's system of "free agency" in which players got a greater say in where they'd play and for what pay.

Easy cases never make it to the United States Supreme Court—only the most vexing, complicated, or politically or socially charged do that. Thanks to important advances in medical technology, society is faced with ethical questions that did not exist only a few decades ago. The concept of a "right to die" has only emerged in the last few decades, and it poses problems as to how our society will decide hard questions, sometimes born of horrific tragedy. Taking his title from words from the Dred Scott opinion, former Missouri Supreme Court Judge Edward "Chip" Robertson, Jr., tells the story of how he and the court had to confront that decision-making process in the context of deciding whether a young woman should live or die. His "In the Midst of All Such Excitement: The Nancy Cruzan Case," concludes this volume. While providing historical context to the Cruzan case, Robertson also offers an invaluable, often amusing, and sometime poignant memoir of how the case was decided by the Missouri Supreme Court, its eventual appeal to the United States Supreme Court, and its tragic aftermath.

Americans are part of a historical stream that has no end. Robertson's essay lies at the bridge of history and memory. The Cruzan case demonstrates how the present turns into the past. Given the riches of Missouri's legal past, it is remarkable how few books have appeared about it. Unsurprisingly, the best work on Missouri's legal history concerns slavery, the Civil War era, and more recent racial issues—although worthwhile books on issues as diverse as frontier society, German immigrants, and abortion have appeared.[4] Still, while the field is ripe, the harvesters have been largely wanting. Given the increasing ease of access to court records the fallow season may have ended, but in the meantime, the essays that follow are mostly pioneering studies of their subjects.

NOTES

1. For an interesting overview of the legal professions' rapid development in the early territorial period, see Stuart Banner, *Legal Systems in Conflict: Property and Sovereignty in Missouri, 1750–1860* (Norman: University of Oklahoma Press, 2000), 101–21.

2. Although it focuses on St. Louis Circuit Court records, an account of my effort to broaden interest in the value of legal records can be found is "Making the Case: Using Court Records to Win Friends and Influence Politicians," in Larry J. Hackman, ed., *Many Happy Returns: Advocacy and the Development of Archives* (Chicago: Society of American Archivists, 2011), 279–96.

3. The number of works theorizing and defining "rights" is immense and beyond the scope of this essay. I have, however, found Richard Primus's history of the evolutionary nature of American rights very useful. See *The American Language of Rights* (New York: Cambridge University Press, 1999).

4. For a fine book on the colonial territorial period, see Banner, *Legal Systems in Conflict*; on slavery, see Lea VanderVelde, *Redemption Songs: Suing for Freedom before Dred Scott* (New York: Oxford University Press, 2014); Melton A. McLaurin, *Celia, a Slave* (Athens: University of Georgia Press, 1991). The volume of material on the Dred Scott case is enormous, and Missouri law and society mostly serve as a prologue to the federal case. Those books with a stronger Missouri focus include VanderVelde's *Mrs. Dred Scott: A Life on Slavery's Frontier* (New York: Oxford

University Press); David T. Konig and Paul Finkelman, and Christopher Alan Bracey, *The Dred Scott Case: Historical and Contemporary Perspectives on Race and Law* (Athens, Ohio: Ohio University Press, 2010); Kenneth C. Kaufmann, *Dred Scott's Advocate: A Biography of Roswell M. Field* (Columbia: University of Missouri Press, 1996); Walter Ehrlich, *They Have No Rights: Dred Scott's Struggle for Freedom* (Westport, CN: Greenwood Press, 1979). Harriet C. Frazier has written prolifically about slavery, race, and crime. See her *Death Sentences in Missouri, 1803–2005: A History and Comprehensive Registry of Legal Executions, Pardons, and Commutations* (Jefferson, NC: McFarland, 2006); *Lynchings in Missouri, 1803–1981* (Jefferson, NC: McFarland, 2009); *Runaway and Freed Missouri Slaves and Those Who Helped Them, 1763–1865* (Jefferson, NC: McFarland, 2004); and *Slavery and Crime in Missouri, 1773–1865* (Jefferson, NC: McFarland, 2001). Dennis K. Bowman has written three Civil War–era studies of note, including *Abiel Leonard, Yankee Slaveholder, Eminent Jurist, and Passionate Unionist* (Lewiston, NY: E. Mellen Press, 2002); *Lincoln and Citizens' Rights in Civil War Missouri: Balancing Freedom and Security* (Baton Rouge: Louisiana State University Press, 2011); *Lincoln's Resolute Unionist: Hamilton Gamble, Dred Scott Dissenter and Missouri's Civil War Governor* (Baton Rouge, LA: LSU Press, 2006). Also of interest is his *The Original Rush Limbaugh: Lawyer, Legislator, and Civil Libertarian* (Columbia: University of Missouri Press, 2012). On German Missourians and World War I, see Petra DeWitt, *Degrees of Allegiance Harassment and Loyalty in Missouri's German-American Community during World War I* (Athens: Ohio University Press, 2012). Gerald T. Dunne's *The Missouri Supreme Court: From Dred Scott to Nancy Cruzan* (Columbia: University of Missouri Press, 1993) is helpful, as are Lawrence Larsen's many books, including *Federal Justice in Western Missouri: The Judges, the Cases, the Times* (Columbia: University of Missouri Press, 1994). On the abortion debate, see Cynthia Gorney, *Articles of Faith: a Frontline History of the Abortion Wars* (New York, NY: Simon & Schuster, 1998). Joshua M. Dunn has explored the Kansas City school desegregation debacle in *Complex Justice: The Case of Missouri v. Jenkins* (Chapel Hill: University of North Carolina Press, 2008.) Finally, there are a number of biographies of Curt Flood, but readers specifically interested in the federal reserve clause should see Stuart Banner, *The Baseball Trust: A History of Baseball's Anti-Trust Exemption* (New York: Oxford University Press, 2013).

CHAPTER ONE

Testing the Limits of American Justice
Indian Trials in Nineteenth-Century Missouri

William E. Foley

WHILE RETURNING FROM THE Pacific in the fall of 1806, Captains Meriwether Lewis and William Clark hungered for news of events that had transpired during their twenty-eight–month absence. A brief encounter with veteran trader James Aird, then on his way up the Missouri, yielded several tantalizing tidbits, including word of the recent jailings in St. Louis of several Indians accused of murder. Two had been tried in Louisiana's territorial superior court, found guilty, and hanged.[1] Far more than subjects for idle river gossip, the trials and executions conveyed a message of lasting import for Native Americans in the trans-Mississippi domains lately claimed by the United States. They signaled the U.S. government's resolve to subject the region's indigenous populace to the dictates of a legal system that differed markedly from the ways of customary Indian law.

Incarceration and hangings may have been the norm for Anglo-Americans intent on assigning blame and punishing offenders, but those practices seemed bizarre to Indian people who had developed systems of ritual recompense that deflected individual punishment and emphasized reciprocity. In the indigenous world, maintaining peace and harmony among the principal disputants was no less important than seeking retribution. While their judicial settlements typically employed restitution, compensation, and banishment as methods for satisfying grieving and injured parties, Indians were not immune from the desire for revenge. In cases of wanton murder, aggrieved tribal members believed it was justifiable to take other lives as recompense for their losses, so long as the retaliation was direct and proportional. The victims did not have to be the actual perpetrators, and that tolerance for substitutions affords a timely reminder that Indian justice was different but not necessarily more benign.[2]

The 1806 trials and executions in St. Louis prefigured major changes to the policies and practices that had governed Indian-white relations in the Louisiana Territory during the French and Spanish regimes. Under their auspices the outnumbered local authorities typically acquiesced to native expectations and embraced restitution and compensation as the preferred solutions for all but the most wanton crimes.[3] The willingness of mid-America's French Creole populace to respect the traditions and autonomy of their powerful Indian neighbors enabled them to coexist in relative harmony and to forge mutually beneficial trading partnerships.[4]

Indian-white killings were a rarity in Upper Louisiana before 1804, but following the territory's transfer to the United States, an influx of land-hungry new settlers with an anti-Indian mindset increased the potential for violent clashes and casualties. When incoming Americans killed five members of the Kickapoo tribe on the Meramec River in 1804, three youthful and disgruntled tribal members struck back by taking the lives of two white hunters at the mouth of the Osage River. General James Wilkinson, Louisiana's newly appointed territorial governor, ordered Kickapoo leaders to hand over the perpetrators, but he made no effort to apprehend the white killers whose actions had provoked the retaliatory attack.[5]

Notwithstanding his forceful response, Governor Wilkinson remained mindful of the residual power and influence of the western tribes and the limited military forces at his disposal. Both he and his Indian counterparts had to walk a fine line. Not wishing to further exacerbate tensions with the Americans, the Kickapoo eventually heeded Wilkinson's directives and surrendered Ouipinicka and Ouabesca to the authorities in St. Louis. While conferring with U.S. officials, tribal leaders invoked the time-honored custom of offering compensation to atone for their misdeeds. In a ritual of recompense intended to settle the matter, a Kickapoo spokesman presented Governor Wilkinson with a white wampum belt and extended his hand in friendship to the American president:

> My father I pray you to listen to me today. I give my hand to my great Father who lives far east on the sea coast and I bring with me this belt to cover the blood which has been spilled with the blood of my father and to erase it from the ground. It is in this way our differences have always been arranged. It is this white belt, which we have always used for this purpose. We therefore hope for your attention.[6]

This was not what the officials in St. Louis had in mind. They were focused on having the U.S. government mete out blame and punishment. Under questioning by the governor in the presence of the Kickapoo leaders, Ouabesca and Ouipinicaka acknowledged their participation in the 1805 Osage River killings. In an effort to shield his tribal elders, Ouabesca stated that he had acted like a fool and lamented that his folly had caused them great pain and grief. For his part, Ouipinicaka simply claimed that he had fallen victim to bad advice.[7] From the governor's point of view, their confessions justified his actions.

In a parallel case, a deputation of Winnebago (Puant) headmen delivered two youthful tribesmen accused of killing a French trader in the Indiana Territory. During an audience with the governor, one frustrated Winnebago elder complained that it was becoming increasingly difficult to restrain the excesses of youthful warriors acting under the influence of alcohol. His lament, no doubt, was intended to suggest that by allowing the illicit liquor traffic to flourish in the Indian country largely unchecked, the American authorities shared the blame for these incidents. Kennebec, one of the accused, admitted that he had been drunk, while the other, Saramenie, attributed his actions to anger emanating from a domestic dispute.[8] Unmoved, Governor Wilkinson, acting under the authority of an 1802 federal statute authorizing U.S. territorial courts to try cases involving Indians who committed crimes within their jurisdictions, issued a commission of *oyer* and *terminer* directing Louisiana's superior court justices to empanel a grand jury to consider the charges.[9]

Indians routinely came and went in St. Louis, but the lingering presence of Winnebago and Kickapoo delegations waiting to learn the fate of their incarcerated tribal brothers provoked an unfortunate altercation between Samuel Hammond, Jr., and Maichiwaighe, a visiting Kickapoo chieftain. When the inebriated Indian brandished his tomahawk in a menacing way, Hammond overreacted by first shooting him and then stabbing him to death. A hastily summoned coroner's jury quickly exonerated the young American who insisted he had acted to defend Colonel Return J. Meigs, Jr., a superior court justice who was standing nearby.[10]

The following week a grand jury indicted the Kickapoo and Winnebago prisoners on charges of murder, but not surprisingly it declined to present a bill against Hammond even though the territory's attorney general had recommended charges against him as well, albeit for partisan political motives unrelated to the case.[11] The next day Judges Meigs and John B. C. Lucas placed the cases of *U.S. v. Ouabesca* and *U.S. v. Ouipinicaka* on the docket for trial. The absence of any further action in the Winnebago cases suggests that the justices had decided that their jurisdiction did not extend to crimes committed in a neighboring territory.[12]

The judges appointed attorneys to represent the Kickapoo defendants, and following brief trials, juries found both guilty of murder. The next morning Judge Meigs sentenced the condemned Indians to be hanged and their executions were carried out four days later.[13] The Americans took satisfaction in the outcomes, but Governor Wilkinson wisely chose to grant Hononquise, also implicated in the Osage River killings, a full and complete pardon.[14] The governor's decision signaled his awareness of Indian adherence to the principle of *lex talionis,* requiring equal and direct retribution. Any attempt to execute three persons for causing the deaths of only two would have been a blatant violation of customary Indian practices.

Notwithstanding this partial nod to native judicial precepts, the 1806 proceedings laid bare the stark differences between the Indian and white systems of justice and conflict resolution and hampered U.S. relations with the powerful Kickapoo nation for years to come. On the eve of the War of 1812, a Kickapoo chief reminded the Americans of the grave injustices his tribe had suffered at their hands:

> We some few years ago went to St. Louis to deliver up murderers, and lost one of our Chiefs at that place—He was killed by one of your young men and you did not deliver up the Murderer, or punish him yourself—You ask us to do justice—You did not do us that justice you ought to have done. How can you suppose that the red skins can have sense, when you, the White skins have none, by not giving us satisfaction for the death of our Chief?[15]

The unhappy events in Louisiana's territorial capital six years earlier remained indelibly imprinted on the tribal memory, and the lingering resentments engendered by those recollections no doubt helped persuade the defiant Kickapoo to join the Indian confederacy organized by the Shawnee chieftain Tecumseh for the purpose of resisting further American usurpation of their lands and livelihoods.[16]

Murder cases evoked strong passions on both sides of the Indian-white divide and remained by far the toughest to adjudicate. A spate of killings along the lower Missouri in 1808 renewed alarm in the American settlements and produced calls for immediate action.[17] Governor Meriwether Lewis, who had replaced Wilkinson, was quick to condemn the killings and reprimand Sac and Ioway leaders for failing to place the alleged perpetrators in U.S. custody. Eventually they acceded to his demands. The Ioway identified Mera Nautais and MaxúThka (also known as Mashashka and White Cloud) as members of the band that had killed the two French traders, but when transferred to

American custody both men claimed self-defense, arguing that they had come under attack and not returned fire until their assailants wounded one of their companions.[18]

The Sacs, for their part, initially declined to hand over Little Crow, who was wanted for an unrelated killing. In traditional Indian fashion they offered instead to ransom him by paying any number of horses demanded by the deceased victim's family. Their plea fell on deaf ears even though U.S. agents regularly resorted to "covering the dead" with gifts when whites killed Indians and went unpunished.[19] This legal double standard was common enough for the secretary of war to authorize two hundred dollars as the usual payment for each wrongful Indian death. After the Americans rejected the Sac offer and threatened to use armed force, tribal authorities relinquished Little Crow to territorial officials under protest, insisting that the killing had been accidental.[20]

Judge Lucas summoned a grand jury to consider the charges against the alleged felons and instructed the jury panel to treat the accused Indians as they would any citizens.[21] His admonition proved no match for the locally pervasive anti-Indian sentiment. Grand jurors rushed to indict all three of the accused on charges of murder, and the sheriff hired a hangman even before the trials got under way. Judge Lucas appointed attorneys to represent the defendants and ordered the clerk and the sheriff to adhere to established legal procedures.

The Ioways, White Cloud and Mera Nautais, were the first to be tried, and juries found them both guilty. When the condemned men returned to the courtroom for sentencing three days later, their court-appointed defense attorney Rufus Easton spent nearly two hours raising legal objections justifying a motion for a new trial. The justices took his request under advisement and proceeded to the trial of Little Crow. Once again a jury returned a guilty verdict, but in this instance the judges immediately sentenced the Sac defendant to be hanged two days later. The hasty sentencing and the silence of his attorneys suggests that the evidence of Little Crow's guilt was a good deal more palpable than the case for convicting White Cloud and Mera Nautais.[22]

The following day Judges Lucas and Otho Shrader granted Easton's request for a new trial in the Ioway cases. Under the circumstances, Governor Lewis felt compelled to stay Little Crow's execution pending a final verdict in the Ioway trials. With representatives of both tribes regularly in the courtroom, he was eager to avoid any appearance of favoritism. Attempts to expedite a second trial went awry as wrangling over jury selection forced a postponement. As the legal maneuvering dragged on, local residents grew impatient, and the hundred or so Ioway and Sac Indians who had come to observe the trials beseeched Governor Lewis and U.S. Indian Agent Clark to end the ordeal with pardons. Experience had taught them that a plea for executive clemency was probably their best hope.[23]

During the second Ioway trial the judges' insistence on a careful screening of potential jurors and their silencing of courtroom outbursts from spectators shouting "hang them, hang them!" moved one observer to comment that their "conduct in this trial and some of their decisions therein would grace even Westminster Hall." After finally receiving the case the jurors deadlocked, with five of them initially favoring acquittal. Their willingness to defy popular opinion suggests that the defendants likely had fired in self-defense. Unable to reach a verdict, the jurors adjourned their deliberations at 1:00 a.m. The following day the holdouts eventually relented and agreed to convict.[24]

The final chapter in these cases was yet to be written. When the defendants were brought back into the courtroom for sentencing, their attorneys filed a barrage of legal challenges. The judges dismissed most of them, but they agreed to take under advisement an assertion that the 1802 law regulating Indian intercourse with the United States failed to assign U.S. officials jurisdiction over Indians who injured whites in Indian country. After carefully reviewing the pertinent federal statutes, Judge Lucas sustained defense pleas to arrest the judgment and dismiss all charges.[25]

Not pleased, Governor Lewis ordered the prisoners returned to the local jail to await a review of the controversial decision. The deputy attorney general asked Judge Lucas to provide the governor with a full explanation of his ruling, but the response failed to satisfy Lewis who communicated his unhappiness to superiors in the national capital. Lucas, however, was on firm legal ground, and his ruling stood.[26]

The outcome occasioned far less outrage on the Potomac than it did in St. Louis. Jefferson urged Lewis to exercise caution noting that:

> We find it difficult, with our regular government, to take & punish a murderer of an Indian—Indeed I believe we have never been able to do it in a single instance. They have their difficulties also, & require time—in fact it is a case where indulgence on both sides is just and necessary to prevent the two nations from being perpetually committed to war by the acts of the most vagabond & ungovernable of their members.[27]

For its part Congress waited until 1817 to change the law and finally grant U.S. officials jurisdiction over crimes committed in the Indian country.[28]

Believing that Indians would view any leniency as weakness, Governor Lewis refused to free the Ioway prisoners and dissuaded the territorial judges from issuing a writ of *habeas corpus* for their release. As a result White Cloud and Mera Nautais languished in the St. Louis jail for nearly a year until their escape, perhaps with assistance, finally ended the stalemate.

A short time later Lewis departed for Washington, D.C., but died while en route to the capital. Acting Governor Frederick Bates, who had long been at odds with Lewis on most matters, countermanded the 1808 arrest warrant after noting the folly of returning the Ioway to U.S. custody, since federal officials lacked legal authority to try them. He concluded that under the circumstances, "the transgression ought to be forgotten as silently as possible."[29]

Bates's action closed the case on the Ioways, but Little Crow still remained in jail. Since the murder for which he had been convicted was committed at a place within the court's jurisdiction, Little Crow's attorney could not use the legal argument that had freed the Ioways. Prior to his departure Lewis had remained noncommittal about the condemned man's future, fearing no doubt that his execution would incite Sac revenge/retaliation. In all likelihood he simply intended to detain him indefinitely, but Bates's decision not to pursue the Ioway fugitives forced a reassessment of the prisoner's status.

Indian agent William Clark recommended that President James Madison pardon him in return for Sac promises of future good behavior. The presidential pardon ended Little Crow's personal ordeal, but Clark's recommendation for clemency came back to haunt him during his unsuccessful 1820 gubernatorial campaign when his opponents used it to label him an Indian lover.[30] The protracted and costly litigation in these cases left a sour taste in almost everyone's mouth.[31] While the defendants avoided execution, tribal members viewed their lengthy incarceration and public humiliation as cruel and inhumane. By contrast most whites decried a judicial process that abetted killers and allowed them to escape their just deserts.

Nonetheless, Indians continued to frequent the territorial capital on a regular basis, and local citizens generally paid them little heed. A deadly domestic altercation involving a man and a woman from the Kickapoo nation did attract considerable public notice in 1811 and prompt a rare attempt by U.S. officials to intervene in a dispute between Indians. In the case of *U.S. v. Askinawa,* the Kickapoo defendant was brought into the territorial superior court to face charges in the death of his female companion, Orthepya. According to eyewitness accounts, both were intoxicated and began arguing prior to Askinawa's striking her in the neck with a bunch of arrows when she attempted to flee with another Indian. The victim ran into a nearby blacksmith shop where she collapsed and died almost instantly from a severed jugular vein. Following a formal inquest, a grand jury indicted Askinawa on a charge of murder, and the authorities placed him in the city jail where he remained for nearly four months. The public spectacle of the dying woman's final moments undoubtedly contributed to the impromptu decision to prefer charges against her assailant.

Once at trial the defendant's court-appointed attorneys challenged the court's right to hear the case. They contended an Indian was neither a citizen nor an alien but a creature *sui generis* and therefore immune from trial on criminal charges in a U.S. court. The trial dragged on for three days, but the jury took only twenty minutes to render a not guilty verdict that allowed the defendant to rejoin his people.[32]

Askinawa's release for killing another Indian failed to provoke a public outcry, but most territorial residents continued to believe that the courts were far too lenient in their dealings with accused Indians. When three Indians were brought to St. Louis in 1814 on charges of having killed Abraham Eastwood, the *Missouri Gazette's* fiery editor Joseph Charless unleashed a tirade against the judicial system in his newspaper. The irate journalist lambasted the current judicial practices employed in Indian murder cases: "The three Osage prisoners were brought to this place to answer for the murder of Eastwood are committed to prison to wait their trial, when we shall have the same **** acted here as was performed some time ago with the Ioway and Sac Indians." He asserted that it was becoming all too common for a band of savages to shoot a white man and subject his body to every indignity, boast of their exploits, deliver themselves up for trial in a style of frolic, plead not guilty, and be acquitted. Charless concluded his editorial with a call for the establishment of military tribunals to try Indian cases.[33]

Not amused by his scathing remarks, the judges ordered Charless to appear before them and show cause why he should not be cited for contempt. The surprised and somewhat chastened editor responded that the court had misinterpreted his remarks. He reaffirmed his respect and esteem for the laws of his country and their sovereignty. His failure to say any more on the subject suggests that after making their point the judges had dropped the matter.[34]

In the meantime, Judge Alexander Stuart had received incontrovertible evidence that the three Indians on trial were innocent pawns. In what appears to have been a classic case of offering up substitutes, the Osage had handed over captives from a rival tribe as scapegoats to stand trial. The jury acquitted the accused trio, and Judge Stuart, who had learned the real killers' identities, expressed a hope that they would be brought to justice.[35] They never were. With war raging, this was not a time for U.S. officials to take further action and risk alienating the powerful Osages who had declined to ally themselves with the British.

Given the widespread belief that the courts were predisposed not to execute Indian killers, it is hardly surprising that on at least one occasion angry local citizens seemingly chose to take matters into their own hands. During the spring of 1820 a combined Shawnee and Seminole hunting party attacked two Mississippi River travelers south of New Madrid, killing one and wounding the other. A sensational account first published in the *Jackson Missouri Herald* accused the Indians of scalping and butchering their victim.[36]

Members of a hastily summoned local militia company set out in pursuit of the alleged assassins. The militiamen fell upon their encampment and captured three Indians, but all others, including the two killers, made a hasty getaway. The captives gave up the murderers' names, but the militia captain ordered the threesome retained as hostages until the guilty parties were handed over. Tribal leaders agreed to deliver the two wanted men, but fearful that the Indians might be stalling while arranging a raid to free the hostages, the local militia commander called for reinforcements.[37]

The troops were at full strength when the chiefs returned with only one of the killers. They claimed that the other perpetrator was well armed and unwilling to surrender peacefully, but the authorities refused to budge from their demands. His eventual delivery facilitated a release of the hostages as promised. While incarcerated in the dungeon of the New Madrid jail, the two accused felons died under questionable circumstances. In a report intended to allay any suspicions concerning the causes of their deaths, the local militia commander assured his superior General William Clark that his men had acted properly and blamed the combative prisoners' premature deaths on their attempts to flee. There is no indication that Clark, then contemplating entering the state's first gubernatorial contest, conducted any sort of investigation, even though there is reason to believe that this was a classic cover-up of American vigilante justice.[38]

Missouri's Indian population declined steadily as a consequence of the U.S. government's dispossession and removal policies. As Missouri's historic tribes exited the state, Indian litigation decreased markedly. The defendants in an 1830 Missouri Indian murder trial served as poster children for the plight of the state's thinning tribal ranks. An 1829 altercation between a breakaway Ioway band desperately trying to cling to its homelands along Missouri's northern border and the inhabitants of a nearby white settlement left three whites and several Indians dead. Tribal leaders had ceded the disputed area to the U.S. government in 1824, but a dissident faction led by Great Walker, also known as Big Neck, had developed second thoughts and resisted attempts to drive its members from the region.

After the bloody clash between Big Neck's recalcitrant followers and local settlers intent on their removal, Missouri authorities called out the militia and asked federal troops from Fort Leavenworth for assistance in capturing the renegades. When the U.S. soldiers caught up with the destitute and starving culprits, they recognized that Big Neck and his band posed no real danger.[39] Once the captives were in federal hands, Missouri officials sought custody after demonstrating that the fatal encounter had taken place within the state's borders. Following the transfer, state officials jailed the prisoners in Fayette, Missouri, and the next spring grand jurors in nearby Randolph County indicted Big Neck and four others for murder. The handover to state officials so alarmed the Ioway prisoners that Indian Superintendent William Clark assigned his clerk Augustin Kennerly to accompany them as a friend and interpreter.

Credible reports that the Indians were not to blame for the incident prompted Clark to hire legal counsel to represent them. A jury, whose members realized that this distressed tribal remnant no longer threatened their safety, acquitted the defendants after determining that the settlers had in fact instigated the skirmish. The Ioway defendants avoided execution, but the ill treatment they received at the hands of the state authorities left them embittered and despairing. Big Neck, who blackened his face as a sign of mourning, ever after regretted that he had been complicit in the transfer of the land and bones of his fathers to the Americans.[40]

Notwithstanding the verdict in this case, the exodus of native people from the state failed to extinguish anti-Indian prejudice, and Missouri juries remained willing to convict native defendants even when the evidence against them was questionable. To their credit, members of the bar occasionally intervened to right such wrongs, especially in capital cases. In 1851 after a jury in Missouri's federal district court found their clients See See Sah Mah and Escotah guilty of having murdered Santa Fe trader Norris Colburn, St. Louis attorneys Frank Blair and B. Gratz Brown went to great lengths to assist the Sac Indians whom they believed had been wrongly convicted.[41]

Colburn had disappeared mysteriously in 1847 while traveling from Santa Fe to Independence, Missouri, with a large sum of money in his possession. Rumors abounded as search parties set out to find the missing man. Following the discovery of his remains several weeks later, there were contradictory reports about the likely cause of death.[42] Suspicion initially pointed to Colburn's brother-in-law, business partner, and traveling companion, Thomas Leitensdorfer, who arrived alone in Independence with the firm's cash. He explained that Colburn had been stranded in Indian country when his mule broke down, and Colburn had sent him ahead to seek help. Reports that renegade Indians likely had waylaid Colburn after he and his partner parted company helped divert attention from the prime suspect. The case remained in limbo for nearly two years until U.S. Indian interpreter Josiah Smart stepped forward to claim credit for solving the crime. In a scheme concocted to collect the thousand-dollar reward offered for the arrest and conviction of Colburn's killer, he produced a confession extorted from See See Sah Mah, a mentally retarded Sac Indian. According to the accused Indian's attorneys, the interpreter and his accomplices had coerced their client into admitting guilt "under circumstances of terror and affright."[43]

During See See Sah Mah's 1851 trial in Jefferson City, bribery, perjured testimony, and flawed and inconclusive evidence proved no obstacles to a guilty verdict. After the trial one juror defended the decision on the grounds, "Any evidence was sufficient to justify the hanging of an Indian." Federal Judge Robert W. Wells declined to overturn the jury's findings in the self-confessed See See Sah Mah's case, but he did set aside the conviction of a second defendant, Escotah, once it was demonstrated that contrary to testimony in court, See See Sah Mah had never implicated him as an accomplice. To no avail Blair and Brown objected to the judge's refusal to consider their client's mental condition, evidence of perjury and coerced testimony, or their allegations that the bailiff had liquored up jurors throughout the trial. After failing to secure a new trial the influential attorneys successfully persuaded President Millard Fillmore to commute See See Sah Mah's death sentence to life in prison.[44] They had requested a full pardon, but the president opted for commutation. Blair and Brown did their best for their client, but in the end they may have done him no favor by securing his placement in the infamous Missouri State Penitentiary where he died of unspecified causes at a time not recorded in the prison records.[45]

Attempts to prosecute whites for killing Indians were rare and universally unsuccessful in Missouri. Grand jurors had refused to indict Samuel Hammond for the 1806 killing of a Kickapoo chief, but in two other pre-statehood incidents local officials went as far as filing murder charges against whites (both identified as common laborers). In 1812 a St. Charles County grand jury indicted Robert Frazier in the death of a Huron (Wyandot) Indian known as Charles, and seven years later similar charges were preferred against

Samuel Thompson for wantonly killing an unarmed Sac Indian boy following a dispute over a pack of dogs. Little is known about the particulars in Frazier's case, but Thompson's unprovoked and deadly assault had aroused fears of Sac retaliation and produced calls from alarmed local residents for his arrest. A grand jury in the territory's northern circuit court returned a true bill against Thompson and ordered him to stand trial. At a preliminary hearing the accused entered a plea of not guilty and shortly thereafter his court-appointed attorneys, having failed to win an outright dismissal, secured a continuation to the next term. In both cases the authorities made a gesture, but in the end both Frazier and Thompson were allowed to flee the scene before they could be tried. It is worth noting that accused Indians often took flight to avoid punishment, but such similarities failed to contribute to any shared understanding.[46]

Following the acquittal of Big Neck and his cohorts in 1830, Ioway subagent Andrew Hughes leveled charges of unprovoked and bloody murder against the settlers who allegedly had instigated the northern Missouri incident, but neither state nor federal authorities ever attempted to hold them accountable.[47] The 1879 killing of Shepalina, a Modoc Indian, in the southwestern Missouri town of Seneca, was by most accounts a clear-cut case of murder. The alleged assassin, storeowner John T. Albert, reportedly shot and killed the Indian in cold blood during a dispute over the sale of a pair of boots. With images of Little Big Horn freshly etched in their minds, Seneca's anxious inhabitants worried that Modocs from the nearby Indian Territory (present-day Oklahoma) might launch a retaliatory raid against their town to avenge Shepalina's death. Officials in the Indian agency, with assistance from tribal leaders, managed to keep the peace, but their efforts to bring the killer to justice eventually ended in defeat.

An agent who represented the Indians at a preliminary hearing aptly noted that most Newton County residents believed that "an Indian has no rights that a white man is bound to respect." His assessment proved to be remarkably prescient. The best the authorities could muster in the case was an indictment for manslaughter in the third degree, and following a series of delays and two mistrials prosecutors failed to sustain even those nominal charges. In 1881 a Neosho jury exonerated Albert from any responsibility for Shepalina's death, and the merchant returned to Seneca where the following year he won election as the town's mayor.[48]

While murder cases attracted far more attention than others, Missouri officials occasionally attempted to prosecute whites on the lesser charge of assaulting an Indian. An early and unique case in Cape Girardeau County offers the only known instance in which such charges resulted in a conviction. In that 1805 proceeding tried in the court of quarter sessions, William Harper pled guilty to having beaten, wounded, and endangered the life of a Delaware man known as Raccoon, causing the judges to fine Harper fifteen dollars and place him on a year's probation. It was likely no mere happenstance that Louis Lorimier, one of the judges who heard the case, was a holdover from the Spanish regime and also married to a Shawnee woman.[49]

Conversely, in 1824 when Hiram and William Howdershell stood accused of having assaulted Kie-sha-so, a Sac Indian known as the Sun, and Kans-Kee-She known as Young Bald Eagle, a Lincoln County jury acquitted Hiram, and following the verdict Judge Nathaniel Beverly Tucker dismissed all pending charges against William. The next year in St. Louis, defendant Howell Powell's failure to appear in court to answer charges that he had assaulted an Indian resulted in the forfeiture of his fifty-dollar recognizance.[50]

Missouri courts considered Indian cases involving theft infrequently. In *U.S. v. Petitso* the Osage defendant was charged with stealing two muslin handkerchiefs and eight silver dollars from Francis Smith. At his arraignment before the St. Charles Circuit Court of Quarter Sessions in January of 1806 he entered a plea of not guilty, but the extant records offer no clues concerning the court's final determination. In all likelihood he simply fled the area. In the same county in 1817 three Ioways—Washaka, Naitaha, and Hocketon—faced charges of horse stealing, but a jury in the territory's northern circuit acquitted them. In Cape Girardeau County whites were hauled into court for stealing horses from their Indian neighbors on at least three occasions. After being indicted in 1809 for the theft of a gray mare belonging to a Delaware known as Little John, William Fuller failed to appear in court for his trial. The court issued a writ of *alias capias* but he too skipped town to evade punishment.[51]

Similar charges were filed against Hiram Hutchcraft, John Forrester, and Ruth Hutchcraft for stealing two black geldings from an unnamed Muskogee Indian and a gray mare from Choppé, a Shawnee, but Forrester and the Hutchcrafts were acquitted and granted a writ of *nolle pros* (abandonment of prosecution). Samuel Jones was brought up on charges of having stolen a horse from an Indian known as Moonshine in 1823. According to the testimony of one witness, Jones boasted that he was not afraid of being found guilty because an Indian's testimony could not be taken in court against a white man. There were, however, other witnesses in the case, and Jones apparently had second thoughts and absconded to be on the safe side.[52]

The paucity of Indian larceny cases reaching the Missouri courts was in large measure the result of a federal depredation claims system that offered government indemnification to Indians or whites for damages sustained at the hands of the other. Intended to forestall retaliation and preserve the peace, the system failed to deliver as promised, but that did not prevent Missourians from seeking to take advantage of its provisions. In 1825 Indian Superintendent William Clark, with assistance from Senator Thomas Hart Benton, unsuccessfully attempted to expedite payments to eighty-nine Missouri residents who had filed depredation claims dating as far back as 1804. The amounts they sought ranged from as little as twelve dollars to as much as several thousand dollars, and the list also contained twenty-two Delaware claims totaling 1,180 dollars for horses stolen by whites (probably including Little John's gray mare).[53]

A handful of civil cases involving Indians likewise found their way into Missouri's courtrooms. Slaves seeking freedom based on their Indian ancestry constituted one of the more interesting and unusual causes for civil action. Spain's hesitant and largely unsuccessful attempts to eliminate Indian slavery from Louisiana placed the mostly female Indian slaves in a legal limbo that emboldened at least a few to seek emancipation.[54]

A landmark Missouri Indian slave case had its origins near the end of the Spanish era when a family disagreement over the attempted sale of Marie Jean Scypion, an aging Afro-Indian slave woman and her three daughters, Celeste, Catiche, and Marguerite, landed their owners before the local magistrate.[55] When the squabbling disputants were advised that under Spanish law their slaves' Indian ancestry precluded a legal sale, they hastily dropped the idea. Marie Jean Scypion died in 1802, but shortly after Louisiana's transfer to the United States two years later, Joseph Tayon resurrected the issue when he petitioned the recently arrived American commandant Captain Amos Stoddard for permission to sell Marie Jean's children and grandchildren to Pierre Chouteau, a member of St. Louis's founding family. Two of Tayon's daughters contested the sale, declaring that the purported slaves were free Indians living voluntarily with them.[56]

The powerful Chouteaus, no strangers to Indian slaveholding, entered the fray, and the wrangling continued as the new American superior court justices attempted to sort through the tangled legal issues surrounding the case. After temporarily losing custody, Joseph Tayon filed suit in 1806 to reclaim ownership of the entire slave family. During a lengthy trial, competing witnesses presented contradictory testimony regarding the defendants' legal status. Hopes for an impartial hearing faded when the jurors elected Pierre Chouteau's brother-in-law jury foreman and ruled in favor of the plaintiff who promptly completed the sale to Chouteau.[57]

Members of the Scypion clan never gave up hope that one day they might gain their freedom, and they were among the first in line to take advantage of an 1824 Missouri statute enabling persons of color being detained illegally as slaves to sue for their freedom. When an attorney representing them petitioned the St. Louis Circuit Court to entertain a suit in their behalf, the judge denied their petition after ruling that the 1806 decision had settled the matter. On appeal the Missouri Supreme Court overturned the lower court's decision and granted a new trial in conformity with the 1824 law. When Chouteau learned that his slaves had initiated legal action against him, he ordered them whipped and confined to their quarters. That retaliation prompted the judge to require that the plaintiffs be brought into court for a physical examination and that the defendant post a surety bond as safeguard against further bodily abuse.[58]

Space limitations preclude a detailed examination of the tortuous legal path of the subsequent cases filed in behalf of Marie Jean's descendants. The first of those suits, *Marguerite v. Pierre Chouteau,* did not come to trial until 1827. Some of Missouri's best legal minds argued the case. Henry S. Geyer and Luke Lawless were members of the defense team, and Hamilton Gamble served as lead attorney for the plaintiffs. When a St. Louis jury once again declared Marguerite a slave, an evenly divided Missouri Supreme Court declined to intervene. Six years later a change in the high court's membership produced yet another appeal, and this time the justices set aside the 1806 verdicts on grounds that the jury in that case had been improperly instructed.[59]

News that the court had granted Marguerite a new trial caused other family members to seek permission to reopen their cases. By mutual consent the contesting parties agreed to have all of the cases decided with one trial and one jury in Jefferson County where the proceedings landed following two changes of venue. Unlike its predecessors this trial was a cut-and-dried affair that ended quickly. Adhering to the dictates of the state Supreme Court's most recent opinion, the jury voted unanimously to award the slaves their freedom, but on the separate count of assault it set the damages in each case at only one cent.[60]

Pierre Chouteau's attorneys appealed the decision to the Missouri Supreme Court, which upheld the lower court's verdict. Chouteau next sought relief before the U.S. Supreme Court, but in 1838 the highest court in the land ruled that it lacked jurisdiction and thereby sustained the state court rulings.[61] The decision in *Marguerite v. Pierre Chouteau, Sr.* officially ended Indian slavery in Missouri, more than three decades after Marguerite and her siblings first sought relief in the American courts.

In separate cases heard in the St. Louis Circuit Court in 1848, two enslaved women filed civil suits alleging wrongful detention and cited their Indian ancestry as justification for their release. When Nancy instituted action against Enoch Steen, a witness at her trial provided compelling evidence of Nancy's Indian heritage: "She was then a girl knocking around with the Indian squaws the same as any other wild Indian not knowing much. She dressed common like the Indians." The testimony may have betrayed a deep-seated ethnocentrism, but it persuaded jurors to rule in Nancy's favor. The verdict, affirmed on appeal the following year, gave Nancy the by then standard one-cent award for damages.[62]

The outcome in the second case is less certain. In a suit filed against Indian trader Joseph Philibert, Peggy Perryman claimed that prior to December 1, 1846, she had lived in Arkansas in the full enjoyment of her freedom and civil rights. Her father was a free man of color, and her mother, legally married to her father, was an Indian of the Blackfoot tribe. She further asserted that her maternal relatives had been free since the memory of man and were distinguished among their tribe. According to her petition, an assailant unknown to her had seized, gagged, and transported her from her home and sold her into servitude. Claiming that Philibert was illegally restraining her, she petitioned the St. Louis Circuit Court for permission to sue for freedom as a poor person. A recent 1845 Missouri statute requiring plaintiffs in freedom suits to post security to cover the costs made it more difficult for poor persons to sue, but notwithstanding the objections of Philibert's attorneys, the court allowed Perryman's case to proceed. The judge ordered that during the course of the suit the plaintiff should have reasonable access to her counsel and court hearings, should not be moved outside the court's jurisdiction, and should not be subjected to any severity on account of her application for freedom. Postponements and delays kept the case from coming to trial for nearly four years. The proceedings ended abruptly in February of 1852 when for unexplained reasons Perryman's counsel withdrew from the case and she failed to appear in court. The judge then issued a final dismissal for want of prosecution. She and the defendant may have reached an agreement to avoid further legal action or, alternatively, she may have lived the remainder of her life in servitude.[63]

By the mid-nineteenth century, Missouri's Indian population had dwindled to the point that, with the exception of a small number of mixed-blood offspring of white traders and Indian wives who filed suits to make claims on their fathers' estates, Indian litigants seldom entered the state's courtrooms. Because most Anglo-Americans held Indian marriage customs in low regard, they were quick to challenge the rights of mixed-blood relatives to share in the division of an estate. While state supreme courts sometimes claimed that principles of comity and the U.S. Constitution required them to recognize informal Indian marriage rites and customs, and inheritance rights for mixed-blood offspring, historian Mark Carroll has pointed out that in actual practice state appellate courts typically relied on habit and repute evidence in probate proceedings involving mixed-blood progeny.[64] That was the case with the rulings of the Missouri Supreme Court where mixed-race children seeking to claim a share of their father's estate generally had to demonstrate some direct evidence of parental support.

While stationed at Prairie du Chien, Colonel John W. Johnson formed a relationship with Tapissee, daughter of the Sac tribal leader Keokuk, who bore him three daughters. When he later moved to St. Louis, Johnson left his Indian wife behind, but his daughters remained in his care. He subsequently married Lucy Gooding, and together they reared and educated the three mixed-blood girls. Johnson died in 1854 and left a will with specific provisions for his daughters and their heirs, including a controversial stipulation that the family's St. Louis residence would go to one of his mixed-blood grandsons upon Lucy Johnson's death.[65]

The widow challenged the proviso and petitioned the St. Louis Land Court to grant her an assignment of dower in Johnson's real estate holdings. The outcome hinged on whether or not Johnson died without descendants capable of inheriting his estate. After a judge instructed them that if they did not "find that John W. Johnson, and the Indian woman with whom he cohabited, mutually agreed to live their whole lives together in a state of union as husband and wife, it was not a marriage, nor are the children born of such union capable of inheriting from their father," jurors ruled for the plaintiff. On appeal a court remanded the case because the jurors had been improperly instructed. Lucy Johnson died before the matter was finally resolved, but the Missouri Supreme Court eventually upheld a verdict favoring Johnson's mixed-blood heirs. Judge William Barclay Napton, speaking for the court, gave a nod to the principle of comity, but the opinion in *Johnson v. Johnson's Administrator* suggested that Johnson's lifelong care and devotion to the defendants was the most telling evidence of their legitimacy.[66]

From its earliest days St. Louis served as a hub in the North American fur trade and as home to many members of the trading community, so it is hardly surprising that other similar suits followed in the St. Louis Circuit Court. Alexander Harvey, a trader living on the upper Missouri River, had taken two Blackfoot sisters as wives, and each of them bore him a daughter. When the girls were four or five years old he placed them in the care of a brother in St.

Louis to be reared and educated. Shortly before his death in 1854 he made a will bequeathing his estate to his mixed-blood daughters, Susan and Adaline, but it was not properly executed. The St. Louis Probate Court chose to follow his wishes and ordered Harvey's property distributed to his daughters, but Harvey's half-brother Joseph Buchanan contested the settlement, asserting that the mixed-blood girls were illegitimate and not eligible to inherit their father's estate. The case eventually landed in the Missouri Supreme Court where the justices upheld the original award to Harvey's mixed-blood heirs.[67]

In a higher profile case, a former Ozarks trader and later prominent Kansas City businessman William Gillis died in 1869 leaving an estate worth a half-million dollars. During his early trading days Gillis had taken several Indian wives, including Kahketoqua, a member of the Piankashaws, who bore him a daughter known as Nancy Gillis. He had two other daughters, Sophia and Mary, by Delaware women. Unlike Johnson and Harvey, Gillis was not particularly close to his mixed-blood offspring, but he did make occasional gestures that acknowledged his paternity. He placed Sophia and Mary under the care of his aunt and provided for their schooling, and in Nancy's case he told a storekeeper to provide her with clothes and goods if she needed them and promised to take care of the bill. The court viewed those actions as sufficient evidence of legitimacy.[68]

Gillis's will made his niece Mary Troost the primary beneficiary, but he did include provisions for Sophia and Mary. Nancy, who was by then deceased, was not mentioned. Aware of their grandfather's sizeable fortune, Nancy's two children, Francis Boyer and James Charley, Jr., filed suit to claim their share. Sophia and Mary, who were given a paltry ten dollars apiece, asked for (and received) permission to be added as plaintiffs in the case. Troost opposed their action, and when she died the administrator of her estate continued to fight the claims of Gillis's mixed-blood progeny. Their case reached the Missouri Supreme Court on appeal, and the high court upheld a lower-court decision awarding the plaintiffs a child's portion of the estate.[69]

La Rivière v. La Rivière, one of the last Indian cases tried in Missouri, provided the state's high court an opportunity to reaffirm its earlier rulings on Indian inheritances and thwart an attempt by members of the La Rivière family to deny their deceased brother Antoine's mixed-blood offspring any portion of his share of their mother's estate. According to a pleading first filed by the plaintiffs in the St. Louis Circuit Court late in 1875, their father had married a mixed-blood Ponca woman in the mid-1850s and lived with her in the Indian Country of northern Nebraska until she died in 1872. In the same year Antoine's mother Mary La Rivière died and bequeathed him a share of her estate, but he was killed before it could be settled. Antoine's siblings challenged the validity of his Indian marriage and rejected the claims of his mixed-blood offspring to a share of their father's inheritance. The court's 1888 ruling upholding the mixed-race plaintiffs' claims provides a fitting finale to the story of Missouri's nineteenth-century Indian trials.[70]

Collectively, Missouri's Indian cases reveal the dramatic decline of Native American power and influence within the state's bounds during the course of the nineteenth century. In the years preceding the Louisiana Purchase, the region's dominant tribes skillfully utilized their superior numbers and their importance as trading partners to sustain their supremacy. Louisiana's Euro-American authorities recognized individual tribes as legitimate entities, chose not to challenge their judicial authority in Indian country, and used treaty-making as the preferred way for settling differences and securing legal rights to Indian lands. Once the region came under the U.S. government's control, the belief that Euro-Americans could live peacefully with native people gradually gave way to growing calls for Indian removal and, in extreme cases, for annihilation. Official efforts to uphold Indian rights and sustain tribal authority in the Indian country frustrated and angered an increasingly numerous Anglo-American populace focused on revenge and retribution. American judges and lawmakers struggled to balance those competing interests and reconcile vastly different notions of law and justice, but the Missouri cases suggest that more often than not, their solutions failed to satisfy either side. Meanwhile, as a consequence of the U.S. government's policies of forced removal and relocation, by the mid-nineteenth century only a relative handful of native people continued to reside within the state. Their diminishing numbers gradually brought this little-noticed chapter in Missouri's legal history to a close, but elsewhere proud and resilient tribal members carried on their relentless quest for justice both in and out of the courtroom.[71]

NOTES

The author thanks Judge Morris Arnold, Jay Buckley, Mark Carroll, Kathleen DuVal, Michael Everman, Patsy Luebbert, Lynn Morrow, Kenneth Winn, and Kristin Zapalac for their assistance.

1. Gary E. Moulton, ed., *The Journals of the Lewis and Clark Expedition*, vol. 8 (Lincoln: University of Nebraska Press, 1983–2001), September 3, 1806, 346–47.

2. Vine Deloria, Jr., and Clifford M. Lytle, *American Indians, American Justice* (Austin: University of Texas Press, 1983), 111–13; Kathleen DuVal, "Cross-Cultural Crime and Osage Justice in the Western Mississippi Valley, 1700–1826," *Ethnohistory*, 54 (Fall 2007), 698–700; and William E. Foley, "Different Notions of Justice: The Case of the 1808 St. Louis Murder Trials," *Gateway Heritage* 9 (Winter 1988–1989), 3. As Willard Rollings noted, only in the most extreme situations, when all else had failed, did Osage tribal leaders, who acted as mediators, sanction executions. Rollings, *The Osage: An Ethnohistorical Study of Hegemony on the Prairie-Plains* (Columbia: University of Missouri Press, 1992), 48.

3. Morris Arnold, *The Rumble of a Distant Drum* (Fayetteville: University of Arkansas Press, 2000), 123–37; Desmond H. Brown, "They Do Not Submit Themselves to the King's Law: Amerindians and Criminal Justice during the French Regime," *Manitoba Law Journal* 28 (2002), 109, and DuVal,"Cross-Cultural Crime and Osage Justice in the Western Mississippi Valley, 1700–1826," 698–707.

4. Jay Gitlin, *Bourgeois Frontier: French Towns, French Traders and American Expansion* (New Haven: Yale University Press, 2009), 26–45.

5. William Henry Harrison to Henry Dearborn, January 1, 1806, *American State Papers, Indian Affairs,* vol. 1, 705.

6. *U.S. v. Ouipinicaka* and *U.S. v. Oaubesca,* May Term 1806, Missouri Supreme Court Case Files, Box 48, Folder 1, and Box 8, Folder 15, Missouri State Archives, Jefferson City, Missouri.

7. Ibid.

8. *U.S. v. Saramenie*, Indian of the Puant Tribe, and *U.S. v. Kennebec*, Puant Indian, May term 1806, Missouri Supreme Court Case Files, Box 7, Folder 39, and Box 8, Folder 27, Missouri State Archives.

9. *2 U.S. Statutes at Large (1845),* 144. The 1804 statute dividing Louisiana into two territories and creating governments for them extended the provisions of the 1802 act to those territories. See, *2 U.S. Statutes at Large (1845)*, 289; and Commission of Oyer and Terminer, May 24, 1806, in Clarence E. Carter, ed., *Territorial Papers of the United States*, vol. 13. (Washington, D.C.: U.S. Government Printing Office, 1934–1962), 541.

10. *U.S. v. Samuel Hammond, Jr.*, May Term 1806, Missouri Supreme Court Case Files, Box 17, Folder 14, Missouri State Archives. Also see Samuel Hammond to Thomas Jefferson, May 28, 1806; Deposition of Samuel Soloman, May 27, 1806; and Findings of a Coroner's Jury, May 23, 1806, in *Territorial Papers,* vol. 13, 514–17.

11. Territorial Superior Court Minute Book I, June 3, 1806, Missouri History Museum Archives (MHMA), St. Louis. It was local politics and not a concern for the Indian victim that motivated Donaldson's surprising decision to seek an indictment against Hammond even though the coroner's jury had found his actions

justified. His attempt was in fact a not so subtle effort to embarrass young Hammond's influential uncle Samuel Hammond, Sr., who recently had parted company with Governor Wilkinson and his protégé Donaldson. Louisiana's partisan political squabbles often found their way into the local courtroom. See James L. Donaldson to William Stewart, July 5, 1806, in *Territorial Papers,* vol. 13, 538–39.

12. Territorial Superior Court Minute Book I, June 4–6, 1806, MHMA.

13. Ibid.

14. Pardon by James Wilkinson, July 8, 1806, in *Territorial Papers,* vol. 13, 542–43.

15. Pemwatome to Governor Ninian Edwards, June 8, 1812, in *Territorial Papers,* vol. 571.

16. Thomas Forsyth to William Clark, July 20, 1813, William Clark Superintendency Records, Kansas State Historical Society (KSHS), Topeka, microfilm reels 1–2.

17. For background on these killings, see Foley, "Different Notions of Justice," 2–4.

18. Ibid., 3–4.

19. William Clark frequently noted Indian insistence on "covering the dead" to effect peace and reconciliation, a practice that he likened to bribing the friends of the deceased with presents. William Clark to Thomas McKenney, [1829?], Clark Superintendency Records, KSHS, Microfilm Reels 3–4.

20. Foley, "Different Notions of Justice," 3–4.

21. Territorial Superior Court Minute Book I, July 20, 1808, MHMA; Transcript of Special Court of Oyer and Terminer, July–August 1808, in *Territorial Papers,* vol., 14, 297–312; and Instructions to Grand Jury, 1808, in Lucas Collection, MHMA.

22. Territorial Superior Court Minute Book I, July 20, 23, and 26, 1808, MHMA; Transcript of Special Court of Oyer and Terminer, July–August 1808, in *Territorial Papers,* vol. 14, 297–312; and *Missouri Gazette,* July 26, 1808.

23. Territorial Superior Court Minute Book I, July 27 and 30, 1808, MHMA; *Missouri Gazette,* August 2, 1808; and William Clark to Henry Dearborn, August 18, 1808, *Territorial Papers,* vol. 14, 208–9.

24. *Missouri Gazette,* August 10 and 17, 1808; and Transcript of Special Court of Oyer and Terminer, July–August 1808, in *Territorial Papers,* vol. 14, 297–312.

25. Territorial Superior Court Minute Book I, August 5 and 6, 1808, MHMA; and Meriwether Lewis to Thomas Jefferson, August 27, 1809 in *Territorial Papers,* vol. 14, 293–97.

26. John B. C. Lucas to Henry Dearborn, February 10, 1807, Letters Received by the Secretary of War Relative to Indian Affairs, Record Group 107, National Archives, Washington, D.C. Microfilm Series M271; rough notes of Judge Lucas, July 1808, Edward Hempstead to Lucas, August 18, 1808, and Lucas to

Hempstead, September 1, 1808, all in Lucas Collection, MHMA; Meriwether Lewis to Thomas Jefferson, August 27, 1809; and William Clark to Henry Dearborn, August 18, 1808, in *Territorial Papers,* vol. 14, 293–97 and 208–9.

27. Thomas Jefferson to Meriwether Lewis, August 21, 1808, in *Territorial Papers,* vol. 14, 219–21.

28. *3 U.S. Statutes at Large (1846),* 383.

29. *Missouri Gazette,* August 17, 1808 and July 26, 1809; Meriwether Lewis to Thomas Jefferson, August 27, 1809, in *Territorial Papers,* vol. 14, 293–297; Captain Horatio Stark to Meriwether Lewis and William Clark, September 15, 1809, National Archives, Microfilm Series M271; and Proclamation of Frederick Bates, October 30, 1809, and Bates to Stark, September 26, 1809 in Thomas M. Marshall, ed., *The Life and Papers of Frederick Bates,* vol. 2 (St. Louis: Missouri Historical Society, 1926), 102, 83–86.

30. *Missouri Gazette,* October 4, 1809; Pardon issued by President James Madison, February 25, 1810, copy in Territorial Superior Court Minute Book II, 1810. On the charges that Clark was biased in favor of Indians see William E. Foley, "After the Applause: Governor William Clark's Failed 1820 Gubernatorial Campaign," in *Gateway Heritage,* 24 (Fall 2003–Winter 2004), 105–11.

31. According to a listing of court fees, the trials and incarceration of the prisoners had cost $146.09, a considerable sum to the average frontier resident in 1809. Territorial Superior Court Minute Book I, Court Fees 1806–1810, MHMA.

32. *U.S. v. Askinawa,* St. Louis Circuit Court Records, November 1811, Box 19, Folder 9, Office of the Circuit Clerk, City of St. Louis, Missouri; and *Missouri Gazette,* September 12, 1811. Sixty-eight years later in the Nebraska case of *Standing Bear v. Crook* a federal judge rejected an argument that Standing Bear was not a citizen and therefore unable to invoke the Fourteenth Amendment to forestall governmental attempts to order the Ponca nation's forced removal.

33. *Missouri Gazette,* June 4, 1814.

34. *Missouri Gazette,* July 16, 1814.

35. Ibid.

36. Report from *Jackson Herald,* April 22, 1820, reprinted in *Missouri Gazette,* May 3, 1820.

37. Ibid., and Stephen Ross to William Clark, April 30, 1820, William Clark Papers, MHMA.

38. Ibid.

39. See Greg Olson, "Navigating the White Road: White Cloud's Struggle to Lead the Ioway along the Path of Acculturation," *Missouri Historical Review,* 99 (January 2005), 93–114; and Dorothy J. Caldwell, "The Big Neck Affair: Tragedy and Farce on the Missouri Frontier," *MHR* 64 (July 1970), 391–412.

40. Ibid.; and William Clark to Secretary of War John Eaton, November 14, 1829; Clark to Thomas McKenney, February 18, 1830; and Clark to Eaton, April 14, 1830 and September 5, 1830, all in Clark Superintendency Records, KSHS, Microfilm reels 3–4.

41. William E. Foley, "Murder on the Santa Fe Trail: *The United States v. See See Sah Mah and Escotah," Kansas History: A Journal of the Central Plains,* 32 (Summer 2009), 90–105. See also U.S. Circuit Court for the Eastern District of Missouri, Eastern Division, and St. Louis, Missouri. Records of the District Courts of the United States, Record Group 21, Law, Equity and Criminal Case files, 1838–1912, Case No. 569, *United States vs. See See Sah Mah and Escotah,* National Archives and Records Administration–Kansas City, and Petitions for Presidential Pardons, Record Group 59, Records of the Department of State, entry 893, Petitions Pardon, entry 893, Petitions of Pardon, 1789–1860, National Archives, College Park, Maryland. The PBS program *History Detectives* featured this case in an episode first aired in July 2009.

42. *St. Louis Daily Union*, April 17, 19, May 6, 11, 1847; *Boonville Observer*, April 2 and May 6, 1847; Columbia *Missouri Statesman*, May 7, 1847; and *Liberty Tribune,* May 15, 1847.

43. Foley, "Murder on the Santa Fe Trail."

44. Ibid.

45. Ibid., and Missouri State Penitentiary Inmate Register, vol. A, 144, and vol. B, 16, Missouri State Archives.

46. *U.S. v. Robert Frazier,* case files in St. Charles Circuit Court Records, February 1812 and June 1812, St. Charles, Missouri. A sheriff's notation on the file dated 1813 states "not to be found in my county." *Missouri Gazette,* February 17, 1819; *U.S. v. Samuel Thompson,* April 1819, Box 46, File 32, Missouri Supreme Court Case Files, Missouri State Archives; and Territorial Superior Court Minute Book III, April 29 and May 8, 1819, MHMA. After his court appearance on May 8, there is no further mention of Thompson in the court records, which suggests that he too had probably fled.

47. Andrew Hughes to William Clark, March 14, 1830, in *Letters Received by the Office of Indian Affairs, 1824–1831, St. Louis Superintendency, 1824–1851, Letters, 1829–1831,* National Archives.

48. Robert E. Smith, "A Life for a Pair of Boots: The Murder of Shepalina," *Chronicles of Oklahoma* 69 (Spring 1991), 26–47.

49. *U.S. v. William Harper*, June 1805, Territorial Files, Box 23, File 9, Cape Girardeau County Archive Center, Jackson, Missouri; and *Abstracts and Indexes of the Early Court Records of Cape Girardeau County Missouri, 1805–1824,* abstracted by Bob and Ann Parkinson (Jackson, Missouri: Cape Girardeau County Archive Center, 2005), 1–2 and 34.

50. *State of Missouri v. Hiram Howdershell* and *State of Missouri v. William Howdershell,* Lincoln County Circuit Court Records, April term 1824, Troy, Missouri; Lincoln County Circuit Court Minute Book, vol. A, 1819–1834, August term 1824, 163–64, Microfilm Reel C3908, Missouri State Archives; *State of Missouri v. Howell Powell,* March term 1825, St. Louis Circuit Court Records, Box 101, File 14; and St. Louis Circuit Court Record Book 4, 81, Office of St. Louis Circuit Clerk.

51. *U.S. v. Petitso*, St. Charles Circuit Court, January 1806, St. Charles Circuit Court Records; *U.S. v. Hocketon et al.,* August 1817, Missouri Supreme Court Case Files, Box 44, Files 4 and 23, Missouri State Archives; and *U.S. v. William Fuller*, 1809, Territorial Records, Box 24, File 6, Cape Girardeau County Archive Center.

52. *U.S. v. Hutchcraft et al.,* 1820, Territorial Files, Box 27, File 23; and *State of Missouri v. Samuel Jones*, 1823, Box 2, File 19, Cape Girardeau County Archive Center.

53. The provisions first outlined in 1796 were continued in the 1802 law and later applied to the Louisiana territories in 1804. See *2 U.S. Statutes at Large (1845),* 141, 143–144; Larry C. Skogen, *Indian Depredation Claims, 1796–1920* (Norman: University of Oklahoma Press, 1996), xv–xvii, 37–39, 56–63, and 227n25; *Missouri Intelligencer* (Franklin), April 28, 1826, and William E. Foley, *Wilderness Journey: The Life of William Clark* (Columbia: University of Missouri Press, 2004), 240–41.

54. Carl Ekberg's recent study *Stealing Indian Women: Native Slaves in the Illinois Country* (Urbana: University of Illinois Press, 2007) documents the persistence of Indian slavery throughout the Spanish era.

55. For a complete account of this lengthy and complex case see William E. Foley, "Slave Freedom Suits before Dred Scott: The Case of Marie Jean Scypion's Descendants," *MHR* 79 (October 1984), 1–23.

56. Notes re slaves' ownership, n.d., testimony of Jacques Chauvin, and testimony of Marie Louise Chauvin and Helene Chevalier in Lucas trial notes, 1806, all in Lucas Collection, MHMA; and Joseph Tayon's petition to Amos Stoddard, May 11, 1804, Chouteau Collection, MHMA.

57. *Joseph Tayon v. Marguerite and other reputed slaves,* May 14–21, 1806 in Territorial Superior Court Minute Book I; Lucas Trial notes, 1806, in Lucas Collection; and Joseph Tayon's sale of slaves to Pierre Chouteau Sr., July 3, 1806, Chouteau Collection, all at MHMA.

58. *Catiche and others v. St. Louis Circuit Court* (1826), 1 Mo 608; and *Catiche and others v. Pierre Chouteau, Sr.,* May 15, 1826, St. Louis Circuit Court Minute Book 4, 349–350.

59. *Marguerite v. Pierre Chouteau* (1828) 2 Mo 71; see also, case file 273, Jefferson County Circuit Court Records; *Marguerite v. Pierre Chouteau* (1834) 3 Mo 540; and Foley, "Slave Freedom Suits before Dred Scott," 20.

60. Jefferson County Circuit Court Records, Hillsboro, Missouri, November 8, 1836, Minute Book 2, 142–47; and trial notes and depositions in case file 273.

61. *Pierre Chouteau v. Marguerite,* Mo. (1828) 12 Peters 507; and Missouri Supreme Court Case Files, Box 150, Folder 13, Missouri State Archives.

62. *Nancy, free woman of color v. Enoch Steen,* April term 1848, Case No. 4, Circuit Court Case Files, Office of Circuit Clerk, City of St. Louis, Missouri.

63. *Peggy Perryman, free woman of color, v. Joseph Philbert,* November term 1848, Case No. 255, and St. Louis Circuit Court Minute Books, No. 18, p 421; No. 19,

pp. 26, 48, 99, 212, and 373, and No. 21, p. and 404. Circuit Court Case Files, Office of the Circuit Clerk, City of St. Louis, Missouri; and Kelly Marie Kennington, "River of Injustice: St. Louis Freedom Suits and the Changing Nature of Legal Slavery in Antebellum America" (Ph.D. diss.) Duke University (2009), 224–30.

64. Mark M. Carroll, *Homesteads Ungovernable: Families, Sex, Race and the Law in Frontier Texas, 1823–1860* (Austin: University of Texas Press, 2001), 27–30.

65. *Johnson v. Johnson's Administrator et al.*, 30 Mo. 72–91 (March Term, 1860) and case files in Missouri Supreme Court Case Files, Box 436, file 8, Missouri State Archives.

66. Ibid.

67. *Buchanan v. Harvey* (1864), Missouri Supreme Court Case Files, Box 527, File 4, Missouri State Archives.

68. *Francis Boyer and James Charley, Jr. v. Michael Dively administrator*, Missouri Supreme Court Case Files, Missouri State Archives; and Lynn Morrow, "Trader William Gillis and Delaware Migration in Southern Missouri," *MHR* 75 (January 1981): 147–67.

69. Ibid.

70. *La Rivière v. La Rivière 97* Mo 84 (October Term 1888); and Missouri Supreme Court Case Files, Box 599, Folder 3, Missouri State Archives.

71. Legal issues addressed in late-nineteenth-century litigation and legislation frequently echoed questions previously raised in the Missouri cases. The cases of Standing Bear (1879) and Crow Dog (1883) and the Major Crimes Act of 1885 offer examples of such similarities.

CHAPTER TWO

The Frown of Fortune: George Sibley Breach of Promise, and Anglo-Francophone Conflict on the Missouri Frontier

Kenneth H. Winn

ON OCTOBER 25, 1812, George Sibley, the Fort Osage Indian factor, asked Ellen Lorr, an illiterate teenager of French descent, to be his concubine. She agreed, or so he would claim. For her part, Lorr, or so she would claim, agreed not to become Sibley's concubine, but his wife. Living on the far western Missouri frontier kept their marriage from being solemnized, but she understood they would take care of that formality upon their return to white civilization.

When the War of 1812 made life on the western frontier too dangerous, Missouri Territorial Governor Benjamin Howard closed off Fort Osage and ordered the Indian factor's return to the safety of St. Louis. Sibley and Lorr arrived back in June 1813. When he did not marry her, she sued him for breach of promise of marriage.[1]

A typical early-nineteenth-century breach of promise suit could be expensive. The father of the would-be bride was usually considered the injured party. His daughter, after all, was damaged goods, and he might be stuck with a financial liability on his hands when no other man would have her. The suit could also prove embarrassing, especially if seduction had been involved. Missouri men of the period were not too embarrassed about such things. The virtue of sexual fidelity within marriage was honored but little observed. Although breach of promise suits had a long history dating over centuries, *Lorr v. Sibley* is the only such case reported in Missouri until 1833, when the numbers began to grow.

George Sibley was a talented, honest, and conscientious government representative to the Osage Indians. Sibley has become historically well known for helping lay out the Santa Fe Trail, as the cofounder of what is now Lindenwood University, and as an evangelical Christian reformer, but he was first noticed for his government service in the far-western Indian trade. He was very sincere in this work. His knowledge that he was more upright and conscientious than other men gave him a streak of self-righteousness. It was not normally an intolerable streak, but it greatly irritated some who knew him. It irritated Fort Osage commander Eli Clemson, for one, who eventually caused Sibley a great deal of trouble. It also irritated the powerful fur trader Pierre Chouteau, who disliked both Sibley and the federal Indian factory system he served. Chouteau would eventually champion Ellen Lorr in her plight, but also in his enmity to the tiresome Indian factor.

Indeed, because of Chouteau, what might have been a relatively minor, if tawdry, domestic dispute became a much larger affair. The original French settlers and the incoming "Yankees," as all Americans were called, persisted in an economic and political rivalry that extended long after the 1803 Louisiana Purchase.[2] Many of the newcomers had unbounded ambition, but the French, especially the powerful Chouteau family, had money and power, and the ability to recruit Yankees looking for both. Though Sibley would deeply offend the French, he would not be without his own partisans. Americans eager to challenge Francophone interests rallied to his side with both legal and social support. The case, thus, became part of an ongoing Anglo-Francophone conflict on the Missouri frontier.

Because Sibley later had strong reasons for suppressing the existence of the case, nearly all evidence of its existence was destroyed. The suit's story and its significance were unknown to history until the recent discovery of the case documents at the Missouri State Archives. The case, however, leads back to Sibley's service as the Indian factor at Fort Osage, near present-day Kansas City, and for that many records exist. It is where most of the participants in the case came to know each other, and where the deep resentments that later played out in the legal system had their origin.

Sibley was born in Great Barrington, Massachusetts, on April 1, 1782. His father, John Sibley, studied medicine as a young man and became a surgeon's mate during the American Revolution, but he became a peripatetic wanderer after the war, eventually landing in French Louisiana in 1801. Well-supplied with letters of recommendation, John quickly found a niche among the territorial elite following the Louisiana Purchase a year and a half later. He soon established a good relationship with Secretary of War Henry Dearborn and, through him, President Thomas Jefferson, with whom John Sibley shared an anthropological interest in Indian culture and language. Favor and patronage followed, including appointment as Indian Agent for Orleans Territory in 1805.[3]

George wished to follow his father into the Indian trade and wrote Dearborn, asking for help. In August 1805 Dearborn offered George a position as the assistant factor at a new trading post, or "factory," planned for an area near the confluence of the Missouri and Mississippi Rivers, "Cantonment Belle Fontaine."[4] Unfortunately Sibley quarreled with the new factor, Rudolph Tillier. Once a better man, Tillier had grown old and corrupt in the service of his country. The combination of a self-righteous twenty-three-year-old and an older, emotionally volcanic, dishonest boss was not a happy one. In November 1807, an exasperated Tillier fired Sibley for insubordination. In response, the indignant George galloped off to Washington, D.C., seeking vindication for his behavior from the superintendent of U.S. Indian affairs, General John Mason. In 1808 Superintendent Mason closed the factory, and Tillier was politely retired.[5] Mason then ordered a portion of Cantonment Belle Fontaine's trading goods transferred up the Missouri River to establish a new factory, "Fort Osage," near present-day Kansas City, with its new factor—George Sibley.

Fort Osage, originally called, "Fort Clark," was built on a cliff seventy feet high over the Missouri River.[6] William Clark had seen the site on his expedition to the Pacific with Meriwether Lewis and thought it would make a good fort location. In need of a new factory near the Osage villages, General Clark, as territorial U.S. Indian Agent, now directed George Sibley and Captain Eli Clemson, his military counterpart, to the fort's general site, which they reached on September 3, 1808.[7]

The new factory was a success. It was not only the nation's westernmost, but its busiest. For a place virtually lost in the woods, there was plenty of divisiveness to keep things agitated: international fur trade rivalries, the resentment of the private fur traders against the government's competition; and the chronic Indian intertribal warfare as Eastern Indians were forced onto the land of those of the West. Earnest and energetic, Sibley got along with the Indians well. He even made money.[8]

Sibley had warm relations with the nonmilitary people who worked at the fort. William Clark initially appointed Territorial Governor Meriwether Lewis's younger brother, Reuben, as the assistant factor. He was followed by Dr. John Robinson, a special subagent to the Osage and later a fort sutler, the civilian merchant who provisions a fort.[9] Robinson and the factor got along well, and Sibley boarded with Robinson's family during their time together. Robinson's tenure overlapped with Marylander Isaac "Ike" Rawlings, another assistant factor, who arrived in 1809.[10] Robinson and Rawlings both figured in the dramas that followed.

In addition to the factory staff and the local Indians, there were occasional visitors. As the last outpost of white civilization on the Missouri River, Fort Osage was the way station for fur-trading expeditions, explorers, botanists, and artists. There were some neighbors who worked to supply the fort, such as James Audrain, after whom Audrain County would be named, and his younger brother, Francis. There was Ira Cottle, who raised cattle, and his family. These, too, would find their way into the legal dispute.

Sibley mostly enjoyed the company of these men, although the private fur traders resented the government's competition. Unfortunately, the most important of them was Pierre Chouteau. The St. Louis fur baron, who with his father Pierre Laclede and his powerful half-brother Auguste founded St. Louis, dominated the regional trade. The Chouteaus were not only successful traders because they enjoyed good relations with the Indians, but because they were also ruthless and politically nimble. They demanded, and for a time, achieved a monopoly on the Osage trade. Government officials both in St. Louis and in Washington worried about the Chouteaus' loyalty to the new American government, and they were highly skeptical of the authenticity of their claims of huge Spanish land grants. Nevertheless, as the territory's dominant family, the American government thought it wise to work with them. In 1804 President Jefferson made Pierre Chouteau the U.S. Indian Agent for Upper Louisiana, although he denied him the monopoly on the Osage Indian trade he desired. In 1807 William Clark assumed responsibility as the territorial U.S. Indian Agent, but Chouteau remained the special Indian Agent to the Osage (his principal tribe of interest).[11]

While the Chouteaus generally provided useful service to the government, they never forgot to look after themselves. In September 1808 William Clark drafted a treaty with the Osage, detailing the factory system's benefits for them, offering them annual annuities and other benefits in exchange for a massive land concession. When the tribe realized the magnitude of their concessions, they were appalled and scuttled the treaty. Governor Meriwether Lewis suspected Pierre Chouteau had agitated the Indians against the treaty, but sent Chouteau to renegotiate its provisions.[12]

When Chouteau arrived in Fort Osage in November 1808, Sibley viewed the fur trader's bargaining methods with contempt, and he made no effort to hide his disapproval. He fumed over what he characterized as Chouteau's hasty and shoddy negotiations with the Osage, and was appalled by Chouteau's threat to employ force to win Indian acquiescence to a treaty that Sibley believed was little different from the one Clark had drawn up.[13]

What really happened in the discussions between Chouteau and the Osage could not have been completely known to Sibley. While Sibley had joined Clark when he made his treaty, Chouteau did not include Sibley in his negotiations.[14] Though they also did not participate, Chouteau asked Fort Commander Captain Eli Clemson and his second-in-command, Louis Lorimier, Jr., to sign as witnesses to the treaty-making, and they obligingly did so. When Chouteau asked Sibley to do the same, the angry factor noted he had "peremptorily refused."[15]

Sibley was not shy about sharing his views of either Pierre Chouteau or his treaty with the Osage and would do so for years to come.[16] But he was not alone. Chouteau's suspected role in scuttling Clark's original treaty seriously damaged relations between Clark and Chouteau and led Meriwether Lewis to contemplate Chouteau's dismissal as the Osage Indian agent.[17]

Although the Senate eventually ratified Chouteau's treaty, the whole affair nearly cost him his relationship with the U.S. government and menaced his privileged Indian trading position. Chouteau and his brother led the region's most powerful fur-trapping enterprise, an international business in which he and his family were amassing a fortune. Government Indian trading, such as that performed by Sibley, posed unwanted competition, especially when the competitor did not have to make a profit. With such distrust each man was bound to find the other an obstacle to his ambition.

Closer at hand, Sibley's development of a ruinous relationship with the local soldiers, particularly their commander, Captain Clemson, hampered his mission, threatened his job, and ultimately harmed his defense against Ellen Lorr's lawsuit. Though the government's goal was to control Indians through trade rather than through arms, troops were stationed at the factories to protect the factors and help secure the regional peace. Sibley and Clemson came to dislike each other fairly early on.[18]

Normally, in these factory-garrison operations, the factor relied on the soldiers to build his factory and living quarters, help with the animal pelts, and perform general work as needed. Part of Sibley's problem—common to other Indian factories as well—was the class division between the factors and the ordinary soldiers. The soldiers were often rough-hewn men compared to the factors, and most were probably illiterate. The Department of Indian Affairs, by contrast, employed more highly educated, politically connected men as factors.[19] Sibley, himself, made things worse. Regarding himself as a "gentleman," he was something of a frontier dandy, wearing formal clothes even in the backwoods.[20] Sibley treated the soldiers like servants, or so they felt. His manners were not only refined, but stiff. He was stubborn, willful, and tended to contradict those who offended him. When he held his tongue, his reserved demeanor usually expressed his thoughts for him.

When the troops worked for Sibley they received only "fatigue pay" and did not consider it part of their "real" mission." Probably because Clemson and his men had already developed a poor attitude toward the factor, or possibly because they had more pressing work in preparing for winter's arrival, building the factory did not progress to Sibley's satisfaction. In early 1809 he complained to Superintendent Mason, who intervened on his behalf with Secretary of War William Eustis. This had the desired effect of pushing Clemson and his troops into greater exertion. By June 1809 construction of the factory had finally progressed toward completion, but Clemson did not appreciate Sibley going over his head and his men provided the factor with the least possible assistance required.[21]

The rift between Sibley and Clemson became irreparable after October 1809, when two boats carrying traders Joseph Robidoux and Francois Dorion heading upstream stopped at Fort Osage. For reasons unclear even at the time, a group of Osage Indians present became hostile to the trading party. Sibley suspected that Paul Loise, Pierre Chouteau's interpreter, had stirred them up against Chouteau's trading rivals. With great effort Sibley and subagent Robinson managed to pacify the Indians, threatening to close the factory to them.[22] The next day the boats attempted to leave, but got caught on a sandbar. When some Indians jumped into the water—whether to push them off the sandbar or take advantage of their difficulty is unknown—a fearful member of the trading party brought down a boat pole on one of the Indian's heads. The unarmed tribesmen then ran for their guns. Robinson plunged into the crisis and made peace. The trading expedition successfully got off and Sibley informed the Indians the factory was temporarily closed to them as a punishment.

At the confrontation's conclusion, a shaken Sibley went to Captain Clemson and demanded to know why the garrison soldiers had not helped to restore order. According to Sibley, Clemson told him that these sorts of disputes were a matter of common intercourse between the Indians and traders and not worth the troops' intervention. At Clemson's response Sibley lost his temper and the two exchanged hard words.[23]

Tension escalated between the factor and his circle and the soldiers. Soldiers may have quietly killed hogs the factor was raising in partnership with St. Louis merchant Risdon Price. On January 8, 1811, Sibley wrote of finding dead animals near the garrison and his belief that the soldiers were responsible for killing them: "The unfortunate coolness that exists between myself and the Gentlemen of the Garrison, among who I include the Sutlers prevents my making as Strict enquiry into these matters as I Should . . . It is easier," he continued, "for a Camel to go through the eye of a needle, than for an Independent American to live near an out post like this, and keep on good terms with those who command the Garrison."[24]

Writing the month before to his brother, Hopkins, George had declared himself well and happy, except for the "disagreeable quarrels" he had "been forced into with Some of the Officers of the Army." Still, he boasted, "I cannot find any diminution of confidence in me on the part of the Govt, but on the contrary am flattered with its being strengthened and increased. This affords me the greater satisfaction because I know that attempts have been made by my enemies to injure my public name and reputation."[25]

The breakdown was worse than he knew, and he would soon find plenty of reason for worry. While Clemson accommodated Sibley on a number of the demands he made the day of the Robidoux incident, he nursed a grudge against the factor. For some reason, on July 10, 1810, Clemson dismissed John Robinson as a sutler. He could not fire Sibley, of course, so he wrote Superintendent Mason to denounce Sibley and Robinson, and now, some eight months after it occurred, used the Robidoux incident as illustration of Sibley's incompetent agitation of the Osage.[26] Not until August 14, 1811, did Sibley receive a letter from Mason asking for an explanation of the incident. Sibley was furious and this created a final break between him and the garrison commander. Mason's letter even led the anxious factor to fear his position might hang in the balance of his response. Seeking support from John Robinson, who then lived in Kaskaskia (and perhaps to keep their stories straight), Sibley wrote him a narrative of events and added: "Whatever may be the Real character of Capt. Clemson, whether good or bad, is a matter of no moment in the present case: the honorable office which he holds necessarily gives a fictitious importance to his name, and Serves to conceal from the world his foibles and his vices; and you have Seen how effectually it has been interposed to Screen him from merited punishment."[27]

Sibley had previously requested a six-month furlough from service to visit his father, but now, as he had in his conflict with Rudolph Tillier, he traveled to Washington during the winter of 1811–1812 to lay his case before Mason. To Sibley his trip was a triumph. He had exaggerated his fears, and Mason eased his mind. Although there appears to have been no reprimand or retaliation against Clemson, Sibley returned to Fort Osage in April with a sense of vindication.[28]

Vindication or not, he was isolated by the friction with the educated officers in the garrison, and he had little in common with the others with whom he came into regular contact. And the truth was that being a factor was often solitary work. It certainly had its dramatic moments, but life in the woods bereft of the accouterments of a larger society was often quite dull, and Sibley sometimes complained of a sense of being cut off. This encouraged his prolific letter writing and it caused him to complain to Hopkins when letters from his family were not forthcoming.[29]

More poignantly, this period at Fort Osage coincided with his late twenties and early thirties and he naturally longed for female companionship. He occasionally wrote to his brother about the attractiveness of the young Indian "princesses," but unlike many traders and soldiers he apparently took no comfort among them.[30] In February 1811 he wrote Hopkins, "I sometimes think pretty Seriously of taking a trip to Kentucky in quest of a wife," but, he confessed, "I am not So certain I can get one.—I am perfectly convinced however that it is now high time for me to marry and Settle myself."[31] It was through the vulnerability borne of his loneliness that Pierre Chouteau and Captain Eli Clemson would exact their revenge.

Sibley lived in a sweaty, remote, masculine world devoid of young unmarried white women. Or mostly so. In addition to the garrison, the subagents, the assistant factors, the Indians, the sutlers, and farm families in the Fort Osage community, there was yet another figure in Sibley's isolated world: his Indian language interpreter Pierre Lorr.[32] Lorr appears from time to time in Sibley's Fort Osage journals and letters as an odd-jobs man around the factory and Sibley's courier between the fort and St. Louis.[33] The interpreter was married with a large and needy family that lived in the small dogtrot next to the factory. So Sibley hired Pierre's wife, Celeste (whom he always referred to as "Madame Lorr") to manage the kitchen and prepare meals, although he thought she did a poor job of it.[34] Yet in his criticism of her kitchen management, Sibley also made reference to his pleasure in helping the Lorr family.

That is the only extant record mentioning Lorr family members other than Pierre and Madame Lorr among Sibley's papers. His journal for this period is missing and his correspondence seems to have been purged. The reason is easy to surmise. The purging, however, would come later. If Sibley's sexual relationship with Ellen Lorr eventually embarrassed him, perhaps after he became a prominent evangelical Christian, it did not at the time; nor did it bother his friends or associates, who apparently considered her suit more vexatious than anything else. The case would never have been discovered except for the survival of the court documents that were beyond Sibley's reach—or the reach of those who later wished to protect his image.

Ellen Lorr was born on September 24, 1797, barely fifteen years old when she began her liaison with George Sibley.[35] She had arrived at Fort Osage with the rest of her family in the fall of 1808. At the time she would have been too young to have a sexual relationship with Sibley, who was twenty-six. But by the fall of 1812 things seemed different. Clemson, himself, implies as much, characterizing her as young girl in 1808, but describing her as a "woman" when discussing her life with Sibley.[36]

Whatever the case, George Sibley initiated his sexual relationship with Ellen Lorr on October 16, 1812. Whether it was to convince himself, or Ellen, or Ellen's parents, or all three, of the honorability of his intention, he wrote a brief "contract" formalizing their relationship. He said Ellen had "voluntarily, freely and willingly placed herself under my protection, to live and abide with me." In a rhetorical allusion to the Declaration of Independence, he wrote that it was only "proper, having a regard to justice and humanity" that he, "desirous of securing the said Ellen against accidents and the frown of Fortune," "solemnly," presented her "this Paper" "pledging myself on the Honor of a Gentleman," to observe the four following articles: First, he would maintain her comfortably, and treat her kindly, honorably, and affectionately. Second, he promised to give her one hundred dollars on the first of every January. (Sibley's salary at the time was $1,000 per year, plus an expense allowance.) In the third article Sibley said so long as she conducted herself faithfully, honestly, and "with strict female propriety," he would honor the first two articles. Last, "this instrument" could be cancelled only by "improper conduct in Ellen or by death." Sibley then signed the agreement. Francis Audrain and the assistant factor, Isaac Rawlings, signed as witnesses.[37]

Nine days later Ellen moved into his quarters. Their relationship lasted nine months. With the outbreak of the War of 1812, the Far West became very dangerous. The British and their far more significant Indian allies menaced St. Louis and St. Charles; a remote little outpost like Fort Osage was beyond protection. Governor Benjamin Howard, accordingly, ordered the fort temporarily abandoned, and in early June 1813 Sibley, Ellen Lorr, and the rest of the factory journeyed to St. Louis. They arrived on June 13.[38]

On July 31, 1813, Ellen Lorr initiated a lawsuit against Sibley for breach of promise of marriage. One of the oddest things about the suit—indeed the whole controversy—is the complete absence of Pierre Lorr. The historical record is thin as to what happened to him after 1812, but it is possible that he had died. Typically, when a man dishonored a female, he would be challenged to a duel or thrashed with a cane by the insulted woman's defender. Pierre Lorr was not of the same social class as Sibley so a duel would have been unlikely, but some form of physical violence was a perfectly viable alternative for many men.[39] Even if an "outraged girl's" father eschewed personal violence for the courts, it was he who was considered to have suffered the potential financial damage caused by the breach of promise or seduction, and it was he who did the suing.[40] This, however, is not what happened in the Lorr suit. Since Ellen was quaintly listed as an "infant" in the court records (a minor), her suit needed to be filed by a "next friend," or legal guardian. Unless the child was an orphan this usually meant the minor's father. So perhaps Pierre Lorr was dead, or perhaps he felt like he needed more a worldly, educated, man to take on his employer.[41] If so, he found one. The person with the sophistication and the money to champion Ellen's case was Pierre Chouteau.

Ellen's parents were very poor, but her mother was not without important connections. Celeste's family, the Dodiers and Bequets, had been with Pierre Laclede and Auguste Chouteau when they founded St. Louis in 1764. The Dodier family, in particular, had prospered. When in 1792 Celeste Dodier wed Pierre Lorr, an Arcadian, of more obscure origins, it was possibly a marriage of diminished social status.[42] Pierre Chouteau would have known Ellen from her birth, just as he had known her mother Celeste from hers in 1775. The idea that someone he despised like George Sibley had mistreated a member of the intimate Francophone community quite likely exacerbated the frictions already present.

For the past five years Sibley and Pierre Chouteau had greatly irritated each other. Sibley had denounced his treaty-making, countenanced his fur trade rivals, and represented the hated factory system to the Osage Indians, a tribe with whom Chouteau had cultivated a trading relationship for decades. After the U.S. government declared war on Britain on June 18, 1812, Chouteau secured the Osage tribe's continued loyalty to the U.S. government. William Clark warmly lauded Chouteau's efforts. Yet as part of this same initiative, Chouteau urged that Fort Osage be closed because of the danger posed in maintaining such an isolated site—despite an Osage pledge to protect the fort. Sibley was furious at Chouteau's suggestion. He regarded the recommendation to close the factory as the fur trader's transparent ruse to get rid of an economic rival.[43] Thus the bad relations begun in 1808 continued without interruption through 1813.

Pierre Chouteau was not known for his gallantry to women. Francophone men, like other frontiersmen, had highly irregular sexual relations by later

Victorian standards. Many, like Chouteau, kept Indian wives, or had black mistresses, even while having Francophone wives. In the French community marriages were often a matter of family alliances. Large disparities in age between a husband and wife were routine. Marital hypocrisies were common. A shortage of Catholic priests and inconvenient church rules led to flexibility in practice. Men did not keep these liaisons private and many wives pretended ignorance of them. Chouteau himself was the son of a long-term liaison between Pierre de Laclede Liguest and Marie Therese Bourgeois Chouteau. Normally, in this period, men would not prosecute other men for the types of sexual liaisons that they themselves might have.[44]

So the meaning was probably clear when on July 31 Louis LeBeaume, a prominent ex-jurist, attorney, and Pierre Chouteau's son-in-law, appeared in the chambers of Territorial Judge J. B. C. Lucas, requested permission to serve as Ellen Lorr's next friend, and proceeded to charge George Sibley with breach of promise of marriage. He submitted Ellen's pleading, signed with an "X," swearing that Sibley had repeatedly promised to marry her if she would "cohabit" with him at Fort Osage. Relying on his sincerity, she had agreed, but Sibley had "utterly forsaken her," and she had "sustained great damage." Moreover, Lorr said, Sibley was a flight risk, who would likely leave the territory before a case came to trial. She therefore requested that he post a two thousand-dollar bond to guarantee his appearance in court. Lucas granted Labeaume's request to serve as Lorr's next friend and required Sibley to post "bond," but thought a thousand dollars sufficient to guarantee his appearance.[45]

Given the absence of private records pertaining to the case, we cannot know Sibley's thoughts on the motivation behind the suit filed against him. It was probably easier on his conscience to think of this as an Anglo-Francophone quarrel and Lorr as merely a French pawn. In the surviving letters to others from the period he seems completely untroubled, bored with his idle time in St. Louis. On the advent of his initial hearing, he complained to his brother Hopkins that his listlessness had been compounded by having found no woman in town worthy of his chase.[46]

Sibley may have been bored, but he took his legal trouble seriously, turning to Rufus Easton, a prominent attorney and an ardent foe of the Francophone elite to mount his defense. Like Sibley, Easton was a New Englander, born in Connecticut. As a young lawyer he moved to upstate New York, where he became involved in Democratic politics and supported Thomas Jefferson for president. After the Louisiana Purchase his effort on Jefferson's behalf won him an appointment in 1805 as a judge to the Upper Louisiana Territorial Court.

Upon his arrival in St. Louis, Easton found escalating tension between the old Francophone residents and the American newcomers, and enthusiastically threw himself into the fray. Easton wrote Jefferson that the French feigned friendliness to American rule only to obtain U.S. confirmation of their land-grant claims, many of which Easton declared fraudulent. When Jefferson sent Easton's letter to Congress, it seriously damaged the Francophone effort to have these grants recognized. This brought Easton the enmity of the Chouteau family, the largest and most aggressive of the land claimants. In late 1805 they exacted a measure of revenge by having a grand jury stacked with Francophones (Pierre Chouteau and land surveyor Antoine Soulard among them) indict Easton himself for land fraud. The American minority on the grand jury took the unusual step of issuing a statement declaring that the indictment was made "to gratify personal hatred" and to seek "cruel revenge."[47] At the subsequent trial, the jury found Easton innocent of any wrongdoing. In 1812 Easton ran to become the first territorial delegate to Congress. In a four-way race, Easton narrowly lost to the French-sponsored candidate, Edward Hempstead.

It was at this time that Sibley approached Easton to defend him from Ellen Lorr's lawsuit. In his response to Lorr's charges against Sibley, Easton responded that Lorr had no grounds for complaint. Sibley had held up his end of the bargain. Lorr had agreed "to live dwell inside and sleep[?] With the said defendant, as his concubine and did so live dwell and bed with him . . . as his concubine and in a state of concubinage." During this time, he "maintain[ed] the said Ellen decently and comfortably and did all that time treat her kindly and affectionately" until "the said Ellen . . . left the service and company and society of him said Defendant and did not thereafter conduct herself toward him faithfully honestly and with strict female propriety."[48]

On September 6 Easton, in the presence of Louis Labeaume, took the deposition of Francis Audrain, witness to the contract between Sibley and Lorr. Audrain detailed how Ellen's uncle had fetched him for a family council. They asked him to explain the "contract" to them and for an opinion of Sibley's proposal. He stated that if she thought she could conduct herself with the female propriety Sibley required, she should agree, and Sibley would be honorably bound to support her. When Audrain implied he thought of the contract as essentially a financial instrument, LaBeaume asked him if he did not think the contract just as binding on Sibley "as a marriage ceremony." Audrain responded he did not. Resuming his story, Audrain said the Lorr family conference continued after his departure. A short time later Pierre and Celeste Lorr and other family members came for him again, and they went to Sibley's quarters. There the parties agreed to the contract's terms. Sibley signed the document, and Audrain and Isaac Rawlings added their signatures as witnesses. Audrain declared that "all the parties concerned knew that the said Ellen was to bed with the said Sibley, & that the father, mother & Daughter all considered the connection an honorable one." Audrain said to the best of his knowledge Sibley had treated Lorr with kindness and that she enjoyed more comfortable circumstances after moving in with Sibley then she had before. In terms of her behavior, it was proper enough, but Audrain added Lorr's "General Character from common report as to chastity was not very fair" prior to her living with Sibley. Indeed, Audrain later claimed it was him with whom she been unchaste.[49]

On October 5, 1813, Easton filed Sibley's pleas. While Labeaume continued to serve as Lorr's next friend, he turned her legal representation over to Easton's political nemesis, Edward Hempstead, and Hempstead's associate William Mears. A highly talented attorney, the Chouteaus entrusted Hempstead with the defense of their Spanish land-grant claims. As a surrogate battle developed between the anti-Francophone faction and the French, the latter sought to strengthen Lorr's representation by turning to Hempstead. Like Sibley and Easton, the handsome Hempstead was a Yankee, born in New London, Connecticut. Upon his arrival in Upper Louisiana in 1804, he realized there was money and advancement to be had through an alliance with the old colonial elite, and he began a dedicated study of the French language. He soon became their advocate, navigating his way through the mists of the American common law for them. In 1808 he further cemented his ties to the French elite by marrying Clarissa Dubreuil, the daughter of the wealthy French merchant Louis Dubreuil. Clarissa's sister Constance was daughter-in-law of Pierre Chouteau. In 1809 Governor Meriwether Lewis had made Hempstead the territorial attorney general, and three years later, thanks in large measure to Francophone support, Hempstead became Missouri's first territorial delegate. He proved effective, and successfully persuaded Congress to liberalize policies recognizing Spanish land grants.[50]

Hempstead's partner in the case, William Mears, was a similarly prominent lawyer. A month after Lorr had filed her lawsuit against Sibley, Mears became the United States Attorney for Illinois Territory. Four years after the Sibley case's conclusion he became the state's second attorney general. He resided in nearby Cahokia, Illinois, but engaged in a number of high-profile legal cases in St. Louis.[51]

On October 18, with Hempstead in Washington, Mears filed Lorr's opening pleas against Sibley. Mears made four major points. Summarizing the contract, he said that Lorr had kept her part of the bargain. That is, she was faithful and honest with Sibley and conducted herself "with strict female propriety." As his second point Mears charged that though Lorr had lived up to her side of the agreement Sibley had not lived up to his. Instead of treating her "kindly affectionately and honorably," he had treated her "cruelly unfeelingly and infamously." He had not given her the one hundred dollars he promised the first of every January. She, moreover, worked for him during the period of their cohabitation. On June 30, 1813, two weeks after their return to St. Louis from Fort Osage, she claimed Sibley told her that he would pay her any reasonable amount she desired for her work. She indicated that her work with Sibley was worth $200, a substantial sum. Sibley, she complained, did not give her this money either. Moreover, because she relied on his promise she had not looked to others as possible marriage partners and remained single. Third, Ellen had always been "ready and willing" to marry Sibley. There simply had been no one legally authorized to solemnize their marriage in the wilderness. Now back in St. Louis, that obstacle had disappeared, but Sibley refused to marry her. She believed he had defrauded her and had never intended to marry her, to her "ruin" as a woman. She, accordingly, asked the court for five thousand dollars in damages.

But she was not done. In the second part of her pleading, Mears said Ellen had always been "a person of good name fame and conversation and always lived in good esteem with her neighbors from her childhood" up until the time Sibley began to court her at Fort Osage. A conspicuous weakness in Lorr's case was that the contract never contained a word about marriage, so Mears asked the court to remember that Ellen was "illiterate unlearned and uncapable to read" and the defendant, knowing that, "deceitfully, craftily, fraudulently," used her ignorance and told her that the document was a marriage contract. Relying on his "representation and promises" through "the false and fraudulent reading of said writing," she permitted him to cohabit with her. Through his repeated and false "protestations of his affection for her and of his design to marry her" he had, in turn, "gained her affections and having insinuated himself into her good will did beguile" to "suffer . . . Sibley to sleep with and cohabit with" her. When this was no longer of interest to him he "utterly forsook" her "to her entire overthrow and public disgrace." And for that disgrace, she requested an additional five thousand dollars in punitive damages from the court. She thus requested ten thousand dollars for the broken contract and damages—ten times Sibley's 1812 salary and probably more than thirty times the wages received by her father.[52] A victory for Lorr would have spelled a financial catastrophe for Sibley.

Sometime after Lorr's deposition was filed on October 18, a new complication arose. In a written addendum, the same hand squeezed in on both the deposition and the original charge the news that Sibley "had begot the said Ellen" with child. Sibley and Lorr presumably had broken off physical relations with each other by June, or maybe early July, making Lorr at least four months pregnant by the time it is noted in the documents. Curiously, her pregnancy is never mentioned again in court documents that stretch on for another eighteen months.[53] While men did not face paternity suits in the manner they do today, pregnancy was not taken lightly by juries who deemed that a virtuous woman had been deceived by a designing man.

Whatever the circumstance, it seems extremely improbable that Sibley ever seriously contemplated marriage with Lorr. He certainly showed no remorse over his actions. Some Americans, Edward Hempstead being one, married into French families. But ambitious and well-educated men did not marry into one like Lorr's. The class, education, ethnic, and religious differences were simply too vast.

In October 1813, the case was essentially Lorr's word against Sibley's and Audrain's. At this point, Hempstead and Mears obtained a continuance to obtain additional testimony to support Lorr's case.[54] They had decided to search for Captain Eli Clemson. It took a long time, but Hempstead and Mears finally tracked him down in New Jersey—still in the military and now a major.

On July 13, 1814, Alexander Stuart, Judge of the Missouri Territorial Superior Court, requested that a Middlesex County, New Jersey, judge pose interrogatories to Clemson written by Hempstead and Easton. Nearly a year later, on May 11, 1815, Clemson gave his answers. These answers were not filed with the St. Louis court until September 4, 1815. By that time the case had gone on for over two years.

In his testimony, Clemson stated that he had known Lorr since 1808. She had then been very young, but as she grew to womanhood he was very impressed that she had resisted the many temptations put in her path in a male-dominated wilderness. He believed that her character and her chastity were very good—at least until she began living with Sibley in the manner of man and wife. I "religiously believe," he said, "that Ellen Lorr lived with Geo C Sibley under the impression of they being regularly married so soon as a person qualified to unite them could be procured," and that she regarded the "certificate" Sibley presented her as a marriage contract. Clemson deemed Sibley's most important witness, Francis Audrain, to be completely untrustworthy. Clemson said he no longer remembered if he and Audrain had discussed Sibley and Lorr's relationship with Audrain, but since Audrain was a liar, it did not really matter. He did remember, however, that Audrain had told him that he himself had "cohabited" with Ellen prior to her living with Sibley. Clemson said he found it hard to believe that Audrain would swear to a falsehood, but he would never believe any oath Audrain made.[55]

Easton began by asking Clemson if there was not "an extreme coolness" between him and Sibley. Clemson straightforwardly affirmed this was true and readily confessed to the hostility that might prejudice his other responses. He not only disliked George Sibley, but he had not spoken to him since 1811. Fort Osage was physically a very tiny community, containing only about one hundred people in its environs. That the community's two leaders—one responsible for the factory and the other for the garrison—did not speak to each other from 1811 until they parted ways in 1813 is remarkable.

Easton then invited Clemson to engage in hearsay and speculation. Had he ever heard that the defendant had promised to marry the plaintiff? Could it really be reasonably believed that the defendant would marry the plaintiff? Did not Sibley merely pay her address as a concubine? Had she not in fact become his concubine by her own consent and that of her parents? Had not Sibley treated her well in her concubinage? Clemson responded he had frequently heard they were going to be married and "to the best of his belief" Ellen's parents thought the same. While Clemson agreed that he had heard nothing but good about Sibley's treatment of Lorr, he reasserted that Ellen had been chaste when he met her and Sibley had obtained her affection with a promise of marriage. Finally, Easton wanted to know how Clemson knew Francis Audrain. Clemson said he had first met Audrain when he was a ten-year-old and they both lived in Detroit. Audrain had come to Fort Osage in 1810, but Clemson had little to do with him. Clemson would not say that Audrain was a malicious liar, but "many thought his stories" redounded "to his own injury."[56]

On March 16, 1816, *Lorr v. Sibley* finally went to trial before Presiding Territorial Superior Court Judge Silas Bent. The draw of Bent was an unhappy choice for Sibley. He was very close to Auguste Chouteau, and Territorial Secretary Frederick Bates scorned him as "Hempstead's creature."[57] If that were not bad enough, in 1814 Hempstead had decided not to stand for reelection as Missouri's territorial delegate to Congress. Easton ran again and won. His departure for Washington left Sibley without his advocate.

Easton turned Sibley's case over to twenty-four-year-old Charles Lucas. Though young, Lucas had made a name for himself as a rising legal star.[58] Easton adored his young protégé, and the Lucas and Easton families were quite close.[59] Easton was friendly with the family patriarch, J. B. C. Lucas, who had served as the first judge in the Sibley case. Though J. B. C. was a French immigrant to the United States, he was a Protestant. He had been a former Pennsylvania congressman, very close to his congressional predecessor, Jefferson's secretary of the treasury Albert Gallatin. Despite his French birth, Lucas regarded the old colonial elite as monarchists who were ill-prepared for republican government.[60] He was, likewise, a fierce opponent of their land-grant claims. Charles had adopted the views of Easton and his father and by 1816 he had become the point person in the opposition to the loose group of Francophone elites and fellow travelers like Hempstead—who were now being termed *the junto*.[61]

In taking on Sibley's case, Lucas recruited as cocounsels Matthias McGirk, who would soon serve as Missouri's first chief justice of the Supreme Court, and a newly arrived former Tennessee attorney named Thomas Hart Benton (who would shoot Lucas dead in a duel eighteen months later).[62] Benton's selection was a curious choice since he had already begun a fast friendship with Edward Hempstead, who had also provided the newcomer with legal work. Although not yet apparent, Benton, according to his biographer William Nesbit Chambers, would soon develop "a reputation in some quarters as a lackey for the local French aristocracy."[63] Of equal curiosity, the Lucas family, especially Charles, was very close to Eli Clemson. (Clemson was Lucas's second when he muffed the firing count, perhaps helping cause Lucas's death).[64] Clemson had never opposed Sibley for political reasons—he just did not like him. In the end, Clemson's his only connection with Pierre Chouteau and his circle was a common enemy.

There are more records about pretrial maneuverings than the trial itself, which went unrecorded. The identities of only two witnesses are known: Fort Osage cattleman Ira Cottle and Upper Mississippi factor John Johnson, both friends of Sibley, and both called by the plaintiff. The Cottle family had boarded with Sibley at the time he and Lorr lived together, and it is unknown what Ira said. Sibley had shown the Cottles much kindness upon their arrival and hired Mrs. Cottle to replace Madame Lorr as his cook.[65] Still, the extant evidence does not say how or what Cottle thought of Ellen Lorr or her relationship with Sibley. Even more difficult to see is what evidence Johnson might have provided. The Fort Madison Indian factor, and future St. Louis mayor, was a Sibley confidant and he had his own Indian concubine, or wife, at the time. In any event, Johnson continued to enjoy good relations with Sibley long after the case had ended.[66]

Whatever the testimony of his friends or the skill of his attorneys, Sibley lost his case. Lucas, Benton, and McGirk immediately filed a motion for a new trial, claiming misbehavior by both the judge and jury. The verdict, they said, was against the law; the verdict was against the evidence; the judge had allowed the jury to leave the courtroom and mingle with others before reaching their verdict; and the judge had not allowed the presentation of testimony that would have reflected negatively on Ellen Lorr's character. Their complaints notwithstanding, the motion for a new trial was denied. Lucas, Benton, and McGirk then asked for an arrest of judgment, asserting that the court had confused a tort with a contractual matter and that a contract for concubinage was against the public good and therefore was unenforceable. This, too, was denied.[67]

The accuracy of these objections is beyond knowing. Without recorded testimony, it cannot be known if the verdict was against the evidence. Surely there were errors if the jury was not properly sequestered. A concubine contract might be considered unenforceable as against the public good, but we do not know if the jury accepted it as a concubine contract. Nor do we know if the jury was assembled in a prejudicial manner, such as stacked with Francophones, or their allies, and who they might have talked to in advance of delivering their verdict.[68]

We also do not know how much Ellen Lorr received in compensation. Unfortunately, the execution books that recorded such judgments were not kept until 1819. There is a clerk's note, however, that says that Sibley forfeited his bond, so perhaps she received $1,000. Happily for Ellen Lorr, her relationship with Sibley did not damage her marital prospects. Given the gender imbalance on the Missouri frontier that would have been unlikely. On June 16, 1817, she wed Francois Bonne, probably in Old Mines, Missouri, where she and her husband lived out the rest of their lives. She would eventually have five children.[69]

The $10,000 Ellen Lorr demanded was an extraordinary sum. A year after the trial was over, Sibley wrote a letter for publication in an eastern newspaper. While he generally lauded the glories of the West, he noted that labor in St. Louis was very dear by eastern standards—$15 to $30 a month, if an employer could find someone to hire. If his assessment is accurate, that would be $180 to $360 a year, so $10,000 would have made for a handsome award, indeed, and $1,000 would have provided nearly three years' wages to St. Louis' s highest-paid workers. Sibley, himself, made $1,000 a year when Lorr sued him.[70]

So Sibley's financial loss was probably quite severe, but apparently not ruinous. Ironically, however, Pierre Chouteau and the Francophones did succeed later in wrecking Sibley financially, albeit inadvertently. After a brief war stint performing his factory duties in the comparative safety of Arrow Rock, he returned to Fort Osage in 1816. In 1822 Senator Thomas Hart Benton, championing the longtime French complaints against the factory system, obtained legislation bringing it to an end.[71] Not only did Sibley get thrown out of a job, he made the mistake of buying the government's leftover inventory, which he could not sell, giving him an enormous burden of debt for many years to come.[72]

Fatefully, it was Sibley's stiff sense of honor, his unwillingness to go along, and his primness, that got him into trouble. These personal qualities, and his sexual loneliness, earned him the right combination of enemies to harm him. There was, however, one happy result to the trial for George Sibley. Rufus Easton argued that Sibley could not have breached a marriage contract because he had contracted for a concubine. What was an attorney to do with a client of such dubious sexual morals? If one is Rufus Easton, you let him marry your daughter. Thirty-three-year-old George Sibley did not breach his promise to fifteen-year-old Mary Easton. They wed mid-trial on August 19, 1815, two years after Ellen Lorr first sued him.[73]

NOTES

The author wishes to thank Karen Holtkamp and Lynn Wolf Gentzler for their assistance in preparing this article. Ms. Holtkamp, a direct descendent of Ellen Lorr, provided the author with information not previously recorded about her ancestor.

1. *Lorr v. Sibley,* Superior Court Files, 1816, Supreme Court of Missouri Collection, Missouri State Archives, Box 38, Folder 13. This suit marks the first appearance of breach of promise in Missouri history and, tellingly, in this highly litigious community, there would not be another for twenty years—after Missouri became a state. *Hill v. Maupin,* Supreme Court of Missouri, 1833, Missouri State Archives, Box 109, Folder 7. The Missouri State Archives Local Records Circuit Court Project may yet turn up other early cases. The civil offense of breach of promise, while anachronistic, is still prosecutable in most states. In its classic Victorian form breach of promise was an unusual hybrid of contract breaking and tort law, which the Lorr-Sibley case anticipated. Cases might involve issues of pregnancy, economic damage, and parental rights, or, less common in this period, protecting women from cruel or irresponsible men. Breach of promise has its origins in the ecclesiastical courts in early modern Britain but by the seventeenth century, it had become secularized, and by the eighteenth, it was employed mostly by wealthy men whose interest was not primarily their daughters' heartbreak,

but property settlement. At the time of Sibley's trial, breach of promise was in a transitional phase. While not necessarily about the rich anymore—it still emphasized economic injury. For general overviews see Michael Grossberg, *Governing the Hearth: Law and the Family in Nineteenth Century America* (Chapel Hill: University of North Carolina Press, 1985), 33–63; Ginger S. Frost, *Promise Broken: Courtship, Class and Gender in Victorian England* (Charlottesville: University Press of Virginia, 1995), 1–57.

2. By the early nineteenth century, people of French descent had lived in America for generations. Not all their ancestors emigrated from France; some of them may have lived in Canada or Detroit before coming to Missouri while others emigrated from the Caribbean or New Orleans and married into other populations. Historians, accordingly, have begun calling these people "Francophones" as opposed to "French" or "Creole." I have mostly used this naming convention in the chapter, though they called themselves "French" during the period under discussion, as did those who did not belong to their community. I have occasionally reverted to this older characterization for reasons of word variation and period usage.

3. For general biographical details concerning John Sibley, see Charles T. Jones, *George Champlin Sibley: The Prairie Puritan, 1782–1863* (Independence, MO: Jackson County Historical Society, 1970), 15–30; A. T. W., "John Sibley," in *Dictionary of American Biography,* vol. 9, ed. Dumas Malone (New York: Charles Scribner's Sons, 1964), 146–47; Joseph Tregle, Jr., "John Sibley," in *Dictionary of National Biography,* vol. 19 (New York: Oxford University Press, 1999), 185–86; G. P. Whittington, ed., "Dr. John Sibley of Natchitoches, 1757–1837, "*Louisiana Historical Quarterly* 10 (October 1927): 468–512.

4. For George Sibley and the history of Cantonment Belle Fontaine see Jones, *George Champlin Sibley,* 26–38; Russell M. Magnaghi, "The Belle Fontaine Indian Factory, 1805–1808," *Missouri Historical Review* 75 (July 1981): 396–416; Kate L. Gregg, "Building the First American Fort West of the Mississippi," *Missouri Historical Review* 40 (July 1935): 345–64; Jeffrey E. Smith, 'George Sibley and the Opening of the Trans-Mississippi West," in George Sibley, *Seeking a Newer World: The Fort Osage Journals and Letters of George Sibley, 1808–1811.* Jeffrey E. Smith, ed. (St. Charles, Missouri: Lindenwood Press, 2003), 25–28, 74; William E. Foley, *The Genesis of Missouri* (Columbia: University of Missouri Press), 1989, 175; For an overview of the factory system see Ora Brooks Peake, *A History of the Indian Factory System, 1795–1822* (Denver, CO: Sage Books, 1954). Jefferson's Indian policy has been the subject of many works, see Anthony F. C. Wallace, *Jefferson and the Indians: The Tragic Fate of the First Americans* (Cambridge: Harvard University Press, 2001); Bernard W. Sheehan, *Seeds of Extinction: Jeffersonian Philanthropy and the American Indian* (Chapel Hill: University of North Carolina, 1972).

5. Though Sibley worried, with the backing of William Clark and Acting Territorial Governor Frederick Bates, his fate was never in doubt. Tillier's brief

stewardship was already a mess, and it had become clear that the factory was not well located for the Indian trade. See Thomas C. Danisi, "George Champlain Sibley: Shady Dealings on the Early Frontier," *Confluence* 2 (Fall/Winter 2010), 38–49; *The Territorial Papers of the United States,* vol. 9. The Territory of Louisiana-Missouri, 1804–1814 (Washington: Government Printing Office, 1949), 151; Frederick Bates, *The Life and Papers of Frederick Bates,* ed. Thomas Maitland Marshall, vols. I–II (New York: Arno Press, 1975), 224–25; Magnaghi, "The Belle Fontaine Indian Factory," 396–416; Kate L. Gregg, "Building the First American Fort West of the Mississippi," *Missouri Historical Review* 40 (July 1935): 345–64; Smith, "George Sibley and the Opening of the Trans-Mississippi West," 25–28, 74; William E. Foley, *Genesis of Missouri*, 175.

6. The standard history of Fort Osage is Kate L. Gregg, "The History of Fort Osage," *Missouri Historical Review* 30 (July 1935), 439–88.

7. The factory opened for business on October 1. William Clark, *Westward with the Dragoons: The Journal of William Clark on His Expedition to Establish Fort Osage, August 25 to September 22, 1808, ed.* Kate L. Gregg (Fulton, MO: Ovid Bell Press, 1937).

8. During his first three years the factory cleared a net profit of $10,291.40. Jones, *Prairie Puritan,* 60.

9. Robinson was a curious figure, an adventurer and a schemer, who accompanied Zebulon Pike's ill-fated 1806–1807 western mission into Mexican territory. Ultimately Robinson became very disliked at Fort Osage. He may have had a friendly relationship with Sibley's father. For more on Robinson see Jones, *Prairie Puritan,* 68–70; and Smith's biographical comments in Sibley, *Seeking a Newer World,* 87–88.

10. Rawlings would remain in the Indian trade for many years in Missouri and Arkansas, before becoming a successful Memphis businessman, who as one of the town's early founders became its second mayor. See Sibley, *Seeking a Newer World,* 99–100.

11. William E. Foley and David C. Rice, *The First Chouteaus: River Barons of Early St. Louis* (Urbana: University of Illinois Press, 1983), 133.

12. Many historians have described the machinations around the 1808 Osage Treaty. See Foley and Rice, *First Chouteaus,* 134–36; Stan Hoig, *The Chouteaus: First Family of the Fur Trade* (Albuquerque: University of New Mexico Press, 2008), 34–37; Willard Rollings, *The Osage: An Ethnohistorical Study of Hegemony on the Prairie-Plains* (Columbia: University of Missouri Press, 1992), 224–27. A copy of both the Clark Treaty and Chouteau's Treaty may be found in Clark, *Westward with the Dragoons,* 64–75. See also *American State Papers: Indian Affairs* 1:763–67

13. In these feelings, however, Sibley was at least partly wrong. Chouteau's treaty did offer the Indians some additional concessions for their land. While it is true the trader made U.S. friendship with the Osage contingent upon their approval

of the treaty, he did so in obedience to Governor Meriwether Lewis's explicit instructions. Foley and Rice, *First Chouteaus,* 136.

14. In further walling off the conversation Chouteau used Paul Loise, often believed to be his, or his brother's, half-breed Osage son, as his official interpreter. Paul Loise was also sometimes referred to as Paul Chouteau. In regards to his paternity, see Foley and Rice, *First Chouteaus*, 45; Hoig, *Chouteau,* 270; see also Smith's comments on Loise in Sibley, *Seeking a Newer World,* 78. Regardless of his blood tie, his closeness to the Chouteau family is not in doubt.

15. Sibley, *Seeking a Newer World,* 85–86, and Smith comments on pp. 144–45.

16. In 1813, after the temporary abandonment of Fort Osage, Sibley wrote a couple of reports rehearsing his dissatisfaction with the treaty's negotiation, the failure to live up to its promises (which he ascribed in part to Chouteau), and Chouteau Indian trade intrigues. See *The Territorial Papers of the United States,* vol. 9, 711–14. See also a report (probably written in late 1813) in which he was also highly critical of Chouteau. In 1819 he gave a copy of this report to Edwin James for inclusion in his memoir of the Long Expedition: Edwin James, *Account of an Expedition from Pittsburgh to the Rocky Mountains, Performed in the Years 1819, 1820* (London, 1823), 108–14.

17. Hoig, *Chouteaus,* 37.

18. The two had known each other at Cantonment Belle Fontaine. George Sibley's tardy August arrival, due in part to his desire to provide himself with a boat with river comforts, spread resentment among soldiers in a hurry to prepare for the danger posed by an unsheltered frontier winter. For this point and my understanding of military life at Fort Osage I am indebted to David Edwards, whose forthcoming essay, "Love and War at Fort Osage" will provide a more comprehensive understanding of fort life than do my general remarks here. Sibley, *Seeking a Newer World*, 71–72.

19. The factors were paid much better than the soldiers. While Sibley initially received $1,000 per year, lived in comfortable quarters, and had a comparatively liberal expense account; the sergeants were paid $86 a year; privates, $60, and they lived in primitive dormitories. Captain Clemson, the fort commander, who lived with his fellow officer in a small officers' quarters, to which he later brought his wife, was paid $420. Jones, *Prairie Puritan,* 58.

20. Ibid., 117.

21. In July 1809, Sibley hired a man named Colar to help with the factory work that troops normally would have performed for a factor. *The Territorial Papers of the United States,* vol. 9, The Territory of Louisiana-Missouri, 1804–1814 (Washington, D.C.: Government Printing Office, 1949), 273–74; Sibley, *Seeking a Newer World*, 93–94, 97–98.

22. Sibley, *Seeking a Newer World,* 186.

23. Ibid., 185–89.

24. Ibid., 123–26; for an example of a more minor harassment, see p. 103.

25. George C. Sibley to Samuel H. Sibley, February 12, 1811, Sibley Papers, Missouri History Museum (hereafter MHM).

26. *The Territorial Papers of the United States,* vol. 9. The Territory of Louisiana-Missouri, 1804–1814 (Washington, D.C.: Government Printing Office, 1949), 400.

27. Sibley, *Seeking a Newer World,* 186.

28. Gregg, "Fort Osage," 453–54; Clemson did not share Sibley's enthusiasm for Fort Osage's mission to the Indians. When the War of 1812 began he wrote to his St. Louis commander, Daniel Bissell, that Fort Osage was at a terrible location, of little use to the Indians, and no good as a military post, providing no significant ability to restrain the Indian war. He called Fort Osage "a moth on the publick purse." The letter was signed by three other officers as well, one of whom was Bissell's nephew (*Territorial Papers,* vol. 14, 587–90).

29. One of the more exciting moments was the night an Indian appeared in his bedchamber holding a severed human head. George C. Sibley to Samuel H. Sibley, December 13, 1808, Sibley Papers, MHM.

30. Ibid., September 16, 1808; February 12, 1811.

31. Ibid., February 12, 1811.

32. Sibley had known Lorr at Cantonment Belle Fountaine. Lorr had heard about the contemplated fort and when he accidentally ran into Sibley on the St. Louis-Bellefontaine Road, he asked if he could serve there as his interpreter. Sibley agreed and put him on the payroll a week later at $1 a day, plus one daily ration. It was unusual for a factory to have a full-time interpreter and the quality of an interpreter's work was usually low, but Fort Osage was apparently considered large enough and important enough to justify the employment. Sibley, *Seeking a Newer World,* 73, 75, see Smith annotation, p. 74.

33. Sibley helped Lorr in other ways as well. He arranged for Lorr's half dozen head of cattle to be delivered to Fort Osage. At Lorr's request he assumed a debt the interpreter owed James Audrain, the fort merchant. Sibley also records Lorr's hand-mangling by an exploding gun. For these and other activities, see Ibid., 103, 116, 177–78.

34. Later cattleman Ira Cottle and his family moved to Fort Osage, and a month later Sibley not only gave Mrs. Cottle Madame Lorr's job, but also temporarily made the interpreter's large family vacate half of a two-room dogtrot structure to give room to the Cottles. Apparently, this demotion did not hurt his relations with the family. There is still a clear record of his using Pierre for various tasks. In Sibley, *Seeking a Newer World,* see the following: on cattle, 82; assumption of debt, 110; inadequacy of Madame Lorr's kitchen service, 110; Mrs. Cottle, 113, 118.

35. She was baptized as "Helene" on September 28. See King of France Cathedral Baptism Records, Record 605, microfilm, Earliest Records of the First Catholic Church in St. Louis, St. Louis Genealogical Society, St. Louis County Public Library.

36. For Clemson's characterization of Ellen Lorr's various ages see his deposition in *Lorr v. Sibley.*

37. Ellen did not sign the agreement (nor mark it with an "X," designating her signature), but then Sibley says he is presenting her with "this Paper," ibid.

38. Ibid.

39. On dueling and less formal types of violence of honor in early Missouri, see Dick Stewart, *Duels and the Roots of Violence in Missouri* (Columbia: University of Missouri Press, 2000). On the relationship between honor, law, and violence in the early nineteenth century, see Lea VanderVelde, "The Legal Ways of Seduction," *Stanford Law Review* 48 (April 1996), 831–38.

40. VanderVelde, "The Legal Ways of Seduction," 867–75; Grossberg, *Governing the Hearth,* 46–47.

41. Celeste, as Pierre Lorr's widow, remarried on September 11, 1817, Marriage Records Ste. Genevieve Catholic Church, Ste. Genevieve, MO (1759–1839). This was four years after Ellen's initial proceeding against Sibley.

42. On Pierre Lorr's family see Pat Weeks, "Researching the Lorr Family," *Diggin's* 10 (Winter 2005): 52–53.

43. George Sibley to William Clark, November 30, 1813, *Territorial Papers*, vol. 9, 712–14.

44. Greater availability of clergy and more settled marital practices grew slowly as the eighteenth century turned into the nineteenth, but the "normative" bourgeois marital relations people associate with the past were still being built many years after the decision in *Lorr v. Sibley.* Stan Hoig takes on the daunting task of outlining the Chouteau clan's complicated sexual relations in an addendum to his book *Chouteaus,* 237–48. See also Katherine T. Corbett, *In Her Place: A Guide to St. Louis Women's History* (St. Louis: Missouri Historical Society Press, 1999), 9; See also Patricia Cleary, *The World, the Flesh, and the Devil: A History of Colonial St. Louis* (Columbia: University of Missouri Press, 2011): 132–61; and Carl J. Ekberg, *Stealing Indian Women: Native Slavery in the Illinois Country* (Urbana: University of Illinois Press, 2007).

45. *Lorr v. Sibley.* The record shows that despite the order, Sibley did not have to put up any actual money. Sibley turned to his old friend John Johnson, the Fort Madison factor, who, like Sibley, was in St. Louis because of the threat posed by Indian warfare, and to Robert Lumpsin, whose background is unknown. Together, on August 2, these three men appeared before St. Louis sheriff John Thompson and swore financial responsibility for Sibley's appearance in court. On Johnson, see Gregg, "A Man Named Johnson," 155.

46. In the surviving letters to others from the period he seems completely untroubled as well. In his letter to his brother he does not even mention the upcoming litigation, George C. Sibley to Samuel H. Sibley, September 25, 1813, Sibley Papers, MHM.

47. *American Territorial Papers*, vol. 9, 43–47. As quoted in Dennis Hahn, "Rufus Easton, Attorney, Public Servant, and First Postmaster of St. Louis," *St. Charles*

County Heritage 18 (April 2000): 66–83; Jo Tice Bloom, "Rufus Easton," in *Dictionary of Missouri Biography*, 271–72; Stuart Banner, *Legal Systems in Conflict: Property and Sovereignty in Missouri, 1750–1860* (Norman: University of Oklahoma Press, 2000): 86–87, 94–95. What the Chouteaus could not do, Aaron Burr did. Easton had met Burr in New York, and when Burr visited St. Louis to seek support for his scheme of western empire, he visited his confederate Governor General James Wilkinson and sought Rufus Easton's support. Easton refused to become involved. Wilkinson had close ties to the French elite, but the stench of the so-called Burr conspiracy attached to Easton, and he lost his federal judicial appointment. Hat in hand, Easton went to see President Jefferson. While the president did not restore his judicial position, Jefferson apparently believed his protestations of innocence and appointed him the United States attorney for Upper Louisiana.

48. Easton, who looked upon the relationship as akin to a business contract, dated their association from October 16 when Sibley presented her with his "paper" until she "broke" their contract when she sued him on July 31, 1813. Their physical association ended sometime between June 13 and July 31, with a date in June being the more probable, *Lorr v. Sibley.*

49. Ibid.

50. Initially, ambitious men moving in after the Louisiana transfer saw that the fastest way to riches and power was by serving, marrying, or partnering with the well-established French. Hempstead, Benton, William Clark, and Alexander McNair, who became Missouri's first governor, all took this route. In 1817, however, a year after the conclusion of the Sibley case, Hempstead had died after being thrown from a horse. William Foley, "Edward Hempstead," in *Dictionary of Missouri Biography,* 391–92; Jay Gitlin, *The Bourgeois Frontier: French Towns, French Trades and American Expansion* (New Haven: Yale University Press, 2009), 58, 63. Foley, *Genesis,* 183–84; Carl J. Ekberg, *French Roots in the Illinois Country: The Mississippi Frontier in Colonial Times* (Urbana: University of Illinois Press, 1998); Foley, *The First Chouteaus,* 211.

51. http://www.jenforum.com/mears/messages/632.html; http://politicalgraveyard.com/bio/meagher-meek.html.

52. Perhaps to emphasize her age and vulnerability, Lorr is referred to as "Ellen" throughout the court documents, whereas Sibley is referred to as "Sibley," *Lorr v. Sibley.*

53. There are, of course, numerous possible explanations: the documents may have disappeared, or subsequent testimony gone unrecorded; Lorr could have miscarried; the baby might have died; or it may have been a cynical play for legal sympathy.

54. *Lorr v. Sibley,* October 1813, Term Jacket Summary.

55. Ibid.

56. Ibid. It is possible that Francis Audrain may have been as untrustworthy a source as Clemson claimed. Born in 1795, Francis was as a hanger-on of his more

respectable brother, James, who ran the post farm for Fort Osage. Francis mishandled his brother's financial affairs and later in life established a reputation as something of a "ne'er-do-well [who was] said to have studied medicine and 'passed himself off as a doctor.'" James ended up in St. Charles, as did Sibley. He was eventually elected a Missouri state senator and sent his daughter to the Lindenwood female academy established by Mary and George Sibley. Carrol Geerling, "Innkeeper, Businessman, Politician, Spy. The Multi-Faceted Life of James H. Audrain of O'Fallon, who gave his name to Audrain County," *St. Charles County Heritage* 25 (October 2007): 161–66, especially, on Francis, p. 165. Francis Audrain was not as central to Sibley's work as his older brother. In his journal Sibley mentions him in passing as someone he used to carry letters St. Louis. See Sibley, *Seeking a Newer World,* 142–44, 147, 165.

57. Foley, *First Chouteaus*, 194; Bates, papers, *Life and Papers,* 271–72.

58. Bianca Adair, "Charles Lucas," in *Dictionary of Missouri Biography*, 505.

59. Rufus Easton to Charles Lucas, March 11, 1815, Rufus Easton Papers, MHM.

60. Historian Jay Gitlin quotes Albert Gallatin as saying the Louisiana French were "but one degree above the French West Indians, than whom a more ignorant and depraved race of civilized men did not exist." "'Avec bien du regret': The Americanization of Creole St. Louis, *Gateway Heritage* 9 (Spring 1989), 6.

61. Foley, *Genesis of Missouri,* 287–88; Stewart, *Duels and the Roots of Violence,* 46.

62. *Lorr v. Sibley.*

63. William Nesbit Chambers, *Old Bullion Benton: Senator from the New West* (Boston, Little Brown, 1956), 65; see also Gitlin, *Bourgeois Frontier*, 69.

64. Stewart, *Duels and the Roots of Violence,* 73. Clemson also served as a second for Lucas (with Frederick Bates) in the proposed duel, later turned aside, that pitted Lucas against the Francophone-supported politician John Scott, who succeeded Easton as a territorial delegate (ibid, 45).

65. Sibley, *Seeking a Newer World*, 118.

66. Gregg, "John Johnson," 154–61. A year after the case was over, John Johnson wrote to Sibley, "I am determined to get a wife. Ask Mrs. Sibley to recommend one. I want to settle down in your neighborhood," John Johnson to George C. Sibley, April 28, 1817, Sibley Papers, MHM.

67. *Lorr v. Sibley.*

68. In some ways, the Lorr-Sibley trial was a harbinger. Few women lost breach of promise suits in Victorian America. A woman's word, when coupled with plausible circumstantial evidence, was generally considered sufficient. Sibley's attorneys denied the verdict as the improper mixing of a tort with a contract. In fact breach of promise developed as such a hybrid. The first definitive expression of the Victorian understanding of breach of promise came in a landmark Massachusetts

case, *Wrightman v. Coates*, two years later. See Grossberg, *Governing the Hearth,* 35–38.

69. Ancestry.com entry for Helene Lor/Lorr/ Lore/ Lord http://trees.ancestry.com/tree/2960/413/person/46337484 (Walz Family Tree)

70. William Darby, *The Emigrant's Guide to Western and Southwestern States and Territories* (New York: n.p., 1818), 305.

71. Chambers, *Old Bullion Benton,* 110–11.

72. Jones, *Prairie Puritan,* 157–63.

73. Ibid., 112–13; Kristie C. Wolferman, *The Indomitable Mary Sibley* (Columbia: The University of Missouri Press, 2008), 45–50.

CHAPTER THREE

The Politics of Slavery and Missouri's First Elected Supreme Court: *Dred Scott v. Emerson*

Paul Finkelman

Dred Scott IS MISSOURI'S most famous—or infamous—case. When this case went to the U.S. Supreme Court, Chief Justice Roger B. Taney concluded: (1) Congress had no power to ban slavery in the federal territories and indeed could only minimally regulate the territories; (2) slavery was a protected form of property under the Constitution; and (3) free blacks, even those in northern states where they could vote and hold public office, could never be citizens of the United States.

Most scholars, judges, and lawyers consider the decision in *Dred Scott* to be one of the Supreme Court's worst. It is roundly condemned from all political perspectives. Conservatives see it as a terrible example of "judicial activism." Liberals point to it as an example of where original intent jurisprudence can lead. Critical race theorists use it to illustrate the endemic racism of American legal culture. Critics of neo-classical economics and jurisprudence point out that *Dred Scott* is the first example of substantive due process—the idea that courts can strike down laws that seem plausible on their face, but that, according to the courts, arbitrarily deny people their "life, liberty, or property" without out "due process of law." Thus, Chief Justice Taney said that it was unconstitutional to deny someone the right to own his constitutionally protected property—in this case the slave Dred Scott—merely because he brought the slave into a federal territory. Opponents of neo-classical economic theory note that the theory that led to the decision in *Lochner v. New York* (1905), denying a state the ability to regulate exploitive working conditions, was illegitimate because it was the intellectual child of Taney's proslavery opinion. Opponents of the right of women to control their own bodies similarly argue that *Roe v. Wade* (1973) was illegitimate because it, too, was based on the substantive due process theories of *Dred Scott.* They see a direct link between the denial of rights to a slave and the denial of rights to a fetus.

Despite the large body of literature on *Dred Scott,* few scholars have focused on the state case, which is usually considered a "prelude" to the more important U.S. Supreme Court decision.[1] But the state case is important in its own right because it illustrates how proslavery jurisprudence pushed the nation closer to civil war. The state opinion perhaps also illustrates the dangers of an elected judiciary. Shortly before the Missouri Supreme Court heard this case, the state went from an appointed judiciary to one elected by the people. This change politicized the court and led it to deny Dred Scott his freedom. Scott had won his freedom before a St. Louis jury, which followed precedents nearly as old as the state itself. But, in 1852 the newly elected justices of the Missouri Supreme Court reversed nearly three decades of Missouri precedents and law in determining that Dred Scott was still a slave. Furthermore, the Missouri decision reflects an over-politicization of the court. The opinion was written by Justice William Scott who had been elected to the court as a proslavery Democrat just a year before the case was heard.[2] His opinion was blatantly and directly political, as he asserted that the changing politics of the nation—and not the settled legal precedents of the state—should guide the court. In the opinion, he made claims about current politics that were incorrect, and indeed, in the context of the times, often absurd. Scott aggressively dismissed the idea that his court was bound by precedent, declaring, "Times are not now as they were when the former decisions on this subject were made."[3]

In the 1830s, Scott was the slave of an army surgeon, Captain John Emerson. Emerson had taken Scott from Missouri to Illinois, where slavery was prohibited by the state constitution, and to Fort Snelling in the Wisconsin Territory (present-day Minnesota), where slavery was banned by a number of federal laws. The simple legal question in this case was whether Scott had gained his freedom by being taken to these free jurisdictions and so remained free when he was taken back to Missouri. These were the facts and issues before the Missouri Supreme Court in 1852.

But as it turned out, neither the law nor the facts of the case were simple. Before turning to how the court dealt with them, and Justice Scott's extraordinary opinion, it is necessary to look at Dred Scott's life, and to recount the existing law of freedom in Missouri before 1852 and the long and complicated factual history of this case.

DRED SCOTT'S LIFE

Dred Scott was born a slave in Virginia sometime between 1795 and 1800. His owner, Peter Blow, moved to Alabama and then to St. Louis, arriving about 1830. Blow died in 1833. Shortly before he died, Blow sold a male slave, and the estate sold another following his death. Dred Scott was one of the slaves. It is not clear which one, but either just before or just after Blow's death, Dr. John Emerson, a St. Louis physician, bought Dred Scott from either Blow or his estate. In December 1833 Dr. Emerson received a U.S. Army commission, and as Captain Emerson he moved to Fort Armstrong, in what is today Rock Island, Illinois. He took his slave, Dred Scott, with him. At the time Scott was in his early or mid-thirties.

Fort Armstrong was in the free state of Illinois, and thus Scott might have claimed his freedom there. But Fort Armstrong was on an isolated frontier. Scott probably had little opportunity to make a claim for freedom and no place to go if he gained it. He was illiterate, and this was his first time living outside a slave state. He may not even have known he had a claim to freedom. In May 1836 the army transferred Captain Emerson to Fort Snelling, in what is today Minnesota, but at the time was the Wisconsin Territory. Congress had banned slavery in the territory in the Missouri Compromise in 1820, and the Wisconsin Enabling Act in 1836. Scott might also have claimed his freedom at Fort Snelling, but again he was in an isolated place where other slaves were held. The only regional authority was the United States Army, and the local Indian agent, Major Lawrence Taliaferro, who was, himself, a slave owner. This was hardly a place to gain freedom.

However, at Fort Snelling, Scott did gain his life's partner, when he married Major Taliaferro's slave, Harriet Robinson, whom Emerson purchased. In October 1837 the army sent Captain Emerson to St. Louis, then a month later he transferred to Fort Jessup in Louisiana. He left the Scotts at Fort Snelling where they were hired out to other officers at the fort. However, in February 1838 everything changed when Dr. Emerson married Irene Sanford, and he now wanted his slaves to help run his new household.

In April 1838 Dred and Harriet traveled by steamboat from St. Paul (in present-day Minnesota) to Fort Jessup on the western edge of Louisiana. On the trip they made no attempt to escape slavery as their steamship passed the free territory of Iowa or the free state of Illinois. Nor did they disembark in St. Louis and try to melt into that city's growing free black community or to sue for their freedom in Missouri. They might also have claimed their freedom in Louisiana, where for at least two decades the courts had emancipated slaves who had lived in free states or territories. But they did not seek their freedom in any of these ways. Five months later Captain Emerson was back at Fort Snelling with the Scotts until they all returned to St. Louis in 1840. In 1842 Emerson left the army and moved to Iowa to begin a medical practice, leaving his slaves and wife in St. Louis, but the next year Emerson died, and his wife, Irene, inherited his estate, including the Scotts. For the next three years she rented Dred to another army officer, and for a brief time Scott lived in the new state of Texas. In 1846, he was finally returned to St. Louis.

Sometime between his return from Fort Snelling and his return from Texas, Dred Scott reconnected with the Blow family. Taylor Blow, son of Peter, tried to purchase Scott's freedom from Mrs. Emerson, but she declined to sell him. In 1846, Scott began a suit for his freedom, arguing that he became free during his residence in the free state of Illinois and at Fort Snelling in the Wisconsin Territory. This suit was based on a long series of precedents, dating from the English case of *Somerset v. Stewart* (1772). In that case Chief Justice Lord Mansfield ruled that a slave became free when brought to a jurisdiction, like England, where there were no laws creating slavery. Mansfield argued that slavery could only exist where there was positive law—statutes—creating slavery. Missouri had followed the *Somerset* precedent in its first case on the subject, *Winny v. Whitesides,* which the state Supreme Court decided in 1824.[4] In that case the state's highest court held that a slave gained freedom by living in a free jurisdiction. Since then there had been more than two hundred cases on this issue in Missouri with slaves almost always winning, if, like Dred Scott, they had spent a substantial amount of time in a free jurisdiction. The Scotts sued in 1846, and the case should have been simple. But poor lawyering on behalf of the Scotts led to a dismissal on technical grounds, and it was another year before a St. Louis judge granted them a new trial. Mrs. Emerson then appealed this ruling to the Missouri Supreme Court, which in 1848 granted the Scotts the right to a new trial.[5] Unfortunately, a citywide fire, a cholera epidemic, and various other delays prevented the case from going to trial until 1850. Finally, a jury heard the evidence and ruled in favor of Dred and Harriet and their two children.

This verdict should have ended the case, which was consistent with a quarter century of Missouri jurisprudence. But in 1850 Missouri jurisprudence was about to change, because the state Supreme Court was no longer appointed, but would now be elected. Proslavery politics would alter the court and Dred

Scott's quest for freedom. To understand this sea change in jurisprudence, we must first understand the law of freedom on the eve of the case going to the state Supreme Court. This understanding begins in England, in 1772.

SOMERSET V. STEWART AND THE LAW OF FREEDOM

From antiquity to the Middle Ages, every country in Europe and the Mediterranean basin recognized slavery. When Columbus set sail for the New World, slavery had disappeared in much of northwestern Europe but could be found in countries all around the Mediterranean, including Spain and Portugal. The civil law traditions and Roman law inheritance of France, Holland, Denmark, and Sweden provided the legal tools to easily reintroduce slavery in the wake of European expansion into the Americas and Africa. In England, by contrast, there were neither laws providing for the creation of slavery nor the laws to sustain the institution. England came late to the colonization of America and was one of the last European nations to become involved in slavery or the African slave trade. The first British settlements in the New World were initially based on free labor. A few blacks had trickled into Virginia, Maryland, and Barbados before 1650, but not all were treated as slaves and they were relatively unimportant to the local economies. By the 1660s Barbados was quickly becoming a slave society and the Chesapeake colonies followed a few decades later. That year the British government chartered the Royal African Company, which received a monopoly to bring slaves from Africa to the New World. By the beginning of the eighteenth century, the British had firmly established slavery in their New World colonies, and Britain had emerged as a major force in the international slave trade. Slavery as such never existed in Britain, but slaves began to appear as servants in upper-class homes.

In 1741, sixteen-year-old Charles Stewart (or Steuart as it was sometimes spelled) moved to America, where he quickly rose from apprentice to a merchant to become an important civil servant. By 1764, he was the highest-ranking custom official in the North American colonies. While in America Stewart acquired a number of slaves, including James Somerset, whom Stewart purchased in 1749 when the eight-year-old African boy first arrived in Virginia. In 1768, Stewart, with Somerset in tow, moved to London. At this time there were an estimated 12,000 to 14,000 slaves in all of England, mostly in London, Liverpool, and a few other cities. Sometime in 1771 Somerset abandoned Stewart. On November 26, 1771, men hired by Stewart captured Somerset, who was then placed aboard a Jamaica-bound ship to be sold.

Immediately Somerset's friends sought legal help, and on November 28 Lord Mansfield, chief justice of the Court of Kings Bench, issued a writ of *habeas corpus* to bring Somerset before him.[6]

Mansfield held hearings between January and June. The chief justice urged the parties to settle the case, implying that Stewart should simply concede Somerset's freedom and perhaps negotiate some sort of wage-labor relationship: "Mr. Stewart advances no claim on contract; he rests his whole demand on a right to the negro as slave, and mentions the purpose of detainure to be the sending of him over to be sold in Jamaica. If the parties will have judgment, fiat justitia, ruat ccelum, let justice be done whatever be the consequence."[7] Stewart, however, did not take up Mansfield's suggestion. Significantly, the proper translations of Mansfield's Latin maxim was "Let Justice be done, though the Heavens may fall." This should have been a hint to Stewart to settle the case.

A battery of antislavery attorneys represented Somerset. These lawyers conceded that their client had been legally a slave in the colonies but argued that there were no laws creating slavery in England. Thus, they asserted, the moment Somerset arrived in England he was free. Three of the five lawyers who represented Somerset made the rhetorically elegant argument that "the air of England" was too pure for a slave to breathe. Francis Hargrave, for example, declared that in England the "air is deemed too pure for slaves to breathe," as did the lawyer John Glyn, who also asserted that "England was too pure an air for slaves to breathe in." Indeed, this argument was so powerful, and so persistently asserted, that Stewart's lawyer, John Dunning felt compelled to respond: "Let me take notice, neither the air of England is too pure for a slave to breathe in, nor the laws of England have rejected servitude. Villenage in this country is said to be worn out; the propriety of the expression strikes me a little. Are the laws not existing by which it was created?"[8] William Davy, another one of Somerset's lawyers, then replied, "For the air of England; I think, however, it has been gradually purifying ever since the reign of Elizabeth."[9]

Lord Mansfield never adopted the poetic language about England's "pure air," but he accepted the argument. At the June term of the court, he recited the facts of the case and concluded: "The state of slavery is of such a nature, that it is incapable of being introduced on any reasons, moral or political; but only positive law, which preserves its force long after the reasons, occasion, and time itself from whence it was created, is erased from memory: it's so odious, that nothing can be suffered to support it, but positive law. Whatever inconveniences, therefore, may follow from a decision, I cannot say this case is allowed or approved by the law of England; and therefore the black must be discharged."[10] Because this case was decided in 1772, the *Somerset* principle was part of American common law at the time of the Revolution. It did not immediately affect anyone in the colonies, because slavery was legal in all thirteen of them. But during and immediately after the war, Massachusetts and New Hampshire ended slavery while Pennsylvania, Connecticut, and Rhode Island passed laws to gradually abolish the institution. Pennsylvania's Gradual Abolition Act of 1780 took the *Somerset* decision into account, specifically providing that masters visiting the state could keep slaves there for up to six months. Massachusetts did not have such a law but did provide for the return of fugitive slaves who escaped into the state. In 1799, New York passed its own gradual abolition law, which allowed visiting masters to bring slaves into the state for up to nine months. However, in all the states ending slavery, if someone moved into the state with slaves (like Stewart had done in England), the slaves would become free immediately.[11]

In the years following the Revolution none of the emerging free states aggressively applied the *Somerset* principle and almost no cases arose under it, although the free states did emancipate slaves that were kept in their jurisdiction. Masters traveling west often brought their slaves through Ohio, Indiana, and Illinois on their way to Kentucky or Missouri. Visiting masters in Pennsylvania and New York were protected by the six- and nine-month exemptions of the gradual abolition laws in those states. Meanwhile, the national Constitution, written in 1787, provided for the return of fugitive slaves and specifically prohibited the free states from applying the *Somerset* principle to slaves escaping into their territory. Congress supported this provision in 1793 with the passage of the first fugitive slave law.[12]

SOMERSET IN THE SOUTH

While northern states did not aggressively apply the *Somerset* principle to slaves coming into their jurisdiction, a number of southern states readily adopted the corollary to this principle: that slave states should recognize the freedom slaves gained if they had lived in free states, territories, or foreign nations. This was precisely the situation in Dred Scott's case, and thus the jury in St. Louis—a jury of twelve white men, some of whom were slave owners—found the Scotts to be free. This is because these jurors were following the precedent, found in many places in the South, that accepted what might be termed the corollary of *Somerset*.

The corollary to the *Somerset* principle arose when slaves who had lived in free jurisdictions but not given court hearings were then brought back to slave jurisdictions by their masters. An alternative might happen when slaves who won the right to be free returned to the jurisdiction to be with family members, even if they risked being held as slaves.[13] The English High Court of Admiralty dealt with this issue in *The Slave, Grace* in 1827.[14] Grace had been brought to England in 1822 and in 1823 she voluntarily returned to Antigua, perhaps thinking she would be a free person. Instead, when she returned she was treated like a slave. Three years later she sued, but William Scott, Baron Stowell, in his last year as a judge of the High Court of Admiralty, held that any right to freedom in Britain was "temporary." Stowell asserted that *Somerset* only prohibited the forced removal of slaves "in irons" from Britain, but once Grace had been "imported in Antigua" she resumed her status as a slave. While in Britain she could not be forced to return to the West Indies, but once she did so, her status was covered by the law of that place, not by the laws of England.[15]

By the time Lord Stowell had rendered his opinion, courts in at least four American slave states had reached the opposite result: if a slave lived in a free state with the permission of the master, the person was free, and once free was always free because there were no laws in these states making a free person into a slave.

Between 1810 and 1816, the Louisiana Supreme Court heard two cases which implied that residence in a free state would emancipate a slave.[16] In both cases slaves who had lived in the North won their freedom in the Louisiana courts, although the outcome of these cases did not rest entirely on free-state residence. However, in *Lunsford v. Coquillon,* Justice François-Xavier Martin cited *Somerset* for the principle that slavery was "a creature of the municipal law," and thus Lunsford became free because she had lived in Ohio, and her subsequent removal to Kentucky and then Louisiana did not take that freedom away from her.[17] Although there were some twists and turns in its jurisprudence, as late as 1857 the Louisiana Supreme Court would uphold the freedom of a slave woman who had been taken to Ohio and emancipated but was returned to bondage in Louisiana.[18] The court recognized the emancipation in Ohio and rejected any idea that the status of slave could "reattach" if she came back (or was taken back against her will) to Louisiana.

In 1818 the brand new state of Mississippi ruled that slaves living in Indiana at the time of statehood became free for two reasons. First, the Northwest Ordinance of 1787 had ended slavery in the territory. Second, the Indiana Constitution of 1816 also prohibited slavery. Thus, the Mississippi Court ruled that Harry was free. The court used stunning language, well beyond that of Lord Mansfield, in reaching this conclusion:

> Slavery is condemned by reason and the laws of nature. It exists and can only exist, through municipal regulations, and in matters of doubt, is it not an unquestioned rule, that courts must lean "in favorem vitae et libertatis ["in favor of life and liberty"]." Admitting it was a doubtful point, whether the constitution was to be considered prospective in its operation or not, the defendants say, you take from us a vested right arising from municipal law. The petitioners say you would deprive us of a natural right guaranteed by the ordinance and constitution. How should the Court decide, if construction was really to determine it? I presume it would be in favour of liberty.[19]

Mississippi would continue to uphold freedom based on out-of-state residence or explicit out-of-state manumission until the late 1850s. In 1858, the Mississippi Court held that slaves taken to Indiana and manumitted by their white father (who was also the owner of their slave mother) were free under Mississippi law, even though they had returned briefly to visit their father.[20] In this case the court rejected arguments, based on the U.S. Supreme Court decision in *Dred Scott v. Sandford,* that free blacks could not inherit property in Mississippi because they were not citizens of the United States. A year later, however, in *Mitchell v. Wells,* the Mississippi Court held that a slave who had been born in Mississippi would always be a slave in that state, even though she had been formally manumitted under the laws of a free state.[21] Thus, the court refused to allow Nancy Wells to inherit from her white father, who had also been her owner before he emancipated her.[22] Rejecting anything that might resemble comity—the respect given to the laws and judicial decisions of another state—Justice William Harris complained that Ohio had no right to make blacks citizens in the United States and that Ohio violated interstate comity by allowing a Mississippi master to emancipate a slave:

> Suppose that Ohio, still further afflicted with her peculiar philanthropy, should determine to descend another grade in the scale of *her peculiar* humanity, and claim to confer citizenship on the chimpanzee or the ourang-outang (the most respectable of the monkey tribe), are we to be told that "comity" will require of the States not thus demented, to forget their own policy and self-respect, and lower their own citizens and institutions in the scale of being, to meet the necessities of the mongrel race thus attempted to be introduced into the family of sisters in this confederacy?[23]

Harris's nonsensical opinion seemed to imply that Ohio had for Mr. Wells to take his slave daughter north and free her. Thus, seven years after Missouri rejected the idea that a slave could become free by living in a free jurisdiction, Mississippi followed suit, with one of the most outrageous opinions in American legal history.

Kentucky also accepted the *Somerset* principle, but unlike Missouri and Mississippi, did not reject it on the eve of the Civil War. In *Rankin v. Lydia* (1820), Judge Benjamin Mills ruled that a slave taken from Kentucky to Indiana became free because slavery was illegal on the northern side of the Ohio River under the Northwest Ordinance of 1787.[24] Mills understood that Lydia was born a slave in Kentucky but concluded that this status was permanently altered when her master took her to Indiana. The Kentucky courts continued to follow this precedent until the Civil War, although with various modifications. A short-term transit through a free state like Ohio or Indiana did not lead to freedom. Even a few days in one of those states might not be enough for freedom. But a longer stay would bring freedom, and so, too, would a decision by a free-state court, even if the transit was very short. Two Kentucky decisions contemporaneous with the Missouri court's ruling in *Dred Scott* illustrate this.

In 1848, a Kentucky slave owner named Rebecca Kirby had taken her slave, Maria, to Pennsylvania. This was a year after Pennsylvania had repealed its six-month-transit law, which meant that a slave like Maria became free the moment she was brought into the state. While in Washington County for three or four days, Maria petitioned for a writ of *habeas corpus* and was declared free by a local judge, who said she was now free "to go where she pleases without coercion or restraint from any one."[25] For reasons that we do not know, Maria then returned to Kentucky with Mrs. Kirby. However, in 1850 Maria sued for her freedom in the Bluegrass State. The Kentucky court rejected her petition. Justice Thomas A. Marshall explained that she had not been in Pennsylvania long enough to be free under the principles of *Somerset,* that the judge who freed her there was from an inferior court that lacked the power to make such a ruling, and that by returning with Mrs. Kirby, Maria freely chose to remain a slave.[26] Marshall's opinion violated a number of legal rules, including the Full Faith and Credit clause of the U.S. Constitution, which required him to uphold a judicial decision of another state. But Marshall simply refused to accept the idea that a few days in Pennsylvania constituted the basis to free a slave. In Justice Marshall's view, the air of Pennsylvania was clearly *not* too pure for a slave to breathe.

This decision came down a year before the Missouri decision in *Dred Scott*, and might indicate that Kentucky, like Missouri, no longer accepted the *Somerset* principle. But, as it turns out, this was not the case. In 1853, a year after the Missouri court denied Dred Scott his freedom, Justice Marshall held that the slave Clarissa had become free in 1838 when her owner kept her in Pennsylvania for more than six consecutive months. In freeing Clarissa, Justice Marshall indicated that he might support a northern law that freed a slave after a stay of "six months, or three months, or even one" because strangers "would have an opportunity of knowing its provisions and avoiding its circumstances."[27] These two cases make clear that Marshall, and the Kentucky Supreme Court, was trying to find a middle ground between freedom and slavery. Kentucky was a border state and understood that smooth relations with its free-state neighbors were critical to interstate harmony. As late as 1865 the Kentucky court would hold that a slave who had lived in Illinois for six months was free.[28]

THE LAW OF FREEDOM IN MISSOURI

In 1824 the Missouri Supreme Court held that a slave named Winny was free because her master had taken her into the Northwest Territory, where slavery was banned by the Northwest Ordinance of 1787. This case illustrated the sometimes torturously slow process of freedom suits. Winny had first sued in the territorial court in 1818 and finally won her freedom in the St. Louis Circuit Court in 1821, and it was this verdict the Missouri Supreme Court upheld in 1824.[29] The Missouri court rejected the arguments of her owner, Phoebe Whitesides, that if Winny had a claim to freedom she had to have made it in Illinois, or that if she became free in Illinois, she lost that freedom by moving into Missouri. The court first asserted that if Whitesides had intended to live in Illinois—and the evidence was clear that was the case—then Winny became free because slaves could not be brought to Illinois and reside there. This analysis assumed that a temporary transit might not have changed Winny's status—that the air or soil of Illinois did not lead to freedom, but residing there did.

The court then explained that *if* Winny gained her freedom when Mrs. Whitesides and her husband took Winny to Illinois, then Winny remained free because "personal rights or disabilities obtained or communicated by the laws of any particular place, are of a nature which accompany the person wherever he goes."[30]

The counterargument to this position might have been that if Winny could gain a new status in Illinois—as a free person—then she could gain a new status (or regain her old status) as a slave when she was brought to Missouri. But this position was not tenable because Missouri had no laws that could actually make someone a slave, while the Northwest Ordinance specifically banned slavery. Missouri law recognized slavery, and slaves brought into the state were held to that status. But there was no law to make a free person—even a free black person—into a slave. Thus, Winny remained free.

From 1824 until 1852 the Missouri courts followed this precedent, although it was refined in a number of ways. Thus, in *La Grange v. Chouteau,* the court held that a Missouri slave who worked on riverboats did not gain freedom for merely being in Illinois for a few days because this was not an attempt "to defeat or evade the [Northwest] ordinance."[31] If the slave owner was "merely passing through the country" with a slave, or lived in Illinois but owned a slave who worked in Missouri and "occasionally" unloaded a boat on the Illinois side, it would do "nothing towards engrafting slavery upon the social system of the State [of Illinois]."[32] Slavery, and not the mere presence of a slave, had to be introduced before emancipation based on free-state residence could take place.

This analysis actually comported, to some extent, with the language of the Northwest Ordinance, which declared that there would not be "slavery" in the territory, rather than that there would be no slaves. More important, the Missouri court was determined to have practical rules that would support the prohibition on slavery in some states while recognizing the necessity of allowing slave owners to travel through free states, or even briefly visit them, while conducting legitimate business.

Subsequent cases clarified these rules but did not stray from them. The rule in Missouri was clear: any significant residence or work by a slave in as free state would lead to emancipation.[33] Under these precedents, St. Louis courts granted freedom to more than one hundred slaves.[34] Dred Scott had a claim to freedom while living in Illinois and again while living in the Wisconsin Territory (modern Minnesota). One Missouri precedent also directly dealt with the possibility that a military officer might be exempt from local law because of his federal service. In *Rachel v. Walker,* the Missouri Supreme Court heard a case on precisely this point at the very time Dred Scott was at Fort Armstrong in Illinois and preparing to relocate to Fort Snelling in the Wisconsin Territory. Rachel's owner, Lt. Thomas Baylis Whitmarsh Stockton, had taken her to Fort Snelling and then to Fort Crawford at Prairie du Chien, in the Michigan Territory, where slavery was prohibited by both the Northwest Ordinance and territorial laws.[35] William Walker, a slave dealer who was about to take Rachel south, argued that her former owner, a military officer, had been required to have a servant and thus he was exempt from local laws.[36] The Missouri Supreme Court would have none of this:

> Shall it be said, that because an officer of the army owns slaves in Virginia, that when as an officer and soldier, he is required to take command of a post in the non-slave holding States or territories, he thereby has a right to take with him as many slaves, as will suit his interests or convenience? It surely cannot be the law . . . that the convenience or supposed convenience of the officer, repeals as to him an others who have the same character, the [Northwest] ordinance and the act of 1821 admitting Missouri into the Union, and also the prohibitions of the several laws and constitutions of the non-slave holding States.[37]

Thus, when Dred Scott sued for his freedom, all the precedents pointed to an easy victory. He had lived for many years in free jurisdictions. He had been rented out at Fort Snelling, which meant Emerson had brought not merely a slave into the territory but the system of slavery itself, which always included a rental market for slaves. Not surprisingly, a jury in St. Louis declared him free.

But all this changed with an amendment to the Missouri Constitution creating an elected Supreme Court. In September two of the incumbent justices lost their elections. One who did not was the new chief justice, Hamilton R. Gamble. A moderate on slavery, he was opposed to any dramatic changes in Missouri law. But the two new justices, proslavery Democrats and political opponents of Missouri's moderate U.S. senator Thomas Hart Benton, were ready to reject past precedent in order to make a political statement about the place of slavery in American society.

SCOTT V. EMERSON: THE DEMISE OF MODERATE SLAVERY JURISPRUDENCE

When the Scotts sued for freedom, Dred Scott's entire family was removed from Mrs. Emerson's custody and rented out. This was to prevent her from retaliating against her slaves. Their earnings were held in an escrow account. By the time the St. Louis jury determined they were entitled to their freedom, a tidy sum had accumulated. There was even more money at stake when the case finally reached the Missouri Supreme Court. Thus, Mrs. Emerson vigorously pursued her appeal. Or, more precisely, her brother, John F. A. Sanford, pursued the appeal in her name. By 1848 or 1849 she had moved to Springfield,

Massachusetts, and in November 1850 the thirty-four-year-old widow married Dr. Calvin C. Chaffee, an antislavery political activist who would eventually serve in Congress as a Republican. Sometime during this period—probably before the case was appealed to the Missouri Supreme Court—Irene Emerson Chaffee sold the Scotts to her brother.[38] Thus, when the loser in the case appealed to the Missouri Supreme Court, the name of the case—*Scott v. Emerson*—was wrong, if not fictitious. In 1852, there was no Mrs. Irene Emerson.[39] Thus, Mrs. Emerson could not have legally pursued the appeal. None of this probably mattered in the long run. However, given that mid-nineteenth-century courts were often obsessed with procedural correctness, it is surprising that Scott's lawyers did not challenge the appeal on these grounds. It is likely such a move would have forced Sanford to refile the case in his own name and delayed proceedings for a year or more. While delays in the 1840s had worked against the Scotts, a delay in 1852 might have worked in their favor, now that they had an 1850 trial judgment supporting their freedom.

None of these issues appear to have been raised before the Missouri Supreme Court, which in 1852 undid Scott's victory and in the process reversed nearly thirty years of state precedents. Speaking for a two-to-one majority on the new Missouri Supreme Court, Justice William Scott announced that Missouri was changing its jurisprudence.

Justice Scott conceded that in past cases of this kind the slaves had gained their freedom. But then he proceeded to exaggerate the nature of previous Missouri cases. He asserted that past Missouri cases were based on "the ground it would seem, that it is the duty of the courts of this State to carry into effect the Constitution and laws of other States and territories, regardless of the rights, the policy or the institutions of the people of this State."[40] This was never the basis of the Missouri decisions. Rather, they were based on specific facts of either residence for a long period or being used as slaves in free jurisdictions, such as having to work crops for a season or being rented out.[41] At no time did Missouri ever assume it must enforce the laws of other states if they were arbitrary or unsympathetic to the needs of masters to cross free states or sometimes visit them with slaves. On the contrary, a number of early Missouri cases upheld a master's claim to his slave, if the slave had been in a free state for only a short time.

The Missouri courts had also always shown deference and respect to federal laws—the Northwest Ordinance and the Missouri Compromise—with the understanding that as part of the Union the state was required to, and also wanted to, respect the supremacy clause of the Constitution. Thus, for example, in *Rachel v. Walker* the court had recognized that the Missouri Compromise, which had led to statehood for Missouri, required that the state recognize the freedom a slave gained from living at Fort Snelling, which was in a federal territory where slavery was banned by the compromise.

Scott argued that these decisions were based purely on comity—rather than ties to other states or the national government or well-settled law throughout the South. He ignored the fact that in 1852 many other states, including Kentucky, Louisiana, and even Mississippi, recognized freedom gained by residence in a free state.

Scott's opinion soon dissolved into a proslavery diatribe that had little to do with the reality of Missouri's actual situation or its relationship with Illinois, where Dred Scott had lived. He claimed it was "a humiliating spectacle, to see the courts of a State confiscating property of her own citizens by the command of foreign law."[42] The problem with this analysis is that it does not comport to any known reality. There are no known instances of an Illinois court emancipating a slave accompanying a visiting Missouri master or traveling with a master from another slave state who was headed for Missouri. In fact, Illinois had gone out of its way to respect slavery and support visiting and traveling slave owners.

Judge Scott went on to rail that the free states "maintain that if a slave, with the consent of his master, touch the soil he thereby becomes free." This was of course an exaggeration, but it was true that by this time Massachusetts and the rest of New England, as well as New York and Pennsylvania, did emancipate slaves who were brought into their states for even a short time.[43] But Illinois and Indiana did not. Ohio courts held that slaves were not emancipated if they were on steamboats that docked at Ohio cities, even if they left the boats for a short while. Only three years before this case a federal judge in neighboring Iowa had declared that masters could cross that state without losing their slaves.[44] Dred Scott's own personal history demonstrated that Illinois and the Wisconsin Territory had been very tolerant of his master visiting with a slave. Furthermore, there had been virtually no change in Illinois since Dred Scott had lived there. In 1852, Illinois was more supportive of slavery than any other northern state except Indiana. Justice Scott was probably responding to the rise of antislavery sentiment in the Northeast and the upper Midwest, but even in those states, on the issue of slave transit the jurisprudence was exactly the same as what it had been in Missouri for nearly three decades: that slaves taken into free states for long periods of time (as Dred Scott was) were free.[45]

Justice Scott asserted, "Some of our old cases say, that a hiring for two days would be a violation of the Constitution of Illinois and entitle the slave to his freedom. If two days would do, why not one? Is there any difference in principle or morality between holding a slave in a free territory two days more than one day? [A]nd if one day, why not six hours? The old cases say, the intent is nothing, the act is the thing."[46] Significantly, he did not cite any of these old cases, because there were no "old cases" from Missouri that said this. On the contrary, in cases like *La Grange v. Chouteau* (1828)[47] and *Nat v. Ruddle* (1834)[48] the Missouri Supreme Court had held exactly the opposite and refused to free slaves based on short-term employment in Illinois.

One can only conclude that either Scott did not know or understand these cases, or had never read them, or that he just did not care what they said. The third analysis seems most likely: that he was not interested in what the Missouri court had done in the past. He was intent on reaching a sweeping proslavery conclusion and ending three decades of moderate, careful jurisprudence that balanced the law of freedom with the realities of a slaveholding Missouri. Justice Scott had other issues on his mind. He was simply not concerned with the facts of Dred Scott's case, the complexity of freedom suits along the Mississippi, or the actual history of his own court's jurisprudence on slave transit. He ignored precedents (like *Rachel v. Walker*) that would have led him to a different conclusion, he misrepresented the legal history of Missouri, and he offered an utterly fictitious account of relations between Missouri and her free-state neighbors.

In dissent, Chief Justice Hamilton R. Gamble berated his colleagues for politicizing Missouri law at a time when the nation had just reached an accommodation over slavery in the Compromise of 1850. He acknowledged that slave owners might be legitimately "exasperated by . . . wanton and unfounded attacks" by abolitionists who denounced slavery. But a court of justice was not the place to deal with such matters, and he admonished the majority for their failure to follow both precedent and settled law. "But, in the midst of all such excitement, it is proper that the judicial mind, calm and self-balanced, should adhere to principles established when there was no feeling to disturb the view of the legal question upon which the rights of parties depend." He reminded his politicized colleagues: "Times may have changed, public feeling may have changed, but principles have not and do not change; and, in my judgment, there can be no safe basis for judicial decisions, but in those principles, which are immutable."[49]

Gamble's dissent fell on deaf ears. His opinion was sophisticated and principled. But it was a futile gesture in the wake of Justice Scott's overwhelming rejection of legal principles, precedent, sound judgment, and even an honest summary of the facts in the case. Thus, Scott ended his opinion with a ringing endorsement of slavery and a bizarre argument that implied that conservative states like Illinois (which had almost always voted with the interests of the South on key issues) were in reality extensions of the most extreme abolitionists of the North. Thus, Scott wrote:

> Times are not now as they were when the former decisions on this subject were made. Since then not only individuals but States have been possessed with a dark and fell spirit in relation to slavery, whose gratification is sought in the pursuit of measures, whose inevitable consequences must be the overthrow and destruction of our government. Under such circumstances it does not behoove the State of Missouri to show the least countenance to any measure which might gratify this spirit. She is not willing to assume her full responsibility for the existence of slavery within her limits, nor does she seek to share or divide it with others. Although we may, for our own sakes, regret that the avarice and hard-heartedness of the progenitors of those who are now so sensitive on the subject, ever introduced the institution among us, yet we will not go to them to learn law, morality or religion on the subject.[50]

The final paragraph of Scott's majority opinion presaged the racism of Chief Justice Taney's opinion in *Dred Scott* in 1857, that under the federal Constitution blacks, even if free, had "no rights" and that slavery was specially protected under the United States Constitution. Justice Scott's opinion was also a precursor of the famous "Cornerstone Speech," given by Confederate Vice President Alexander Stephens in 1861, before the Civil War began. In that speech, Stephens declared that slavery and racism were the cornerstones of the new Confederacy. He condemned northern proponents of racial equality, declaring: "Our new government is founded upon exactly the opposite idea; its foundations are laid, its corner-stone rests, upon the great truth that the negro is not equal to the white man; that slavery subordination to the superior race is his natural and normal condition. This, our new government, is the first, in the history of the world, based upon this great physical, philosophical, and moral truth."[51]

Thus, Justice Scott concluded his opinion defending slavery and racism:

> As to the consequences of slavery, they are much more hurtful to the master than the slave. There is no comparison between the slave in the United States and the cruel, uncivilized negro in Africa. When the condition of our slaves is contrasted with the state of their miserable race in Africa; when their civilization, intelligence and instruction in religious truths are considered, and the means now

> employed to restore them to the country from which they have been torn, bearing with them the blessings of civilized life, we are almost persuaded, that the introduction of slavery amongst us was, in the providence of God, who makes the evil passions of men subservient to His own glory, a means of placing that unhappy race within the pale of civilized nations.[52]

THE MISSOURI SUPREME COURT'S SELF-INFLICTED WOUND

The Supreme Court decision in *Dred Scott v. Sandford*[53] is often called a "self-inflicted wound" by the court.[54] The reason for this does not seem to be based on the outcome of the case. The final outcome—that Dred Scott would not get his freedom—was not difficult to reach, or even legally wrong.[55] The court initially planned to accept an opinion written by Justice Samuel Nelson of New York (which became his concurring opinion) that the status of blacks, as slaves or free people, was entirely based on state law and that the Supreme Court had no jurisdiction to overturn the Missouri Supreme Court. Had the court done this, Dred Scott would not be a household word in the United States, and the case would be long forgotten except by specialized scholars. Almost no scholars doubt that the court could have taken this route with ease.[56]

Indeed, virtually everyone condemns the U.S. Supreme Court decision, but scholars have trouble explaining exactly why. At a symposium on "Supreme Mistakes" in *Pepperdine Law Review,* one scholar argued that *Dred Scott* was a mistake but oddly did not think it was decided incorrectly.[57] How can that be? The best explanation is the outcome was correct, or at least jurisprudentially defensible, but Chief Justice Taney's analysis was wrong, over the top, racist even by the standards of the mid-nineteenth century, and unnecessarily harsh and sweeping.[58] But if Taney's opinion was over the top, he was following the path laid out by the Missouri Supreme Court.

The Missouri Supreme Court might have reached the same result—that Scott was a slave—by many alternative routes. The court could have analyzed the case in the context of a statute of limitations. Many slaves sued as quickly as they could to gain their freedom. The Scotts waited. The court might have noted that by voluntarily going to Louisiana from Fort Snelling, the Scotts had implicitly rejected the freedom they might have acquired in the Wisconsin Territory. The court might have also used this case to signal that it would no longer support freedom claims based on free-state residence without an actual decision in a free-state court. Alternatively, the court might have held that freedom did not accrue in Illinois but that the court would recognize the power of the Missouri Compromise to emancipate a slave as part of the cost of being in the union. All but the last of these would have led to the same result—that Scott was a slave. All of these alternatives would have supported slavery.

But Justice Scott, like Taney five years later, was intent on a larger outcome. He wanted to assert, once and for all, that Missouri would stand firmly for slavery and against liberty. He did so by ignoring history, law, precedent, the political relations between Missouri and its neighbors, and most of all, the state's obligation to respect federal law under the supremacy clause of the Constitution. Unnecessarily, he abused his role as a judge and disgraced his own court. It was truly a self-inflicted wound by a determined, proslavery, racist majority on the Missouri Supreme Court. Indeed, with this decision the Missouri court emerged as more proslavery than other upper-South state courts and even more proslavery than some deep-South courts.

NOTES

1. See, for example, Don E. Fehrenbacher, *The Dred Scott Case: Its Significance in American Law and Politics* (New York: Oxford University Press, 1978); Paul Finkelman, *Dred Scott v. Sandford: A Brief History* (Boston: Bedford Books, 1995); Mark Graber, *Dred Scott and the Problem of Constitutional Evil* (New York: Cambridge University Press, 2006); David Thomas Konig, Paul Finkelman, and Christopher Alan Bracey, *The Dred Scott Case: Historical and Contemporary Perspectives on Race and Law* (Athens: Ohio University Press, 2010); Austin Allen, *Origins of the Dred Scott Case: Jacksonian Jurisprudence and the Supreme Court, 1836–1857* (Athens: University of Georgia Press, 2006).

2. Obviously he was no relation to the plaintiff Dred Scott.

3. *Scott v. Emerson,* 15 Mo. 576, at 586 (1852).

4. 1 Mo. 472 (1824).

5. *Emerson v. Harriet (of color),* 11 Mo. 413 (1848); *Emerson v. Dred Scott (of color),* 11 Mo. 413 (1848).

6. See generally, Steven M. Wise, *Though the Heavens May Fall: The Landmark Trial That Led to the End of Human Slavery* (New York: Da Capo Press, 2005), 1–11.

7. *Somerset v. Stewart,* 98 Eng. Rep. 499 (1772) at 509. The actual translation of the Latin phrase is "Let Justice Be Done, Though the Heavens May Fall."

8. *Somerset* at 506.

9. *Somerset* at 500, 506, and 509; Wise, *Though the Heavens May Fall,* quoting Glyn, 143.

10. *Somerset* at 510.

11. The history of these laws is found in Paul Finkelman, *An Imperfect Union: Slavery, Federalism, and Comity* (Chapel Hill: University of North Carolina Press, 1981).

12. For a history of these issues see Finkelman, *An Imperfect Union,* and Paul Finkelman, *Slavery and the Founders: Race and Liberty in the Age of Jefferson,* 3rd ed. (Armonk, NY: M. E. Sharpe, 2014).

13. Such a case occurred in Massachusetts when a twenty-five-year-old slave woman refused the opportunity to be free so she could return to her husband in Tennessee, *Betty's Case, 20 Monthly Law Reporter* 455 (1857). This and a few other similar cases are discussed in Finkelman, *An Imperfect Union*, 120–22.

14. *The Slave, Grace*, 2 Hagg. Admiralty 94 (1827).

15. *The Slave, Grace,* at 98–99, 106–7, 124, and 127; Finkelman, *An Imperfect Union*, 186.

16. *Adelle v. Beauregard*, 1 Mart. O.S. (La.) 183 (1810); *Forsyth v. Nash,* 4 Mart. O.S. (La.) 385 (1816).

17. 2 Mart. N.S. (La.) 401 (1824).

18. *Barclay, f.w.c. v. Sewell*, 12 La. Ann. 262 (1857). The entire line of cases is discussed in Finkelman, *An Imperfect Union*, 206–16.

19. *Harry v. Decker & Hopkins*, 1 Mississippi (Walker's Reports) 36 (1818), at 42–43.

20. *Shaw v. Brown*, 35 Miss. 246 (1858).

21. *Mitchell v. Wells*, 37 Miss. 235 (1859).

22. See Finkelman, *An Imperfect Union*, 228–34; 287–95.

23. *Mitchell v. Wells,* at 263.

24. *Rankin v. Lydia*, 2 A.K. Marsh. (Ky) 467 (1820). For more discussion of Kentucky, see Finkelman, *An Imperfect Union*, 190–205.

25. *Maria v. Kirby*, 12 B. Mon. (Ky.) 542 (1851), at 542.

26. *Maria v. Kirby*, at 542–43, 545–51.

27. *Maria v. Kirby,* at 547–48.

28. *Joe Henry (of color) v. Graves*, 2 Duv. (Ky.) 259 (1865).

29. Information on this case is from a marvelous article by David Konig on freedom suits in St. Louis, David Thomas Konig, "The Long Road to Dred Scott: Personhood and the Rule of Law in the Trial Court Records of St. Louis Slave Freedom Suits," *University of Missouri Kansas City Law Review* 75 (Fall 2006), 72.

30. *Winny v. Whitesides,* 1 Mo. 472 at 475 (1824).

31. 2 Mo. 19 (1828).

32. Ibid., at 21–22.

33. These cases are discussed at length in Paul Finkelman, *An Imperfect Union*, 221–28.

34. Konig, *The Long Road to Dred Scott*, 69, noted that existing records identify 98 people who gained their freedom with such suits just in St. Louis, but added that the records were fragmentary. Since the time of his writing, additional cases have come to light, boosting the numbers even higher.

35. 4 Mo. 350 (1836).

36. See Konig, "Long Road to Dred Scott," 73–74. For background on Stockton, see also: http://www.findagrave.com/cgi-bin/fg.cgi?page=gr&GRid=74238323.

37. *Rachel v. Walker,* at 354.

38. Marriages Registered in the Town of Springfield, database Ancestry.com (http://.ancestry.com/search_accessed 22 December 2013): Calvin C Chaffee-Irene Emerson, November 21, 1850; citing Hampshire County, Massachusetts, *Massachusetts, Marriage Records, 1840–1915* (database online), 51.

39. The legal term for this is the "caption" of the case.

40. *Scott v. Emerson,* at 582.

41. See *Vincent v. Duncan,* 2 Mo. 214 (1830) and *Ralph v. Duncan,* 3 Mo. 194 (1833).

42. Ibid., 584.

43. Finkelman, *An Imperfect Union*.

44. *Daggs v. Grazer,* 6 F. Cas. 1112 (1849).

45. See generally, Finkelman, *An Imperfect Union*.

46. *Scott v. Emerson,* at 584.

47. 2 Mo. 19 (1828).

48. 3 Mo. 400 (1834).

49. *Scott v. Emerson*, at 590–91.

50. Ibid., 586.

51. Alexander Stephens, "The Cornerstone Speech," in *Public and Private: With Letters and Speeches, Before, During, and Since the War,* ed. Henry Cleveland, Alexander H. Stephens (Philadelphia: n.p., 1886), 717–29.

52. *Scott v. Emerson,* at 586.

53. 60 U.S (19 How.) 393 (1857).

54. Charles Evans Hughes, *The Supreme Court of the United States* (New York: Columbia University Press, 1928), 50.

55. For a discussion of why the outcome in Dred Scott, at the federal level, might be correct, see Paul Finkelman, "Was *Dred Scott* Correctly Decided? An 'Expert Report' for the Defendant," *Lewis & Clark Law Review* 12 (2008), 1219–52.

56. See Ibid.

57. Daniel A. Farber, *Fatal Loss of Balance: Dred Scott Revisited*, 39 *Pepperdine Law Review* 39(2012).

58. Ibid, Finkelman, *Was Dred Scott Correctly Decided?,"* 1219–52.

CHAPTER FOUR

The Judicial Ouster Ordinance of 1865 and Radical Reconstruction in Missouri

Dennis W. Belcher

"That is no progress which progresses backward."[1]

THE STAMP OF BOOTS echoed in St. Louis Courthouse on the morning of June 14, 1865. Leading a determined group of men through the halls toward the Missouri Supreme Court there in session was Brigadier General David C. Coleman, Adjutant General of the Missouri Militia, followed by a group of St. Louis police officers. In Coleman's pocket was an order from Governor Thomas Clement Fletcher instructing him to remove two Missouri Supreme Court judges, John D. S. Dryden and William V. N. Bay, from their seats. Fletcher's order also required the confiscation of all the records, documents, and papers of the Supreme Court and the arrest of the judges if they failed to voluntarily give up their positions on the bench.

Coleman served a copy of Fletcher's order on Dryden and Bay. When they refused to relinquish their seats, Coleman declared they should consider themselves removed by force. Again the judges declined to accept Coleman's authority. Coleman then placed the judges under arrest and asked the police officers waiting to escort the judges to the office of St. Louis Recorder C. D. Wolff to face the charge of disturbing the peace by interfering with the operations of the Missouri Supreme Court. Three new judges then proceeded to the bench. Coleman had just implemented the "Ouster Ordinance" passed by the Missouri Constitutional Convention, a key part of the Radical Republican agenda of Reconstruction for Missouri.

The replacement of judges was part of the overall strategy of the Radicals to insure that the judiciary would not impede the changes made in the new constitution. As the Civil War neared its end, a new constitution was written which made significant changes to the laws of Missouri, changes that included the enfranchisement of some, the emancipation of slaves, and the ouster of judges from all of Missouri's judicial offices.

Before the war, Missouri had been divided on the issue of secession. From 1861 to 1865, the state government was sharply divided, perhaps more so than the government of any other state, and this division led to the judicial ouster ordinance of 1865. Missouri's fourteenth governor, Democrat Claiborne Fox Jackson, had been elected in 1860, and he wanted to align Missouri with the slaveholding southern states. In 1860, the population of Missouri was 1.2 million; but there were only 24,320 slave owners in the state. Twelve counties contained over half of the slaves. In February 1861, Missouri convened a constitutional convention of ninety-nine delegates to consider the state's relation to the United States. In March, the convention's Federal Relations Committee offered a formal report which opposed Missouri's secession, stating, "To involve Missouri in revolution, under the present circumstances, is certainly not demanded by the magnitude of the grievances of which we complain; . . . nor by the hope that they would be remedied, or even diminished by such revolution." The results of the 1860 census, which collected information on the geographic concentration of slaves, reinforced the conclusion that only a minority of the people supported secession, and the decision of Missouri to remain in the Union confirmed this belief. However, when the convention failed to push for secession, Governor Jackson and many in the Missouri legislature were greatly disappointed.[2]

Events in the spring and early summer of 1861 further exposed deep divisions within the state. The pro-Southern Missouri State Guard was formed; Federal troops moved into the state, and open hostility began. In the face of the imminent arrival of Union troops, the governor and the rest of the executive branch fled the capital on June 13. Two days later Brigadier General Nathaniel Lyon, with two thousand troops, arrived there. The pro-Southern troops of Governor Jackson and former governor General Sterling Price moved to Cowskin Prairie in southwestern Missouri. Meanwhile, Union troops from Kansas, Iowa, and Illinois joined Lyon's command.

With much of the civil government in flight, it soon became apparent the state could not function without the necessary authorities to run the government. The constitutional convention reconvened in Jefferson City in July 1861 to decide how the government would operate during the Civil War. Eighty of the original ninety-nine delegates attended the convention. Provisional executives Hamilton R. Gamble, William Hall, and Mordecai Oliver were elected to the offices of governor, lieutenant governor and secretary of state, respectively, offices they were to hold until there could be a general election in November 1861.[3]

The Civil War in Missouri was a bitter experience. Guerrilla warfare, which included "bushwhacking," attacks on individuals and families, reached a level hardly matched elsewhere in the country. The intensity of the experience led to increasing political extremism that shaped the bitter politics at the war's end. A radical, pro-emancipation political party gained strength in the polarized political climate. On September 30, 1863, a delegation of self-professed "Radical Union Men" led by Charles Drake of St. Louis and James Lane of Kansas met with President Lincoln at the White House. The delegation, primarily from St. Louis, heartily endorsed the Emancipation Proclamation and strongly supported the use of African American soldiers to fight in the war. In addition, they wanted better support from the Union army in the state and a guarantee that slavery would be abolished when the war was over. The Conservative Unionist Governor Hamilton Gamble came under fire from the emerging political party as a foot-dragging, native Virginian who would not move quickly to abolish slavery in Missouri. Drake's committee unsuccessfully urged the president to withdraw his support of Gamble as the division among Missourians widened.[4]

A year later the state's polarizing politics propelled the Radical Republicans—called simply Radicals or, sometimes, Charcoals—into office. The Radicals, with Thomas C. Fletcher as their head, carried eight of nine congressional districts and 80 of 114 counties in the 1864 general election. While their victory was decisive, Radical Republicans received a considerable boost from the disenfranchisement of voters believed to harbor pro-Confederate sympathies. Those able to vote were frightened and angered by four years of conflict, bushwhacking, guerrilla actions, and the efforts of Copperheads, northerners who tried to undermine the war effort. These sentiments translated into votes for the Radicals, and Fletcher won the governorship with greater than 70 percent of the popular vote. He was inaugurated on January 2, 1865.[5]

It was against this backdrop that the 1865 Missouri Constitutional Convention convened. The political power was held by a group that believed itself a model for the country. Slavery had been abolished in the Confederate states by the Emancipation Proclamation, but on January 1, 1865, in "loyal" Missouri, slavery was still legal. On January 11, 1865, Radicals voted to abolish slavery, and the decision was announced in an executive proclamation by the new governor, Thomas Clement Fletcher.[6]

During the preceding four years of harsh war, much of the state's infrastructure had been destroyed or neglected. The war was expensive, and the state had the highest taxes in its history. While much of the convention's attention was devoted to war-related issues, the Radicals also had a political agenda designed to advance the state economically and socially—advancement they believed had been held up before the war by the Conservatives or their pro-Southern opponents.[7]

Convention delegates, backed by their perceived overwhelming electoral support, met first on January 6, 1865. When only four delegates opposed the emancipation of the slaves, the momentum to progressively change the constitution increased. Instead of drafting amendments to the existing constitution of 1820, the delegates proceeded to draft an entirely new constitution, rewriting the constitution in only seventy-eight days.[8]

The document's master spirit was Charles Drake, who had actually drafted much of the new constitution in advance of the convention. So important was Drake to the new constitution that it became popularly known as the "Drake Constitution." A native Ohioan, Drake had immigrated to St. Louis in 1834 and taken up the practice of law. He served in the U.S. House of Representatives in 1859–1860. An intense, driven man, Drake frequently irritated people in his attempts to achieve his goals. He gained national attention as he led the Committee of Seventy in its unsuccessful attempt to persuade President Lincoln to withdraw his support for then-governor Hamilton Gamble. He had unsuccessfully proposed emancipation for slaves in Missouri to begin on January 1, 1864. From 1863 to 1864, Drake worked tirelessly against the Gamble administration's moderate position toward Missouri's Southern partisans. He had also strongly opposed, as unsuitable, the 1863 emancipation legislation passed under Hamilton Gamble's leadership that would formally end slavery in 1866 but create a system of involuntary apprenticeship preparatory to real freedom in 1874.[9]

Having been frustrated in his attempts to advance his agenda throughout the war, Drake was not to be denied at the constitutional convention. The Radicals distrusted the general assembly and feared it would undermine the agenda set by the new constitution. Their electoral ascendency might prove all too transitory. So the Radicals set about creating fundamental laws that would more permanently enshrine their will in the state's guiding document.[10]

A key portion of the Drake Constitution was a constitutional provision designed to insure that those who had served in the Confederate army or even sympathized with the South during the war were forever excluded from the affairs of the state. This disenfranchisement was accomplished through an oath that required individuals to swear that they had always been loyal to the United States government and opposed to all enemies of the country, which, in this case, meant the Confederacy. In addition, the citizens of the state vowed, without "reservation or evasion," to support the U.S. Constitution and promised to defend the country, including resisting any dissolution of the government.[11]

The oath referred to specific terms contained in Article II, Section Three of the new Missouri Constitution. Section Three denied the right to vote to anyone who had committed any of the specified violations contained in the article. The amendment also included language declaring a person could not practice law, serve on a corporate board, or serve in any capacity as a clergyman without signing the oath. The full inclusiveness of the "Ironclad" Loyalty Oath required any Missourian who wished to vote, hold office, teach, practice law, serve on a jury, or preach to swear he had not committed any of the forty-five violations included in the oath. The requirements were so strict that anyone who had even written a letter to a person in the Southern states from 1861 to 1865 was disenfranchised from any participation in the operations of the state.[12]

When some objected to the oath, the Radicals replied that such oath-taking was an accepted practice, one that had been in effect since 1862. While the 1862 oath was widely used and supported during the war, it was not as extensive as the one approved in 1865. Certainly, the loyalty oath had an immediate impact on lawyers and those who held office, but the convention delegates were not through. Early in the convention, a resolution made by Moses P. Green of Hannibal called for the reorganization of the state's judiciary, beginning with vacating of all judicial offices. His proposal found a ready audience. The committee on the judicial department, headed by a forty-one-year-old attorney from St. Louis, Henry A. Clover, feared the existing judiciary might derail the Drake Constitution's determination to remake Missouri society. Clover's committee accordingly adopted Green's resolution proposing an ordinance that "vacate[d] certain civil offices, to harmonize the workings of the government, and to protect citizens from injury and harassment from persecution for acts done by them in support of the government."[13]

The result was the "Ouster Ordinance." To accomplish the harmonization of state government, it was apparently necessary to remove all the judicial officials of the state. The committee felt that disloyal judicial officeholders were concentrated in the more pro-Southern areas of Missouri, and it feared these officeholders would block the emancipationist intention of the new government. The committee noted that the value of a slave had been recognized by Missouri law since the state's beginning, and it concluded: "Property in man exists and has always heretofore been recognized in this state, and if rightfully existing at one time, it may always rightfully exist." The committee felt it was important to move forward without becoming entangled in interminable legal battles that might attempt to derail the convention's intent to free the slaves by raising thorny questions about compensation for slaveholders. It believed the judiciary was the key to implementing the proposed changes; with the executive and legislative branches firmly in Radical hands, the committee viewed the judiciary as the Achilles heel to the Radicals' plans. The state had just passed through four years of bloody division, and the delegates were determined not to have these important changes undermined by "unfavorable and hostile construction and interpretation of term or phrase."[14]

With this reasoning the entire platform of the Radical Republicans was pulled together. Missouri's emancipation of slaves, the loyalty oaths, and the disenfranchisement of Southern sympathizers were all critical to the new postwar Missouri; but the power of the judiciary was recognized as the key to guarantee these laws would be unimpeded in their implementation. The committee questioned whether all the matters of the convention should be "drawn into controversy and adjudication by the civil or criminal courts of the lands? In the opinion of the committee it would not be the part of wisdom to have this be." The committee needed to insure the efforts of the constitutional convention were not undermined by individuals sympathetic to ideals that supported the old system of slavery and those who showed leniency for ex-Confederates.[15]

The Ouster Ordinance, or Vacating Ordinance, as it was also known, was passed by the convention on March 17, 1865. The ordinance specified that the judges of the "supreme court, of all circuit courts, and of all courts of record"; the justices of county courts, circuit attorneys and assistant, sheriffs and county recorders would be removed from office on May 1, 1865. All of the vacated offices would be filled by appointment by the governor.[16]

This ordinance had little opposition during the convention. Among the delegates, Isidor Bush, a prominent Jewish businessman from St. Louis, and a few supporters argued that most of the judiciary and other officeholders were loyal citizens. The wholesale ousting of 1,000 officeholders was unnecessary. Bush attempted to change the wording so that an officeholder would be ousted only after proven disloyal. Benjamin Hughes, delegate from Pettis County, similarly demanded proof of disloyalty and stated, "Mere difference in opinions in politics ought not to be enough to depose a man."[17]

But Bush and his small group were shouted down as Samuel Gilbert, a delegate from Platte County, sharply retorted: "'Hustle these officers out,' he said—'Don't put these Copperheads and sympathizers to the trouble of proving their loyalty—make a clean sweep of all who disagree with you in politics.'" Another convention delegate, Emory Foster of Johnson Country, exclaimed, "I am in favor of cleaning them out. I believe the Supreme Judges now on the bench, although Union men, were elected by Rebels [*sic*] votes." Bush was only able to find four additional supporters, and the ordinance easily passed the convention 43–5. Following its passage, members of the judiciary were removed from their offices, and the governor was given power to appoint new ones as he saw fit.

The tactic chosen by the Radical Republicans was not a new one. Missouri judges had been ousted by constitutional amendment in 1822, 1834, 1848, 1850, and 1861. The 1822 and 1834 constitutional amendments put judges out of office by ending their terms, while the 1848 and 1850 amendments fixed prescribed term limits for the officeholders. Only the 1822 decision to vacate judicial offices was exactly similar to the ousting ordinance of 1865. In regard to the 1822 amendment, historian Perry McCandless posited that legislators feared that already seated judges would derail the legislation that had been enacted by the general assembly. Thus, the action taken in 1865 was not new, but it was extreme; the scale of removals was both breathtaking and unprecedented.[18]

Henry Clover recognized that, in giving the governor such sweeping power of judicial appointment, "an extraordinary amount of patronage and power is lodged in the hands of a single citizen of the State." Still, he dismissed such concern by arguing that because the governor had been elected, his appointments simply ensured the will of the electorate. What went unnoted, by Clover at least, was that Radical delegates were, of course, putting new power in the hands of a Radical governor.[19]

Ousting the members of the judiciary began early in Fletcher's term. Anxious office-seekers had widely anticipated such an action, and angled for patronage even before the ordinance's passage. For example, two months earlier, David Wagner, who would himself win a Supreme Court appointment, began lobbying for a judicial clerkship for Captain D. S. Hooker. Many others across the state began doing the same.[20]

Certainly the most visible impact of the new Ousting Ordinance concerned the judges of the Missouri Supreme Court. In 1861, the Supreme Court had three proslavery judges on the bench, William Scott, William B. Napton, and Ephraim Ewing. Many recognized the power these judges held and sought a method "to wrest away control." The first attempt was a plan to increase the number of judges from three to seven, placing four new judges on the bench to ensure a majority; but Governor Hamilton Gamble, who had served as a Missouri Supreme Court judge with William Scott, opposed this idea. When the constitutional convention reconvened after Governor Claiborne Fox Jackson vacated his office, a loyalty oath was required for Supreme Court judges, and the "oath" had to be signed within forty days. This finally did the trick. Scott, Napton, and Ewing all refused to sign, and Barton Bates, William V. N. Bay and John D. S. Dryden were appointed to the bench. While these judges were initially appointed due to the "emergency" within the state, in 1863 all three were elected to their positions. Although the circumstances were different in 1865, there was a certain irony in the ousting of three judges who had gained their seats when their predecessors had refused to sign loyalty oaths.[21] Judge Bay had been a Republican before the war and Dryden had been a Democrat. Justice Barton Bates, son of Lincoln's conservative attorney general, Edward Bates, decided to resign from the bench in February 1865. These men planning the judicial reform in Missouri were men with a personal stake in the reform. In 1863, the three unsuccessful Radical candidates for judgeship of the Missouri Supreme Court were St. Louis attorney and chairman of the judicial committee of the 1865 constitutional convention, Henry A. Clover; Arnold Krekel, president of the 1865 constitutional convention; and David Wagner, who would be appointed to the Supreme Court.[22]

The new constitution was presented to the voters on June 6, 1865; however, the official election results were not known until July 1. The St. Louis *Daily Missouri Republican,* a Democratic paper, noted on June 13 that some counties were still lagging in providing vote totals. Because the vote was so close, and because those in distant military units were also included in the election, the secretary of state, Francis A. Rodman, delayed in certifying the new constitution. On July 1, he finally announced that it had been approved.[23]

In the meantime, the Supreme Court had convened a special session in St. Louis on June 12, three weeks before the new constitution was passed through the popular vote. Bay and Dryden, in opposition to the ordinance, presided as usual. In response, Governor Fletcher instructed Adjutant General Coleman to deliver a letter to Bay and Dryden on June 13 to vacate their seats or be subject to enforcement of the law under the new constitution. Coleman also demanded that the clerk of the court, Andrew W. Mead, turn over documents and records of the court on June 13, which he refused to do. Mead then filed a petition in St. Louis Circuit Court to prevent Fletcher's appointees from forcibly seizing these materials. The court agreed with Mead's argument and issued an order which "enjoined, prohibited and restrained seizing, taking or carrying away, handling or in any manner meddling" with any of the documents or records of the Supreme Court. Charles Drake would write this action was an "astonishment of almost everyone" because those who constructed the constitution regarded the judges and Mead as "mere usurpers."[24]

The letter from Governor Fletcher had set the stage for confrontation on June 13 when the court was again called into session. Sensing the drama of events yet to come, the *Daily Missouri Republican* noted the exchange between the newly appointed judges to the Supreme Court and the two "ousted" judges. Wagner and Lovelace entered the courtroom, while attorney James O. Broadhead, a prominent opponent of the new constitution, was involved in arguing a case before the court. The Republican reported, "Waiting a suitable opportunity Mr. Wagner approached Judge Dryden, and after the usual salutations, between personal friends (which we understand these gentlemen to be), Mr. Wagner informed the Judge he had in his pocket a commission from Gov. Fletcher, appointing him a Judge of the Supreme court, coupling the information with the remark—'But I suppose you do not intend to recognize the appointment,' or words to that effect." Dryden told Wagner his supposition was correct, and Wagner and Lovelace then left the courtroom.[25]

The events of June 14 were trumpeted in the headlines of the *St. Louis Daily Republican:* "The Supreme Court of Missouri Stricken Down by the Military Power—Gov. Fletcher as a Dictator." Despite the circuit court's order, Coleman arrived at the courtroom of the Supreme Court with a group of police officers, ushered Dryden and Bay out of the courtroom, and seized the previously demanded documents and other property. Fletcher had ordered Coleman, "In putting the Judges into possession of the Court room and clerk's office, you will as far as is convenient in your judgment, avoid the use of violent means, but if, in your judgment necessary, do not hesitate to employ all the force it may require." Dryden and Bay were taken to a police justice and charged with disturbing the peace for interfering with the operation of the Missouri Supreme Court. The now ex-Supreme Court judges were ordered to appear in circuit court the next morning, but no one appeared to prosecute the charges, which were then dismissed.[26]

Drake, the mastermind behind the new constitution, viewed the Supreme Court judges' resistance as a part of a "bold conspiracy among the opponents of the constitution." While many opposed the actions to remove the Supreme Court judges, many others supported Fletcher's actions. The state was fiercely divided, many newspapers across the state agreed with Drake and supported removal of the judiciary. Governor Fletcher anticipated civil demonstrations against these actions and ordered the 48th Missouri Infantry to circle the

St. Louis Courthouse where the Supreme Court was meeting. He also summoned the Seventh Regiment Missouri Enrolled Militia to duty to insure the new judges presided without disturbance.[27]

Throughout the state, duly elected civil officers were ousted from their posts beginning in May, based on decisions made by the governor. The ordinance demonstrated the immense power and influence focused on ensuring a single political agenda. While no one has tabulated the number of judicial officials removed from office, its application varied widely, falling most heavily on those sections of the state holding pro-Southern or proslavery opinions. Thus, many Republican-dominated counties, such as Adair and Sullivan, were scarcely touched, while central counties along Missouri's slave belt such as Clay and Lafayette were heavily impacted. For example, in Taney County in southwest Missouri, all the judiciary was replaced. In neighboring Greene County, the clerks and judges were all removed; an observer later noted that: "Those who were removed in Greene county submitted without an audible murmur!" Generally, throughout the state officeholders were removed or retained based on the judgment of the governor without controversy.[28]

One notable exception to the passivity of ousted officeholders occurred in Lafayette County where the Conservatives refused to leave their offices and gained local support to protect the officials. Lafayette had overwhelmingly disapproved the new constitution with only 295 votes in favor and 895 votes cast opposing it. In a calculated insult to local authorities, Governor Fletcher responded by sending a company of African American militia men to enforce the ordinance. Two county judges identified as the organizers of the protest were arrested and placed in jail. They appealed to a circuit court judge who had recently been reappointed by Fletcher. The judge contacted Fletcher before ruling on the case, and the governor reassured him the Ouster Ordinance would be enforced throughout the state regardless of judicial opposition. Seeing the futility of further protest, the two judges and other county officials vacated their offices.[29]

The intent of Governor Fletcher in dispatching an African American regiment to suppress the Lafayette County dissent cannot be overlooked. Before emancipation, slaves made up 32 percent of the population. Harsh Union patrols throughout the war had done little to suppress Southern sentiment in this county. Even after the ousting of the judiciary in 1865, a conservative, prowhite newspaper, *Lexington Weekly Caucasian,* defiantly began publishing in April 1866. The newspaper, true to its name, opposed equal rights not only for the African American, but also for the "Mongolian" and the "Indian." The *Weekly Caucasian* reflected the residual proslavery sympathy of some of the citizens within the state, highlighting the concerns of the Radical Republicans. By 1868 the Ku Klux Klan was operating openly within the county.[30]

Lafayette County was part of "Little Dixie," an area in the center of the state just north along the Missouri River in which the slave population ranged from 26 to 37 percent before the war. Many who had settled in this area were from slaveholding states to the east. The reactions from "Little Dixie" varied, but most counties opposed the actions of the constitutional convention. In Boone County, the actions of Governor Fletcher were positively received, but the convention was taken to task in an editorial by William F. Switzler, who had opposed emancipation, in the *Missouri Statesman,* which referred to the Ousting Ordinance as the "last great wrong" of the convention. "What a grave insult is here, what unparalled [*sic*] audacity! . . . That many of the members of the convention had a personal interest in the passage of this Ordinance the country has a loud suspicion . . . The Convention is serving its party, not the State, and the eight hundred offices created vacant are intended to be divided out as so much booty." In Fulton, the *Missouri Telegraph* simply stated: "This is infamous." But not everyone who had supported the South during the war engaged in prolonged resistance to the actions of the convention. Howard County was one of the counties in the heart of "Little Dixie" and was the home of Missouri's pro-secession governor Claiborne Fox Jackson. Just after the announcement of the passing of the new constitution in July 1865, Editor Francis M. Taylor of the *Howard Union* wrote: "We have had enough rebellion. No lesson can be plainer taught by the events of the past four years than the duty of obedience to the law." The new constitution was soundly defeated in each of these counties, but overall, the actions of the newly approved constitution were accepted in "Little Dixie" and across the state.[31]

For those who opposed the Ousting Ordinance on the basis of philosophy or politics, the next battles were fought in the courts as the authority to remove judicial officials was challenged in a series of cases. The hopes of those who objected to the Ouster Ordinance initially were encouraged by the state courts. In *Conrad v. Bernoudy,* Alfred C. Bernoudy, an elected recorder for St. Louis County, challenged his ouster, which occurred prior to the ratification of the new constitution. J. C. Conrad had been appointed by the governor to fill this office. Bernoudy took his case to the St. Louis Circuit Court and it ruled that the convention exceeded its power by ordering the ouster before the constitution was passed by popular vote and therefore, the office was not vacant. On May 19, the *Liberty Tribune* in Clay County, Missouri, and other Democratic newspapers across the state reported, "Vacating Ordinance of the Convention Unconstitutional!" The *Daily Missouri Republican* echoed the message with headlines, "The Case of Conrad vs. Bernoudy—The Vacating Ordinance Unconstitutional." However, the state continued to act based on the Ouster Ordinance even though the new constitution had yet to be voted upon; and not surprisingly, the state immediately appealed the *Bernoudy* ruling.[32]

The Ouster Ordinance resulted in additional suits that served to test the elements of the new constitution. The new Missouri Supreme Court heard the case of *James S. Thomas v. Andrew W. Mead and James C. Moodey* in September 1865. This case stemmed from Andrew Mead's attempt on June 13 to withhold the records as Governor Fletcher's new appointees seized the documents of the Missouri Supreme Court when the judges and clerk of the court were ousted. In Mead's petition for the restraining order, he named nine men, including St. Louis mayor James S. Thomas, as confederates in the plan to seize the court's documents. Mead succeeded in obtaining a restraining order from Judge James Moodey's circuit court; however, the restraining order was ignored and the materials were taken from Mead. In the case before the Supreme Court, Thomas, who was formally in contempt of court by ignoring the restraining order issued by Moodey, argued that the failure to turn over court material, and the subsequent restraining order were in contempt of the State of Missouri and violated the constitution. Henry A. Clover, whose committee authored the Ousting Ordinance, argued Thomas's case.

Thomas v. Mead would be one of many defeats of the actions protesting the Ouster Ordinance. There, of course, was a certain irony to arguing the case before three sitting judges who had benefitted from the ordinance. Writing for the court, Nathaniel Holmes declared: "The books, records, papers, and seal of the court, are public property of the State, and belong to the court." The ruling stated Mead could maintain possession of these materials only so long as he was clerk of the court, and the court had the right to compel him to relinquish control once his office was vacated by the order of the new constitution. The ruling addressed the nature of the Ousting Ordinance: "Both defendants appear to have assumed willfully, or by mistake of law, that the ordinance vacating civil offices was null and void. . . ." The court overturned the lower court decision and lifted the restraining order.[33]

That same September, the Missouri Supreme Court in *Missouri v. Garesche* reviewed the ordinance's constitutionality in disbarring an attorney who failed to sign the loyalty oath. Alexander J. P. Garesche asked the Supreme Court to vacate an order that disbarred him due to the *ex post facto* nature of the law. The court overruled his request, stating that attorneys and counselors were officers of the court and "are subject to ordinary legislation as the public judgment and good government may demand."[34]

In October 1865, the Missouri Supreme Court took up the *State v. Bernoudy*. Bernoudy was removed from office despite the verdict rendered by circuit court, which ruled the constitutional convention had exceeded its powers, stating "the defendant's term of office had not yet expired, and that the ordinance vacating the office was illegal, inoperative and void." Bernoudy also failed to take and file the loyalty oath required by the new constitution. Bernoudy again argued there was no evidence of overwhelming support for a constitution which had not even been put to the public vote and he was within his rights to maintain his office. For the Ouster Ordinance's opponents, the optimism of May gave way to the harsh reality of October, as Judge Nathaniel Holmes dismissively wrote that Bernoudy's arguments "contain nothing which constitutes any valid defence in law or fact to the information."[35]

The Supreme Court finally heard the appeal of *Conrad v. Bernoudy* in the March 1867 session of the court. In the fall of 1865, the court had handled any immediate cases regarding the ousting order. In ruling on the 1867 case, the court focused on the issue of the validity of the Ousting Ordinance. Once and for all, it put any questions about the constitutionality of the ordinance to rest. Bernoudy again lost, as the court pointed out that vacating ordinances had been adopted five times previously in Missouri. The court further noted, "All courts sitting under the State government were bound to take notice of the political action of the State Convention, and of the action of the Governor in recognizing the ordinance." The court ruled, "No authority has been produced to shake the legal foundations of these decisions."[36]

The legal rulings on the Ousting Ordinance were watched with keen interest by many judges outside the boundaries of Missouri. Judge J. F. Dillon of Davenport, Iowa, writing in the *American Law Register* in 1865, summarized the constitutionality of the Ousting Ordinance in Missouri: "The people are the source of all political power: but this power may be . . . conferred upon delegates or representatives." Delegates of the convention received "plenary and unrestricted power from the people" to act on their behalf, which included the passing of the Ousting Ordinance. Dillon declared: "This view has the sanction of high judicial authority." So ended the question of the legality of the Ouster Ordinance.[37]

Next, with the loyalty oath and Ousting Ordinance firmly in hand, Governor Fletcher and his party were faced with holding onto the offices with Fletcher appointees during upcoming elections. Since some of the appointees were simply serving the remaining terms of the ousted officials, this meant some faced general elections in November 1866. In an October 1866 *Advisory Opinion upon the Election of Circuit Attorneys,* the Supreme Court judges officially responded to a query by Governor Fletcher. The court opined that these attorneys would not have to face the general election until 1868, although Judge Nathaniel Holmes dissented, stating the general assembly was charged with prescribing how and when the circuit attorneys would be selected.[38]

Those who failed to fall in line with the spirit of the new constitution felt the weight of the politics of the time press against them. Judge James Moodey's opposition to the Ouster Ordinance in *Thomas v. Mead* did not go unpunished by his political opponents. The irascible Moodey continued to battle the Radicals by failing to adhere to prescribed regulations regarding oaths by the jurors and the lawyers who appeared in his court. The general assembly impeached Moodey and convicted and removed him from office in the summer of 1867.[39]

After the overwhelming victory of the Radical Republicans and their rewritten constitution, Governor Fletcher had secured his political agenda with the Ouster Ordinance. The Radical Republicans seemed poised for a long run of controlling the policies of Missouri, but the party's dominance was relatively short-lived. The state courts ruled in favor of the Ouster Ordinance, but the "Ironclad Oath of Loyalty" was successfully challenged on the federal level. The loyalty oath was strongly resisted, particularly by members of the clergy and other professions. A Roman Catholic priest, the Reverend John A. Cummings of St. Joseph's Church in Louisiana, Missouri, eventually derailed the oath. On January 14, 1867, the United States Supreme Court, in *Cummings v. Missouri,* declared the ironclad oath unconstitutional as it applied to certain professions, though it remained in effect in all other situations. In the 1870 election, the Missouri electorate had had enough. A majority of the seats in the legislature were won by the Democrats and Liberal Republicans, the latter group, led by U.S. Senator Carl Schurz, had split with the Radicals over the issue of the right of suffrage. The constitutional amendment to abolish the loyalty oath was submitted to the electorate in 1870, and it was approved overwhelming by 127,000 to 16,000.[40]

After his removal from the Supreme Court in June 1865, Judge John Dryden sued Thomas C. Fletcher for $50,000 in the Court of Common Pleas in St. Louis. Dryden's case came to trial the following year and the court ruled against Dryden and in favor of the Ousting Ordinance. Both Judge Dryden and Judge Bay retired from public life after their removal from office. Judge Nathaniel Holmes resigned in 1868; Judge David Wagner retired in 1877; and Judge Walter Lovelace served on the Supreme Court until his death in 1866.[41]

CONCLUSION

The full analysis of the 1865 Missouri Constitution Convention is generally positive. Historian Martha Kohl noted that the Radicals believed if Missouri were allowed to fall under Conservative influence at the end of the war then the state would fall back into the "Union as it was," which is exactly what the Southerners had wanted before the war. For Missouri to progress into a socially, politically, and economically thriving state, the Radical Republican policies were necessary. Kohl argued, "Radicals believed that they could build the industrial, industrious, Free-Soil community that they had advocated before the war." It is difficult to argue that the growth in Missouri from 1860 to 1870 was insignificant. The number of farms grew by 60 percent, the number of factories increased by greater than 300 percent, and the population increased by over 45 percent after the Civil War under the policies of the Radical Republicans.[42]

The events of 1865 have to be understood in the context of postwar circumstances. After achieving the victory of the Civil War, and by winning office with overwhelming public support, the Radicals felt they had a mandate to complete their agenda. While some of their actions were controversial, their efforts in many ways yielded positive results. William Parrish noted the Radicals provided a framework for the encouragement of industrial and corporate growth, and the proper utilization of the state's natural resources. In addition, they provided "equitable funding" for public education of both races. Increased power was given to the electorate by broadening the referendum power and by limiting terms of office under Radical rule. Most important, the constitution of 1865 provided for the emancipation of slaves, though it failed to extend the right to vote to the freed slaves. These advances, or so it seemed to them, were predicated on preventing the resurgence of the Southern sympathizing politicians, thus ensuring a state that was more progressive despite the less than equitable manner, in some cases, of achieving these results.[43]

As a result, the furtherance of human rights was much more successful in Missouri than in a neighboring border state, Kentucky, which lacked Radical influence. The Conservative Party gained control of Kentucky after the Civil War and restricted some of the more progressive efforts instituted in neighboring states. Although the Thirteenth Amendment abolished slavery throughout the nation, Kentucky did not abolish slavery in its own constitution until 1890 and would not ratify the Thirteenth Amendment until 1976.[44]

The Radicals made mistakes in the construction and implementation of the constitution in 1865. Most egregiously, the judges who reviewed the constitutionality of the Ousting Ordinance owed their position to it, a clear violation of professional ethics and basic principles of law. In addition, the removal of duly elected officials solely because those officials held different political opinions was remarkable and self-serving to any political party in power and antithetical to democratic principles. In addition, ex-Supreme Court judge and Democrat William Barclay Napton wrote of the actions of the constitutional convention: "Their object is to drive every one from the State who differed in opinion from them on the policy of the government"; but those charged with the civil responsibility of Missouri faced the reactionary environment of Lafayette County and similar areas within the state. There can be little doubt that the Radicals, despite their errors, propelled Missouri's evolution into a state that valued human rights and a more progressive way of life, into the last third of the nineteenth century. The conclusion of the Ouster Ordinance was best summed up by remarks made by William Taylor Hughes in *Blair v. Ridgeley*, which challenged the loyalty oath, "A law is constitutional, although it is immoral, unjust, and against natural justice." Certainly, the intent of those drafting the constitution of 1865 was the advancement of a society they believed had been crippled by the enslavement of human beings, and the desire to insure the ideals fought for in the Civil War were fulfilled.[45]

NOTES

1. Water Lovelace, "Speech of the Honorable Walter L. Lovelace," *St. Louis Daily Missouri Republican,* February 3, 1865, 1.

2. Jeffery C. Stone, *Slavery, Southern Culture, and Education in Little Dixie, Missouri, 1820–1860* (New York: Routledge, Taylor & Francis Group, 2006), 18–21; Walter Barlow Stevens, *Missouri: The Center State 1821–1915* (Chicago: J. S. Clark Publishing Company, 1915), 252. The census of 1860 established the distribution of slavery in the United States. The map produced from the census "introduced to American political and intellectual leaders the potential for thematic cartography to both shape and serve public policy" (Susan Schulten, "Visualizing Slavery," in *Disunion: Modern Historians Revisit and Reconsider the Civil War,* ed. Ted Widmer [New York: Black Dog and Levanthal Publishers, 2013], 19–22).

3. *Journal of the State Convention Held at Jefferson City, July 1861* (St. Louis, 1861), 23–26.

4. Walter Stevens, "Lincoln and Missouri," *Missouri Historical Review* 10 (January 1916), 93–106; Carl Sandburg, *Abraham Lincoln: The War Years,* vol. 2 (New York: Harcourt, Brace & Company, 1939), 403–6.

5. *Journal of the Senate of the State of Missouri at the Regular Session of the Twenty-Third General Assembly* (Jefferson City, 1865), 33; Mark E. Neeley, Jr., *The Civil War and the Limits of Destruction* (Cambridge: Harvard University Press, 2007), 216.

6. Thomas C. Fletcher, *Missouri's Jubilee Speech of Thomas C. Fletcher* (Jefferson City, 1865), 1–7. Fletcher was born in Herculaneum, Missouri, on January 21, 1827. Early in his public life, he was elected as county court clerk in Jefferson County, Missouri. Fletcher decided on law as his profession and was admitted to the Missouri Bar in 1856. He worked diligently in the formation of the Missouri Republican Party, and he served as a delegate to the 1860 Republican National Convention. He served as a provost marshal in Missouri and was elected colonel of the 31st Missouri Volunteer Infantry. He later served as colonel in the 47th Missouri Infantry and was brevetted brigadier general of volunteers. He left the army and was elected governor of Missouri on November 8, 1864, and assumed his office in January. "Historical and Biographical Notes," Thomas Clement Fletcher, 1865–1869, Office of Governor, Record Group 3.18; Missouri State Archives, Jefferson City; *The War of the Rebellion, A Compilation of the Official Records of the Union and Confederate Armies,* series I, volume 31, number 1 (Washington, D. C.: U. S. Government Printing Office, 1880–1901), 818; *Official Records,* volume 61, number 3, 730.

7. Thomas C. Fletcher, *Governor Thomas C. Fletcher to the Twenty-Third General Assembly* (Jefferson City: W. A. Curry, Public Printers, 1865), 3–13; Lawrence O. Christenson, William E. Foley, Gary Kremer, and Kenneth Winn, eds., "Thomas Clement Fletcher," in *Dictionary of Missouri Biography* (Columbia: University of Missouri Press, 1999), 303; Federal Worker's Project, *Missouri: A Guide to the Show Me State* (New York: Duell, Sloan and Pearce, 1941), 54.

8. Isidor Loeb, "Constitutions and Constitutional Conventions in Missouri," *Missouri Historical Review* 16 (January 1922), 202; Walter Barlow Stevens, *Centennial History of Missouri: One Hundred Years in the Union,* vol. 1 (Chicago: S. J. Clarke Publishing Co., 1921), 203; Richard Fulton and Jerry Brekke, *Understanding Missouri's Constitutional Government* (Columbia: University of Missouri Press, 2010), 10–11.

9. John Hay, *Inside Lincoln's White House: The Complete Civil War Diary of John Hay,* ed. Michael Burlingame and John R. Turner Ettlinger (Carbondale: Southern Illinois University Press, 1997), 78–90; David D. March, "Charles D. Drake and the Constitutional Convention of 1865," *Missouri Historical Review* 47 (January 1953), 110–23; Marguerite Porter, "Hamilton R. Gamble, Missouri's War Governor," *Missouri Historical Review* 35 (October 1940), 25–71.

10. William E. Parrish, "Reconstruction Politics in Missouri," in *Radicalism, Racism, and Party Realignment: The Border States during Reconstruction,* ed. Richard Curry (Baltimore: Johns Hopkins Press, 1968), 12.

11. A. F. Denny, *The General Statutes of the State of Missouri* (City of Jefferson, 1866), 45.

12. The New Constitution of the State of Missouri (St. Louis: n.p., 1865), 7; Stephen C. Neff, *Justice in Blue and Gray: A Legal History of the Civil War* (Cambridge: Harvard University Press, 2010), 155.

13. William E. Parrish, *Missouri under Radical Rule: 1865–1870* (Columbia: University of Missouri Press, 1965), 31; Thomas K. Skinker, "The Removal of the Judges of the Supreme Court of Missouri, in 1865," Missouri Historical Society Collections 4, (1914), 243–74.

14. *Journal of the Missouri State Convention, Held at the City of St. Louis, January 6 — April 10, 1865* (St. Louis: n.p., 1865), 97, 243–74; Thomas S. Barclay, "The Liberal Republican Movement in Missouri," *Missouri Historical Review* 20 (October 1925), 21–22.

15. Jeremy Neely, *The Border between Them: Violence and Reconciliation on the Kansas-Missouri Line* (Columbia: University of Missouri Press, 2007), 157; Silvani Siddali, *Missouri's War: The Civil War in Documents* (Athens: Ohio University Press, 2009), 218; *Journal of the Missouri State Convention,* 99.

16. Denny, *The General Statutes of the State of Missouri,* 47–48.

17. Carol Ferring Shepley, *Movers and Shakers, Scalawags and Suffragettes: Tales from Bellefontaine Cemetery* (St. Louis: Missouri History Museum, 2008), 338; Skinker, "The Removal of the Judges of the Supreme Court of Missouri, in 1865," 256.

18. Skinker, "The Removal of the Judges of the Supreme Court of Missouri, in 1865," 257–59; Laurance Hyde, "Origin and Development of Missouri Appellate Procedure," *Missouri Law Review* 2 (1937), 281–99; Perry McCandless, *History of Missouri, 1829–1860,* vol. II (Columbia: University of Missouri Press, 1971), 67; Loeb, "Constitutions and Constitutional Conventions in Missouri," 194–95; C. H. McClure, Early Opposition to Thomas Hart Benton, *Missouri Historical Review* 10 (April 1916), 158.

19. *Journal of the Missouri State Convention,* 98.

20. David Wagner, letter to Thomas Clement Fletcher, January 16, 1865, Thomas Clement Fletcher, 1865–1869, Office of Governor, Record Group 3.18, Missouri State Archives, Jefferson City.

21. Joseph Fred Benson, "Ages of the Law—A Brief Legal History of Missouri Part II—1860–1918," *Journal of the Missouri Bar* 68 (July–August 2012), 200–207.

22. Marvin Cain, *Lincoln's Attorney General: Edward Bates* (Columbia: University of Missouri Press, 1965), 318–24; James O Broadhead, "Reminiscences of Fifty-Years of Practice," in *The History of the Bench and Bar of Missouri,* ed. A. J. D. Stewart (St. Louis: n.p., 1898), 11.

23. The new constitution was approved 43,670 to 41,808 votes. Drake's own tally showed the constitution failed to pass until 3,995 favorable votes were added from Union soldiers. The military vote was decisive; it resulted in a majority of 2,827 votes in favor of the constitution. Before the soldiers' ballots were counted, the constitution was a mere 965 votes shy of approval. Charles Drake, "Autobiography," Charles D. Drake Papers (C1003), Folder 40, p. 1149, State Historical Society of Missouri, Columbia; "Result of the Election," *St. Louis Daily Missouri Republican,* June 13, 1865, 2; Parrish, "Reconstruction Politics in Missouri," 14.

24. "The Supreme Court Case," *St. Louis Daily Missouri Republican,* June 14, 1865, 2; Drake, "Autobiography," Folder 40, pp. 1128–35.

25. "The Supreme Court," *St. Louis Daily Missouri Republican,* June 13, 1865, 2.

26. "The Supreme Court of Missouri Stricken Down by the Military Power—Gov. Fletcher as a Dictator," *St. Louis Daily Missouri Republican,* June 15, 1865, 2; Frank O. Bowman III, "Stories of Crimes, Trials, and Appeals in Civil War Era Missouri," *Marquette Law Review* 93 (2009), 372; Charles C. Whittelsey, *Reports of Cases Argued and Determined in the Supreme Court of Missouri,* vol. XXXV (St. Louis: n.p., 1865), v.

27. "The Supreme Court Question," *Missouri State Times* (Jefferson City), June 23, 1865, p. 2, col. 2; "The Government Sustained," *Morning Herald and Daily News* (St. Joseph), July 2, 1865, p. 2, col. 1; "Ratification Meeting," *Missouri Weekly Patriot* (Springfield), June 29, 1865, p. 2. col. 2; Drake, "Autobiography," Folder 40, p. 1139.

28. "Bar Meeting," *Liberty Tribune,* May 1, 1865, 1; Missouri Secretary of State's Office, Register of Civil Officers, 1865–1904, MSA, Record Group 5, Reel No. S80–81; *History of Adair, Sullivan, Putnam, and Schuyler Counties, Missouri* (Chicago: Goodspeed Publishing Company, 1888), 54–60, 268–70, 670–72; *The History of Southeast Missouri,* (Chicago: Goodspeed Publishing Co., 1888), 390–92; Christopher Phillips, "'A Question of Power, Not One of Law:' Federal Occupation and Politics of Loyalty in the Western Border Slave States during the American Civil War," in *Bleeding Kansas, Bleeding Missouri,* ed. Jonathan Earle and Diane Mutti Burke (Lawrence: University Press of Kansas, 2013), 131–51; Missouri Secretary of State's Office, Register of Civil Officers, Volume 5: Reynolds—Wright Counties, 1865–1904, MSA, Record Group 5, Reel No. S83, 319; *The History of Greene County, Missouri* (n.p., n.d.), 485.

29. William Young, *Young's History of Lafayette County Missouri,* vol. 1 (Indianapolis, 1901), 77; Parrish, *Missouri under Radical Rule,* 51.

30. Philips, "A Question of Power"; Aaron Aster, "The Lexington Weekly Caucasian: White Supremacist Discourse in Post–Civil War Western Missouri," both in *Bleeding Kansas, Bleeding Missouri,* ed. Earle and Burke, 189–90; John Starrett Hughes, "Lafayette County and the Aftermath of Slavery: 1861–1870," *Missouri Historical Review* 75 (October 1980), 51–63.

31. "New Constitution," *Missouri Statesman,* May 19, 1865; State Convention—Its Last Great Wrong," *Missouri Statesman,* "March 24, 1865, p. 2., col. 1; "The New Constitution," *Missouri Telegraph, May 12, 1865;* "The New Constitution," *Howard Union,* p. 2, col. 1, July 13, 1865; *Missouri State Times* (Jefferson City), "Official Return of the Vote," July 7, 1865; For statistics regarding slavery in various counties, see Jeffrey C. Stone, *Slavery, Southern Culture, and Education in Little Dixie, Missouri* (New York: Routledge, Taylor & Francis Group, 2006), 20–21.

32. *Missouri v. Bernoudy,* 36 Mo. 279, 1865 WL 2672 (Mo.); "Vacating Ordinance of the Convention Unconstitutional," *Liberty Tribune,* May 19, 1865, 1; "The Supreme Court Case," *St. Louis Daily Missouri Republican,* June 14, 1865, 2.

33. *Thomas v. Mead,* 36 Mo. 232, 1865 WL 2671 (Mo.).

34. *Missouri v. Garesche,* 36 Mo. 256, 1865 WL 2586 (Mo.).

35. *Conrad v. Bernoudy,* 40 Mo. 192, 1867 WL 4709 (Mo.).

36. Ibid., Judicial offices were ordered vacated in 1822, 1834, 1848, 1850, and 1861.

37. Dillon wrote a summary of the constitutionality of the actions in Missouri during the summer of 1865, including the citations of various cases from across the nation. Dillon noted the problems with the actions in Missouri as well as the case law that supported these actions. J. F. Dillon, "The Missouri Supreme Judgeship," *American Law Register* 4 (October 1865), 714–15.

38. *Advisory Opinion upon the Election of Circuit Attorneys,* 38 Mo. 419, 1866 WL 4283 (Mo.).

39. Parrish, *Missouri under Radical Rule: 1865–1870,* 229.

40. *Cummings v. Missouri,* 71 U.S. 4 Wall. 277 277 (1867); Harold Bradley, "In Defense of John Cummings," *Missouri Historical Review* 57 (October 1962), 1–15; Jonathan Lurie, *The Chase Court: Justices, Rulings, and Legacy* (Santa Barbara: ABC-CLIO, Inc., 2004) 58–59; Eugene M. Violette, *History of Missouri* (Boston: D. C. Heath & Co., 1918), 421.

41. D. A. Divilbiss, "The Ousting of the Judges," *Missouri Supreme Court History Journal* 1 (Spring 1986), 1–10.

42. Martha Kohl, "Enforcing a Vision of Community: The Role of the Test Oath in Missouri's Reconstruction," *Civil War History* 40 (December 1994), 298.

43. William E. Parrish, *The History of Missouri, 1860–1875,* vol. III (Columbia: University of Missouri Press: 2001), 123–24.

44. Laura Hromyak Hendrix, *Constitution of the Commonwealth of Kentucky,* Informational Bulletin No. 59 (Frankfort, KY: Legislative Research Commission, 2013), 29; House of Representatives, *The Constitution of the United States as Amended,* 102nd Congress, Second Session, Document Number 102–188 (Washington, D.C.: GPO, 1992), 18.

45. The summary of errors in the execution of the Ousting Ordinance was made by St. Louis University Law School professor Gerald T. Dunne in *The Missouri Supreme Court: From Dred Scott to Nancy Cruzan* (Columbia: University of Missouri Press, 1993), 63; William Barclay Napton, *The Union on Trial: the Political Journals of William Barclay Napton 1829–1883,* ed. Christopher Phillips and Jason Pendleton (Columbia: University of Missouri Press, 2005), 238; William Taylor Hughes, *Datum Posts of Jurisprudence* (Chicago: Usonia Publishing Company, 1907), 137. William Barclay Napton, *The Union on Trial: the Political Journals of William Barclay Napton 1829–1883*, ed. Christopher Phillips and Jason Pendleton (Columbia: University of Missouri Press, 2005), 238. William Taylor Hughes, *Datum Posts of Jurisprudence* (Chicago: Usonia Publishing Company, 1907), 137.

CHAPTER FIVE

Disfranchised and Degraded
Virginia L. Minor and the Constitutional Case for Women's Suffrage

Bonnie Stepenoff

IS VOTING A FUNDAMENTAL human right? In the 1870s, Virginia Louisa Minor lost her suit against a St. Louis County official who refused to add her name to the list of registered voters. In taking the case all the way to the United States Supreme Court, she and her husband, Francis Minor, argued that voting was one of the "privileges and immunities" of citizenship protected by the Fourteenth Amendment to the United States Constitution. While the Minors were pressing their case, the Supreme Court adopted a very narrow definition of the "privileges and immunities" to be protected by the federal government. During Reconstruction, as the nation quickly retreated from its post–Civil War commitment to equality, the Minors continued to insist on full civil rights for all citizens. Long after the court battle ended, the Minor case inspired activists and scholars to reexamine assumptions about civil rights, political rights, states' rights, and the meaning of citizenship. Because these assumptions are central to the functioning of a democratic republic, the case of *Minor v. Happersett* deserves another careful look with a focus on its far-reaching legal implications.

With great detective skill, historian LeeAnn Whites has ably uncovered biographical information on Virginia Minor. Minor was born on March 27, 1824, in Caroline County, Virginia. She married a distant cousin, and so her maiden name and married name were the same. Her parents, Warner and Maria Timberlake Minor, had six other children. Their second-born, Virginia, received most of her education at home and grew to be an attractive and popular young woman. She spent a short time at an academy for young ladies in Charlottesville, where her father served as hotel-keeper for the University of Virginia. On August 31, 1843, she married Francis Minor of Orange, Virginia, and moved with him to St. Louis in 1845. Francis carried on a successful law practice, and the couple occupied a substantial house in town. By 1853, they had moved to a ten-acre property, which they named Minoria, on the outskirts of the city. They had one child, Francis Gilmer. He was born in 1852 and died in 1866 in a shooting accident.[1]

Historians have discovered few clues as to why Virginia Minor challenged the norms of her society. Friends in St. Louis regarded her as a loving wife and Francis as a devoted husband. By studying deeds, wills, and other public records, LeeAnn Whites concluded that Francis did his best to give Virginia some financial independence, despite customs and laws denying property rights to married women. Initially, Francis Minor acquired the house and lot in St. Louis in his own name, but in 1846 he placed all his property, real and personal, and any property he might acquire in the future, in trust for his wife. Using his legal expertise, he made certain that his wife had the power to sell, mortgage, or bequeath the property as she saw fit. In 1853, she purchased their country estate and sold their house in town in separate transactions involving two other married women. In both cases, the buying and selling of land by women was made possible through the use of trusts, although by this time Missouri had confirmed married women's rights to control their own separate property. The Minor trust gave Virginia considerable power to assign the family's property to her heirs as she saw fit. Francis Minor's motivation may have stemmed from his childhood experience of living in a household headed by a widowed mother, who had many children, a large plantation, and many slaves to manage.[2]

It is instructive to consider the legal status of women in nineteenth-century Missouri, where Virginia Minor's financial independence was unusual, but not unique. Because of its French colonial roots, Missouri had a long-standing tradition of allowing women to take an active role in their own affairs. In colonial Ste. Genevieve, as historian Susan Boyle has shown, French customs supported women's rights to inherit from their fathers and maintain property separate from that of their husbands. After the Louisiana Purchase, women in Ste. Genevieve continued to exercise these rights under the American regime. For example, the twice-married and twice-widowed Marie LaPorte engaged in farming, innkeeping, slave-trading, and money-lending, and defended her interests in a series of legal disputes. By 1823, she owned at least four houses, and in 1839 she registered her own personal brand for free-roaming hogs. As a widow in her fifties, she adopted an infant son. She died in 1849 at the age of eighty-three, having demonstrated that Missouri women had legal rights to sue, testify in court, sign deeds, make wills, adopt children, and own slaves.

In the year of her death, Missouri passed a statute allowing married women to own separate property that could not be taken from them to cover their husbands' debts.[3]

The Civil War and the end of slavery challenged the dominance of white male heads of households. Traditionally, political power, including the right to vote, belonged to those who owned property, supported families, and were in a position to act and think independently. Before the war, women, children, and slaves, who were dependent on white males, were denied political autonomy. When slavery ended, the position of white masters became uncertain. Black men, who should have been in a position to assume their place as heads of households, faced terrible obstacles of racism and economic injustice. The position of white and black women became a subject of debate, as the hierarchical basis of society, particularly that of Southern society, shifted.[4]

Minor, a Southern-born woman, supported the Union during the Civil War. When the Minors left Virginia, they brought no slaves with them, nor did they acquire any once in Missouri. Missouri had entered the Union as a slave state, and St. Louis's French and Spanish roots connected it to the slaveholding societies of the eighteenth century. However, by the 1840s, German immigration and commercial growth were changing the city's social and economic character. Although many St. Louisans sympathized with the Confederacy during the Civil War, the Minors staunchly supported the Union. After 1861, Virginia joined the Ladies' Union Aid Society, an auxiliary of the Western Sanitary Commission, which provided aid to injured soldiers and their wives. After the war, Francis received an appointment as St. Louis County's claim agent for veterans seeking pensions.[5]

The Union victory required Americans to grant citizenship to millions of freedmen and, consequently, to examine the nature of citizenship. Before the war, slavery had a more coherent legal definition than did freedom. The federal system, allowing as it did for sovereignty shared by national, state, and local governments, resulted in many variations in laws that regulated property ownership, family relationships, criminal codes, court procedures, and other matters that impinged on the rights of independent citizens. The United States Constitution was more concerned with limiting the powers of the federal government than with defining the rights of the governed. The Bill of Rights protected some of the rights of individuals and states, but it neglected many important issues, including marriage, privacy, and voting. During Reconstruction, the nation adopted the Thirteenth, Fourteenth, and Fifteenth Amendments, which affirmed the rights of "persons" and "citizens" but did not address gender.[6]

Minor belonged to a group of St. Louis women who participated in wartime relief work and subsequently embraced the cause of women's rights. These women gathered in St. Louis on May 8, 1867, to form a new organization to fight for the vote. The women had served their country and naturally felt entitled to the benefits of citizenship. They could not have remained unaware of the issues surrounding the end of slavery and the conferral of citizenship on the former slaves. In addition, during their wartime work, the women had learned to work together and had formed lasting personal bonds. In 1867, they gathered 355 signatures on a petition to the Missouri General Assembly, demanding the vote for women. The legislature rebuffed them. On February 20, 1868, a second petition went down to defeat. Thereafter, Missouri women went repeatedly to the state legislature and petitioned unsuccessfully for voting rights, but even while pursuing the issue at the state level, the Woman Suffrage Association of Missouri also made connections with the national suffrage movement.[7]

Historians have recognized the importance of Francis Minor, who vigorously supported his wife's cause by pointing out that women were taxpaying citizens of the republic. Early in 1868, he wrote a letter to *The Revolution,* the newspaper published by Elizabeth Cady Stanton and Susan B. Anthony, arguing that if women paid taxes they ought to have the right to vote. His wife, he had made certain, owned property and therefore paid property taxes. In 1869, Virginia signed a letter to the city assessor, demanding to know how much tax money the city collected from women. The assessor reluctantly reported that there were two thousand female taxpayers, who owned property valued in the millions. Phoebe Couzins, a brilliant young speaker, used this information in a speech to the legislature, asserting that women were taxed without being represented in government.[8]

Monia Cook Morris, an early historian of Missouri's suffrage movement, wrote that in 1869 the St. Louis group began to make real progress, holding meetings twice each month. A committee took on the task of recruiting working women to the cause. About thirty women agreed to participate in a Working Woman's Meeting under the auspices of the Woman Suffrage Association. Two delegates from the St. Louis organization attended a national convention in Washington, D.C. Another delegation traveled to Jefferson City, where a number of representatives and senators expressed support for the cause.[9]

On October 6–7, 1869, St. Louis hosted a national convention of the American Equal Rights Association. Anthony, the most famous of all suffrage advocates, and Julia Ward Howe, author of "The Battle Hymn of the Republic" and leader of many women's clubs, attended the meeting. Participants from the St.

Louis association included Rebecca Naylor Hazard, who had helped organize the Ladies' Union Aid Society. Also present was Couzins, a Washington University student, who would soon become the second woman in the United States to graduate from law school. Couzins's mother, Adaline Weston Couzins, had worked as a nursing volunteer for the Ladies' Union Aid Society.[10]

At this historic meeting, Virginia Minor, as president of the Missouri organization, gave an impassioned opening address, in which she asserted that women were entitled to exactly the same rights as men. She pointedly questioned a then-popular notion that women occupied a pedestal well above the world of politics and were too pure and virtuous to mingle with the riffraff at the polling places. In Minor's view, women were being not uplifted but demeaned. "Disguise it as you may," she said. "The disfranchised class is ever a degraded class."[11]

Francis Minor stunned this gathering by taking the position that women had already been enfranchised by the Fourteenth Amendment (1868), which stated that all persons born or naturalized in the United States were entitled to the privileges and immunities of citizenship. The wording of section one of the amendment is important enough to be quoted here in full:

> All persons born or naturalized in the United States and subject to the jurisdiction thereof, are citizens of the United States and of the State wherein they reside. No State shall make or enforce any law which shall abridge the privileges or immunities of citizens of the United States; nor shall any State deprive any person of life, liberty, or property, without due process of law, nor deny to any person within its jurisdiction the equal protection of the laws.[12]

The intent of the amendment was to confer citizenship on former slaves, but in the years following its adoption, the nation brought the former slaveholding states back into the Union, and by the early 1870s, politicians and federal judges had backed away from the notion of equality. The judicial system placed limits on federal responsibility for protecting individual rights.[13]

Minor stoutly rejected arguments that would allow the federal government to avoid its obligation to protect the rights of citizens. He insisted, simply and forcefully, that women were persons and therefore entitled to all the benefits of citizenship, including the right to vote. In defense of this position, he offered a series of six resolutions. First, he argued, the privileges of citizenship derived from the national government and were paramount to state authority. Second, in his view, the states had the power to regulate, but not to prohibit, the right to vote. Third, excluding women from the electorate violated both the letter and the spirit of the United States Constitution. Fourth, he said, according to the Fourteenth Amendment, naturalized citizens were guaranteed equal protection of the laws. Women could be naturalized; therefore they could not be denied equal protection. Fifth, in his view, justice and equity demanded that the laws be the same for men and women. Sixth, he advocated not only equal protection of the laws, but also equal participation in government by men and women.[14]

The Fourteenth Amendment was ambiguous on the issue of gender. Section One used the word *persons* rather than the word *men* in asserting the rights of citizenship. However, section two, one of the enforcement clauses, provided for sanctions against any state that denied voting rights to adult *male* residents. In the context of the times, this must have referred to adult freedmen. The punishment for states that denied voting rights to black males would be a proportional reduction in the population figures used in calculating the numbers of representatives the state could send to Congress. This stipulation introduced the word *male* into the language of the Constitution. Minor did not address this issue but based his argument on section one, which used the non-gendered term *persons*.[15]

The adoption of the Fifteenth Amendment in 1870 undercut Minor's argument by specifically prohibiting states from denying the right to vote on the basis of race, creed, color, or national origin, but not listing there sex. If, in fact, the Fourteenth Amendment protected the franchise, what was the purpose of the Fifteenth Amendment? The Fourteenth Amendment left the gender issue unsettled. At the very least the Fifteenth Amendment failed to clarify this matter while implying that voting rights remained outside the parameters of the previous amendment. Despite this setback, the suffrage movement pressed forward with the argument that women's voting rights had constitutional protection.

Historian Ellen Carol DuBois has credited Francis and Virginia Minor with providing the philosophical basis of the New Departure, a militant effort by suffragists to go to the polls and claim the right to vote. This effort began as early as 1868, when nearly two hundred women in Vineland, New Jersey, cast their votes in a separate ballot box and tried to get them counted along with the men's votes. In the 1870s, many other women went to the polls in groups, and some of them tested voting restrictions in the courts. A group of more than seventy women sued election officials in the District of Columbia in 1871, but lost their case. Other women, including seasoned veterans of the suffrage cause, went to the polling places and tried to exercise what they believed were their constitutional rights.[16]

On March 7, 1870, Sarah Grimke and her sister Angelina Grimke Weld committed an act of civil disobedience by voting in Massachusetts. The Grimke sisters had left South Carolina half a century earlier after freeing their deceased father's slaves. For many years, they had lectured on abolitionism and women's rights in New England. When they cast their ballots in 1870, the action was more symbolic than serious. At an agreed-upon time, a group of women met at a hotel, where male supporters greeted them with bouquets of flowers. The women and their escorts proceeded to a specially arranged section of the polling place. A jeering and hissing crowd broke into applause when the elderly Grimke sisters, who were national celebrities, appeared at the head of the procession. In a sort of stately pantomime, the women cast their votes and then left. Election officials did not count their votes.[17]

Victoria Woodhull, a controversial young champion of women's rights, brought the issue to the attention of the United States Congress. On January 11, 1871, Woodhull read a "Memorial" to the Judiciary Committee of the House of Representatives, urging Congress to recognize women's right to vote under the Fourteenth Amendment. On this historic occasion, she became the first woman ever to address a congressional committee. She had pulled all sorts of strings to get there, and she benefitted from the sponsorship of retired Civil War general and Massachusetts Republican Benjamin Butler. Woodhull's argument was convoluted, but it boiled down to this: the United States Constitution made no distinction between male and female citizens. The Fourteenth Amendment provided that no state should abridge the privileges and immunities of citizens. Congress had the power to make laws carrying out the intentions of the Constitution. Therefore, Congress should make laws that protected women's voting rights from the unconstitutional actions of the states. Woodhull pushed Congress to take action, while the Minors would press the matter in the court system.[18]

Before the end of the month, the committee rejected Woodhull's request. Butler and one other member of the committee supported her position. John Bingham of Ohio wrote the majority opinion, stating that this was not an issue for Congress, but for the courts and the states to decide. In the opinion of the committee, the Fourteenth Amendment did not confer any rights of citizenship beyond those mentioned in the original text of the Constitution (Article IV Section Two) and the Bill of Rights. The committee further determined that the Bill of Rights did not limit the power of the states to limit the electoral franchise. Undeterred, Woodhull remained in Washington and continued to push for congressional action.[19]

Many women in the suffrage movement had reservations about embracing Woodhull because of her colorful past, sexual notoriety, and belief in free love. With financing from Cornelius Vanderbilt, she and her sister, Tennessee Claflin, published *Woodhull and Claflin's Weekly,* a New York City paper that advocated divorce, spiritualism, abortion, and communism, as well as feminism. In 1871, the paper publicized Henry Ward Beecher's affair with a parishioner. Woodhull's subsequent arrest and trial on charges of obscenity ended in an acquittal but became an embarrassment to the suffrage movement. Unabashed, Woodhull ran for president of the United States in 1872. Historian Amanda Frisken has argued that Woodhull's notoriety hurt the movement and may have been partially responsible for a concerted effort by later suffragists to emphasize the maternal and moral strengths of women as qualifications for voting.[20]

Nevertheless, in 1871 Woodhull had gained access to Congress and moved the movement at least a small step toward its goal. Swallowing her pride, the redoubtable Anthony publicly admitted that she had been unable to get a petition before the congressional committee and gave her support to Woodhull's "Memorial." In the excitement of this breakthrough, "Aunt Susan," the most formidable woman in the suffrage movement, urged women to go out and register and, if necessary, sue for the right to vote under the Fourteenth Amendment. An impassioned Quaker schoolteacher, she practiced what she preached. On November 1, 1872, Anthony, several of her female relatives, and as many as fifty other women entered voter registration sites in Rochester, New York. In the Eighth Ward, Anthony intimidated the registrar by brandishing a copy of the Fourteenth Amendment. A total of sixteen women, including Anthony and her sisters, managed to register.[21]

Four days later, on November 5, all sixteen went to the polls and voted in the presidential election. On Thanksgiving Day, 1872, deputy marshals knocked on doors and handed out warrants to the women for casting illegal votes in a federal election. Prosecutors, who concentrated their efforts on Anthony, alleged that her vote was illegal because New York's constitution limited the franchise to men. During her trial in the United States Circuit Court for the Northern District in Canandaigua, New York, in June 1873, the judge would not let her speak in her own defense. He famously fined her one hundred dollars, and she refused to pay a penny of it. She did not go to prison for her defiance of the law, and she did not take the case to higher courts.[22]

After sentencing, the judge did allow her to make a statement, and she took full advantage of this opening. Historians have often quoted her eloquent speech. In terms of the controversy about voting and the Fourteenth

Amendment, she made one extremely important point. Denying a woman the vote, she asserted, inevitably denied her the most basic human rights under the Constitution. As she stated it to the court, "Your denial of my citizen's right to vote is the denial of my right of consent as one of the governed, the denial of my right of representation as one of the taxed, the denial of my right to a trial by a jury of my peers as an offender against the law, the denial of my sacred rights to life, liberty, [and] property."[23]

The following spring, Rosella Buckingham and two sisters, Abby and Julia Smith, demanded that officials in Glastonbury, Connecticut, list their names on the register of voters. The registrars wrote their names on forms and promised to pass them along to the town selectmen, but nothing happened. Several months later, the Smith sisters went to New York City for a suffrage convention, where women from many parts of the country described their efforts to vote. Frances Ellen Watkins Harper gave an impassioned address on black women's need for voting rights. When the Smith sisters returned to Connecticut, they found that their property taxes had gone up to two hundred dollars. Believing the increase to be unjust, the sisters refused to pay. The tax collector confiscated the women's cows, and the poor penned-up cows became symbols of women's oppression. Eventually, a tenant of the sisters bought the cows back, probably with the sisters' own money. The Smith sisters vociferously defended their rights, but the battle turned from the issue of voting to the issue of fair and just taxation.[24]

Virginia Minor may have been the ideal person to take the suffrage fight through the court system. She was respectably married and had the full support of her husband, an attorney, to press the matter in the courts. She and her husband had the political connections and financial resources to persevere through three years of legal wrangling. No scurrilous past undermined her credibility. She embodied the virtues of the wife and mother. Tragically, she had lost her only son at a young age. Perhaps this loss strengthened her resolve to press her case and leave a legacy to the women of America. She lacked the name recognition of Anthony, but of all the women who tested restrictions on voting in the 1870s, Minor was the only one to take her case to the United States Supreme Court.[25]

On October 15, 1872, one of the designated days for voter registration, Minor appeared before Reese Happersett, the St. Louis registrar of voters, and asked to have her name placed on the rolls. Happersett refused because she was not male, and Article II, Section Eighteen of the Missouri State Constitution specified that only male citizens could vote. Because she was married, she needed the permission of her husband to file a lawsuit. Her husband not only gave permission but acted as her chief counsel. Working with him were prominent attorney and former St. Louis mayor John M. Krum and former United States Senator John B. Henderson. While serving in the senate, Henderson introduced a constitutional amendment for the immediate abolition of slavery. This became the Thirteenth Amendment. When Henderson lost his bid for reelection in 1869, he returned to Missouri to practice law.[26]

In a petition to the St. Louis County Circuit Court, Minor's attorneys argued that Article II, Section Eighteen of the Missouri's state constitution violated the Constitution of the United States. Specifically, they alleged that the elective franchise was one of the privileges of citizenship. In fact, they argued, suffrage was the chief political right that maintained the human rights of life, liberty, and the pursuit of happiness. Because these rights inhered in the individual, no state could deny or abridge them. The Fourteenth Amendment specifically stated that no state should abridge the privileges or immunities of citizens of the United States. The State of Missouri must yield to the paramount authority of the United States Constitution. Therefore, the state had violated Minor's rights and owed her damages in the amount of one thousand dollars.[27]

Reese Happersett filed a demurrer to this petition on January 2, 1873. His attorney, Smith P. Galt, filed a brief asserting that everyone knew that the Fourteenth Amendment was about granting citizenship to the freed slaves and not about women's suffrage. The use of the word *person* in the amendment signified that black females, as well as black males, became citizens of the republic. It did not mean that every person thereby gained the right to vote. If it did, argued Galt, "neither age nor sex [was] any barrier, and children and puling infants in their nurses' arms [could] vote." He concluded that the Fourteenth Amendment did not overturn the Missouri State Constitution, which granted voting rights only to adult males. Virginia Minor did not have the right to vote in the general election or register to vote. Happersett simply did his duty by refusing to place a woman's name on the list of registered voters. The Circuit Court of St. Louis County sustained the demurrer and denied the Minors' petition.[28]

The Minors appealed the case to the Missouri Supreme Court. Francis argued once again that the right to vote was a privilege of citizenship according to the spirit of the United States Constitution. States could regulate the franchise by stipulating qualifications for electors, but the states could not deny the franchise to an entire category of people based on sex. He further stated that there could be no partial citizenship; a person was either a citizen or not. Women were citizens under the terms of the Fourteenth Amendment. Galt countered that the Fourteenth Amendment did not apply in this case.[29]

The Missouri Supreme Court considered the question of whether the state's voting laws violated the federal Constitution. Before the adoption of the Fourteenth Amendment, Missouri and all the other states had restricted the franchise to males. The purpose of the Fourteenth Amendment, in the view of the court, was to ensure that the recently freed slaves had all the rights of other citizens. If white males over twenty-one years of age had the right to vote, then black males over twenty-one years of age should have the right to vote. The writers of the amendment had not intended to extend this right to women. The court upheld the lower court's decision and denied the Minors' petition.[30]

When they appealed their case to the United States Supreme Court, the Minors argued that the privilege of voting for federal officials did not depend on state authority. In their opinion, the state had the right to regulate the franchise but not to actually prohibit voting by imposing impossible conditions on voters. Therefore, the state constitution violated the federal Constitution, specifically with respect to section one of the Fourteenth Amendment. Henderson and Krum's names appeared on the brief, but the oral argument was made by Francis Minor alone.[31]

This argument had little chance of swaying the Supreme Court in light of its ruling in the Slaughterhouse Cases in 1873. In those cases, New Orleans butchers had argued that a state-sanctioned monopoly violated their rights under the Fourteenth Amendment, and the Supreme Court ruled against them. Responding for the majority, Justice Samuel F. Miller asserted that the Fourteenth Amendment applied solely to the recently freed slaves. Ironically, the court's decision relegated the protection of the rights of the freedmen to the control of the states that had previously held them in slavery. The court made a distinction between citizenship in the state and citizenship in the nation, allowing the federal government a very limited role in defining and protecting individual rights. In particular, the states retained authority over the election process.[32]

A dramatic moment in the Minors' case came when Justice Stephen Johnson Field asked some pointed questions. Field had previously challenged the court majority by arguing that the federal government, not the states, should be the guarantor of human rights.[33] During the Minor hearing, Field asked Minor whether children were citizens, and Minor answered that they were. Most people, then and now, would agree that the states were justified in denying the franchise to people under a certain age. Missouri's legal voting age was twenty-one. For Field, this raised an obvious question, which he prefaced by asking, "So you hold that citizenship confers the right to vote?"

Minor answered, "Yes, sir."

Field then asked, "Have children the right to vote?"

Minor again answered, "Yes, sir." But he offered no further explanation, even when other justices tried to prompt him. This would seem to have rendered his argument absurd, because it would mean, as Galt had argued, that babies in their nurses' arms could vote.[34]

This exchange established the principle that it was reasonable for states to deny some citizens the electoral franchise. Children, the argument implied, could be disqualified because of their immaturity and lack of experience. It also seemed to imply that women could be disqualified for the same reason. But here is where the argument broke down. Women, like men, grew up and left their childhood behind. Minor missed the opportunity to make this very important point. But perhaps he saw the danger in conceding that the government could deny the vote to any group, even children. Eventually, most suffragists would agree that children, felons, and people with mental illnesses could be excluded from the electorate. Unfortunately, many people believed that this exclusionary policy could logically be extended to new immigrants and racial minorities, as well as women, in a society that was retreating from its Revolutionary ideals.[35]

The justices of the United States Supreme Court unanimously agreed that the Fourteenth Amendment did not add voting rights to the privileges and immunities of citizenship. The justices pointed out that the Fifteenth Amendment would have been unnecessary if the Fourteenth Amendment guaranteed suffrage to everyone. What were the privileges and immunities guaranteed to all citizens under the Constitution? It guaranteed a republican form of government and also stipulated that no person could be deprived of life, liberty, or property without due process of law. It did not guarantee the franchise.

The court did not deny that women were citizens. They had always been citizens. Unlike the former slaves, women did not become citizens after passage of the Fourteenth Amendment. Women had been citizens since the beginning of the republic. The Fourteenth Amendment did not change their status in any way.

United States citizens were not necessarily members of the electorate. In fact, the United States had no national electorate. The states elected Congress and sent electors to choose the president, and the states had always set the qualifications for voters. No state permitted all of its citizens to vote; all the states placed restrictions on voting rights. If citizenship automatically conferred the right to vote in any state, then voters could leave their places of residence and go and vote in any other state at will. But this had never been allowed.

When the United States Constitution was adopted, every state but Rhode Island and Connecticut had its own constitution and all had republican forms of government accepted under the Constitution. Voting was a matter for state laws and state constitutions. In all the states (except New Jersey[36]), suffrage had been granted to men only. These governments had ratified the United States Constitution. Thus, the matter was settled and had been for more than ninety years.[37]

Or was it? The court's decision gave wide latitude to the states in conferring citizenship and protecting human rights, but questions remained. What should be the role of the federal government? Did the Bill of Rights limit the power of the states, or did it merely prohibit federal encroachment on people's rights? The Waite court clearly recognized the dual sovereignty of the federal and state governments. In the view of this court, the Fourteenth Amendment did not give the federal government sweeping powers to interfere in the affairs of the states. All it did was require the states to apply the law equally to all citizens. But equality was precisely the issue at hand, and *Minor v. Happersett* left the issue unresolved.[38]

In the 1870s, the Supreme Court's interpretation of the Fourteenth Amendment made it possible for states to limit the rights not only of women, but also of African Americans. According to Earl M. Maltz, the decision that the Constitution could confer citizenship, but not suffrage, and that the states had the right to limit suffrage had an impact on future court rulings. For instance, in 1876, the Supreme Court validated the states' right to use poll taxes to keep black citizens from voting. Historian Joan Hoff has argued that the response of the justice system to Minor's case was probably racist as well as sexist. Judges dealt harshly with the question of women's rights in order to keep to a minimum the rights of the freedmen. Decisions enforcing second-class citizenship for women could set precedents for Jim Crow laws.[39]

Many suffragists, including Stanton and Anthony, continued to defend voting as a natural right and pushed for a voting rights amendment to the United States Constitution. Stanton had been the driving force behind the Seneca Falls Convention's Declaration of Sentiments (1848), which had asserted that the elective franchise was an unalienable right. In 1876, she and Anthony presented a Declaration of Rights for Women that echoed both the Declaration of Independence (1776) and the Seneca Falls Declaration. Phoebe Couzins endorsed this new document with a florid speech presented at the First Unitarian Church in Philadelphia, Pennsylvania, on July 4, 1876. Against the wishes of the centennial commission, the women had put forward their declaration, proclaiming, in Couzins's words "that taxation without representation is tyranny, the divine right of one-half the people to rule the other half is also despotism." Beginning in 1878, Stanton and other leaders appeared regularly before committees of the United States Senate, supporting a women's suffrage amendment.[40]

While the fight for a federal amendment gathered momentum, four states in the Far West granted women suffrage. In 1869, the Wyoming territorial legislature gave its approval to women's voting rights, and on September 6, 1870, women voted for the first time in that far western territory. During the same year, Utah embraced women's suffrage, partly to discredit the argument that Mormonism debased and dehumanized women. The women of Utah lost the franchise in 1887, but reclaimed it in 1896. In 1894, Phoebe Couzins went to Colorado to support a Populist campaign for women's voting rights. With her help, Colorado became the first state to grant women the ballot by popular referendum. In 1896, another Populist crusade helped pass an equal-suffrage amendment in Idaho. All these victories took place in the Rocky Mountain region, where populations were small and people were willing to experiment with social and political change. In all these states, officials viewed voting rights as a privilege bestowed by the government and not as a fundamental human right. But by example, they proved that women's suffrage bolstered and did not weaken the republic.[41]

Some states granted partial suffrage in local elections or on issues directly related to taxation. In 1879, Massachusetts adopted a statute granting the right to vote for local school committees to females over twenty-one years of age who could read and write and had paid state, county, or local taxes within the past two years. Two years later, the privilege was extended to property-owning women who paid a poll tax. This, of course, limited suffrage to affluent women. Beginning in 1887, women in Kansas could vote on municipal matters. By the early twentieth century, some states had given partial suffrage to all women, regardless of property ownership, in local elections relating to school policy, bond issues, and taxes. Despite these gains, the women's movement had been unable to establish voting as a fundamental human right. The injustice of poll taxes continued to limit voting by African American men and women until the latter part of the twentieth century.[42]

From the 1870s until her death, Minor kept working for the cause, but Missouri's suffrage movement divided into factions. After the St. Louis meeting in 1869, Couzins joined with Anthony and Stanton to found the National Woman Suffrage Association (NWSA). In 1871, the Missouri association affiliated with the more conservative American Woman Suffrage Association (AWSA). Hazard remained with the organization and became president of the AWSA in 1878. The local affiliate of AWSA continued meeting until 1886, but Minor and Couzins resigned in protest. The Minors continued their suffrage work outside the organization. In 1878, Francis Minor retired from his law practice, but continued to write articles on women's rights. In 1879, a St. Louis branch of NWSA organized, and Virginia Minor became its president. In 1889, she spoke before a United States Senate committee on the subject of women's suffrage. Three years later, she resigned from the suffrage association, citing an unspecified illness of her husband's. Francis passed away in 1892, and Virginia died two years later.[43]

From middle age on, she enjoyed local renown as a fighter for women's rights. On August 14, 1874, she passed away at the Baptist Sanitarium, Nineteenth and Carr streets. The funeral took place in her residence on Lucas Avenue, with burial in Bellefontaine Cemetery. A quartet played several hymns, but she had requested that there be no religious service because the clergy opposed the women's movement. Obituaries identified her as a women's rights advocate who left her mark on judicial history as the plaintiff in *Minor v. Happersett.* With a codicil to her will she bequeathed $1,000 to Susan B. Anthony.[44]

At the time of her death, the suffrage movement was in the doldrums. In Illinois, the movement sank into a kind of lethargy during the late 1870s. Historian Steven M. Buechler has argued that other reform movements, particularly the temperance movement, drew energy and attention away from women's rights in Illinois and other states. Many women joined the Women's Christian Temperance Union (WCTU), which supported suffrage as a means to the end of passing legislation against the sale and consumption of alcohol. Missouri's Hazard and Couzins both turned their attention to the anti-liquor crusade. In the 1880s, a smartly dressed and charismatic Couzins traveled the country, speaking to appreciative audiences on both temperance and suffrage. Many women supported both causes, but the temperance movement drew a larger following among middle-class women, who tended to embrace their traditional role as protectors of family, morality, and the sanctity of the home. Some women believed that temperance had a better chance of success than suffrage and channeled their energies in that direction.[45]

Missouri's situation seemed particularly bleak. In their *History of Woman Suffrage,* Stanton and Anthony wrote that at the turn of the century "Missouri was one of the blackest spots on the suffrage map" and showed no signs of reviving. Early leaders like Minor, Hazard, and Couzins, they wrote, were "no longer living or [were] past the age for strenuous work."[46] Minor had died, but Hazard was alive and well, although she had turned her attention to other causes, including temperance. In the final decades of her life, she wrote essays on Dante and hosted a women's literary society at her home in Kirkwood (St. Louis County). The women's rights movement did not remain at the center of her life.[47]

Couzins became difficult and intractable toward the end of her life. She did not rejoin the Missouri association even after 1890, when the AWSA and the NWSA resolved their differences and formed NAWSA. By the end of the 1890s she expressed disillusionment not only with the suffragists, but also with the temperance movement, which she had previously supported. In 1897 she thumbed her nose at temperance by becoming a lobbyist and lecturer for the United Brewers Association. Early in the twentieth century, she had a change of heart and apologized for her actions. But her last years were difficult. Increasingly erratic in her behavior and suffering from arthritis, she died in poverty in 1913.[48] By then Missouri's suffrage movement had revived.

Aileen Kraditor and others have noted that during the 1890s, when many of the old guard suffragists died or retired, a younger group with a different ideology rose to prominence. The earlier generation of suffragists had taken their inspiration from the leaders of the American Revolution, who demanded liberty and equality as inalienable rights. By the end of the nineteenth century, however, many middle-class Americans retreated from the idea of equality and made a concerted attempt to restrict immigration and enforce racial segregation. Suffragists, who tended to come from the white middle class, also withdrew from their previous insistence on equality and justice. Southern suffragists rationalized the disfranchisement of black men by espousing the idea that voting was not a right, but a privilege granted only to those qualified to exercise it. Many leading suffragists in both the North and the South openly asserted that educated white women deserved the franchise far more than did uneducated black men. Some suffragists argued that enfranchising white women would help to "clean up" politics. Rather than an end in itself, the vote became a means of effecting change in society. According to Kraditor, these latter-day suffragists argued for the vote based on expediency and not natural rights.[49]

By the turn of the century, a wide variety of women's clubs began actively working for reform. Missouri's State Federation of Women's Clubs had formed by 1896. These clubs often moved from social and charitable activities to serious involvement in civic and political affairs. In St. Louis, the Wednesday Club led a vigorous campaign for clean air legislation. Cape Girardeau's Wednesday Club addressed issues of health and welfare, including the quality of local dairy products, child labor reform, and working conditions for women in factories. Working women participated in strikes and demanded better wages and working conditions, and the WCTU continued to campaign against alcohol consumption. Through involvement in these reform efforts, women became more aware of the limitations in their political power and more convinced of their need to participate in the electoral process.[50]

In 1910, the St. Louis Wednesday Club helped rejuvenate the voting rights movement by sponsoring a suffrage meeting at the home of Marie Garesche. An initial group of ten women issued a call to others who might be interested in forming a new organization. Fifty women responded to the call, establishing the St. Louis Equal Suffrage League. Within months, the organization had attracted a mixed group of male and female members, including clergymen, lawyers, physicians, and businessmen. Branch organizations formed in public libraries around the city. By the end of the year, the league had 250 members. One year later, the St. Louis group joined with organizations in Warrensburg and Webster Groves to form the Missouri Equal Suffrage Association. By 1913, the state had eleven clubs, bringing well-known speakers to spread their message in the state.[51]

Jane Addams, founder of Hull House, came to Missouri in 1914 to promote the idea that women needed the vote in order to bring about social change. In a booklet entitled "Why Women Should Vote," Addams argued that women could use the ballot to protect their homes and their families from the bad effects of industrialization and urbanization. According to Addams, women were naturally more compassionate and gentle than men and therefore had a deeper understanding of the problems faced by children growing up in unsafe and unhealthy environments. With the power of the vote, women could force the government to address these problems. Her message resonated with Missourians. In Cape Girardeau, for example, she gave three addresses at three different locations on October 24, 1914. The local newspaper reported that she "took the Cape by storm," attracting and captivating large audiences.[52]

At the time of Addams's speaking tour, Missouri was one of several states gearing up for a statewide referendum on women's suffrage. In 1908, the progressive state administration had made the initiative and referendum part of Missouri politics, providing openings for the women's rights movement to take its issue to the polls. From 1910 through 1912, voters passed women's suffrage referenda in the states of Washington, California, Arizona, Kansas, and Oregon. In 1913, Illinois gave women the right to vote in presidential elections. In 1914, seven states, including Missouri, held referenda on women's suffrage. Enthusiastic women traveled around the state in automobiles, horses and buggies, on horseback, and on foot to get the necessary signatures to place the issue on the ballot. Missouri voters defeated the referendum, as did voters in South Dakota, North Dakota, Nebraska, and Ohio. Only Montana and Nevada approved the vote for women. One year later, in November 1915, Pennsylvania, New York, New Jersey, and Massachusetts defeated suffrage referenda, although the pro-suffrage vote was substantial.[53]

In 1916, Emily Newell Blair, an editor and activist from southwest Missouri, came up with the idea for a silent, elegant protest at the Democratic National Convention in St. Louis. Weeks before the convention, suffragists recruited women for a pageant called the Golden Lane on Locust Street between the Jefferson Hotel and the Coliseum. On June 14, the opening day of the convention, thousands of women in white dresses, carrying yellow parasols and wearing yellow sashes or streamers, formed a double line, with the front row seated and the back row standing. Inside the hall, women's voting rights were a primary topic of discussion.[54]

The 1916 Democratic platform supported women's suffrage but did not endorse the "Susan B. Anthony Amendment" to the United States Constitution. Instead, the convention reaffirmed the right of each state to determine qualifications for voters. Southern Democrats adamantly championed states' rights in order to prevent black women from voting. President Woodrow Wilson, campaigning for reelection on the Democratic ticket, recognized the growing power of the movement and addressed a NAWSA convention in Atlantic City in September 1916. The president praised the suffragists' spirit but did not budge from his party's official position."[55]

After militant suffragists picketed the White House, President Wilson finally spoke out in support of a constitutional amendment. The picketers, led by Alice Paul, had concluded that the suffrage movement could not win by using its traditional tactics. NAWSA condemned the militants, but women showed up day after day with signs that insulted the president. Beginning in June 1917, police arrested the pickets and jailed them. Paul and other imprisoned women went on hunger strikes. In October wartime volunteers and Red Cross workers joined in a suffrage parade in New York City, showing that women were patriots as well as citizens. At the end of November, authorities released all the jailed women in Washington, D.C. Under intense pressure, Wilson endorsed the suffrage amendment in 1918. In 1919, Congress passed the Nineteenth Amendment and sent it to the states for ratification. Missouri's Fiftieth General Assembly ratified it in July of that year.[56]

Virginia Minor belonged to an earlier generation of suffragists, and her legacy was a quiet one. She was not an icon like Anthony, not a celebrity like Woodhull, not a firebrand like Alice Paul. But in one very important respect, she took a radical stand. She insisted that voting was a fundamental right that belonged to all citizens, including women, and she forced the Supreme Court to examine the issue of citizenship. On several points, the court affirmed the Minors' position. After all, the court determined that women were citizens and that they had been citizens since the early days of the republic. As citizens, they had some fundamental rights, including life, liberty, and the enjoyment of their property. But the court found that citizenship, in and of itself, did not include the right to vote. The burden of protecting that right remained with the states.

A committed and impassioned group of suffragists succeeded in passing the Nineteenth Amendment to the United States Constitution, but this amendment did not establish voting as a fundamental human right. While barring the states from denying suffrage on the basis of sex, the amendment still treated voting as a privilege granted by state governments and not as the inalienable right of every citizen. Had the Minors won their case, voting would have been protected by the Fourteenth Amendment as a human right. This may seem like a fine distinction, but it is not. What the Minors demanded was far more revolutionary than the content of the Nineteenth Amendment.

As a basic human right, the franchise would belong to the individual, not the state. Denial of the vote, based on any criterion, including sex, would be a violation of human rights. Felons might still be denied the right to vote after "due process of law." Children might still be exempt, temporarily, until they reached adulthood. But all citizens would have an equal right to vote, regardless of race, sex, creed, economic status, educational level, place of residence, or the ability to pay a poll tax.

In the twenty-first century, states have attempted to deny the vote to those citizens who could not produce a government-issued photo-identification card on demand. The elderly, the disabled, the poor, and those who lack drivers' licenses were those most likely to lack such a "photo-ID." In 2006, the Missouri State legislature passed a law requiring that voters present a valid, unexpired federal or state identification card with a photograph before casting their ballots. A group of registered voters sued the state, arguing that they lacked appropriate photo-identification and that obtaining such identification would cost them money. On October 16, 2006, the Missouri Supreme Court upheld a lower court's ruling that the voter-identification law violated the equal protection clause of the state's modern constitution. The legislature contended that the voter-identification law was needed to prevent voter impersonation fraud, but the court found no evidence that this kind of fraud had in fact occurred. In the opinion of the court, the state did not have a compelling reason to restrict voting rights in this way.[57]

Missouri's voter-identification law did not survive through the 2006 election, but other states passed similar laws. It seems likely that the United States Supreme Court will review some of these laws. The court will have to consider also the question of whether the federal government or the states should bear the burden of protecting the rights of citizens.

Virginia Minor made an important contribution to the discourse on citizens' right to vote by fervently arguing that a disfranchised person was a degraded person. She shared this conviction with Anthony, Stanton, and others, who maintained that voting was a fundamental human right. To deny this right was to deny a person her full status as a human being. Of these early suffragists, Minor was the only one who took her case all the way to the United States Supreme Court. She lost her case, and the subsequent passage of a women's suffrage amendment seemed to make her effort irrelevant. But the Minor case raised an issue that transcended gender, an issue that has yet to be resolved. Is the denial of the electoral franchise to anyone, without due process of law, a violation of basic human rights?

NOTES

1. LeeAnn Whites, "The Tale of Two Minors: Women's Rights on the Border," in *Women in Missouri History: In Search of Power and Influence,* ed. LeeAnn Whites, Mary C. Neth, and Gary R. Kremer (Columbia: University of Missouri Press, 2004), 106. Other sources of biographical information on Virginia Minor include *Dictionary of Missouri Biography,* edited by Lawrence O. Christensen, William E. Foley, Gary R. Kremer, and Kenneth H. Winn (Columbia: University of Missouri Press, 1999), 552–53; Mary K. Dains, ed., *Show Me Missouri Women: Selected Biographies* (Kirksville, MO: Thomas Jefferson University Press, 1989), 234–35; and an obituary in the *St. Louis Republic,* August 16, 1894. It appears, unfortunately, that Minor left no diaries or collections of letters that might help scholars to understand her motivations or feelings.

2. Whites, "Tale of Two Minors," 106–15; Stuart Banner, *Legal Systems in Conflict: Property and Sovereignty in Missouri, 1750–1860* (Norman: University of Oklahoma Press, 2000), 130–33.

3. Bonnie Stepenoff, *From French Community to Missouri Town: Ste. Genevieve in the Nineteenth Century* (Columbia: University of Missouri Press, 2006), 97, 109–14; Banner, *Legal Systems in Conflict,* 130–33. See also Susan C. Boyle, "Did She Generally Decide? Women in Ste. Genevieve, 1750–1805," *William and Mary Quarterly* 44 (October 1987): 775–89; and N. Renae Farris, "French

Roots, American Woman: Marie LaPorte of Ste. Genevieve, 1766–1849" (master's thesis, Southeast Missouri State University, 2002).

4. Laura F. Edwards, *Gendered Strife and Confusion: The Political Culture of Reconstruction* (Urbana: University of Illinois Press, 1997), 7–9.

5. "Virginia Louisa Minor," in *Show-Me Missouri Women*, 234; Whites, "Tale of Two Minors," 105.

6. An excellent article on this topic is Patricia Lucie's "On Being a Free Person and a Citizen by Constitutional Amendment," *Journal of American Studies* (Great Britain) 12, (1978), 343–58.

7. Laura Staley, "Suffrage Movement in St. Louis during the 1870s," *Gateway Heritage* 3 (Spring 1983), 38.

8. Linda K. Kerber, *No Constitutional Right to Be Ladies* (New York: Hill and Wang, 1998), 103; Whites, "Tale of Two Minors," 104–5.

9. Monia Cook Morris, "The History of Woman Suffrage in Missouri, 1867–1901," *Missouri Historical Review* 25 (October 1930), 69–70.

10. *Missouri Democrat*, October 7, 1869; "Phoebe Wilson Couzins" in *Dictionary of Missouri Biography*, 211.

11. Staley, "Suffrage Movement in St. Louis," 38; Elizabeth Cady Stanton, *History of Woman Suffrage,* edited by Elizabeth Cady Stanton, Susan B. Anthony, and Matilda J. Gage, vol. 2 (New York: Arno Press Reprint Edition, 1969), 410.

12. Elizabeth Frost and Kathryn Cullen-DuPont, *Women's Suffrage in America: An Eyewitness History* (New York: Facts on File, 1992), 381.

13. Michael Kent Curtis, *No State Shall Abridge: The Fourteenth Amendment and the Bill of Rights* (Durham: Duke University Press, 1986), 154–70.

14. Stanton, *History of Woman Suffrage,* vol. 2, p. 408.

15. Frost and Cullen-DuPont, *Women's Suffrage in America,* 210, 381.

16. Ellen Carol DuBois, "Taking the Law into Our own Hands: Bradwell, Minor, and Suffrage Militance in the 1870s," in *One Woman, One Vote,* ed. Marjorie Spruill Wheeler (Troutdale, OR: New Sage Press, 1995), 86–88.

17. Catherine H. Birney, *The Grimke Sisters* (Westport, CT: Greenwood Press, 1885; reprint, 1969), 296; *Appleton's Cyclopedia of American Biography,* vol. II (New York: D. Appleton, 1892), 768.

18. Mary Gabriel, *Notorious Victoria: The Life of Victoria Woodhull, Uncensored* (Chapel Hill, NC: Algonquin Books, 1998), 73–77.

19. Gabriel, *Notorious Victoria*, 82; Curtis, *No State Shall Abridge*, 168.

20. The growing literature on Woodhull includes Amanda Frisken, "Sex in Politics: Victoria Woodhull as an American Public Woman, 1870–1876," *Journal of American History* 12 (2000), 89–110; Barbara Goldsmith, *Other Powers: The Age of Suffrage, Spiritualism, and the Scandalous Victoria Woodhull* (New York: Knopf, 1998); Emanie Sachs, *The Terrible Siren: Victoria Woodhull* (New York: Arno Press Reprint, 1972).

21. Katharine Anthony, *Susan B. Anthony: Her Personal History and Her Era* (New York: Russell and Russell, 1954), 277–78; Gabriel, *Notorious Victoria*, 77; Sachs, *Terrible Siren*, 78–80.

22. Anthony, *Susan B. Anthony*, 279–99; Eva D. Adams, "*Minor v. Happersett*: A Case of Woman's Suffrage," *Proceedings and Papers of the Georgia Association of Historians* 14 (1993), 142.

23. Anthony, *Susan B. Anthony*, 297.

24. Kerber, *No Constitutional Right*, 87–92.

25. Joan Hoff, *Law, Gender, and Injustice: A Legal History of U.S. Women* (New York: New York University Press, 1991), 170.

26. Adams, "*Minor v. Happersett*," 143; "John B. Henderson," in *Dictionary of Missouri Biography*, 394.

27. "Statement, Brief, and Petition in the Case of *Virginia L. Minor, et al., vs. Reese Happersett*," on file at the Missouri State Archives, Jefferson City.

28. Adams, "*Minor v. Happersett*," 143; Galt's demurrer to the "Statement, Brief, and Petition," previously cited; Marshall Hier, "Virginia Minor's Struggle to Vote," *St. Louis Bar Journal* (Winter 1992), 39.

29. Adams, "*Minor v. Happersett*," 143.

30. Ibid.

31. *New York Times*, February 10, 1875.

32. Kermit L. Hall, William Wiecek, and Paul Finkelman, *American Legal History: Cases and Materials*, 2nd ed. (New York: Oxford University Press, 1996), 238–41; Curtis, *No State Shall Abridge*, 174–79; Charles W. McCurdy, "Waite Court," *Society* 24 (November–December 1986), 40–45.

33. *Dictionary of American Biography*, vol. 6 (New York: Scribner's, 1931), 372–76.

34. *New York Times*, February 10, 1875.

35. Aileen Kraditor has argued that by the end of the nineteenth century many suffragists coupled their support of women's rights with racist, antiforeign, and antilabor beliefs, see *The Ideas of the Woman Suffrage Movement, 1890–1920* (New York: W. W. Norton, 1981), 254.

36. Mary Beth Norton explains that New Jersey experimented with the enfranchisement of women in the late eighteenth and early nineteenth centuries. Women voted there in several elections until a state law disfranchised them in 1807, see *Liberty's Daughters: The Revolutionary Experience of American Women, 1750–1800* (Boston: Little, Brown, and Company, 1980), 191–93.

37. *Minor v. Happersett*, Supreme Court of the United States 88 U.S. 162: 21 Wall. 162 October, 1874, Term; *New York Times*, March 30, 1875.

38. William E. Nelson, *The Fourteenth Amendment: From Political Principle to Judicial Doctrine* (Cambridge: Harvard University Press, 1988), 168–69.

39. Earl M. Maltz, *The Fourteenth Amendment and the Law of the Constitution* (Durham: Carolina Academic Press, 2003), 116–17; Hoff, *Law, Gender, and*

Injustice, 173–75. Hoff found it strange that the *Minor v. Happersett* decision has never been harshly condemned by legal scholars.

40. Frost and Cullen-DuPont, *Women's Suffrage in America*, 233; Akhil Reed Amar, "How Women Won the Vote," *Wilson Quarterly* 29 (2005), 30; Hoff, *Law, Gender, and Injustice*, 187–88.

41. For a fuller treatment of the battle for suffrage in the West, see Beverly Beeton, *Women Vote in the West: The Woman Suffrage Movement, 1869–1896* (New York: Garland, 1986).

42. Kerber, *No Constitutional Right*, 117–19.

43. Cook, "History of Woman Suffrage," 73–75; "Phoebe Wilson Couzins," in *Dictionary of Missouri Biography*, 211; *Missouri Democrat*, October 7, 1869; Katharine Corbett, *In Her Place: A Guide to St. Louis Women's History* (St. Louis: Missouri Historical Society Press, 1999), 132–34; Hier, "Virginia Minor's Struggle to Vote," 38–40.

44. *St. Louis Republic*, August 16, 1894; Clippings in the Hardcastle Scrapbook, 19, 21, and the Necrology Scrapbook II-C, 79, Collections of the Missouri Historical Society, St. Louis.

45. Steven M. Buechler, "Elizabeth Boynton Harbert and the Woman Suffrage Movement, 1870–1896," *Signs* 13 (Autumn 1987), 88. Returning to St. Louis after a speaking tour in Massachusetts, Couzins told a reporter that the subject of her lectures was "temperance and suffrage and reform, etc," *St. Louis Post-Dispatch*, March 24, 1884.

46. Stanton, *History of Woman Suffrage*, vol. 6, p. 342.

47. "Rebecca Naylor Hazard," in *Dictionary of Missouri Biography*, 387.

48. *Dictionary of Missouri Biography*, 211–12.

49. Kraditor, *Ideas of the Woman Suffrage Movement*, 44–45; Marjorie Spruill Wheeler, *New Women of the New South: The Leaders of the Woman Suffrage Movement in the Southern States* (New York: Oxford University Press, 1993), 100–102.

50. Cook, "History of Woman Suffrage," 75–76; Lynn Michele Lansdown, "The Defeat of the 1914 Missouri Woman Suffrage Initiative" (master's thesis, Southwest Missouri State University, 2005), 17–31; Heather Marin Haynes, "Public Action from the Private Sphere" (master's thesis, Southeast Missouri State University, 2005), 36–38; David Morgan, *Suffragists and Democrats* (East Lansing: Michigan State University Press, 1972), 84; Buechler, "Elizabeth Boynton Harbert," 96–97.

51. Mary Semple Scott, "History of Woman Suffrage in Missouri," *Missouri Historical Review* 14 (April–July 1920), 300–304.

52. Jane Addams, *Why Women* Should *Vote* (New York: National Woman Suffrage Publishing Company, 1912), 1; Haynes, "Public Action from the Private Sphere," 45–48; *Cape Girardeau Daily Republican*, October 26, 1914.

53. Frost and Cullen-DuPont, *Women's Suffrage in America*, 295; Morgan, *Suffragists and Democrats*, 72, 97–98; Kraditor, *Ideas of the Woman Suffrage Movement*, 231.

54. Scott, "History of Woman Suffrage," 312–13.

55. Virginia Laas, "Breaking into Politics: Emily Newell Blair and the Democratic Party in the 1920s," in *Women in Missouri History*, ed. Whites, Neth, Kremer, 220–21; Frost and Cullen-DuPont, *Women's Suffrage in America,* 296; Morgan, *Suffragists and Democrats,* 108–12.

56. Kraditor, *Ideas of the Woman Suffrage Movement,* 231; Frost and Cullen-DuPont, *Women's Suffrage in America,* 318–19; and Scott, "History of Woman Suffrage," 285.

57. Missouri Supreme Court Slip Opinion in Case Number SC88039, October 16, 2006.

CHAPTER SIX

Missouri's Long Road to Juvenile Justice

Douglas E. Abrams

"I could talk for half a day and not convey how important it is to have a place like Missouri that we can look to."
David Utter, 2003

IN 2003, DAVID UTTER and other Louisiana state officials had come to Missouri to tour juvenile corrections facilities operated by the state's Division of Youth Services (DYS), an agency within the Department of Social Services. Louisiana, like more than thirty other states, had sent inspection teams to learn from the nationally recognized DYS program for delinquent youth because it was struggling with juvenile prisons beset by years of turmoil.[1] Dozens of youths incarcerated in Louisiana's juvenile prisons had suffered broken jaws, fractured eye sockets, and other bloody injuries. Guards enlisted youths to beat one another, denied them medical and psychological treatment, and even brutally assaulted them, sometimes attacking while the youths slept.[2] The U.S. Justice Department had sued the Bayou State under the Civil Rights of Institutionalized Persons Act of 1980 (CRIPA),[3] which Congress had enacted after finding nationwide conditions of juvenile confinement "barbaric."[4]

The pervasive and unstemmed violence within these facilities was no secret. Even the president of the National Juvenile Detention Association (which represents the heads of the nation's juvenile detention facilities) acknowledged that "[v]iolence against offenders, lack of adequate education and mental health [care] . . . crowding and . . . poorly paid and poorly trained staff [were] the norm rather than the exception" in America's juvenile prisons.[5] A few months after Utter spoke, *U.S. News & World Report* found "[j]uvenile justice facilities across the nation . . . in a dangerously advanced state of disarray, with violence an almost everyday occurrence and rehabilitation the exception rather than the rule. Abuse of juvenile inmates by staff is routine."[6]

Acting under its CRIPA authority, the Justice Department has documented that more than a century after creation of the nation's first juvenile court in 1899, many states still confine delinquent youths in institutions that the *New York Times* calls "quasi penitentiaries."[7] Mentally ill and otherwise vulnerable youths in these states are beaten by guards, physically and sexually assaulted by other inmates, and sometimes left in fear for their lives. The prison cells are frequently overcrowded, and youths are often denied needed mental health and medical treatment as well as education guaranteed them by both state and federal law. Younger inmates, both male and female, are particularly vulnerable to sexual assault, which is reported in these facilities at rates as much as ten times higher than in adult lockups.[8] Many released youths return to their local communities in worse emotional and physical condition than when they entered the juvenile justice system. Some incarcerated youths attempt suicide, and some succeed.[9]

In the face of this grim national scorecard, the "Missouri Model" has emerged as the lodestar for states contemplating reform of their broken juvenile corrections systems. Missouri did an about-face in the 1970s, when the state finally acknowledged that for a century and a half, its prisons and reform schools had not enhanced personal accountability, emphasized rehabilitation, or protected public safety. Today, says the *New York Times,* Missouri's DYS program focuses on "rehabilitation in small groups, constant therapeutic interventions and minimal force."[10]

The DYS recidivism rate is among the lowest in the nation, an outcome that the agency achieves at a considerably lower cost per youth than other states' punitive programs incur.[11] Dr. Barry Krisberg, president of the National Council on Crime and Delinquency, says that Missouri "gives children a way to redeem themselves, and most of the kids do it."[12] Effectiveness plus efficiency prompt leading foundations and professional organizations to single out DYS as "a guiding light for reform"[13] and "a national model."[14]

Missouri's national leadership did not come quickly or easily. When still a territory and for decades after achieving statehood in 1821, Missouri incarcerated children with hardened adult criminals in prisons barely fit for human habitation. The downward spiral continued even after Missouri opened two austere juvenile institutions in 1889—the Missouri Reform School for Boys at Boonville and the State Industrial Home for Girls at Chillicothe. With racial segregation the law of the state, a third institution—the State Industrial Home for Negro Girls—opened at Tipton in 1916.

Missouri closed the Tipton home in 1960 with the end of official segregation, but that did not end decades of disarray. The state continued to use the facility in Chillicothe until 1981 and the one in Boonville until 1983. By that time, according to former DYS director Mark D. Steward, Missouri maintained "a dysfunctional system, and we had to change our mindset" about how to deliver juvenile justice to boys and girls in the public interest.[15]

"The great strength of history in a free society," wrote historian Arthur M. Schlesinger, Jr., "is its capacity for self-correction."[16] Contemplating the state's tortuous path to national leadership in the area of juvenile justice can be unsettling, but in turning from that path, Missouri redesigned its compass for one it can share with states that still struggle to escape the sort of failure that Missouri overcame by summoning political will to pursue self-correction more than a generation ago.[17]

JUVENILE JUSTICE IN NINETEENTH-CENTURY MISSOURI

Missouri began its long journey to effective juvenile justice during territorial days in the earliest years of the nineteenth century. Juvenile justice was harsh business in those days because the common law exposed all but the very youngest children to the full force of criminal punishment. The general age of majority was twenty-one, but the law deemed children over fourteen as conclusively capable of criminality and, thus, as subject to adult punishment. Children between seven and fourteen were presumed incapable of committing a crime, but the presumption could be (and often was) rebutted with evidence that the child accused could distinguish between right and wrong. Only children under the age of seven were conclusively incapable of committing a crime.[18] The four Missouri children executed in the nineteenth century were between twelve and sixteen when they committed their homicides.[19]

For most of the nineteenth century, children and adults were arrested under the same laws, tried in the same courts, and incarcerated in many of the same prisons because the law perceived children as miniature adults, not as individuals with developing cognitive faculties, moral sensibilities, and emotional needs. The nation had not yet embraced compulsory education statutes, child labor laws, juvenile court acts, and other protective legislation that, by the end of the century, would begin to distinguish children from adults in the public mind. Childhood and adolescence in America are largely twentieth-century concepts stemming from progress in psychology and the social sciences.[20]

Exposing children to the full force of the criminal law was no small matter in early-nineteenth-century America because prisoners on the frontier and in cities alike might be sentenced to whipping with the lash or to standing in the pillory. An 1813 Missouri territorial law, for example, provided that a person convicted of larceny "shall be whipped on his or her bare back, not exceeding thirty-nine stripes, at the discretion of the court."[21] Whipping and the pillory ended for whites in Missouri by the early 1830s, but slave children, like their parents, remained at the lowest rung of the state's criminal justice ladder. The "lowest rung" meant whipping, other corporal punishment, or death, with little or no legal protection.[22]

After 1836, imprisonment of adults and children in Missouri usually meant confinement in the new state penitentiary, a county jail, or, in rural counties without jails, a military prison.[23] Among prisoners, disease and premature death were rampant. By the mid-1850s, the penitentiary was already the worst in the nation, a "loathesome stone purgatory" with cells that were "little more than kennels" and guards who included "all manners of men from sadists to drunkards."[24]

For their part, Missouri's county jails were filthy "fortresses" with little light or sanitation.[25] An 1835 statute required counties to maintain their jails "in good and sufficient condition and repair," but authorities frequently ignored the mandate because Missouri, like the rest of the nation, did not yet perceive rehabilitation as even a peripheral goal of incarceration, except insofar as inmates—including children—might change their ways by the threat of harsh confinement.[26]

The state penitentiary, the St. Louis Workhouse (which opened in 1843), and most county jails were barely habitable for adults and were totally unfit for children. Disease and filth were only part of the story. State law required separation of debtors and other civil prisoners from criminals, and female prisoners from males, but said nothing about separating children from adults.[27] Reformers, called "child-savers," found few supporters among the general public when they decried prison conditions that enabled adult convicts to prey on confined children and teach them the ways of the criminal world.[28]

The cruel irony is that relatively few incarcerated children were violent criminals. Some had committed petty theft or other antisocial conduct, some were jailed for disobeying their parents, but many had committed no crime at all by today's standards. Because vagrancy and begging were then considered crimes, poor or homeless or orphaned children were often locked up with hardened adult criminals when authorities had no other place to put them after their parents died or could no longer care for them.[29] Not until the twentieth century did states enact abuse and neglect laws that treated dependent children as blameless victims rather than common criminals.

By the 1840s, state criminal justice systems had begun inching toward more compassionate treatment of wayward children. In his 1833 study of emerging American penal institutions, French political writer Alexis de Tocqueville observed that some judges "hesitate[d] to pursue young delinquents, and the jury to condemn them" when imprisonment with hardened adult criminals awaited.[30] Accused children often received lighter sentences, or more frequent pardons, than did adults. Particularly in Missouri's larger cities, judges sometimes released children informally to responsible private citizens or children's aid societies for supervision similar to today's probation.[31]

Missouri's largest urban center was St. Louis, which in the 1840s grew from a frontier town into the nation's eighth-largest city. Fueled by immigration and industrialism, this explosive growth produced a desperate class of urban poor, including hordes of rootless, unhoused children who roamed the streets unsupervised and unprotected. Before the private St. Louis Reform School opened in 1851, overwhelmed authorities usually committed destitute children to the workhouse or prison for poverty or relatively minor offenses. With the private reformatory filled to capacity by 1853, the city's Common Council authorized establishment of Missouri's first public institution for children, the St. Louis House of Refuge, which admitted both white and free African American children. Slave children were still entitled only to bondage.[32]

The St. Louis House of Refuge was a secure facility (that is, one that youths could not leave without permission), and it quickly descended to the depths occupied by the prisons it sought to replace. In 1872, the mayor of St. Louis reported that the institution was already "a prison-house for the juvenile offenders, where compulsory educational discipline assume[d] the form of punishment."[33] Windows and doors had iron bars; children wore uniforms; and authorities shaved the children's heads. The children had no directed play and little indoor or outdoor recreation.[34] In 1873, public concern about cruelty at the House of Refuge led the state legislature to require separation of its criminal and dependent children for the first time, but severe overcrowding left the statutory command a virtual dead letter for the rest of the century.[35]

In 1893, the house's superintendent pleaded with St. Louis lawmakers: "We have 100 boys sleeping in one room 40 by 80 feet, low ceiling and the beds are 'two story'; there are no bathroom privileges of any kind in the building. . . . Can we not prevail upon this assembly to give us relief? In the name of humanity!"[36] The plea went unheeded, and by 1902 the House still confined some children at hard labor, including work on public roads or breaking rocks. Children who had committed only petty crimes, as well as those who were blameless but poor, were not spared.[37]

Often the first step toward the House of Refuge was the St. Louis Court of Criminal Correction, which tried felony cases of both adults and children.

Prisoners of all ages would wait in an iron cage just outside the courtroom until the judge called their case.[38] In 1897, the city's Progressive group the Humanity Club secured state legislation authorizing courts to parole persons under twenty-five who had been convicted of felonies other than murder, rape, arson, or robbery. Courts exercised this authority only rarely, however, largely because of public perception that parole meant releasing a criminal. Children received parole more often than adults, but no child was guaranteed such relatively lenient treatment.[39]

In 1895, the state legislature prohibited commitment of any boy under eighteen to the state penitentiary or a county jail. Instead, the boys would be committed to the new state training school at Boonville. The legislation also authorized transfer to Boonville of any boy under twenty-one who was then-incarcerated in the penitentiary.[40] Governor William J. Stone reported, however, that many boys sixteen and even younger continued serving long sentences in the penitentiary. The governor assailed the practice as "almost inhuman, and a disgrace to our civilization."[41]

The Humanity Club redoubled its reform efforts in 1899 after finding between thirty and forty boys under sixteen imprisoned in the St. Louis city jail, including boys bound over to the grand jury which might not meet for weeks or even months. The boys were confined in cells separate from those that held adult men, but prisoners of all ages mingled during recreation hour.[42] The prisoners included two ten-year-olds who had already spent months in jail awaiting trial for grand larceny because they had taken a farmer's wagon and later been found asleep in it.[43]

Most rural Missouri counties (that is, most of the state) had no public institutions similar to the St. Louis House of Refuge because maintaining such large facilities for a relatively small number of wayward children made no economic sense. Those same areas likewise lacked orphanages, charities, and other private entities that could keep children out of prison by providing probation-like supervision. Courts outside St. Louis still frequently imprisoned dependent children as young as seven. Foster care to protect dependent children in family-like settings outside institutional walls would not appear until the twentieth century.[44]

Imprisoned children continued to endure squalid conditions. Between 1897 and 1910, the State Board of Charities and Corrections found Missouri's prisons filthy, with all ages, both sexes, and the insane often mixed together.[45] In 1912, the board found that most Missouri counties still maintained "old-fashioned jails, dark and unsanitary, vermin-laden and disinfectant soaked, and impossible properly to administer." In one rural county jail, the board found eighteen persons, including six boys under eighteen, crammed into three cells.[46]

Missouri's first Children's Code Commission, appointed by Governor Elliot W. Major in 1915, found more than five hundred children under eighteen living in jails and "associating with criminals and tramps." The commission also reported that the state penitentiary still confined children, including a fifteen-year-old serving a twenty-five-year sentence, and that another fifteen-year-old had recently been paroled.[47]

THE EARLY "CHILD-SAVERS" AND THE PROGRESSIVES

With harsh imprisonment of delinquent and dependent children still widespread late in the nineteenth century, juvenile justice reform throughout the United States felt the influence of the Progressive movement, which from the early 1890s until the eve of World War I, advanced government's role in improving American life. According to juvenile justice professor Franklin Zimring, the "public optimism of the 'progressive era' provided a mandate for" a governmental role to protect delinquent children.[48] States pursued this mandate with two major institutional innovations, the juvenile courts and government-operated training (or reform) schools.

The impulses that motivated progressives and earlier child-savers still invite spirited debate today. The traditional view, embraced by most historians and by the Supreme Court, is that juvenile court legislation culminated decades of essentially humanitarian advocacy by reformers who sought to extricate delinquent children from harsh adult prisons, and to improve the lives of dependent children and their families.[49]

Some revisionist historians, however, have asserted that although many reformers undeniably perceived child welfare as a moral imperative, the reformers were "middle class, conservative and culturally ethnocentric" women and men who perceived the juvenile court as a vehicle for imposing traditional agrarian values on an increasingly urban nation and particularly on poor immigrant children.[50]

Early juvenile court acts defined delinquency broadly to include not only conduct that would be crimes if committed by adults, but also "status offenses," noncriminal conduct sanctionable only when committed by a juvenile. "It was not by accident," writes revisionist Anthony M. Platt, "that the behavior selected for penalizing by the child-savers—drinking, begging, roaming the streets, frequenting dance-halls and movies, fighting, sexuality, staying out late at night, and incorrigibility—was primarily attributable to the children of lower-class migrant and immigrant families."[51]

The revisionists, in turn, have faced criticism for minimizing the reformers' child-protective aims, and for exaggerating their class-based impulses. Ellen Ryerson, for example, maintains that the child-savers defined delinquency broadly, not to place blameless children in the clutches of the law, but to permit juvenile court treatment of children who might otherwise have landed in criminal court for disorderly conduct, vagrancy, or some similar offense.[52] "No doubt there was a good deal of middle-class snobbery and condescension" in the child-savers' attitudes, writes legal historian Lawrence M. Friedman, but "children were not, by and large, dragged into court by social workers, policemen, upper-class snoops and hegemonists. More often than not they were brought in by their very own parents."[53]

THE JUVENILE COURTS

As debate about the child-savers' motives continues, a group of leading juvenile justice experts correctly calls the juvenile court "the most widely and immediately popular legal reform in American history."[54] Cook County, Illinois, created the first juvenile court in 1899, and by 1911, Missouri and twenty-one other states had followed suit. By 1925, forty-five states maintained these specialized courts, and the final three states followed by the end of World War II. Never before or since have so many states created entirely new court systems so swiftly, in such unison, and with such general enthusiasm.

The nation's early juvenile courts were in effect quasi-social welfare agencies whose judges exercised broad discretion over parents and children, virtually free from due process, the rules of evidence, or other legal constraints. Such judicial discretion concerned some contemporary observers, notably Roscoe Pound, who commented in 1913 that compared to the juvenile courts, "the powers of the court of Star Chamber were a bagatelle."[55] Unease fell largely on deaf ears, however, because procedural informality comported with prevailing perceptions of the juvenile court's rehabilitative mission after decades of harshness. (Not until 1967 did the Supreme Court begin the "constitutional domestication" of the nation's juvenile courts by imposing due-process formalities on delinquency cases.)[56]

Governor Alexander M. Dockery strongly endorsed juvenile court legislation in his January 8, 1903, message to the Missouri General Assembly.[57] Two months later, the lawmakers responded by unanimously creating Missouri's first juvenile court after energetic advocacy led by the St. Louis Humanity Club, the Missouri Conference of Charities, the State Board of Charities and Corrections, police court and circuit judges, and many law enforcement officers.[58]

For more than a decade, Missouri inched toward the juvenile court ideal one step at a time. The bill Governor Dockery signed created the court only in St. Louis City and in counties with populations of 150,000 or more.[59] Because Jackson County (Kansas City and its outlying areas) was the only county that qualified, much work remained to be done. "[I]f it is well to have in the two largest cities of the State a [juvenile] court," asked Missouri Bar Association president William Muir Williams, "why should not the provisions of the law be extended to smaller places, and even to every county in Missouri?"[60]

Legislation in 1905 extended the juvenile court to Missouri counties with populations between 150,000 and 500,000, and repealed the 1903 act insofar as it applied to counties with less than 500,000 population.[61] In 1907, Governor Joseph W. Folk (the former reform-minded St. Louis circuit attorney) strongly urged the general assembly to extend juvenile courts to smaller counties in light of the positive experiences that other states had reported with their juvenile courts.[62] New legislation created juvenile courts in counties with populations between 100,000 and 150,000.[63]

At the end of this four-year flurry, Missouri's juvenile courts still reached only a small percentage of the state's children and families. Even St. Louis County, with a population of only 50,000 at the time, was left on the outside.[64] Governor Folk again urged the legislature to extend the juvenile courts to other areas of the state because "[y]outhful violators of law deserve different treatment from hardened criminals."[65]

In 1909, the general assembly extended the juvenile court to counties with populations of 50,000 or more.[66] By that time, the private Missouri Conference of Charities and Corrections (later renamed the Missouri Conference of Social Welfare) maintained a strong voice in children's affairs. Reform efforts by its professional social workers spurred legislation that, by the eve of U.S. entry into World War I in 1917, extended juvenile courts to the state's smaller counties.[67]

By 1921, Missouri's juvenile courts reached all major populated counties and the state Supreme Court praised the new courts for their "wise and beneficent purposes."[68] The court concluded that children were "no longer regarded as criminals to be punished without effort at reformation and after their detention to continue as menaces to society; but as wards to be aided, encouraged and educated, that they may . . . become assets instead of liabilities."[69]

With children removed from the criminal courts for most criminal charges, juvenile courts in Missouri's two largest cities quickly became among the nation's busiest. In 1920, for example, the St. Louis City juvenile court formally disposed of 2,064 cases, more than the number heard that year by juvenile courts in most other major cities, including Boston, Minneapolis, Seattle, Los Angeles, and San Francisco.[70] In 1936, Jackson County's juvenile court heard 2,288 cases.[71]

BOONVILLE: FALSE HOPES AND HARD REALITY

In Missouri and several other states, legislatures coupled creation of juvenile courts with construction of large congregate state training schools as dispositional alternatives for delinquent or dependent children who might otherwise face time in adult prisons. "Nothing is so costly to the State as jails and penitentiaries," Governor Thomas T. Crittenden said in 1885. "If the state is the guardian of its children, it should be prepared to take charge of the little waifs of society."[72]

Expressing similar lofty motives four years later, Governor Albert P. Morehouse told the legislature that "[t]he State cannot engage in a more laudable undertaking than caring for and reforming its youth, whom circumstances over which they had no control have started on the wrong road in life." Governor Morehouse estimated that 90 percent of youths sent to training schools would "make good and honorable citizens" later on.[73]

In 1887, the legislature authorized construction of two training schools that opened two years later, the Missouri Reform School for Boys at Boonville and the State Industrial Home for Girls at Chillicothe. The State Industrial Home for Negro Girls followed in 1916.

Conditions in Missouri's training schools quickly deteriorated, particularly at Boonville. The legislature had confidently predicted that the boys' institution would be "not simply a place of correction, but a reform school where the young offender of the law, separated from vicious associates, may receive careful physical, intellectual and moral training, be reformed and restored to the community with purposes and character fitting for a good citizen, an honorable and an honest man."[74] The institution never lived up to these expectations.

The earliest documentation of Boonville's long descent came in 1911 from the St. Louis Municipal Commission on Delinquent, Dependent and Defective Children, which Mayor Frederick H. Kreismann appointed at the behest of the reformist St. Louis Civic League. After visiting juvenile facilities in Missouri and other states, the commission called conditions at Boonville "almost intolerable."[75] The three commissioners charged that after barely twenty years, the institution had "slumped from its previously high standards to a juvenile prison similar to a penitentiary,"[76] where dependent children as young as eight found little protection against predatory, older juvenile criminals.[77]

The St. Louis Commission concluded that Boonville was "not in spirit or in fact an institution with an educational program." The institution was "physically in a bad condition, and suffer[ing] from lack of funds for the proper care of its inmates." The boys ate and slept barracks-style with a hundred or more in a large room, a barren institutional setting that prevented "anything like a home atmosphere or a constant individual influence." Boys were regularly assigned to menial, and sometimes dangerous, labor that served no purpose but to help the institution maintain its skimpy budget without hiring outside workers.[78]

The commission's three members included its secretary, Roger N. Baldwin, one of Missouri's leading juvenile justice progressives. Baldwin's pedigree warrants attention here, not only because his later national prominence has shrouded his Missouri professional roots, but also because his early Missouri initiatives highlight the Progressives' inability to reform the statewide juvenile training schools that accompanied creation of the juvenile court.

Baldwin was born to a wealthy Boston-area family in 1884, entered social work after earning bachelor's and master's degrees from Harvard, and went west to teach sociology at Washington University in 1906 at the urging of his father's lawyer, Louis D. Brandeis, who had practiced law in St. Louis for a few months after graduating from Harvard Law School in 1879. In 1907, Baldwin became the St. Louis juvenile court's second chief juvenile probation officer, a position he held until 1910.[79]

In 1908, Baldwin helped create the National Probation Association. After the St. Louis Municipal Commission issued its final report in 1911, he founded the St. Louis Council of Social Agencies, a clearinghouse that arranged private treatment for children and families. In 1912, he founded the St. Louis Board of Children's Guardians, the city's public child protective agency. He also remained active in the Missouri Association for Social Welfare.[80]

In 1914, Baldwin's St. Louis experiences led him to coauthor *Juvenile Courts and Probation,* an influential treatise that remained a leading national authority on juvenile justice well into the 1950s.[81] With a national reputation, Baldwin was named one of the ten most influential people in St. Louis in 1915.[82]

When his critique of Boonville went unheeded, Baldwin left Missouri to organize the American Civil Liberties Union in 1920. He went on to achieve national attention as the organization's executive director for the next three decades. Years after his early forays into Missouri progressivism, he died in

1981 at the age of ninety-seven, a few months after President Jimmy Carter awarded him the Medal of Freedom, the nation's highest civilian honor.[83]

On the heels of the St. Louis Commission's report, Governor Herbert S. Hadley reported in 1911 that Boonville held about a hundred older boys who were so vicious that they belonged in a special state facility away from younger inmates.[84] When Governor Elliot W. Major cited serious overcrowding at the institution in 1915, the legislature made matters worse by opening its doors to first-time male offenders under thirty.[85] Courts freely assigned adult criminals to Boonville until 1927, when the state opened a prison at Algoa for male offenders over twenty-one, the general age of majority at that time.[86]

In 1931, a state commission reported that Boonville's buildings were "in bad shape, almost beyond repair," and that "living conditions are far from what they should be for young men and children." The commission concluded that Boonville had "outlived its usefulness and should be abandoned."[87] Like the report of Baldwin's St. Louis Commission twenty years earlier, the state commission's report went unheeded.

Perhaps partly to keep boys out of Boonville unless they were serious or repeat offenders, some larger Missouri counties maintained their own juvenile confinement facilities. Most children confined in the St. Louis area, for example, were sent to the St. Louis House of Refuge, an institution still unworthy of praise. Because many smaller counties did not have funding to maintain alternative juvenile institutions, however, rural youths were often committed to Boonville for offenses that did not land metropolitan youths there.

As Boonville adhered to the juvenile prison model in the 1930s, the state placed the three training schools within the Department of Penal Institutions, the agency that managed the state penitentiary.[88] In 1934, Boonville's new superintendent frankly told the legislature that the reformatory was "in a deplorable condition. The equipment is inadequate and nearly all the buildings are old and in a bad state of repair."[89] Smaller boys were housed in two crumbling, decaying buildings that leaked in the rain and were "serious fire-traps." Mattresses were infested with bedbugs, and the dining room, kitchen, and hospital were filthy. Boys sometimes refused to eat because the food was infested with bugs, flies, and roaches (dead ones if authorities used bug spray just before the meal).[90]

Later that year, a visiting Minnesota prison warden found that Boonville's boys "carr[ied] themselves with the air of the oppressed and the hopeless" because of "overcrowding, poor food, unsanitary conditions, fear of physical punishment, and an inadequate system of recreation."[91] "It is not my policy to coddle criminals," the warden continued, but Boonville warehoused "many children who are not responsible for their condition and who should be treated as children and not as dangerous criminals. The state of Missouri has sadly neglected its delinquent youngsters and under the present system there is no hope for their improvement."[92]

In 1937, the Osborne Association, a national corrections organization, condemned Boonville as one of the nation's worst juvenile reformatories. The institution was marked by "bad housing, negative discipline, mass treatment, an ineffectual program, and poor parole work in common with some of the others" the association inspected, but "it stood alone in the extent to which it followed the pattern of the old-time prison."[93]

The Osborne Association harshly criticized Boonville's assignment of nearly all its boys to daily physical labor that "emphasize[d] production and custody rather than training." To the association, backbreaking hazardous labor for no wages at the institution's profit-making quarry "fairly shouted 'convict labor.'"[94] The criticism fell on deaf ears, as did the 1938 recommendation of the federal Prison Industries Reorganization Administration that Boonville shift emphasis from "work for the institution's maintenance" to "training for the boys' future."[95]

The Osborne Association found Boonville's prison-like atmosphere reinforced by "[s]haved heads, typically prison uniforms, V's cut in the heels of the shoes [to help identify escapees], and the use of numbers instead of names." "Modern principles and methods of dealing with delinquents did not receive even lip service," and staff members who took rehabilitation seriously were "thoroughly discouraged by the lack of support from the administration."[96]

Conditions at Boonville declined still further throughout the 1940s, even after the constitution of 1945 classified the three training schools as educational institutions, and created the State Board of Training Schools to administer them.[97] In 1947, Governor Phil M. Donnelly reported that Boonville's inmates included "children eight and nine years of age who are committed primarily because of neglect in their homes. These children are not essentially incorrigible but need the guidance and the discipline comparable to that of a model home life. At the other extreme are boys sixteen to seventeen years of age, who . . . have become potential criminals. It is impossible to adjust many of them to normal social attitudes."[98]

Throughout the 1940s, many Boonville citizens demanded the training school's removal because they feared violence from the reformatory's many escapees.[99] On the night of March 17, 1948, after violent inmates killed two boys at the school and committed a series of assaults, a Highway Patrol convoy carrying Governor Donnelly and armed officers drove there. In the so-called "Midnight Ride of Governor Donnelly," the officers forcibly removed seventy-one of the most violent boys and transferred them in chains to the state penitentiary.[100]

Later in 1948, the State Board of Training Schools reported that Boonville had fallen into "a state of physical and moral collapse," a familiar refrain by that time. "[I]f 300 model boys from even the best families in Missouri were placed in this institution," the board explained, "within a reasonable time they would deteriorate and become juvenile menaces." Cattle on the institution's farmland, the board admitted, were treated better than the confined boys.[101]

Soon after losing his position in 1949, Boonville's former superintendent told the St. Louis *Post-Dispatch:* "I saw black eyes, battered faces, broken noses among the boys. . . . The usual corrective procedure among the guards was to knock a boy down with their fists, then kick him in the groin. . . . Many of the men were sadists."[102]

In 1950, social worker Albert Deutsch found Boonville's boys still "mixed indiscriminately—the younger with the older, dangerous mental cases with the normals, the first offender with the hardened repeater, the frightened child with the sadistic hoodlum." He reaffirmed frequent beatings by guards. "[T]error-stricken and desperate boys had been escaping from the institution in great numbers," about four hundred in 1948 alone. Deutsch condemned Boonville as a "hellhole" with a "long-standing tradition of sadistic maltreatment and a grossly inadequate budget."[103]

Boonville confined both white and black youths, but courts sometimes sent black youths there under circumstances that would have landed white youths in a private institution or other alternative placement. Boonville was the last resort because many private institutions refused to accept blacks until the 1960s.[104] Without success, the Missouri Association for Social Welfare recommended that Boonville's black children be permitted to "share in all the programs provided for white boys," to eat in the same dining hall rather than in a separate isolated unit, and to receive more vocational opportunities.[105]

CHILLICOTHE: "VICIOUS ASSOCIATES AND EVIL INFLUENCES"

Reflecting the social roles expected of women during the Gilded Age, the 1887 legislation creating the State Industrial Home for Girls noted that the Chillicothe institution would offer "thorough systematic teaching of all domestic industries [and] a thorough education in every branch of household work."[106] Chillicothe's rules and regulations said that "girls, removed from vicious associates and evil influences, may receive careful physical, intellectual, and moral training, participate in the enjoyment of a true home life, be reformed, and become good domestic women prudent in speech and conduct, cleanly, industrious and capable housekeepers." The phrase "vicious associates and evil influences" had particular meaning because girls were usually committed for sexual indiscretions, while boys committed to Boonville for crimes had usually acted against persons or property.[107]

The decline of the Chillicothe institution began later than that of the Boonville school. When Roger N. Baldwin and his colleagues on the St. Louis Municipal Commission condemned Boonville in 1911, they found Chillicothe still a "pleasing contrast" to the boys' counterpart. "The girls are housed in large cottages; there is a good deal of home life; the institution is kept in splendid physical shape, and the girls have a fair amount of schooling and training."[108] The State Board of Charities and Corrections nonetheless reported that overcrowding had led Chillicothe to refuse admission to some girls committed by the courts.[109]

By the end of the 1920s, the verdict on Chillicothe was mixed, but a 1929 researcher still found the institution's vocational program to be one of the best in the nation's juvenile reformatories.[110] In 1938, however, the Osborne Association ranked Chillicothe low among midwestern training schools because of "shameful overcrowding, dissension among staff members, precarious disciplinary control, and the housing of girls in dilapidated firetraps under physically and morally unhealthy conditions." The school's annual expenditure of $419 per girl fell far short of the national average of $600, but Chillicothe was one of the few institutions for delinquent girls that offered a high school education.[111]

TIPTON: SEPARATE BUT NOT EQUAL

Boonville segregated boys by race, but Chillicothe refused court commitments of African American girls because, according to the institution's superintendent in 1903, "intermingling of the races would inevitably result in the demoralization of the whites and nullify, to a great extent, the good we are now doing."[112] A twelve-year-old black girl committed to the state penitentiary in 1908 was released only when the Federated Negro Women's Clubs of Missouri appealed to the state attorney general.[113]

In 1909, the legislature authorized construction of the State Industrial Home for Negro Girls. The state purchased twenty-eight acres northwest of Sedalia, but objections from local residents forced abandonment of plans to build the training school there. Other towns also objected, and it was not until 1913 that the lawmakers appropriated funds to purchase 165 acres a mile north of Tipton, where the institution opened three years later.[114]

Chillicothe and Tipton were assuredly separate, but not equal. Despite its budget woes, Chillicothe had an adequate school building—a three-story structure with classrooms, a large gymnasium, auditorium, and a library with about 4,000 purchased and donated books, some in disrepair because the institution had no librarian. Chillicothe's buildings were located in a residential section on the outskirts of town and its rented farm offered soil suitable for the agriculture taught at the school. By 1940, daily meals at the institution featured meat at least once, three cups of milk per girl, fruit and vegetables, hot cereal at breakfast in the winter, and a sweet dessert at least once. Each girl could have as much food as she wished.[115]

Tipton was another story. Deliveries were often slow to the school, which was located on a country road only partially graveled and almost impassable in wet weather. Low water pressure could barely reach the second floor of the living quarters, and the water was so hard that it had to be softened with the school's antiquated water softening equipment. Sewage disposal was poor, and most of the school's facilities were ill equipped.[116]

Efforts to attract quality staff to Tipton were hampered both by salaries considerably lower than those paid at Chillicothe and by the surrounding community's animosity and racial discrimination. Tipton's entire staff was black, and the superintendent often had to hire any applicant who came through the door. The superintendent also served as nurse, secretary, discipline officer, recreation director, religious leader, and parole officer. The budget allowed the school only minimal food, with little meat, milk, or fresh fruit. The school's milk cows sometimes had to be slaughtered for food. "[T]he only adequate source of food," a 1943 study found, "was the vegetable garden, and it was not too productive because of the poor soil."[117]

The study also found that Tipton's girls were "dressed in rags with little immediate possibility of securing any better clothing." "The supply of winter jackets is so limited that three or four girls must wear the same jacket. Heavier clothing for outside work is more or less community property because it is placed in the main office and is worn by any of the girls as needed. There are no supplies of galoshes, hats, long stockings, or heavy underwear. Many of the shoes are in a condition beyond all possible repair; in fact, some of the shoes have no soles at all, yet the girls continue to wear them."[118]

In 1943, the governor vetoed an appropriation of about $5,000 for Tipton, an amount he said exceeded the school's needs by $4,297.[119] The budgetary imbalance between the two schools for girls had widened by 1950, when the Missouri Association for Social Welfare reported gingerly that "[t]raining, in general, at Tipton, is not as complete as at Chillicothe."[120]

Despite these persistent impediments, recent scholarship concludes that Tipton served a positive purpose for the one thousand delinquent, orphaned, neglected, and impoverished girls who were assigned there during four decades marked by official segregation, Jim Crow legislation, poverty, and rampant racism and sexism that the girls encountered on the outside.[121] Professor Leroy Milton Rowe concludes that Tipton's "all-African American staff with access to public appropriations was able to successfully prepare many girls to live out their lives, not just as productive citizens, but also as the future mothers of their race."[122] "[I]t was vital," he says, "for these poor black females who grew up in a society constrained by racism and sexism to be institutionalized at a place where they learned to negotiate these challenges from individuals who shared this very experience with them."[123]

THE REFORMATORIES' FAILURE AND COLLAPSE

Well into the 1960s, some Missouri courts avoided sending boys to Boonville because judges knew about beatings by staff, violent youth-on-youth assaults, and other constant dangers.[124] Courts in the state's smaller counties had fewer options, as the counties often could not afford to maintain their own facilities. To avoid Boonville, some judges sent boys outside Missouri for treatment.[125]

A 1969 federal report roundly condemned Boonville's "quasi-penal-military" atmosphere, lack of adequate rehabilitation programs, substandard educational program, understaffing, outdated physical plant, and deteriorating buildings.[126] Particularly notorious was "The Hole," a dank solitary-confinement room located atop the administration building and used for decades. In 1971, the president of the Northern Missouri Juvenile Officers Association said that Boonville could not attract quality staff because "the reputation of the treatment program and the professional climate within the institution are so poor" that professionals aspiring to juvenile justice careers did not want their employment histories to show service there.[127]

Like other states in the late nineteenth century, Missouri built the training schools in remote rural areas because America's "agrarian ideal"—admiration for the hardworking, simple, honest farmer—equated farm life with personal growth and redemption. By the early 1970s, however, most boys confined at Boonville were from the inner cities and benefited little from the institution's farming regimen, nor did they relate well to the staff members, largely drawn from rural areas.[128]

In 1971, Boonville's superintendent said the training school "cannot exist as it is" because a third of the inmates were rapists, murderers, or armed robbers, including some inmates who were mentally ill.[129] Many of the remaining two-thirds were easy marks, having been confined not for crimes but as victims of abuse or neglect or for running away from home.[130] A year later, the Missouri Law Enforcement Assistance Council reiterated that the state's juvenile justice system was plagued by "glaring inadequacies, fragmentation, and great service gaps, low quality of services, and lack of measures of effectiveness."[131] Boonville's superintendent himself derided the institution as a place for "warehousing of bodies."[132]

In 1975, the federal district court in Kansas City entered a consent decree in a class action filed two years earlier challenging conditions at Boonville. State officials agreed to close the Hole, and to improve conditions in detention cells that held the most violent boys. Under the state Reorganization Act of 1974, the Board of Training Schools became the Division of Youth Services within the Department of Social Services.[133]

In 1976, investigative journalist Kenneth Wooden wrote *Weeping in the Playtime of Others,* which recounted his visits to juvenile correctional facilities in thirty states. He reported that Boonville inmates told him about staff members "having sexual relations with the children, beating them, throwing them into solitary confinement for no substantial reason, pushing drugs, etc."[134]

In 1979, escapes from Boonville doubled during a six-month period. When a fifteen-year-old inmate ran away, eluded the institution's bloodhounds, and drowned in the Missouri River, officials said little but that the drowning was Boonville's first suicide in at least seven years.[135]

Boonville's closing in 1983 left a haunting legacy: atop a hill on the reformatory's grounds was a small cemetery with fifty white markers, only three inscribed with names. People could not quite remember whether the interred boys were beaten to death by guards, beaten to death by other inmates, or victims of an influenza epidemic. What was certain was that every marker stood above the coffin of a boy whose family or friends had not bothered to claim his body.[136] Today, detailed historical essays on the websites of the cities of Boonville, Chillicothe, and Tipton make no mention that the reformatories ever existed.

NATIONAL LEADERSHIP FOR MISSOURI DYS

As Boonville and Chillicothe stumbled throughout the 1970s, Missouri judges and prominent lawmakers urged the state to move from an incarceration-based juvenile corrections system to a therapeutic approach. Similar calls had failed to resonate for decades, but now more Missouri leaders began to listen, even though the message meant summoning the political will to swim against the national and state tide that stressed "getting tough on crime" to preserve "law and order."

Calls for therapeutic reform were led by two respected statewide Republican officeholders who could not plausibly be challenged as "soft on crime." Attorney General John C. Danforth urged replacing Boonville with foster homes or group homes where children supervised by probation officers could live in noninstitutional settings closer to their own home communities. The attorney general called his proposal "nothing less than a total shift of philosophy in dealing with juvenile offenders in Missouri." "We must learn how to rehabilitate juvenile offenders and we are not doing a good job in Missouri now."[137]

In 1973, Governor Christopher S. Bond told a statewide gathering of juvenile justice professionals that "[e]xisting institutions in too many instances are monuments to the mistakes of the past, reflecting our propensity for trying to solve social problems by building an enclosure to keep them out of sight and mind." The governor urged creation of "new programs for community-based treatment services, group treatment techniques and diversification."[138]

Missouri's first step toward a therapeutic approach to juvenile corrections was the "Positive Peer Culture" (PPC) pilot experiment at the Sears Youth Center in Poplar Bluff beginning in 1970. Departing from Boonville's large congregate model, PPC placed about ten to twelve delinquent boys in a group. Each small group remained with the same small number of staff throughout schooling, recreation, and other daily activities. Once the experiment demonstrated enhanced accountability, safety, and rehabilitation while markedly reducing violence and escapes, the Department of Social Services introduced PPC at other juvenile facilities.[139]

Momentum to close Boonville, and to move from congregate institutions to small-group therapy also spread to Chillicothe. While the girls' school had never been as notorious as its counterpart, thoughtful policymakers realized that the large congregate model also disserved the special unmet needs of girls, who often arrived at the depressing, prisonlike Chillicothe institution after suffering physical and emotional abuse, victimization typically different from the life experiences of most confined boys.[140]

For boys and girls alike, the result today is the Missouri Model, administered by the DYS. Missouri has become the national exemplar because (according to former DYS director Tim Decker) the model has "traded coercion, threats and punishment for a model of structure, development and healthy relationships."[141] Other states, Decker adds, "put their money into fences and isolation cells and all kinds of hardware security, which doesn't really make anyone any safer, nor does it help young people turn their lives around."[142] According to one DYS youth, staff members "don't judge us on our crime; they just treat us like regular human beings."[143]

DYS divides the state into five regions, with thirty-two residential facilities that house the more than 1,300 youths who are assigned to the agency each year for committing crimes.[144] Decentralization enables the agency's college-educated, highly trained staff to treat most youths within thirty to fifty miles of their homes. DYS deems family and community support so important that when parents, guardians, or other family members lack transportation, agency staff drive them to and from residential facilities to participate.[145]

Each of Missouri's five juvenile justice regions maintains a diverse range of residential facilities that separate violent offenders from other youths. Each incoming youth receives a comprehensive needs and risk assessment.[146] DYS then fashions an Individual Treatment Plan for each youth in the region's residential care facility that provides "the least restrictive environment possible without compromising public safety."[147] Each youth is assigned an individual case manager whose supervision and support continue throughout the youth's stay and after release into the community. Diverse programming seeks to treat both urban and rural youth in an ethnically sensitive environment.[148]

No DYS facility contains more than eighty-five beds, and all but three contain thirty-three beds or fewer.[149] For youths who have committed status offenses or misdemeanors, the agency maintains six nonsecure group homes (each with ten to twelve beds) under twenty-four-hour responsible-adult supervision, and proctor homes where youths live with college student mentors in structured, supportive, supervised settings. One such group home for eleven girls is located on the William Woods University campus in Fulton, and the girls eat in the university dining hall and attend university activities. Youths in group homes generally spend time in schools, jobs, group projects, community service, and individual and family counseling.[150]

For youths who have committed more serious crimes and require more supervision, DYS maintains eighteen moderately secure group homes (each with twenty to thirty beds) throughout the state in residential neighborhoods, state parks, and two college campuses. These youths also spend time on community service projects, and youths who demonstrate trustworthiness may get jobs at local nonprofit or government agencies.[151]

DYS maintains secure care facilities that provide violent offenders and chronic repeaters education, counseling, and vocational guidance in groups of ten to twelve. The facilities are enclosed by a locked perimeter fence, but maintain atmospheres conducive to treatment.[152]

Ten DYS day-treatment facilities provide youths a minimum of six hours of daily education, counseling, and tutoring before they return home in the evening. These year-round facilities are the first stop for some younger teens who are relatively minor offenders. For youths previously confined in residential treatment, day treatment helps smooth reintegration into the community. Day treatment enables staff to provide supervision and support and enables youths to continue their education without having to await the start of the new semester.[153]

Some DYS youths participate in local community service activities, including working at hospitals, senior centers, homeless shelters, and children's mental health facilities. Other DYS youths join scout troops and other local organizations. Many DYS youths earn their high school diplomas or high school equivalency certificates while in the DYS program, and many proceed to postsecondary education.[154]

When a youth completes the DYS program, the agency's comprehensive aftercare program keeps the individual case manager involved, supervising the youth's return to the community and sometimes helping the youth find employment or admission to further education. The DYS Job Readiness/Work Experience Program provides a variety of employment experiences in cooperation with not-for-profit enterprises. College students studying social work and similar disciplines serve as "trackers" who monitor youths released into the community so they will not drift back to peer influences that contributed to crime in the first place.[155]

The Missouri Model has won the attention and support of the Annie E. Casey Foundation, perhaps the national leader in promoting solutions for vulnerable children and families. For nearly twenty years, foundation grants have enabled DYS to host delegations from more than thirty other states that wish to inspect and learn from Missouri facilities. The foundation explains the model this way: "The three most important DYS beliefs are: (1) that all people—including delinquent youth—desire to do well and succeed; (2) that with the right kinds of help, all youth can (and most will) make lasting behavioral changes and succeed; and (3) that the mission of youth corrections must be to provide the right kinds of help, consistent with public safety, so that young people make needed changes and move on to successful adult lives."[156]

"COULDN'T WE JUST HIRE SOMEBODY FROM MISSOURI THIS TIME?"

Missouri's national influence in juvenile corrections has paid dividends. Recall Louisiana, whose distressed juvenile corrections system opened this chapter. With funding from the Casey Foundation, the Bayou State has adopted the Missouri Model to create low-, mid-, and secure-level facilities that are tailored to a youth's offense and located within fifty miles of youths' homes. Each facility will treat a small number of youths through development programming.[157] According to the New Orleans *Times-Picayune*, "Missouri has become a model for juvenile justice reformers around the country, and it has earned its reputation."[158]

New challenges beckon. In 2009, the U.S. Justice Department found four New York state juvenile facilities rife with routine staff-on-inmate brutality that left youths with broken bones, shattered teeth, concussions, and dozens of other serious injuries. At one of the four, an emotionally disturbed fifteen-year-old died after two staff members pinned him to the ground.[159]

In 2014, the Justice Department charged that a "deep-seated culture of violence"[160] pervades facilities that confine sixteen- and seventeen-year-old boys at Rikers Island in New York City, a prison that the *New York Times* condemns as a "chamber of horrors."[161] The department found that adolescent inmates suffer (1) "serious physical harm from the rampant use of unnecessary and excessive force used by DOC [Department of Corrections] staff," and (2) "harm caused by violence inflicted by other inmates, including inmate-on-inmate fights." Adolescents "have sustained a striking number of serious injuries, including broken jaws, broken orbital bones, long bone fractures, and lacerations requiring sutures. [A]t an alarming rate and for excessive periods of time," the prison's staff also "relies far too heavily" on solitary confinement of mentally ill inmates.[162]

A 2009 New York gubernatorial task force called for adoption of the Missouri Model, whose "rehabilitative approach has been shown to better protect public safety and produce more impressive outcomes than punitive alternatives."[163] Four years later, New York City's former corrections commissioner reiterated the call to replicate Missouri's program, charging that New York "demoniz[es] its own . . . children" and "send[s] a not-so-subtle message to the staff that the community doesn't want these kids, and the community doesn't really care what happens to them."[164]

How does a state begin systemic reform in the twenty-first century? As Maryland struggled to reform its violence-plagued juvenile prison system in 2010, the Baltimore *Sun* urged that the state "needs to follow the highly successful Missouri model for juvenile justice."[165] When the head of Maryland's Department of Juvenile Services resigned with the agency in disarray, a *Sun* editorial asked a simple question: "Couldn't we just hire somebody from Missouri this time?"[166]

MISSOURI'S STATEWIDE JUVENILE JUSTICE SYSTEM IN HISTORICAL PERSPECTIVE

Despite the Division of Youth Services' national renown, Missouri's long road to juvenile justice has not yet reached its destination. In 2013, the National Juvenile Defender Center alleged that the state's juvenile indigent defense system "is in crisis and has endured at least two decades of crushing caseloads and inadequate resources to provide its mandated services."[167]

In 2015, the U.S. Justice Department reported "reason to believe that the St. Louis County Family Court fails to ensure that children appearing for juvenile justice proceedings receive adequate due process," and that the court "engages in conduct that violates" equal protection.[168] As it began negotiations with state authorities to remedy the alleged constitutional violations, the department acknowledged "the recognized innovations of the Missouri juvenile justice system."[169] "Missouri has been at the forefront of a community-based approach to juvenile corrections, closing its training schools–large prison-like institutions located away from most communities–and replacing them with smaller, treatment-focused facilities located closer to youths' homes."[170]

"If the house is to be set in order," wrote historian John Hope Franklin, "one cannot begin with the present; he must begin with the past."[171] Missouri's therapeutic approach to juvenile justice demonstrates the wisdom of summoning political will in response to harsh lessons learned over time. Freeing itself from the undertow of the "get tough on crime" mood that characterized America in the 1970s, Missouri chose to jettison its reformatories after decades of demonstrable failure. Like the traveler who reached a fork in Robert Frost's celebrated poem "The Road Not Taken," Missouri chose the road "less traveled by/ And that has made all the difference."[172] Further challenges remain on travels down that road.

NOTES

1. Matthew Franck, "Juvenile Justice in Missouri Serves as Model for Nation," *St. Louis Post-Dispatch*, October 5, 2003, A1 (quotation).

2. Douglas E. Abrams, "Reforming Juvenile Delinquency Treatment to Enhance Rehabilitation, Personal Accountability and Public Safety," *Oregon Law Review* 84 (2005), 1001, 1002, 1022–27; *State ex rel SD*, 832 So2d 415, 430–32, 437 (La Ct App 2002) (Louisiana juvenile prison guards "maintained order through fear, force and violence," and that nearly a quarter of confined youths each month

suffered injuries inflicted by guards and other youths, including broken jaws and other fractures; discussing fear, force, violence and injuries).

3. United States Code, vol. 42, secs. 1997–1997j (Washington, D.C.: U.S. Government Printing Office, 2012).

4. Senate Committee on the Judiciary, The Civil Rights of Institutionalized Persons Act, 96th Cong., 2d sess., 1979, Senate Report No. 96–416, 2; H.R. Conference Report, 96th Cong., 2d sess., 1980, H.R. Report No. 96–897, 9 (discussing the "barbaric treatment of . . . juvenile prisoners").

5. Fox Butterfield, "Profits at a Juvenile Prison Come with a Chilling Cost," *New York Times*, July 15, 1998, A1.

6. Angie Cannon, "Juvenile Injustice: Overcrowding, Violence, and Abuse," *U.S. News & World Report* (August 9, 2004), 28.

7. Solomon Moore, "Missouri System Treats Juvenile Offenders with Lighter Hand," *New York Times*, March 27, 2009.

8. Alan J. Beck and David Cantor, *Sexual Victimization in Juvenile Facilities Reported by Youth, 2012* (Washington, D.C.: U.S. Bureau of Justice Statistics, 2012), 4–5; Andrea J. Sedlak, Karla S. McPherson and Monica Basena, *Nature and Risk of Victimization: Findings from the Survey of Youth in Residential Placement* (Washington, D.C.: U.S. Justice Department, 2013), 8.

9. Abrams, "Reforming Juvenile Delinquency Treatment," 1001, 1004–63.

10. Moore, "Missouri System Treats Juvenile Offenders."

11. Dick Mendel, "Small Is Beautiful: The Missouri Division of Youth Services," *AdvoCasey* 29 (Spring 2003), 35–36.

12. Barry Krisberg, interview with author, Columbia, MO, December 8, 2002.

13. Richard A. Mendel, *Less Cost, More Safety: Guiding Lights for Reform in Juvenile Justice* (Washington, D.C.: American Youth Policy Forum, 2001), 11–13.

14. Annie E. Casey Foundation, "Moving Youth from Risk to Opportunity," *Kids Count 2002* 1 (July 2006), 19 (calling Missouri "a national model in juvenile corrections" and providing grants to enable the state to demonstrate its program to other states).

15. Stephanie Chen, "Teen Offenders Find a Future in Missouri," CNN, August 25, 2009 (quotation).

16. Arthur M. Schlesinger, Jr., "Folly's Antidote," *New York Times*, January 1, 2007, A19.

17. Abrams, "Reforming Juvenile Delinquency Treatment," 1071–77.

18. *State v. Tice*, 90 Mo 112, 2 SW 269, 269 (1886); *State v. Adams*, 76 Mo 355 (1882) (discussing the common law standards).

19. Concerning nineteenth-century executions in Missouri, see *State v. Barton*, 71 Mo 288, 290 (1879); Missouri Revised Statutes, sec. 1666 (1879); Missouri Revised Statutes 167, 168 sec. 3 (1835); Victor L. Streib, *Death Penalty for Juveniles* (Bloomington: Indiana University Press, 1987), 199; Harriet C. Frazier,

"The Execution of Juveniles in Missouri," part I, *Journal of the Missouri Bar* (December 1990), 633, 634.

20. Douglas E. Abrams, *A Very Special Place in Life: The History of Juvenile Justice in Missouri* (Jefferson City, MO: Missouri Juvenile Justice Association, 2003), 19.

21. Laws of a Public and General Nature, of the District of Louisiana, of the Territory of Louisiana, of the Territory of Missouri, and of the State of Missouri, up to the Year 1824, vol. 1, ch. 91, § 3 (1813), 267.

22. For instance, *Scott, A Man of Color v. Emerson*, 15 Mo 576 (Mo 1852); *Dred Scott v. Sandford*, 60 US 393 (1857).

23. Duane G. Meyer, *The Heritage of Missouri,* 3rd ed. (Jefferson City, MO.: River City Publishers, 1982), 296–98.

24. Bob Priddy, *Across Our Wide Missouri,* vol. 1 (Independence, MO: Independence Press, 1982), 42; Gary R. Kremer, "Politics, Punishment, and Profit: Convict Labor in the Missouri State Penitentiary 1875–1900," *Gateway Heritage* 13 (Summer 1992), 28–29; William Nesheim, "A History of the Missouri State Penitentiary 1833–1875" (master's thesis, University of Missouri-Kansas City, 1970), 35.

25. William T. Cross and Charlotte B. Forrester, *County Almshouses and Jails of Missouri* (Jefferson City, MO: Missouri State Nurses' Association, 1913), 3–4.

26. Missouri Revised Statutes 334, 335 sec. 1 (1835).

27. Missouri Revised Statutes 334, 335 secs. 4–5 (1835); Missouri Revised Statutes 88, 89 secs. 4–5 (1845); Missouri Revised Statutes 895, 896 secs. 4–5 (1855); Missouri Revised Statutes 1200, 1201 secs. 6073–74 (1879).

28. Joseph Fred Benson, "The Case of the Murdered Dandy," *St. Louis Bar Journal* 56 (Summer 1982), 29.

29. Abrams, *Very Special Place in Life*, 11–12.

30. Gustave de Beaumont and Alexis de Tocqueville, *On the Penitentiary System in the United States and Its Application to France* (Paris: n.p., 1833), 133.

31. Abrams, *Very Special Place in Life*, 12.

32. Evelyn Roberta Koenig, "The History of the Episcopal House for Children in St. Louis" (master's thesis, Washington University, 1935), 20, table 1; Walter L. Rutnam, "History of the Juvenile Court in St. Louis, Missouri" (master's thesis, Washington University 1931), 8.

33. *Report of the Municipal Commission on Delinquent, Dependent and Defective Children* (St. Louis, MO, 1911), 13.

34. Landau, Gaylord E., "A History of the St. Louis Board of Children's Guardians in Relation to the Care of Dependent and Neglected Children from 1912–1938" (master's thesis, Washington University, 1939), 20.

35. Act of Feb. 24, 1873, 1873 Missouri Laws 353, 356.

36. Landau, "A History of the St. Louis Board," 24.

37. *In re Lorkowszki*, 94 Mo App 623, 624, 68 SW 610, 611 (St L Ct App 1902).

38. Benjamin Clay Weakley, "The St. Louis Juvenile Court" (master's thesis, Washington University, 1913), 11.

39. Rutnam, "History of the Juvenile Court in St. Louis, Missouri," 15.

40. Act of Mar. 18, 1895, 1895 Missouri Laws 190 § 5; Act of Mar. 18, 1895, 1895 Missouri Laws §§ 5–6, 19.

41. Messages and Proclamations of the Governors of the State of Missouri, vol. 8 (Columbia, MO: State Historical Society of Missouri, 1926), 4–5.

42. Weakley, "St. Louis Juvenile Court," 10–11.

43. Rutnam, "History of the Juvenile Court in St. Louis, Missouri," 15.

44. Abrams, *Very Special Place in Life,* 88–89.

45. Jack David Muraskin, "Missouri Politics during the Progressive Era, 1896–1916" (Ph.D. diss., Washington University, 1969), 26.

46. Deborah Shirley Portnoy, "The History of the State Board of Charities and Corrections in Missouri" (master's thesis, Washington University, 1934), 75.

47. Missouri Children's Code Commission, *A Complete Revision of the Laws for the Welfare of Missouri Children* 6, 33 (Jefferson City, MO, 1916).

48. Franklin E. Zimring, *American Juvenile Justice* (Oxford: Oxford University Press, 2005), 6–7.

49. *In re Gault*, 387 US 1, 15–16 (1967).

50. Douglas R. Rendleman, "*Parens Patriae*, From Chancery to the Juvenile Court," 23 *South Carolina Law Review* (1971), 205, 217.

51. Anthony M. Platt, *The Child Savers: The Invention of Delinquency,* 2nd ed. (Chicago: University of Chicago Press, 1977), 3, 139.

52. Ellen Ryerson, *The Best–Laid Plans: America's Juvenile Court Experiment* (New York: Hill and Wang, 1978), 46.

53. Lawrence M. Friedman, *Crime and Punishment in American History* (New York: Basic Books, 1993), 414–15.

54. Margaret K. Rosenheim et al., eds., *A Century of Juvenile Justice* (Chicago: University of Chicago Press, 2002), xiii.

55. Roscoe Pound, "The Administration of Justice in the Modern City," *Harvard Law Review* 26 (1913), 302, 322.

56. *In re Gault*, 387 U.S. 1, 22 (1967).

57. Messages and Proclamations of the Governors, vol. 9 (1926), 33.

58. Act of Mar. 23, 1903, 1903 Missouri Laws 217 sec. 21; Elizabeth J. Clapp, *Mothers of All Children: Women Reformers and the Rise of Juvenile Courts in Progressive Era America* (Harrisburg, PA: State University Press, 1998), 92–93; David J. Rothman, *Conscience and Convenience: The Asylum and Its Alternatives in Progressive America* (Boston: Little, Brown 1980), 229.

59. Act of Mar. 23, 1903, 1903 Missouri Laws 213, 213 sec. 2.

60. *Proceedings of the Twenty-First Annual Meeting of the Missouri Bar Association*, vol. 9 (1904), 65, 76.

61. Act of Apr. 8, 1905, 1905 Missouri, Laws 56, 57 sec 2.

62. Messages and Proclamations of the Governors, vol. 9 (1926), 315.

63. Act of Mar. 19, 1907, 1907 Missouri Laws 217, 218 sec. 2.

64. *Twelfth Census of the United States 1900*, vol. 2, pt. 1, (1902) 631; Joseph Fred Benson, "One Hundred Years of Justice: A History of the Circuit Court of St. Louis County, Missouri, 1877–1978" (unpublished manuscript, St. Louis County Government 1981), 45.

65. Messages and Proclamations of the Governors, vol. 9 (1926), 382.

66. Act of June 12, 1909, 1909 Missouri Laws 423, 425 sec. 2, 431 secs. 25, 25a.

67. Act of Apr. 10, 1917, 1917 Missouri Laws 195, 197 sec. 2, 199 sec. 7.

68. *Ex parte Loving*, 178 Mo 194, 202, 77 SW 508, 509 (1903).

69. *State ex rel. Cave v. Tincher*, 258 Mo 1, 12–13, 166 SW 1028, 1029 (1914).

70. Katherine F. Lenroot and Emma O. Lundberg, *Juvenile Courts at Work: A Study of the Organization and Methods of Ten Courts* (Washington, D.C.: U.S. Children's Bureau, 1925), 23, table 3.

71. M. Ruth Vance, "The Juvenile Court of Jackson County" (master's thesis, University of Missouri-Columbia, 1938), 13.

72. Messages and Proclamations of the Governors, vol. 6 (1924), 396.

73. Ibid., vol. 7 (1926), 159.

74. Act of Mar. 30, 1887, 1887 Missouri Laws 278, 279 sec. 4.

75. *Report of the Municipal Commission*, 69.

76. Jack Reichenstein. "A History of the Missouri Training School for Boys, Boonville, 1917–1944" (master's thesis, Washington University, 1950), 9.

77. Osborne Association, *Handbook of American Institutions for Delinquent Juveniles* (1938), 206, 244, 270.

78. *Report of the Municipal Commission*, 10, 25, 38.

79. "Roger Baldwin, 97, Is Dead; Crusader for Civil Rights Founded the ACLU," *New York Times*, August 27, 1981, D18.

80. Thomas D. Eliot, *The Juvenile Court and the Community* (New York: Macmillan, 1914), 81.

81. Bernard Flexner and Roger N. Baldwin, *Juvenile Courts and Probation* (New York: Century Co., 1914), 62–63; "Roger Baldwin, 97."

82. Samuel Walker, *In Defense of American Liberties* (Oxford: Oxford University Press, 1990), 32.

83. "Roger Baldwin, 97."

84. Messages and Proclamations of the Governors, vol. 10 (1928), 62.

85. Ibid., vol. 11 (1928), 56; Act of Mar. 15, 1915, 1915 Missouri Laws, 209.

86. Act of Mar. 15, 1915, 1915 Missouri Laws 209; Osborne Association, *Handbook of American Institutions*, 206; Act of May 8, 1933, 1933 Missouri Laws 330; Act of Apr. 6, 1927, 1927 Missouri Laws, 381.

87. Reichenstein, "A History of the Missouri Training School for Boys," 28–29, 49–50.

88. *Report of the Children's Code Commission to the Honorable Lloyd C. Stark* (Jefferson City, MO, 1939), 24.

89. Reichenstein, "A History of the Missouri Training School for Boys," 51.

90. Harry Roberds Struder, "Two State Institutions for the Treatment of Delinquent Boys" (master's thesis, University of Missouri-Columbia, 1937), 3–4, 12.

91. Reichenstein, "A History of the Missouri Training School for Boys," 49.

92. Ibid.

93. Osborne Association, *Handbook of American Institutions,* 206.

94. Ibid., 221.

95. Prison Industries. Reorganization. Administration, *The Prison Problem in Missouri: A Survey by the Prison Industries Reorganization Administration* (Washington, D.C.: Prison Industries Reorganization Administration, 1938), 9.

96. Osborne Association, *Handbook of American Institutions,* 206.

97. *A Report of the Missouri Children's Code Commission* (Jefferson City MO, 1946), 90.

98. Messages and Proclamations of the Governors, vol. 16 (1951), 28.

99. Ibid., 5.

100. Ted Gest, "Training Schools Head Likely to Resign Soon," *St. Louis Post-Dispatch*, August 15, 1971; Jacob H. Wolf, "Boys' School's Violent History," *St. Louis Post-Dispatch*, August 18, 1971.

101. Albert Deutsch, *Our Rejected Children* (Boston: Little, Brown, 1950), 130–31.

102. Mendel, "Small Is Beautiful," 29.

103. Deutsch, *Our Rejected Children*, 126–27.

104. Betty Conyers Patton, interview with author, Jefferson City, MO, September 5, 2002.

105. Missouri Association for Social Welfare, *Missouri's Three Training Schools*, 16.

106. Act of Mar. 30, 1887, 274, 276, sec. 11.

107. Jonan Haskell, "Institutional Treatment of Delinquent Girls in Missouri: A Study of the Institutional Homes for Girls at Chillicothe and Tipton" (master's thesis, University of Missouri-Columbia, 1943), 76.

108. *Report of the Municipal Commission*, 8.

109. Portnoy, "The History of the State Board of Charities and Corrections," 127.

110. Haskell, "Institutional Treatment of Delinquent Girls," 76–78, 124–25, 210–11.

111. Osborne Association, *Handbook of American Institutions*, 218.

112. Nancy Ellen Cole, "Missouri State Industrial Home for Negro Girls, Tipton, Missouri, 1909–1944" (master's thesis, Washington University, 1926), 11.

113. Ibid., 12.

114. Leroy Milton Rowe, "Becoming Good Girls and Useful Citizens: Growing Up Poor, Black, and Female in Jim Crow Missouri, 1909–1944" (Ph.D. diss., University of Missouri-Columbia, 2012), 39–40.

115. Ibid., 96, 100–102, 123–24.

116. Cole, "Missouri State Industrial Home for Negro Girls," 16.

117. Haskell, "Institutional Treatment of Delinquent Girls," 184.

118. Ibid., 90, 130, 155, 156, 161, 162, 163, 178–79, 181, 183, 184, 209, 210.

119. Act of Mar. 28, 1941, 1941 Missouri Laws 60, 78.

120. Missouri Association for Social Welfare, *Missouri's Three Training Schools, Reports and Recommendations No. II* (Jefferson City, MO, 1950), 6.

121. Rowe, "Becoming Good Girls and Useful Citizens," 1.

122. Ibid.

123. Ibid., 25.

124. Andrew Jackson Higgins, interview with author, Jefferson City, MO, August 24, 2002.

125. Robert Hoester, interview with author, Jefferson City, MO, September 12, 2002; James A. Finch, Jr., "The State of the Judiciary In Missouri," *Journal of the Missouri Bar* 31 (1971), 514, 517.

126. "Missouri's 'Warehouse for Bodies,'" *St. Louis Globe-Democrat*, September 11–12, 1971.

127. "Juvenile Officer Group Assails State Board," *St. Louis Post-Dispatch*, August 14, 1971.

128. Ronald L. Larkin, interview with author, Jefferson City, MO, September 12, 2002.

129. Dennis J. McCarthy, "'Hard Core' Juvenile Facility Needed," *St. Louis Globe-Democrat*, February 6–7, 1971.

130. Patton interview.

131. Missouri Law Enforcement Assistance Council, *Juvenile Justice in Missouri: A Report of the Task Force on Juvenile Delinquency* (Jefferson City, MO, 1972), 34.

132. Wolf, "Boys' School's Violent History"; *St. Louis Globe-Democrat*, "Missouri's 'Warehouse for Bodies."

133. Abrams, *Very Special Place in Life,* 200.

134. Kenneth Wooden, *Weeping in the Playtime of Others: America's Incarcerated Children,* 2nd ed. (Ohio State University Press, 2000), 117.

135. Michael A. Robinson, "The Dilemma of Discipline," *Kansas City Times*, November 19, 1979.

136. Wooden, *Weeping in the Playtime of Others*, 117.

137. "State Training Board Said to Have Quit," *St. Louis Post-Dispatch*, September 9, 1971 (quotation).

138. Second Governor's Conference on the Prevention of Juvenile Delinquency: A Report to the Governor and to the People of Missouri (Jefferson City, MO, 1973), 6, 8.

139. Mark D. Steward, interview with author, Columbia, MO, October 17, 2014.

140. Ibid.

141. Elizabeth Stuart, "Fixing the Time in Youth Crime," *Deseret Morning News* (Salt Lake, Utah), February 20, 2012 (quotation).

142. Chris Cuomo, "Jails That Treat Kids Like Kids," *ABC News*, September 9, 2009.

143. Nancy Cambria, "'Missouri Model' Lets Kids Be Kids – But Grow Up," *St. Louis Post-Dispatch*, September 14, 2008, C1.

144. Abrams, *Very Special Place in Life*, 205.

145. Mendel, *Less Cost, More Safety*, 11.

146. Missouri Department of Social Services, *Missouri's Division of Youth Services: Programs and Services* (Jefferson City, MO, 2003), 1.

147. Ira M. Schwartz and Russell K. Van Vleet, *Incarcerating Youth: The Minnesota and Missouri Experiences* (Philadelphia: Center for the Study of Youth Policy, 1996), 6.

148. Mendel, *Less Cost, More Safety,* 10–13.

149. Ibid.

150. Missouri Department of Social Services, *Missouri's Division of Youth Services*, 5–6.

151. Mendel, *Less Cost, More Safety,* 14.

152. Jenifer Warren, "Spare the Rod, Save the Child," *Los Angeles Times*, July 1, 2004, A1.

153. Abrams, *Reforming Juvenile Delinquency Treatment,* 1067.

154. *The Missouri Approach: Results*, http://missouriapproach.org/results/ (2014).

155. Abrams, *Reforming Juvenile Delinquency Treatment*, 1067.

156. Richard A. Mendel, *The Missouri Model: Reinventing the Practice of Rehabilitating Youthful Offenders, Summary Report* (Baltimore: Annie E. Casey Foundation, 2010).

157. Jim Mustian, "'Missouri Model' Inspires New Juvenile Center," *Baton Rouge (La.) Advocate*, May 15, 2013.

158. Editorial, "A Model for Juvenile Justice," *New Orleans Times-Picayune*, October 7, 2004, 159; Nicholas Confessore, "4 Youth Prisons in New York Used Excessive Force," *New York Times*, August 25, 2009.

160. U.S. Department of Justice, CRIPA Investigation of the New York City Department of Corrections Jails on Rikers Island (Washington, D.C., 2014), 3.

161. Editorial, "New York's Jails Need Federal Oversight," *New York Times*, October 10, 2014.

162. U.S. DOJ, CRIPA Investigation, 3.

163. Charting a New Course: A Blueprint for Transforming Juvenile Justice in New York State: A Report of Governor David Paterson's Task Force on Transforming Juvenile Justice (New York, December 2009), 8, 15.

164. National Public Radio, "'Culture of Violence' Pervades Rikers' Juvenile Facilities," October 15, 2014, http://www.npr.org/2014/10/15/356165968/culture-of-violence-pervades-rikers-juvenile-facilities.

165. Editorial, "The Current [Department of Juvenile Services] Secretary Is Leaving His Agency in a Mess," *Baltimore Sun*, November 21, 2010.

166. Ibid.

167. National Juvenile Defender Center, Missouri: Justice Rationed 7 (2013).

168. U.S. Department of Justice, Investigation of the St. Louis County Family Court, St. Louis, Missouri, 2 (report), July 31, 2015; see also Christine Byers, Feds Accuse St. Louis Family Court of Rights Violations and Racial Bias, *St. Louis Post-Dispatch,* Aug. 1, 2015, at A1; Richard Perez-Pena, Federal Report Finds Bias against Black Youths in Missouri County Court, *New York Times,* Aug. 1, 2015, A11.

169. U.S. Department of Justice, Investigation of the St. Louis County Family Court, 2 (cover letter).

170. Ibid.

171. John Hope Franklin, "Rediscovering Black America: A Historical Roundup," *New York Times*, September 8, 1968, http://www.nytimes.com/books/99/08/15/specials/franklin-roundup.html.

172. Robert Frost, "The Road Not Taken," in *The Poetry of Robert Frost: The Collected Poems, Complete and Unabridged,* ed. Edward Connery Lathem (New York: Holt, Rinehart & Winston, 1969), 105.

CHAPTER SEVEN

The Living Example: Laurance M. Hyde and the Missouri Nonpartisan Court Plan

Kenneth H. Winn

IN THE 1930S LAURANCE Hyde set out to remake the judicial landscape. He believed that his values ran opposite to those dominating the judiciary when he became a Missouri Supreme Court commissioner in 1931. There were many good judges to be sure, but by his reckoning, the courts had been corrupted by those on the bench who were partisan and self-seeking. A regeneration of the courts required new methods by which to reestablish the truly independent judiciary envisioned by the Founding Fathers—one composed of educated, high-minded men, whose integrity remained unsoiled by political consideration. As partisans are wont to do, of course, Hyde failed to recognize the degree to which he pursued his own self-interest in his desire to take power into his own hands, which he thought considerably cleaner than his opponents'.

Missouri often manifests a provincialism in its politics that depends on more venturesome states to pioneer innovative policies. In 1940, however, it led the nation by adopting the "non-partisan court plan," a groundbreaking way to pick state judges. Gradually, many other states embraced what became known as the "Missouri Plan," or "merit selection," as the method by which they also chose their judges. Laurance Hyde's greatest legacy is his championship of that plan. Indeed for many, including himself, he became its living embodiment. As a commissioner he helped formulate the plan. In 1940, he advocated its adoption by voters, and he later became the first Missouri Supreme Court judge selected under its provisions. Hyde spent the rest of his life celebrating the Missouri Plan and defending it against its critics.

The court plan was born at the mid-century collision of judicial professionalism and politics. Missouri came early to this clash because of a 1938 power struggle over a state supreme court election that turned into a vicious proxy fight between Kansas City Democratic Party boss Thomas Pendergast and Democratic Governor Lloyd Stark. The plan—placed on the ballot through initiative petition, passed in 1940, reaffirmed in a referendum in 1942, and included in the 1945 constitution—attempted to take politics out of judicial selection and to ensure a professional and independent judiciary by replacing partisan judicial elections with a nonpartisan appointment procedure.[1]

In the plan's original design, all appellate judges as well as the lower court judges in St. Louis and Kansas City were to be chosen by commissions composed of representatives of the governor and of the Missouri Bar, and chaired by the chief justice of the Missouri Supreme Court, or, in the two named cities, the presiding judge of the circuit court possessing the vacancy. A commission would produce a panel of three candidates, each of whom was qualified to be a judge. The governor would then choose from among the three. The selected judge would face one retention election by the voters in the general election following his first year of service and another after a number of years, that number depending upon the specific court.

Hyde is a curious figure by twenty-first-century standards—conservative in temperament, politically moderate, and ardently elitist. He was Missouri's most influential twentieth-century judge, though more as a bureaucrat than as a jurist. His greatest service was as a legal modernizer and institution builder. His career, more so than those of his contemporaries, symbolizes the trend toward professionalization of judicial administration occurring across the country.

Even as the nonpartisan plan attempted to raise merit above political influence in judicial selection, Hyde, himself, came from a highly partisan background. To appreciate his energetic advocacy of the nonpartisan court plan one needs to understand the cultural inheritance of region and family imparted to him and later the political environment in which he aspired to become a judge. This legacy was one of moral uprightness, which included a liberal evangelical religion, gentlemanly economic ambition, and a dedication to public service. Hyde would later refer to himself as a "country lawyer" while pointedly noting that John Marshall and Abraham Lincoln were country lawyers. Like the Virginia elite he admired, his was a privileged birth. Male ancestors on both sides of his family were almost all lawyers, back to his great-grandfather, and he took lifelong pride in this fact.[2]

Hyde was born in 1892 in Princeton, Missouri, a village centrally located about twenty-five miles south of the Iowa border. It is better known as Calamity Jane's birthplace than Laurance Hyde's and is now the headquarters of factory-farm giant Premium Standard Farms. Princeton, the seat of Mercer County, was formed in 1845 by westering Yankees, who in earlier generations had swept down through the Old Northwestern states like Ohio and Indiana. During the twentieth century its population and economy steadily declined. In 1900, Mercer had a strong rural economy and 14,706 people. In 2012, the U.S. Census Bureau estimated that Mercer, now a relatively poor county, had 3,729 residents, one thousand of whom lived in Princeton.[3]

Missouri was a factionalized state during the Civil War, but Mercer County was ardently pro-Union. Ira Hyde, Laurance's father, was born in upstate New York in 1838. On the eve of the war he attended Oberlin College in Ohio, a hotbed of evangelical Republicanism. After his graduation he moved to Minnesota where he served as an attorney until he joined the Minnesota Mounted Rangers, and he spent the war fighting Indians rather than Confederates. Following a brief stint in Washington, D.C., at the war's end he moved to Princeton, where in 1866 he became a successful railroad lawyer, banker, and gentleman farmer. A decade after his arrival, he won a single congressional term as a Reconstruction-era Republican, but his political career could survive neither the national recession nor reenfranchised pro-southern Missouri Democrats. Though supporting the losing side in a Democratic state, he remained politically active for the rest of his life.[4]

Ira prospered in other ways. He built the rambling "Hyde Mansion" in Princeton (over which Laurance would one day preside). He populated it with children. Twice widowed, he already had three sons when his third wife gave birth to a fourth, Laurance. Two more children would follow. Laurance's older brothers, like their father before them, became lawyers. The oldest, Edward, moved west and pursued a successful legal career. The third, Arthur, grew wealthy as the owner of car dealerships across sixteen northern Missouri counties. But Arthur followed their father's other example and entered politics. He became a Progressive Party activist (i.e., a Theodore Roosevelt "Bull Mooser"). In one dramatic speech he waved a knife, announcing, "If I had a drop of Republican blood in my veins, I would take this knife and let it out."[5] Times changed, Arthur returned to the Republican fold, and he was elected Missouri's governor in 1920. He subsequently became President Herbert Hoover's secretary of agriculture. As partisan politics blessed Arthur, he, in turn, blessed his older brother, Ben C. Hyde, an owner of regional telephone companies, by making him Missouri's superintendent of insurance. Ben would start an interminable quarrel with the insurance companies that would, many years later, bring down political boss Tom Pendergast and would give brother Laurance a seat on the state supreme court.[6]

Laurance, like the rest of his family, was a lifelong Republican, and an ardent one, but circumstances eventually led him to a less conspicuously political path. As a young man he went to the University of Missouri, where he distinguished himself as a Phi Beta Kappa scholar-athlete, a "miler" on the track team, and a member of the Order of the Coif in law school. Hyde won admission to the Missouri Bar in 1916, but when the United States entered the First World War, he joined the army as a first infantry lieutenant and subsequently served in the judge advocacy corps. At the war's end he settled into a successful Princeton law and banking practice with his father.

In 1922, Hyde married Florence Fuller, the attractive daughter of a banker and lumberyard owner of New England descent. Both Hydes were Anglophiles. While Laurance wrote admiringly of English law, Florence spent a good deal of her adult life tracing Laurance's descent from British nobility, in particular his connection to Edward Hyde, Earl of Clarendon. Her own pedigree, no more humble, included the "nobility" conferred on her as a direct descendant of Mayflower Pilgrims. This background was more than a source of family pride, it gave the couple their sense of identity and prescribed a personal code of gentility, principled virtue, and an unquestioned sense of self-worth.[7] Hyde's soft-spoken manner and social grace would later set him apart from some of his more rough-hewn court colleagues, as well as give him the assurance needed to challenge the judicial realities these colleagues represented.

In 1931 Laurance received a Republican appointment to the Missouri Supreme Court Commission, which had been established as a response to an exploding docket by creating a class of subordinate judges to help with the court's workload. The first commissioner system was virtually stillborn in 1883, and disbanded in 1884, as other institutional arrangements were tried. They all failed to master the problem. By 1911 plaintiffs and defendants had to wait an average of three years and two months *after* their appeal had been initiated for the court to hear their appeal and over four years before the court delivered its opinion. To deal with this congestion, new legislation was passed, with an emergency clause, creating a new commission system. With minor adjustments it gradually evolved into a six-person commission. The bipartisan commissioners were chosen by the judges themselves for four-year terms, with the possibility of renewal.

Commissioners sat in on cases—three on civil and three on criminal—and they were opinion-writing machines. In fact, they wrote more opinions than the judges themselves. They received the same compensation as the judges, but they were not allowed to vote on the adoption of any opinion. They had offices rather than chambers and received markedly less deference. Their second-class status occasionally grated, or at least made for a distinction that commissioners rarely forgot, as some possessed greater legal skills than the judges for whom they worked.[8]

The commission's bipartisan membership was fortunate for Hyde. He was a Republican during a severe economic depression blamed largely on Republicans. With Franklin Roosevelt's smashing presidential victory in the offing, there was not a statewide position to which a Republican could have been elected in Missouri in the 1930s.

And as if to prove it, he tried. He fervently wished to be a judge on the state supreme court, but there was only one way to become one. Despite the odds, Hyde ran for a seat in 1934. His opponent was Judge C. A. Leedy.[9] Leedy symbolized everything Hyde disapproved of about judicial elections and the judiciary's involvement in politics. Born in 1895, Leedy came up through the legal apprentice system, which was not uncommon at the time. In 1912 he became a court reporter for Platte County Circuit Judge Alonzo Burns and studied in his chambers and at St. Joseph Law School. During World War I he became General Charles Dawes's stenographer (Dawes later became Calvin Coolidge's vice president). Leedy's work for Dawes led to his becoming the American delegation's official shorthand reporter during the crafting of the Versailles Treaty that ended the war. After his return to the United States, Leedy obtained his law degree in 1921, got involved in politics, and in 1925 moved to Kansas City.

In the 1920s, "getting involved in politics" in Kansas City meant (as it did for another World War I veteran, Harry Truman) working for Tom Pendergast's political machine. Leedy, for his part, thrived in the organization. By 1932 he had become a significant political operative, serving as the campaign manager for a Pendergast-favored candidate, Francis Wilson, the Platte City lawyer who had lost the gubernatorial election in 1928. While Wilson was widely expected to win in 1932, he suddenly died of a heart attack less than a month before the election. In the nomination crisis that followed, Pendergast initiated a hasty search for a new candidate. An advisor proposed Wilson's former law partner, Judge Guy P. Park—a man the boss hardly knew. Pendergast, accordingly, asked Leedy, who had once worked as Park's court reporter, to bring the judge in for an interview. Park was subsequently anointed. At a statewide meeting the Democrats were nonplussed. They had never heard of Park and found his candidacy hard to swallow. But Pendergast insisted, and he had the votes. The boss subsequently installed Leedy as Park's campaign manager. The irregular nature of these events hardly mattered. Given the Depression-era bias in favor of Democrats, the newly minted candidate glided to easy victory. Park's gratitude for his newfound eminence was unbounded, and he demonstrated it so slavishly that wags soon dubbed the governor's mansion "Uncle Tom's Cabin."[10]

Just as Park had obtained his governorship by the unexpected death of Francis Wilson, C. A. Leedy obtained his vacancy appointment to the court from Parks upon the unexpected death of Judge Clarence Burney, a Pendergast-backed judge who had just taken office.[11] When Hyde and Leedy faced off in the 1934 election, Leedy was a thirty-nine-year-old rough-and-tumble political lawyer, and Hyde was a forty-two-year-old blue-blooded commissioner. Legal historian Gerald Dunne called Leedy the "manifestly inferior candidate" but one "who had the good fortune of being a Democrat."[12]

As anyone could have predicted, Hyde lost, and by a large margin. Leedy won 60 percent of the statewide vote, while Hyde took in 39.5. These figures, however, are somewhat misleading as to the nature of the vote. In Kansas City, Hyde received only 16.7 percent of the vote. When the equally lopsided vote from the smaller Jackson County electoral district is added in, 53 percent of Leedy's statewide margin of victory came from the Kansas City area.[13] Leedy did not "steal" the election, but even by Depression-era standards Hyde's trivial vote count in the Kansas City–Jackson County electoral districts was impressive.

In his role as a commissioner, the defeated Hyde worked as Leedy's inferior for another eight years. In his voluminous writings over the years Hyde frequently mentioned that there had been problems with judicial elections in Missouri's big cities. But he never made a specific reference to either Pendergast's intervention in supreme court politics or his own campaign. One might readily infer from his judicial activities that he felt the loss keenly.[14]

So, for eleven years, Hyde waited in the shadows and wrote opinions for men whose politics and judicial values he disapproved. With only thirty-eight employees in 1935, the court provided a challenging environment for a dissenting commissioner. Still, Hyde strove to be courteous to his "errant" colleagues, and his legal talent was recognized. He accordingly won reappointment as a Republican commissioner in 1935 and again in 1939, by which time he had even become something of a national figure within judicial circles.

Better days for Hyde were ahead. During the Progressive era, many Americans, especially those in the middle class, revolted against the predatory capitalism of the late Gilded Age, which they characterized as amoral and the source of the era's excesses. "The people," often styled as the sober, upright, white middle class (now including middle-class women), were being squeezed by the irresponsible rich and the irresponsible poor. Part of the problem was the American party system and the political corruption that members of the middle class largely perceived as emanating from the nation's big cities. If "democracy" meant thuggish political bosses, unwashed immigrants from southern and eastern Europe, illiterate Negroes, drunks, and the poor who did the political machine's bidding, then democracy had become degraded.[15]

Many reformers turned to government regulation to check the abuses of capitalism, and to good government measures to control the huddled masses yearning to vote for evil politicians. To a remarkable degree, both the left and right lost confidence in conventional politicians and turned to "experts," who extolled professionalism and scientific management as the means of solving the nation's social problems.

This urge, with its elitist subtext, cut across virtually every field, and it was markedly strong even in the conservative field of the law. In 1906 Progressive Nebraska Republican Roscoe Pound announced his appearance on the legal scene with his landmark essay, "The Causes of Popular Dissatisfaction with the Administration of Justice." Pound argued that the sorry state of the American judiciary would be improved by the appointment of candidates qualified to be judges rather than by the election of those who had merely received "recommends" from their local ward heelers. As unrevolutionary as that later appeared, Pound's emphasis on professionalism in his attack on judicial elections struck like a thunderbolt, and helped catapult Pound—a Ph.D. botanist-turned-legal-scholar—into the position of long-term dean of Harvard Law School. (Laurance Hyde adored Pound and would come to take great pride in a friendship with the older man.) Pound's opening salvo helped inspire a judicial reform movement that would find institutional expression in the founding of the American Judicature Society in 1913, and over the following decade, ideas about judicial selection became more sophisticated and refined. Particularly important were the points put forward by London School of Economics Professor Harold Laski. In his seminal 1926 essay, "The Technique of Judicial Appointment," Laski provided reformers with many of the concrete ideas that would later find implementation.[16]

By the early 1930s, the American Bar Association (ABA) was actively seeking opportunities in various states to implement judicial merit appointments. Failures in California, Michigan, and Ohio led to a more sophisticated honing of strategy.[17] It was at this juncture that a major rupture in 1938 between Tom Pendergast and Missouri Governor Lloyd Stark gave Missourians and the state bar their chance. Pendergast grew vexed when a Stark vacancy appointee to the supreme court, James Marsh Douglas, cast the deciding and unfavorable vote in an insurance case that was important to the boss. (This is the case that had its origins many years before in Superintendent of Insurance Ben Hyde's quarrel with the insurance companies over their rates.) Feeling both political and personal financial pressure related to the case, Pendergast decided to purge the offending judge and offer a show of strength to an increasingly hostile governor. The Kansas City politician recruited southeast Missouri judge James M. Billings to run against Douglas in the 1938 Democratic primary. A bitter political war followed in which the two candidates disappeared beneath the ugly battle fought between the governor and the Pendergast political machine. At great cost to the Democratic Party and Stark himself, Judge Douglas emerged the victor.[18]

At the same time, the struggle created an atmosphere in which the guarantee of a politically independent judiciary seemed imperative. It was in this unique environment that the Missouri Bar formed the Missouri Institute of Judicial Administration (MIJA) in 1939, a coalition of lawyers and laypeople, to establish a nonpartisan court plan by initiative petition. The MIJA ran a veritable crusade through a decentralized regional leadership that adapted to local conditions. In the end, Republicans and good-government Democrats triumphed over Democrat machine votes and rural skepticism—somewhat to their own surprise.[19] In November 1940 state voters gave the initiative a 90,000-vote majority, making Missouri's seminal nonpartisan court plan part of the state's constitution. Subsequent reactionary attempts by state legislators to destroy the plan with a new amendment in 1942, along with the work of other opponents during the Missouri constitutional deliberations of 1943–1944, failed.

Laurence Hyde would later boast that it was the popularity of the nonpartisan court plan that helped ensure approval of the 1945 Missouri Constitution.[20] The commissioner, himself, had been tireless in his support, and it paid off for him personally. In late December 1942 Republican Governor Forrest C. Donnell announced Hyde's appointment to the court, making Hyde the first high-court judge appointed under the new nonpartisan plan.[21]

The 1945 Missouri constitution solidified and expanded the judicial triumph by giving the supreme court the broad new powers with which Hyde planned to reinvent the judicial system along more professional lines. In his 1945 article "Work of the Missouri Supreme Court under the Old and New Constitutions," Hyde said that "the adoption of the new Constitution by the people of Missouri, on February 27, 1945, began a new era of greatly increased responsibility and work for the Supreme Court of Missouri, and one which is unique in American history. No other state has imposed so many duties upon its highest court as the new 1945 constitution requires of the Supreme

Court of Missouri." Rationalizing Missouri's court system would be a terrible burden, he said, and an awesome responsibility. He proceeded to outline the daunting administrative challenges that lay ahead, but he had worked assiduously for the court to gain these new powers and relished the challenge. As he triumphantly noted in his conclusion, this was a singular opportunity "to increase the prestige of the legal profession."[22]

The end of World War II marked a governmental divide for both America and Missouri. In the larger view, the nonpartisan court plan was part of the rise of the administrative state that had been progressing on the federal and state levels since the Great Depression. In many ways Laurance Hyde was a perfect bridge between the Progressive era's doubts about politicians and its love of technical expertise to solve problems, and the general postwar consensus among the American elite on "best and brightest" problem-solving. Administrative government would prove a source of unease for some Americans. It served as a target for politicians who inveighed against unelected bureaucrats, much less unelected judges. Yet in the postwar world, the basic questions of the postindustrial age in economics, politics, and foreign policy had seemed settled. Ideology was exhausted, sociologist Daniel Bell famously observed.[23] What the rising American century needed, said others, were men like the optimistic "whiz kid" technocrats, epitomized by Ford Motors executive Robert McNamara, and youthful "can-do" politicians like John Kennedy. The American professional class that had become conspicuous at the turn of the twentieth century boomed in the decades following the Second World War.

If it is unsurprising that the Republican Hyde became a staunch spokesman and authorial advocate on professionalism and judicial nonpartisanship during such a Democratically dominated era, Hyde's partisan heart followed his nonpartisan head. Like many others, Hyde was enthralled with professionalism in a period that was obsessed with leaving irregular education, standards, and practices of the past behind. He spoke of the law in tones of religious awe and despised the blasphemers whom he thought degraded it. Hyde's friend and former fellow commissioner Norwin Houser said of him that the law was "his life. He lived and breathed it; delighted in it."[24]

As a highly self-conscious professional, Hyde took professionalism to mean not only the possession of specialized knowledge, but a relentless commitment to better a calling. In a 1932 address to new members of the Missouri Bar, he said: "The Public expects lawyers not only to practice law but improve law. The best way to do this is through local state and national bar organizations."[25] Hyde was describing his own career path. The number of his professional associations, the state, national, and international task forces, and his boards and commissions, many of which he chaired or for which he served as the organization president, makes for mind-numbing reading. Most of these were designed to strengthen the judicial system, but even the others were meant to modernize some aspect of the law. For example, Hyde was very active in the ABA and in 1942 undertook a study of national appellate methods on its behalf; he helped found and was the first chairman of the Conference of Chief Justices, which had its organizational meeting in St. Louis in 1949.[26] He was a director of the American Judicature Society from 1946 to 1960, serving as its board chair from 1951 to 1955. For thirty years he sat on the council of the American Law Institute under whose aegis he worked on the Second Restatement of the Law; he helped create a national model for the uniform commercial code and a model criminal penalty code. He helped author a study of the division between state and federal courts. Awards for this kind of service followed. Many people find administrative committee work boring, but Hyde thrived on it. All of this work fit, part and parcel, with the kind of judicial professionalism he helped to create through his advocacy of the nonpartisan court plan, which he considered his most important work.

Concomitant with his indefatigable committee work, Laurence Hyde wrote more than any other Missouri Supreme Court judge of the twentieth century. He was delighted to be told that Harvard Law School Dean Roscoe Pound regularly read his opinions, which numbered one thousand by the time his career ended.[27] But his approximately one hundred professional articles, published mostly in law reviews and legal journals, were more nationally influential than were his opinions, and his most read articles were his many on the Missouri nonpartisan court plan.[28]

Hyde had written on the plan from its inception. His first and shortest essay in the series was "Selection and Tenure of Judges," an address to the ABA that was published in the *American Bar Association Journal* in December 1941.[29] After World War II he continued to write energetically, defending and celebrating the plan and encouraging other states to use it as a model. His last article, styled by the American Judicature Society as an "interview," appeared in 1957. In the postwar years he published these articles in a wide range of venues such as the *Alabama Lawyer* and the *Journal of Criminal Law and Criminology*.[30] His most influential article on the plan was published in *The New York Law Quarterly Review* in 1947.[31] Typically these essays varied little. Each article used an introduction and conclusion suitable to the audience, and some included an occasional update, but the heart of these essays was the same. Each recounted the bad old days, the advent of the Missouri Plan, and the good days that now lay ahead (or had just been realized). The articles were often supported with the same anecdotes, and the same word-for-word passages appeared numerous times.

Hyde's view of judicial selection rested on his sweeping view of Anglo-American history. The principle of judicial independence, he argued, had its origins in Britain's Glorious Revolution of 1688. Americans received this principle as part of their British heritage, and it was forcibly underscored by the British attempts to take away judicial independence during the events leading up to the American Revolution. The Founding Fathers, accordingly, adopted the principle of life tenure for judges based on "good behavior." Regrettably, this wise legacy was cast aside when the serpent of "Jacksonian Democracy" came into the judicial garden. Democracy, the good tree of American civic life, produced the fruit of judicial evil. By the 1830s new states coming into the Union—then one by one the old states—began abandoning the wisdom of America's Revolutionary generation in favor of the direct election of judges held to short terms. Hyde saw this "radical" change rooted in a variety of historical causes, but however understandable, he argued, "it is fairly obvious that the movement went too far, resulted in the impairment of judicial independence and lowered the standing of the judiciary in our state governments."[32] Following in the path of late-nineteenth-century British observer James Bryce, Hyde put forward a syllogism that equated popular election with party rule, which he then equated with boss rule—the very antithesis of real democracy.[33]

In addition to the flaws inherent in the boss system, Hyde argued that light voter interest in judicial elections often meant that irrelevant national issues, which had no bearing on a judicial candidate's professional qualifications, determined the winning candidate. A favorite illustration that he repeated over the years was that only two judges in the twenty-year period between World War I and World War II (1919–1939) were reelected to ten-year terms after previously serving full ten-year terms. Although he did not say so, only five judges met his analytical criteria (others died, retired, or resigned). Hyde liked to cite the example of Fred Lincoln Williams, a Democratic judge, though without mentioning him by name. Williams, according to Hyde, claimed that he had been elected in 1916 to a vacancy term on the court because Woodrow Wilson had kept America out of war but was then defeated in the 1920 general election because Wilson had failed to keep the country out of war.[34] Indeed, whatever the case, the Republicans swept the elections nationally that year, and in Missouri they were led to power by Arthur Hyde.

Williams's story was a good one for Hyde, not only because it illustrated that judicial talent had nothing to do with who got elected to the supreme court, but since Williams was a Democrat, it showed that the Republican Hyde was not simply a partisan complainer. Aside from Williams, the other four judges who lost their seats during the interwar period were all Republicans. A fifth Republican judge, Frank Atwood, apparently didn't even run for reelection.[35] Each of these judges had originally won in the "Republican" 1920s; all had lost their seats in the "Democratic" 1930s, just as Hyde lost his election in 1934. Thus, from the perspective of a Republican wedged between Roosevelt and Pendergast, the nonpartisan court plan looked pretty good indeed.

And things had changed. By 1949 Hyde was serving as Missouri's chief justice. In October of that year New Yorkers invited him, as the high priest of judicial merit selection, to tell them how they might copy Missouri's example. Judicial reformers, organized as the "Citizens Committee on the Courts," invited Hyde to address a large formal gathering at the Biltmore Hotel on the virtues of the plan and on how they might imitate it. In a speech well covered by the daily newspapers, Hyde told his audience that a judicial golden age awaited their imitation of Missouri's example. The party system, he said, provides "some good judges, but its batting average is poor." After nearly ten years of operation the Missouri Plan had proven its value. High-quality judges had come to the bench and continued to do so. "It has taken our courts out of politics," he said. "Court dockets have been brought up to date, delays lessened and expense of litigation reduced because judges spend no time campaigning for re-election. But are free to use all their time on their work [*sic*]." "Our judges," he continued, now "work on the next case and not on the next election."[36] *The New York World-Telegram* editorialized that New York "has few sorrier spectacles than the all-too-common one of a judge going hat in hand to a political boss to beg support for a campaign no judge should ever have to make. Missouri has ended all that. So can New York." This effort, the editorial observed, had failed in the last state legislative session, but "it may prove easier after Justice Hyde's impressive first hand testimony."[37]

Hyde had had a remarkable run since his accession to the Missouri Supreme Court. Great success was not determined by Missourians in Hyde's eyes, but by New Yorkers, his hero Roscoe Pound, the ABA, and, the British legal establishment. That he had been measured and not found wanting was very satisfying. Roscoe Pound—the midwesterner who had become the quintessential representative of the American eastern legal establishment—had become his friend and admired his opinions. In 1957, to his utter delight, Hyde helped lead an ABA delegation to Britain. His Anglophilism reflected his taste for the decorous and the orderly as well as his sense of professionalism—all things he found in the British judiciary. Party bosses, like Pendergast and his ill-scrubbed followers who threatened to drag judges into the gutter, or out of the gutter to the bench, were an offense to all he admired. Hyde's advocacy of the nonpartisan court plan, which proclaimed that a man was selected for honor and authority by merit, not obeisance to a political machine, was part of being a scholarly gentleman jurist, the class to which he aspired. It was his principal vehicle for winning both American and British admiration.[38]

The recognition that validated his career may have eventually become a bit too heady for him—maybe for his colleagues as well. Decades later, former fellow Republican commissioner Paul Barrett contemptuously observed, "I've seen some of the finest people I ever knew [make] perfect damn fools by becoming Chief Justice! . . . One of them was not only a personal friend[,] but I am the person who thought of him as becoming a judge. And I once saw him strut as he walked past the post office. And he was built like a plow jockey and was a plow jockey! He was a country boy but by becoming Chief Justice, and especially after he had been to an American Bar Association meeting in London and visited the Inns of Court, he was a perfect fool. He never recovered and did less work all of the time."[39]

Barrett was a decade younger than Hyde, and it would not be surprising if the judge's drive cooled in his mid-sixties. Perhaps more important, while Barrett was a Republican from southwest Missouri, he had become an intimate of Pendergast machine confederate Judge Ernest Tipton. Whether influenced by his friendship with Tipton or not, Barrett came to regard the nonpartisan court plan as greatly overrated. Even so, there was probably as much personal rancor as court factionalism in Barrett's statement. Given Hyde's unabashed Anglophilia and his self-satisfied boasting that the nonpartisan plan had ended the threat of more judges like his colleagues might have proven tiresome, especially to those prone to dislike him anyway.

Tiresome or not, the accolades for his life's work kept rolling in. In 1957 *Life* magazine published a pictorial on seven "eminent jurists." Hyde was featured not only for having "fought for the clean administration of Justice and for speedy trials for the accused," but naturally enough, for the "Missouri Court Plan, which he helped formulate, [taking] the election of judges out of politics" and which inspired other states to follow Missouri's example.[40] Major recognition came again in 1964 when the American Bar Foundation made Hyde an honorary fellow. Addressing Hyde, the official citation expressed the foundation's "gratitude for your notable contributions to the improvement of the judiciary by advancing the standards for the selection of judges." Hyde was told, he was "a living example of the desirability of non-partisan selection of judges" who had "served as a disciple of the Missouri plan by preaching and teaching its virtues to countless judges and lawyers throughout the nation until you have become the acknowledged leader for non-partisan judicial selection."[41]

Hyde and his old antagonist C. A. Leedy were in early middle age when they met in their electoral contest. After Hyde's judicial appointment they went on to serve together as colleagues for another twenty-one years. The differences between the two were publicly muted, but they maintained their mutual dislike and stark differences in their views on both politics and the judiciary. Yet, Hyde won in the end. In a *Kansas City Times* editorial written at the time of Leedy's death, the paper noted how much things had changed during Leedy's half-century involvement with courts. At the start of Leedy's career judicial politics had been marked by sharp elbows. By the time of his retirement in 1964, the *Times* said, the supreme court had "become a quiet reflective place to serve in comparison with the politically raucous years when judicial candidates waged hard-hitting election campaigns."[42] Leedy had become an anachronism.[43]

Upon Hyde's retirement from the court on January 1, 1967, a lengthy article, which drew on his close cooperation, appeared in the *Jefferson City News and Tribune.* The story touched on many subjects, including his pleasure in the growing legal professionalism and the stringency of new law school requirements. But appropriately, the article dwelt most centrally upon Hyde's role in the nonpartisan court plan's success. When asked about the biggest changes in the law during his eleven years as a commissioner and twenty-four as a judge, Hyde said that "politics is no longer so strong an influence in legal decisions," which he attributed to the plan. Among the letters he received was one from Glenn Winters, the longtime director of the American Judicature Society. Winters wrote that hearing of Hyde's retirement "took me back to that day almost 25 years ago when your appointment to the Court was announced. I remember so well the announcement of that appointment was hailed as one of the first indications of the wisdom of the non-partisan court plan."[44] As memorialist Henry Andrae notes, the "Plan might have been enacted without the help of Laurance Hyde but it might not have been. He believed in it, gave it his all to enact it and later to keep it."[45]

Laurance Hyde's values continue to challenge political powerbrokers. In his time, political muscle was used to select judges and to bend justice to private advantage. Today those with enough money may still bend law to their advantage. People who share Hyde's values of probity, professionalism, and sense of public responsibility have a challenge to defend those values not only in the courts, but throughout government. Since 1940 the court plan Hyde championed has come under periodic attack both from serious people who have good reason to push modifications to the plan and from those who do not. To date, the challengers have not prevailed, and the judicial revolution Hyde and his allies wrought has endured.

NOTES

The author thanks Claire Kates for her assistance in the preparation of this essay.

1. Since the plan's inception it has had opponents both in Missouri and across the country. The intensity and composition of that opposition has varied over the years. For more on circumstances leading to the adoption of the Missouri Court Plan, along with a fuller description of its working, see Jack W. Peltason, *The Missouri Plan for Selection of Judges* (Columbia: University of Missouri Press, 1945); Richard Watson and Rondal G. Downing, *The Politics of the Bench and the Bar: Judicial Selection under the Missouri Nonpartisan Court Plan* (New York: John Wiley and Sons, 1969); Gerald T. Dunne, *The Missouri Supreme Court: From Dred Scott to Nancy Cruzan* (Columbia: University of Missouri Press, 1993), 115–26; D. A. Divilbiss, "Politics and the Courts: *Douglas v. Billings*—Primary Election, 1938," *Missouri Supreme Court Historical Journa*l 7 (February 2000), 1–14. How many states have imitated the plan, and how deep its influence runs, is often a matter of dispute, typically depending on whether the person doing the tabulating likes or dislikes the plan. See, for example, the diverse collection of essays on the plan appearing in a special thematic issue of the *Missouri Law Review* 74 (Summer 2009).

2. Laurence M. Hyde, "The Practice of Law," *Missouri Bar Journal: Official Publication of the Missouri Bar Association* 37 (July 1932), 115; the reformatted essay may also be found on the Missouri Bar's website: http://www.mobar.org/uploadedFiles/Home/Publications/Journal/2010/05–06/The%20Practice%20of%20Law.pdf. Hyde's daughter, Florence, and his son, Laurance, Jr., also became attorneys. Florence for a time would work for Rush Limbaugh, Sr., in Cape Girardeau. For biographical information on Hyde and his family, see Florence Fuller Hyde, *The Hyde Family in England and America and the Fuller Family in England and America* (Jefferson City, Mo: privately printed, 1967). Henry Andrae, "Laurance Mastick Hyde," *Missouri Supreme Court Historical Journal* 7 (Summer 1988), 2–4; "Judge Laurance M. Hyde Leaves Court—but Not Law," *Sunday News and Tribune* (Jefferson City), January 1, 1967; "Rites Tuesday for Judge Hyde," *News Tribune* (Jefferson City), January 22, 1978; and Jean C. Carnahan, *If Walls Could Talk: The Story of Missouri's First Families* (Jefferson City, MO: MMPI, 1998), 179–82.

3. Princeton became the headquarters for Premium Standard Farms in 1988, populating the county with more pigs than people. http://mcdc.missouri.edu/cgi-bin/uexplore?/pub/data/popests/intercensal20xx.; the Census Bureau estimates there were 1,148 people living in Princeton in 2012: http://en.wikipedia.org/wiki/Princeton,_Missouri.

4. http://bioguide.congress.gov/scripts/biodisplay.pl?index=H001023; John T. Barker, *Missouri Lawyer* (Philadelphia: Dorrance, 1949), 105–6.

5. *Princeton Post* (Missouri), October 31, 1912, as quoted in Robert Phillip Friedman, "The Candidate Speaks: Arthur M. Hyde," *Missouri Historical Review* 61 (October 1966–67), 52.

6. Arthur mostly returned to the fold; his attempts to "modernize" the Republican Party during his governorship were strongly resisted by Republicans who did not wish to be reformed. For more on Arthur Hyde's administration see Richard S. Kirkendall, *A History of Missouri, V*olume V, 1919–1953 (Columbia: University of Missouri Press, 1986), 29–34; and Carnahan, *If Walls Could Talk,* 179–82. On Ben C. Hyde, see Gerald T. Dunne, *The Missouri Supreme Court: From Dred Scott to Nancy Cruzan* (Columbia: University of Missouri Press, 1993), 111–14; George Slavens, "Lloyd C. Stark as a Political Reformer" (master's thesis, University of Missouri—Columbia, 1956), 64–77. Hyde served as superintendent of insurance from 1921 to 1929. The youngest brother, Ira Barnes Hyde, Jr., the owner of two local newspapers, became a state representative in 1944.

7. See Florence Hyde, *The Hyde Family*. Even granting the celebratory nature of the occasion, there was truth in Norwin Houser's remarks when he declared upon Hyde's retirement ceremony that the judge "is [a] man of humility and gentility. I never heard him speak ill of any man. He operates quietly, without fanfare, politely and smoothly. He is a gentleman in the finest and truest sense of the word." Houser's remarks are reprinted in full on p. 38.

8. The commission was eventually phased out with the retirements and resignations of its incumbents after a new judicial reorganization in 1970. For an overview of the commission system see Norwin D. Houser, "Missouri Supreme Court Commissioners: 1883–1885; 1911–1982," *Missouri Supreme Court Historical Journal* 1 (Spring 1992), 2–11; Dunne, *The Missouri Supreme Court*, 100–104.

9. Unless otherwise noted, the Leedys' biographical details may be found in the following: "Kansas Citian, Ex Chief Justice, Dies," *Kansas City Times*, October 10, 1978; "Judge C. A. Leedy Jr.," *Kansas City Times,* October 11, 1978; Gordon M. Connelly, comp. and ed., *The Leedy Family History* (Baltimore: Gateway Press, 1985); "The Leedy Family" http://www.leedyfamily.com/index.html. The official Leedy family history makes for a very interesting counterpoint to that put forward by Florence Hyde regarding her family. The high-minded Hydes and Fullers have behaved well for centuries. The Leedys are not slow to point out their family celebrities, but they also take pleasure in some of their eccentric and colorful relatives. Harold, C. A. Leedy's brother, headed the U.S. Federal

Reserve Bank in Kansas City in 1941, but other members include Robert, "Sky-Hi Lee," a professional wrestler; Samuel, who founded the "Leedyite Church" after being "disfellowshipped" over foot washing; Val "Dogface," a martial arts fighter; as well as George Lucas, a well-known star warrior. See also Dwight Brown, comp., *State of Missouri Official Manual, 1935–1936* (Jefferson City, Mo: Office of Secretary of State, 1935), 123; Warren A. Hearnes, comp., *State of Missouri Official Manual, 1963–1964* (Jefferson City, MO: Office of Secretary of State, 1963), 211.

10. Lawrence Larsen and Nancy J. Hulston, *Pendergast!* (Columbia: University of Missouri Press, 1997), 90; Kirkendall, *History of Missouri,* 155, 158–59; James P. Alyward, oral history, interview by James Fuchs, June 12, 1968; Harry S. Truman Library & Museum, 1968, 31–60, http://www.trumanlibrary.org/oralhist/aylward.htm#transcript.

11. Pendergast's effect on the selection of supreme court judges was palpable. Besides Burney and Leedy, for example, Ernest M. Tipton was not only associated with the court, but was also a Pendergast insider. See Alyward, oral history, 1968. In the original manuscript, which is denoted in the online version, the portions regarding Leedy are pp. 28–29, 33–34, 142; for Tipton, see pp. 57, 77–78, 82, 140–41.

12. Dunne, *The Missouri Supreme Court,* 198.

13. In St. Louis, then a more Republican-friendly city, Hyde received 41 percent of the vote (figures are slightly rounded). One half of 1 percent of the statewide vote went to the Socialist Party candidate, who did better in some rural areas than in Kansas City. The Pendergast organization, of course, was vigorously backing other candidates in addition to Leedy. Brown comp., *Official Manual, 1935–1936,* 302–3.

14. Indeed, Hyde's only reference to Pendergast that I have seen in print concerned the boss's control of the Kansas City Police Board and appeared in a retirement interview: "Judge Laurance M. Hyde Leaves Court," *Sunday News and Tribune* (Jefferson City), January 1, 1967.

15. See Michael McGerr, *A Fierce Discontent: The Rise and Fall of the Progressive Movement in America* (New York: The Free Press, 2003); Kenneth Winn, "It All Adds Up: Reform and the Erosion of Representative Government in Missouri, 1900-2000," in Rebecca Cook, comp., *Official Manual State of Missouri, 1999–2000* (Jefferson City: Office of Secretary of State, 1999), 28–52, 926–31, http://www.sos.mo.gov/archives/pubs/article/article.asp; Steven L. Piott, *Holy Joe: Joseph W. Folk and the Missouri Idea* (Columbia: University of Missouri Press, 1997).

16. Roscoe Pound, "The Causes of Popular Dissatisfaction with the Administration of Justice," presented at the annual convention of the American Bar Association in 1906, reprinted in *American Bar Association Report,* part 1 29 (1906), 395–417, http://law-test.unl.edu/splash/Roscoe_Pound-Causes_of_Popular....pdf.; Harold J. Laski, "The Technique of Judicial Appointment," *Michigan Law*

Review 24 (April 1926), 529–43. In recent years Laski has been touted for his socialism by some critics of the plan, but you would not know it by his essay, which shares a dedication to meritocracy found more in the arguments of more conservative critics of the judiciary. See Carrie Severino, "Missouri: Trial–Lawyer Heaven." *Nationalreview.com* September 7, 2011, http://www.nationalreview.com/bench-memos/276512/missouri-trial-lawyer-heaven-carrie-severino.

17. Peltason, *The Missouri Plan for Selection of Judges,* 38–40.

18. The best version of this oft-told story is Patrick McLear, "Pendergast vs. Stark: Politics, Patronage, and the 1938 Supreme Court Democratic Primary," *Missouri Historical Review* 96 (April 2002), 188–210; see also Divilbiss, "Politics and the Courts."

19. M. B. Marshall to John Perry Wood, April 15, 1941, Laurance M. Hyde Papers, State Historical Society of Missouri, Collection 3390, Folder 796.

20. Laurance M. Hyde, "Judges: Their Selection and Tenure," *New York University Law Quarterly Review* 22 (1947), 397. Hyde used the same title for an article in *Alabama Lawyer.* To distinguish between the two, this essay is noted hereafter as *NYLQR* in the short title.

21. It made him also the first judge in the nation appointed under a merit plan. Many sources, including some with which Hyde cooperated, say that he was appointed in 1942; others list him as a member of the court in 1943. Both are based in fact. While his appointment was announced in late December, he was sworn in as a judge on January 4, 1943. "Laurance M. Hyde Appointed Judge Missouri Supreme Court," *Missouri Bar Journal: Official Publication of the Missouri Bar Association* 14 (January 1943), 9. William H. Killoran, of the St. Louis circuit, was the first judge sworn in under the nonpartisan court plan.

22. Laurance M. Hyde, "Work of Missouri Supreme Court under the Old and New Constitution," *Journal of the Missouri Bar* 2 (September 1946), 65–69 (quotations on pp. 65, 69).

23. Daniel Bell, *The End of Ideology: On the Exhaustion of Political Ideas in the Fifties,* 2nd ed. (Cambridge: Harvard University Press, 1960, reprint, 2000).

24. Quoted in Andrae, "Hyde," 2. Indeed, Hyde wore his professionalism on not only his sleeve, but his shoes. As Hyde's memorialist, Henry Andrae, observed, "Judge Hyde was always impeccable and conservative in his dress. He believed that this helped to inspire confidence and that a professional should give the appearance of being one. . . . His 'uniform' was a dark suit, a white shirt, a four-in-hand tie, and polished dark shoes. . . . It may be that he thought that a casual habit of dress bespoke a casual habit of thinking." Hyde was always the gentleman. He may have been insufferable to his more mortal colleagues: he never smoked, gossiped, or contested people by name, and he got plenty of regular exercise.

25. "Judge Laurance M. Hyde Leaves Court—But Not Law," *Sunday News and Tribune* (Jefferson City), January 1, 1967; Laurance M. Hyde, "The Practice of Law," *Missouri Bar Journal: Official Publication of the Missouri Bar Association*

3 (July 1932), 115–17. http://www.mobar.org/uploadedFiles/Home/Publications/Journal/2010/05–06/The%20Practice%20of%20Law.pdf

26. Hyde founded the conference with Nebraska Chief Justice Robert Simmons and his friend New Jersey Chief Justice Arthur T. Vanderbilt. Unsurprisingly, during Hyde's two tenures as chief justice, 1949–1951 and 1960–1962, judicial selection and tenure would be among the limited topics chosen for discussion by the conference those years. Robert F. Stephens, ed., *History of the Conference of Chief Justices* (Williamsburg, Virginia: National Center for the State Courts, 1986, 1993), 13–14, 60–61. http://ccj.ncsc.dni.us/B995A84B-B3B5–4FB9–BB4E-C01BE146FC3E/FinalDownload/DownloadId-9F19975BD68E574673C4DACF2DDD019A/B995A84B-B3B5–4FB9.

27. Pound to George Rossman in conversation, and later related to Hyde by Rossman in a letter April 3, 1950, reprinted in Florence Hyde, *Hyde Family,* 38; see also Andrae, "Hyde," 2.

28. Hyde formally spent thirty-five and a half years on the court as a commissioner and judge. The (then) constitutional requirement that he leave the court at seventy-five years old had only a modest effect on Hyde's career. From 1967 to 1977, Hyde served as a special commissioner for the supreme court, during which he wrote over a hundred opinions and was also active in legal professional associations. "Judge Laurance M. Hyde Leaves Court—But Not Law," *Sunday News and Tribune* (Jefferson City), January 1, 1967; "Rites Tuesday for Judge Hyde," January 22, 1978.

29. Laurance M. Hyde, "Selection and Tenure of Judges," *American Bar Association Journal* 27(December 1941), 763–65.

30. Laurance M. Hyde, "Judges: Their Selection and Tenure," *Alabama Lawyer* 9 (April 1948), 211–21; Laurance M. Hyde, "The Missouri Plan for Selection and Tenure of Judges," *Journal of Criminal Law and Criminology* 39 (September-October 1948), 277–87.

31. Hyde, "Judges: Their Selection and Tenure," *NYLQR,* 389–400.

32. Ibid., 391.

33. Ibid., 391–92.

34. Ibid., 395. Other judicial writers, probably following Hyde, liked to cite the same anecdote. See for example, Harry A. Hall, "The Missouri Nonpartisan Court Plan: A Quarter Century Review," *The University of Missouri at Kansas City Law Review* 33 (Summer 1965), 164.

35. Atwood was keen on the nonpartisan court plan, too. After his term he was elected president of the Missouri Bar, and in 1938 he became president of the American Judicature Society. He would run for a supreme court seat in 1940 and lose.

36. *New York Times,* October, 1949; see also *New York Herald Tribune,* October 5, 1949; *New York Daily News,* October 5, 1949; *New York Sun,* October 4, 1949; *New York World-Telegram,* October 5, 1949. Hyde clearly enjoyed his time and the attention, saving the various articles covering his speech. "Hyde Vertical File," Supreme Court of Missouri Library.

37. *New York World Examiner*, October 5, 1949.

38. Florence Hyde gives a rather gushing space in *The Hyde Family* to the British trip, illustrated with photographs and a full reprint of a letter from Lord Chancellor Jewett praising Laurence. It was clearly a high moment. Laurence was one of two American judges to preside over the meeting, see pp. 55–62. In the same section Florence reprints another letter from Lord Chancellor Jewett, from 1948, praising Hyde's 1947 article in the *New York University Law Quarterly Review*, 62.

39. E. A. Richter., ed., "A Conversation with Judge Paul W. Barrett," *Missouri Supreme Court Historical Society Journal* 6 (March 1996), 18.

40. John Osborne, "The Qualities of Justice," Crime in the U.S.: Part III, *Life* magazine, September 23, 1957. Laurence Hyde is featured as one of seven "Eminent American Jurists" in a special color pictorial inner article, 64; see also Florence Hyde, *The Hyde Family,* 36.

41. Florence Hyde, *The Hyde Family*, 36.

42. "Judge C. A. Leedy, Jr.," *Kansas City Times,* October 10, 1978.

43. As if that time together was not enough, they are buried next to each other at Jefferson City's Riverview Cemetery, both presumably rolling in their respective graves.

44. He also noted with understated discomfort United States Supreme Court decisions concerning criminal rights, which led to a flood of criminal cases into Missouri courts, issued without adequate guidance from the Court as to what its lofty decisions meant. Quoted in "Judge Laurance M. Hyde Leaves Court—But Not Law," *Sunday News and Tribune* (Jefferson City), January 1, 1967; see also "Illustrious Records Well Kept By Judge Hyde in High Court," *Kansas City Star,* December 1966, included in Florence Hyde, *The Hyde Family,* 38c (*sic).*

45. Andrae, "Laurance Mastick Hyde," 2.

CHAPTER EIGHT

Constitutional Mollycoddling: How Women Won the Right to Serve as Jurors in Missouri (but only if they wanted to)

Karen Anderson Winn

IN 1944, DELEGATES TO Missouri's constitutional convention debated an amendment they believed had the potential to undermine Missouri's farms, homes, and families. It would tear down respect for women. Cows would go unmilked, chickens untended, and children unfed. Women would neglect their duties at home, and their peace of mind would suffer. Worst of all, the amendment would contribute to the causes of delinquency among children. Its inclusion in the new constitution would cause the people to reject the entire document at the polls.

The delegates were discussing whether women in Missouri should serve as jurors.

Many people think of the period between the culmination of the women's suffrage movement and the 1960s as a quiescent one for the women's rights movement. The former was the "first wave" of feminism; the latter, the "second wave"—and the sea was calm between the two. In 1973, one author wrote, "After 1920 the women's rights movement in Missouri lay dormant for more than forty years. Very little in the area of women's rights was accomplished or even sought by the women of this State. Then in the early 1960s the movement awoke from its long rest and once again become an active force in Missouri politics."[1]

During those decades, however, not all Missouri women had lost interest in politics or forgotten the battle for equal rights. After they won the right to vote, members of the League of Women Voters[2] worked tirelessly to educate voters, get out the vote, and promote various good-government causes.[3] And they actively worked on behalf of women's interests and rights, especially the right to serve on juries.

The fight to gain that right was part of a larger national struggle that lasted roughly one hundred years, from the late 1860s to the late 1960s. In Missouri, it began in earnest in the 1920s after women gained the right to vote. The League of Women Voters, in particular, began a dogged, if initially ineffectual, campaign that lasted twenty-five years. Its eventual vehicle for success was Missouri's constitutional convention of 1943–1944.

The convention became the scene of a prolonged and impassioned debate as to whether women should be allowed to serve as jurors, and if so, whether they should be *required* to serve. The convention delegates debated the issue in plenary session for nearly two weeks against a backdrop of intense lobbying from women's organizations. They revisited the issue and voted on it several times. Months after it seemed the issue had been settled, a delegate attempted, in a last-minute maneuver, to remove the provision entirely. When the dust settled, women had won the right to serve on juries, but they had not gained the equal status that many desired.

American women gained the right to serve on juries state by state, with stops and starts along the way. Some of the western American states experimented with jury service for women very early, but those experiments were typically short-lived. The first chief justice of Wyoming Territory included women on juries after women gained the right to vote in the territory in 1869. The second chief justice put an end to the practice in 1871; then Wyoming women again served on juries from 1890 to 1892. Women in Washington served on juries from 1883 to 1887, and gained the permanent right to do so in 1911. Colorado, Utah, and Idaho permitted women to serve on juries in the 1890s, but few women actually did so in the early years, and women did not win the statutory right to do so in Colorado and Idaho until the 1940s.[4]

Although some forward-thinking American women demanded the right to serve on juries in the nineteenth century, the campaign accelerated after the enactment of the Nineteenth Amendment to the United States Constitution, granting women the right to vote.[5] In the 1920s and '30s, several women's groups took up the cause of jury service. The National Women's Party, led by Alice Paul, lobbied for a number of women's rights issues such as the Equal Rights Amendment. It also campaigned for jury service for women, lobbying state legislatures in the 1920s. In the 1930s, it changed its tack and focused, unsuccessfully, on bringing test cases.[6] Local women's bar associations and the National Association of Women Lawyers advocated for the issue.[7] The League of Women Voters pressed the cause through publicity and education and lobbied state legislatures throughout the country.[8]

Missouri enacted legislation enabling partial women's suffrage shortly before the ratification of the Nineteenth Amendment, and the voters approved an amendment to the state constitution allowing women to hold political office in 1921.[9] But jury service was not so quickly achieved in Missouri or in many other states. In some states that allowed women to vote before passage of the Nineteenth Amendment, jury service for women was also allowed relatively early as, for example, in Utah (1898), Washington (1911), Kansas (1913), California (1917), and New Jersey (1917). In others, jury service for women quickly followed the passage of the Nineteenth Amendment. Ten states enacted such laws in 1920 and 1921. But women did not gain the right to serve on juries in Alabama, South Carolina, and Mississippi until 1966, 1967, and 1968, respectively.[10]

From 1920 on, the Missouri League of Women Voters supported jury service for women. At each annual convention, the organization officially adopted it as a plank in the program. The topic was frequently discussed at league conventions, and the league hosted speakers and wrote advocacy pieces on the issue. But Missouri's constitution and its statutes as well as the state legislature proved formidable obstacles to achieving the goal.

The league lobbied the Missouri General Assembly for more than two decades without success. One barrier was Missouri's 1875 constitution, which guaranteed the right to trial by jury in Article II, Section Twenty-Eight:

> The right of trial by jury, as heretofore enjoyed, shall remain inviolate, but a jury for the trial of criminal or civil cases in courts not of record, may consist of less than twelve *men* as may be prescribed by law. . . . Hereafter a grand jury shall consist of twelve *men*, any nine of whom concurring may find an indictment or true bill . . . [emphasis added].

The 1875 constitution's references to a jury of "twelve men" were frequently cited as a barrier to such a law in permitting women to serve on juries. In 1926, two prominent St. Louis lawyers published a report concluding that a constitutional amendment would be required before women could serve on juries. They added, however, that "experience [in other states] seems to have shown that they make at least as good jurors as men[.]"[11] The next year, in response to a request from the Missouri League of Women Voters, two other lawyers wrote an opinion concluding that no such amendment was necessary. They wrote that the 1875 constitution had used "men" in the generic sense of the word; therefore, a constitutional amendment was unnecessary. However, they noted that § 6607 RSMo, 1919, provided that every juror "shall be a male citizen of the state[.]" If this statutory restriction were removed by the legislature, they believed, women would be qualified for jury service.[12] In 1931, in response to a request from a league member, an assistant attorney general wrote an opinion to the same effect.[13]

In 1927 and 1929, bills were introduced in the Missouri General Assembly to allow women to serve as jurors, and league members lobbied for them. A bill passed the house of representatives in 1929—causing the *Kansas City Star* to report that the reactionary house briefly "went red"[14]—but failed in the senate. After the failure of the 1929 bill, members of the Missouri league wrote and presented a skit, "An Inquest on the Body of Bill Jury Service." The subject of the inquest is "whether the murder of Bill was justifiable homicide, or whether it was a foul murder." Before a verdict can be rendered, however, the body of Bill stirs, and "Mrs. League of Women Voters rushes to Bill, promising to restore him to health and strength and to follow his career in the School of Legislature more carefully that no such illness may occur again."[15] League members were optimistic about the bill's chances in 1931.

To no avail, however: unsuccessful bills were introduced in 1931, 1933, and 1937. During the general assembly's 1939 session, Representative Gladys Steward tried a different tack, introducing a constitutional amendment for women's jury rights, but it did not pass.[16] In 1942, the league capitalized on "the manpower problem" of World War II when it issued a press release urging the enactment of a law permitting women to serve as jurors—"another means whereby they can serve their country."[17] In 1943, league members wrote scores of letters to state representatives supporting such a bill introduced by St. Louis Representative Milton F. Napier.

Letters, lobbying, and publicity had met with little success, but then the call came in 1943 for a new state constitutional convention—for which the league had also campaigned. Suddenly, the constitutional barriers weakened, and women were able to link this opportunity to demographic changes caused by World War II, including the shortage of manpower and the participation by women in traditionally male sectors of the workforce.[18] Finally, their arguments fell on receptive ears.

There were eighty-three elected delegates to the 1943–1944 convention: a Republican and a Democrat from each of Missouri's thirty-four senatorial districts, largely chosen by party insiders, and fifteen "at-large" delegates. Civic groups, particularly the League of Women Voters, played a major role in the election of the at-large delegates. Eight at-large delegates were endorsed by the league.[19]

Demographically, the delegates were overwhelmingly white, male, and mature, with an average age of fifty-five. They were *less* diverse than the delegates to the short and unsuccessful 1922–1923 constitutional convention, which had boasted four women delegates and one African American. Among the delegates to the 1943–1944 convention, there were no African Americans and only two women.[20]

The delegates were relatively well educated. Forty-one of the eighty-three were lawyers, of whom a number had served as prosecuting attorneys and judges. Four were college professors. Most, but not all, had been politically active, with a former governor, two former congressmen, twenty-four former members of the general assembly, and numerous party committeemen in their ranks.[21]

The delegates first took up the topic of women's jury service on April 11, 1944, as it had been referred to them from the Bill of Rights Committee.[22] Various constituencies had been lobbying delegates since the convention committees had convened in 1943. In addition to women's groups like the League of Women Voters and the Missouri Federation of Business and Professional Women's Clubs, the president of the St. Louis Chamber of Commerce, George C. Smith, weighed in on the issue. Smith wrote in 1943 that "there seems to be no logical reason why [women] should not be eligible to serve on juries."[23]

Smith addressed his letter to E. McDonald Stevens, chairman of the Committee on Suffrage and Elections. Stevens was a Republican attorney from University City. He had been a member of the general assembly from 1920 to 1922. At the time of the convention, he was in private practice as an attorney in St. Louis. For three months in 1942 he had served as a circuit judge, filling out the term of a judge who had left for war service, and his fellow delegates sometimes addressed him as "Judge." More than other delegates, he empathized with the desire of the members of some women's groups to be treated as men's equals. He argued that the word "male" should come out of the constitution every place it appeared, and that the state should have the right to draft women as well as men into the militia if necessary.[24] He was also a fervent supporter of allowing women to serve on juries, and his committee had supported the measure unanimously. But in October 1943 he referred the matter to the Bill of Rights Committee, to which, he said, "the matter properly belongs."[25] That committee, chaired by P. M. Marr, a Democratic attorney from Milan, also supported the measure, and Marr introduced it to all the delegates on April 11.

The provision allowing women to serve on juries fell within a larger section that read, in pertinent part:

> SECTION 26. Trial by jury inviolate—majority verdicts—grand jury, twelve men.—*That the right of trial by jury as heretofore enjoyed shall remain inviolate; provided that a jury for the trial of criminal and civil cases in courts not of record may consist of less than twelve citizens as may be prescribed by law[.] . . . Hereafter, a grand jury shall consist of twelve citizens[.] . . . No person shall be disqualified from jury service on account of sex.* Every citizen over the age of twenty-one years and otherwise qualified, and not exempted by law, shall be eligible for jury service unless otherwise shown upon examination at the trial [emphasis added].[26]

This section contained three new provisions, including the one that qualified women to serve on juries. In his introductory remarks, Marr stated that he thought there "could be no valid objection" to the provision allowing women to serve on juries.[27] That afternoon, however, there was no quorum, and the matter was postponed until the following morning.

But there *were* objections, as delegates found out almost immediately upon taking up the amendment on April 12. J. A. Hemphill, a Democratic farmer and gin operator from Kennett, informed the convention that he had an amendment to "knock out that portion of this particular Section dealing with forcing women to serve on juries."[28] The actual amendment was introduced by George Heege, a Republican attorney from Kirkwood, and James E. Sater, a Democratic attorney from Monett, who made a motion to reinsert the word "male" in front of "citizen" both times it appeared, and to delete the sentence "No person shall be disqualified from jury service on account of sex." As Heege saw it, there was no demand from the "rank and file" of women for jury service.[29]

Hemphill seconded the motion. He argued that serving on juries was not a privilege but an imposition, saying that this amendment would only "tear down the respect for women" by adding another burden to "these many things we are expecting of" them during the war. Hemphill thought the work women were already doing in war plants and on the battlefield was taking them "away from their homes, and in this country today we are missing them in the work they should be doing."[30]

A heated debate followed. O. C. Tee, a Republican attorney from Caldwell County, opposed women serving on juries because he was for "preserving the high and respective position of motherhood in the State of Missouri and protecting it from the things that I deem to be unnecessary impositions in order for justice to function and prevail in our great state."[31] He thought that jury service would be not only an imposition on women, but a source of mental anguish for some. "Now, imagine if you will, a mother who has a small child in her home who is ill and she's summoned by the call of a Sheriff or a Deputy to be in court on a certain day to serve on a jury. Is that going to . . . increase her peace of mind and quietude in that home or not?"[32]

Delegates complained that women's extended absences from the home on account of jury service would disrupt the lives of men and their families. Clyde Cope, a Democratic attorney from Clayton, complained that "it would be a little inconvenient" for him as "I don't know how to cook and I don't know how to make beds, and household help is mighty scarce these days."[33]

Sater said the amendment "only adds and contributes to the causes of the delinquency of children."[34] He quoted extensively from an article by J. Edgar Hoover.[35] He also quoted the president of Stephens College: "While we are fighting the international gangsters, we are breeding in our own midst countless young gangsters who might have been decent, useful citizens if their mothers had not put activities outside the home ahead of their duty to their children and society."[36]

William Allen, a Democratic attorney from Kansas City, quickly tried to counter the Heege amendment by offering his own amendment.[37] Allen wanted to strike the word "male" from the Heege amendment, delete the last sentence of the committee amendment, and substitute the word "citizen" for "person." Thus, this iteration of the constitutional amendment contained the sentence: "No citizen shall be disqualified from jury service on account of sex."

The debate was joined, as members who favored women's jury service fought back with a number of logical and tactical gambits. Attorneys who had practiced in neighboring states invoked their own experiences in favor of women serving as jurors. Rex Moore, a Democratic attorney from Trenton, in the northeast corner of the state, pointed out that the citizens of Iowa, Illinois, and Kansas seemed to have coped with women on juries, and he would "certainly hate to have to admit that the State of Kansas is more progressive than the State of Missouri," since "all that we ever got out of Kansas was windstorms and grasshoppers."[38]

Other delegates pointed out that judges were reasonable in excusing people from jury service. Farmers were routinely excused during their busy seasons, and their wives would be, too. Furthermore, as Allen remarked, all of the circuit judges in Missouri outside of St. Louis and Kansas City were still elected and had all the more reason to be accommodating:

> Every Circuit Court has the right to excuse any juror from jury service. In the country districts, about which Mr. Hemphill spoke, those Circuit Judges are still elected by the people, and I can't conceive of any Circuit Judge compelling a mother of a large family to leave her home to go and sit in a jury room on a panel for weeks at a time while her children run about unattended, or while Senator Cope is unfed or has to go to a restaurant.[39]

Still other delegates argued that extending jury service to women could improve the quality of jury pools. Ethan Shepley, a prominent Republican St. Louis attorney, was convinced that "by extending this jury duty to include women as well as men, the net result will be to ease the burden on both or on all; to elevate, generally speaking, the type of juror that we have in cases by a larger number of people to whom we can look for this service."[40] Frank Wesley, a Republican attorney and realtor from St. Louis, argued that "if we give this duty to the women . . . we will get some of the best qualified women to serve," because women would not ask for excuses as much as men.[41] Marshall Ford, a Democratic attorney from Maryville, worried that worthwhile women, like their male counterparts, would seek to be excused. On the other hand, he thought, "It may be that the best qualified women will have more time for jury service than the best qualified men. If that be true, and if they accept the responsibility and don't duck the blow as men do who are qualified, then the administration of justice will be even better with women sitting on the jury."[42]

In some cases, the delegates who favored jury service for women fought stereotypes with stereotypes. Stratford Morton, a Republican attorney from Clayton, dismissed opponents' arguments as the same ones they had made about women's suffrage. But in response to Sater's argument about increased juvenile delinquency, he asked whether there was "any substitute for a good, loving mother on a jury to decide the fate of a first offender, 18, 19, or 20 years of age."[43] Frank Williams, a Democratic attorney from Springfield, conceded that jury service was a duty, and, implicitly, that a woman's primary responsibility was to care for her home and family. But this was even more reason for women to serve on juries, because "the protection of our civil rights, the protection of our lives, our liberty and our property, is fundamentally referred to a jury . . . and if those rights drawn in question affect the home, then they affect immediately and directly the mother who presides over that home, and it is her interest as much as it is her husband's to discharge the duty as a jury woman and which will protect that home."[44]

Some delegates to the convention had a broader perspective on matters. Republican L. E. Meador was a professor at Drury College in Springfield who held a Ph.D. from the University of Chicago. He argued repeatedly that the task of the convention was to draft a document for the ages, and that there was no reason, scientifically or politically, for having such a sex-based distinction in the constitution. As for differences between the sexes, he contended:

> Science dispels these differences. . . . What are the differences in sex? Not very much. . . . No one knows and certainly we shouldn't put in our Constitution a statement based on apparent differences. It will quickly be dispelled. I do not know that women wish to serve on juries at the present time. There will be a demand for it as time goes on. We are writing this Constitution not only for today but for a century and certainly before that century expires we will find the differences now apparently existing between the sexes as will have been to a very great extent dispelled, no longer exist . . . [O]ur Constitution should be a democratic document without any discrimination in sex whatsoever.[45]

Some delegates were able to articulate the perspective of women's rights activists. Rather than seeing jury service primarily as a duty, they saw it simply as one of the rights women should have to put them on an equal footing with men. Several delegates who argued from this vantage point saw it as a matter of logic, fairness, and justice. Others who did so resorted, ironically, to the casual but widespread racism of the time, comparing the status of deserving women to that of African American men, whom they saw as less deserving. Marr, the attorney who reported the women's jury service amendment to the full convention, said: "Only recently, since this Convention started, on one Saturday I was trying a jury case in the County, not terribly far from here, and on my jury was a negro, and I thought to myself then we certainly should give the women of this State the rights that we accord the Negro."[46]

Stevens took an active role throughout this debate and vigorously argued that women had the right to serve as jurors. He read aloud an article from *The Christian Science Monitor* that stated that after the "Scottsboro case," in which the United States Supreme Court had reversed the conviction of an African American man who had been convicted by an all-white jury from which African Americans had been excluded, "women alone" were being denied the equal protection of the law.[47] "There isn't any doubt since 1921 the women of the State of Missouri have been trying to get this right from the Legislature and they have been unable to get it. They have been insisting on this right and privilege and it is a right and a privilege and it's the only civil right that has been denied to the women of this State in the State of Missouri."[48]

As Stevens saw it, this was the logical next step for women: they had the right of suffrage, they served as election judges and clerks, they were eligible to hold office, and now, "they should have the right, the duty, and the privilege of serving on juries."[49] Stevens called the ability to serve on a jury "the fundamental right that [women] have as citizen[s] of this state."[50]

At the end of the day, and with barely a quorum present, the Allen amendment passed on a roll-call vote, 37–9.[51] But during the debate, Claude Arnold, a Democratic attorney from Puxico, had mentioned the idea of allowing women to exempt themselves upon request. Arnold favored allowing women to serve on juries as a right or a privilege, but not if it was imposed as a duty.

> Now as a country lawyer, knowing something about the ratification of court procedure in a small county, I would not like for my mother or my sisters or my wife to be summoned and dragged over to Bloomfield, a distance of twenty miles and have to sit around over there a day or two, waiting to be called for jury service, neglecting their duties at home if they have any, and I assure you they do have, and yet have to go over there and sit around and be dragged around by order of court.[52]

Immediately after the vote on the Allen amendment, Cope proposed just such an amendment as an addition: "But any woman shall be excused from jury service if she requests the court for exemption before she is sworn as a juror in any case or proceeding which is pending." The Cope amendment, with its exemption clause for women, ignited days of controversy.[53]

The tenor of the debate at the constitutional convention, as well as the lopsided vote in favor of the Allen amendment, suggests that an amendment to permit women to serve on juries was not in serious doubt, although a few delegates such as Heege and Hemphill earnestly opposed it. But clearly, the debate had participants in one camp who firmly believed in the preservation of a woman's traditional role and that granting women the right to serve on juries would undermine that role. It had participants in another camp who believed that women should be recognized as men's equals in all matters of the rights, duties, and privileges of citizenship. This was the goal of a number of women's organizations, including the League of Women Voters.

But many more delegates were between the two camps. In 1944, they understood that if women wanted the right to serve on juries, they could hardly be denied. On the other hand, the delegates were by no means sure that women really wanted the right. And even if women wanted it, many people had reservations about what the new right represented.

The result of this tension was that when the debate was on a binary proposition—jury service for women or no jury service for women—few delegates spoke up, and the vote was fairly lopsided. But when a third option was added—the women's exemption—more delegates participated, and the votes became much closer. The Cope amendment allowed delegates to resolve their discomfort with this "new thing in Missouri"[54] by dividing women into two groups—those who adhered to traditional values and lifestyles and those who pressed for their rights and a broader role for women in society—and accommodating the perceived desires of both.

At the time of the convention, Clyde Cope was an attorney in Clayton, but he had cut his political teeth in smaller towns. He was for many years the prosecuting attorney of rural Dent County, and he had represented that county in the state senate. He had also served on the Committee on Suffrage and Elections, which had unanimously supported the women's jury-service provision. But Cope clearly divided women into two groups. Of his own family, he said, "Why I even pour my daughter a high-ball now and then. When I go home over the week-end we smoke cigarettes together. . . . I believe that my wife and daughter have already heard as much about murder and rape and seduction as they will ever hear in the court room and I don't think that it has hurt them any either."[55] He knew such women were not babes in the woods, and he had supported the amendment when it was reported out of the committee. But he later changed his mind. He explained that, at the time, he "honestly thought the women of Missouri wanted to serve on juries," but since then, he said,

> I've made some inquiries and I have changed my mind about the attitude of the women, if you will exclude the Suffragettes. This morning one of the delegates in this Convention told me that while we were debating this subject, he went around and talked to thirteen women in the galleries here on the lower floor. That's all there were here this morning, thirteen, he said. He asked them if they wanted to have the right and the duty and the obligation to serve on juries, and what do you suppose was the result of that poll he took? I could

> give you the name of the delegate. He said that of the thirteen women here this morning nine of them said they didn't want this written in the constitution.[56]

Thus, he believed,

> [A]ny woman ought to have the right to be excused from jury service because of the fact that she is a woman. We all know, those who are lawyers as well as those who are not lawyers, that all the proceedings in court are held with open doors. Any requests for exemption from jury service are made in public where all can hear. I don't think that any woman in this state would be required to stand up in open court and make a public excuse for exemption because of any periodic sickness.[57]

Not only would women be embarrassed to ask to be excused if they were having their periods, there were some "whose faces still will flush when they are called upon to hear the evidence in some of the filthy trashy trials that are held in public."[58]

After little debate, the Cope amendment passed on April 12, 26–21.[59] But Stevens voted "aye," he explained, for the sole purpose of being able to move to reconsider it on another date. He made the motion to reconsider immediately after the vote was taken, and the convention then adjourned for the day. The debate was carried forward from that Wednesday to the next Tuesday, April 18.

Over the weekend, the idea of dividing women into two camps took hold. When J. T. Opie, a Republican brush manufacturer from Kansas City, returned to the convention, he argued that, although for "women in the business world," jury service would "be a vacation," the woman with a large family or a child at her breast had not been at the convention asking for jury service and ought to have the option of the women's exemption. When told that such a woman had only to call the judge to get excused, Opie replied, "She don't have a telephone. I am not talking about us aristocrats."[60]

Cope reported that some of his next-door neighbors were members of the League of Women Voters, and he happened to know they did not want to sit on juries.[61] Others made similar arguments. Kirk Jones, a veteran Republican legislator and auto dealer from Desoto, asserted that there was no demand among the women of Missouri to serve on juries. To the extent there was, "I know where that demand comes from. It doesn't come from the rank and file of the women of this state. It doesn't come from the house-wife of this state. It comes largely from the people who are engaged in promoting women's rights in the state and a few organizations of that kind."[62]

Hemphill, who had previously advocated continuing the outright ban, jumped on the bandwagon:

> I drove three hundred and twenty nine miles yesterday and went down on Friday and came back on yesterday all though this great territory of south east Missouri, heavily populated. I never saw but one woman that clamored about this matter of serving on the jury and she is an old maid, didn't have any work. She thought it would be fun. But through all that vast territory they're not making any clamor to be on the juries and those I did talk to said, "Well, we have too much work to do, too many things that we can do to accomplish more for our community and for our families and our nation than being drug down to jury service."[63]

So did Amanda Hargis of Springfield, who was a Republican, a former teacher, a former labor and industrial inspection commissioner, and one of the two women delegates at the convention. She said she had held "a number of state offices," was for women's rights, had stood at the polls and begged men to vote for measures women wanted, but she supported Cope's amendment because she was "one of the women that certainly would not want to serve on a jury."[64]

But others called the Cope amendment "ridiculous," including the other woman delegate, Helen Crome, who finally spoke up during the reconsideration debate:

> I don't believe that women want to be excused from serving on juries. I don't belong to the League of Women Voters; I am not a member of a profession. I am just a woman and I don't think they want to be excused and I think Senator Cope's amendment is superfluous and I think it's really ridiculous, as our Chairman said. I think that we should serve and become equal with the men on the jury service.[65]

Delegates who opposed the Cope amendment also believed that debating such an amendment meant that they were running the risk of making *themselves* look ridiculous.[66] They pointed out that similar arguments—like the argument that only a few organizations really were concerned with the matter—had been made during the debate over women's suffrage.[67] They characterized the Cope amendment as infantilizing. Mayer, who had served as a circuit judge, did "not believe the women of Missouri wanted to make a plaything out of their duty to serve on juries."[68] Marr said, "We don't need to treat [women] like babies."[69] Ford echoed this sentiment:

> [S]o far as conferring on women or placing on them the responsibility of serving on juries, that question has been settled. The sole question now is shall we treat these women as if they were doll babies instead of adult human beings. Every one that I have talked to resented this clause in the constitution. . . . If we are going to put this responsibility on women let's treat them as if they were adult human beings ready to accept the responsibilities of citizenship and perform their duties the same as anybody else. I think they want to be treated as human beings, adult intelligent—not treated like . . . we would treat children.[70]

Undeterred, Opie shot back: "Do I understand that you're in favor of pushing our American women around out in the snow and cold and rain and leave the kids at home to starve?"[71] Mr. Garten asked, "[D]o we ask women taxpayers whether they want to pay their taxes or not? . . . Aren't they forced to serve as a witness and as litigants in the court?"

> I don't believe that [women] want us to preserve this lavender and old lace attitude that we are. I believe they want this as a duty and a responsibility of citizenship and that they should have and expect to be obligated just as much as our men on this matter of jury service.[72]

Over the weekend, too, supporters of women's jury service were busy. The League of Women Voters had long supported compulsory rather than permissive service, and Edna Gellhorn, president of the St. Louis league, wrote to several convention delegates entreating them to redouble their efforts for the former. They politely answered that they agreed with her position but believed the die was cast.[73] Mary Bryant, president of the Missouri league, wrote a letter to the editor of the *St. Louis Star-Times* in which she expressed her dismay at the prospect of such "constitutional mollycoddling."[74]

Marr read aloud a telegram from the Missouri Federation of Business and Professional Women's Clubs, which declared that "Missouri women will accept the full duties and responsibilities of citizenship in a democracy by willingness to serve on juries. Today women are sharing equally with men in the work of defense and the horrors of war and should be permitted to assume equal duties on the home front."[75] The messages from the women's groups that invoked women's service during the war gave the delegates who favored equal rights and responsibilities for women their most powerful arguments.

Of course, some had argued for years that women were entitled to the full panoply of civil rights. But some of those civil rights, such as jury service or employment-related rights, were traditionally confined to males. As historian Linda K. Kerber and others point out, many saw this not as discrimination against women, but discrimination to their advantage.[76] Women were seen as privileged in the sense that they did not have to undertake some of the more onerous duties of citizenship such as jury service and military service. Women had rights, but one of their rights was *not* to have to do those things. Early on, Opie had expressed this view:

> I believe a great deal of equality should be preserved, but equality is not so served when that equality or that which brings it about, brings also undue and unnecessary impositions upon those who are brought into the field of activity by that step. Now, I know that there are certain men in the country today who are such firm believers in equal rights with reference to men and women that they are perfectly willing, and insist in some cases, that their equality go so far that their women be the breadwinners of their families and support their children and even themselves in supplying them with tobacco money, in some cases I have heard of. Now, that's carrying equal rights too far in my opinion.[77]

But that was precisely the point for many women, particularly league members: they wanted to have the same rights and responsibilities as men. In 1944, their participation in the war effort gave them the ideal position from which to pursue their quest for these double-edged rights.

The war broadened the appeal of the argument that women were entitled to rights on the same basis as men. Because of manpower shortages during the war, diverse voices ranging from Franklin Roosevelt's to *Fortune* magazine's urged women to enter the work force, and about six million did.[78] In the fall of 1943, when the convention's committees were meeting, seventeen million women were in the work force—one-third of the total. Five million of those were working in war industries such as airplane factories. They often did dangerous work for less pay than men—a patriotic effort indeed.[79] Many Americans like Tee, Sater, and Hemphill were ambivalent about this trend of "carrying equal rights too far" and leaving children at home without mothers. Some warned of the long-term effects this phenomenon might have on the home and the postwar workforce.[80]

Many delegates, however, simply saw women's war effort as evidence that they deserved rights and status equal to men's. They linked women's participation in the war effort to their argument that jury service was a civil right that women should enjoy. This theme was present from the beginning of the debates. Allen noted that "for the first time in the history of this country, they are not only our equals in civil rights, but we have a vast army of women today serving in the armed forces of the United States."[81] Vance Julian, a Democratic attorney from Clinton, argued early in the debate that the original Heege amendment should be defeated: "If jury service, Mr. President, is a duty, and we have the ladies of our country in the armed forces and they are voting as they are in every state in the union, I see no reason as a lawyer, why women should not be allowed to serve on juries."[82]

Democrat Edward Stayton, a retired army general from Independence, said that while his "old family" had always put their women on pedestals, "today we see the women doing a perfectly magnificent job in the factories all over the land . . . Women are demanding their rights, equal rights, every kind of right, and they're gradually getting them." Therefore:

> Well, I've made up my mind to go the whole way and grant them every right and absolute equality with men. I think as a matter of justice they are entitled to it if they want it. I regret it, but I realize that it is very definitely there and I for one am going to vote to give them every right that man has and along with it every responsibility that goes with those rights . . . I want to give them, along with the rights, all of the privileges that they have demanded and are getting. I want to place the responsibility there just the same and I think if women want equal rights with men, and I want to give them equal rights with me, they should assume the same responsibility that I am required to assume.[83]

Leslie Deason, a Republican insurance agent from Hannibal, pointed out:

> Women are wearing overalls nowadays and driving trucks, switching freight cars and if you would try to take the women out of the election booths, or rather out of the precincts as Election Judges and Clerks, you wouldn't have enough people to staff the elections

> and they go down there at six o-clock in the morning, and stay until midnight and apparently they like it and they make excellent officials. I go to town frequently in a taxicab, operated by one of three female taxi drivers from one of the taxi agencies in my town. They wear overalls; they haul drunks; they haul me and I've not heard anything to the contrary but what they fulfill their mission well . . . I told the other day what I knew about the duties of a jury commission and for brother Opie's benefit I'll tell him that there will be no women driving in from the R.F.D. who have no telephones and no shoes to wear to sit around the Courthouse waiting to be dismissed from jury service.[84]

Stevens made an eloquent speech invoking women's war experiences:

> . . . I read the other day in the newspaper of a woman in this war that was riding a fighting plane on the eastern front who gave birth to a baby two weeks after she shot down a German plane and then three weeks afterwards she was up in that same plane and she shot down three planes. That woman didn't ask for an excuse. Senator Cope takes me to task for trying to strike out the word, "male" when we are working on the Militia, as I knew he would at some later date when I filed that motion, but I say the women of this country don't want to be treated any different from men.
>
> They are doing their work today in these war plants and if they weren't doing it, you and I wouldn't be here because we'd be behind those machines. Go down to St. Louis and see who's doing the work, making the shells in the Small Arms Plant out there on Goodfellow Avenue, the biggest plant of its kind in the world. It isn't the men; it's the women of this country that's doing it and they haven't asked for any preferential status there. They go in and they take their place alongside of the men. Go out to the West Coast in the Kaiser Shipyards and see who is doing the heavy work out there, voluntarily, of their own free will. They haven't asked to be preferred; they say, "Let us stand up alongside of men because it is our duty; it's our responsibility now." Now the only civil right that the women of this state don't have is the right to serve on juries. We've given them that right. We've given it to them in the way they want it and now we try to take it away from them by letting women, because they're women, say "Well, I just won't serve on a jury."[85]

The arguments linking war service with jury duty were powerful but ultimately ineffective. When Stevens's motion to reconsider the Cope amendment was brought to a vote, the delegates were evenly divided: 31–31. Robert Blake, the convention president, broke the tie. Blake, a prominent Democratic attorney from St. Louis, had been nominated for the presidency by none other than Clyde Cope. Ironically, Blake was one of the at-large delegates for whom the League of Women Voters had successfully campaigned.

So strong were the feelings on both sides of this issue, however, that later that day, because of a motion to reconsider another part of section 26, V. E. Philips, a Democratic attorney from Jackson County, seized the opportunity to reconsider the Cope amendment yet again, offering an amendment to strike the last sentence of line 26—the one containing the women's exemption. He argued that this would remove the disqualification for women, making it possible for the general assembly to "pass the necessary laws for the panel of juries to utilize the services of women upon juries . . . with the proper types of exemptions."[86]

Many delegates protested vigorously that such an amendment was improper under the convention's rules, and that they had already debated the issue into the ground. The chair overruled them, stating that the delegates had not yet considered the issue in light of a motion to strike out the sentence. But many delegates had already left for the day. After brief debate that afternoon, the delegates voted to continue the discussion the next day.

On April 19, delegates wearily resumed the debate. In general, the delegates who favored jury service for women on an equal basis with men liked the Philips amendment, considering it preferable to the "ridiculous" Cope amendment. Conservatives disliked it, considering that it undermined the "good work" the delegates had done in the last few days.[87] One delegate grumbled, "The only purpose of this Philips amendment is to get rid of the Cope amendment."[88]

Tee reported the results of a "survey" conducted by delegate Joe Manlove, a Republican attorney from Joplin. Manlove had sent questionnaires to "responsible citizens in various walks of life throughout southwest Missouri," asking: "Do you favor jury service for women?" followed by a question in parentheses: "Do you favor extending all privileges in government now enjoyed by men to women?" The result was 292 in favor and 349 in opposition. Tee called the results "the expression of ordinary common sense in that rural part of this state."[89]

Opie raised a familiar issue argument again, calling the campaign for women's jury service "an underhanded movement to wreck the family life of America. We are talking about juvenile delinquency."[90] Stevens, in whose committee the measure had originated, asked Opie if he had any evidence that family life in the twenty-eight states that permitted women on juries had been disrupted. Opie replied, "I'll answer this. I don't think there is anything that takes the place of good common horse sense."[91]

Jones Parker, a Republican attorney from St. Louis, former speaker of the Missouri house, and self-described "hill-billy,"[92] repeated the concern of other delegates that the constitution would not survive a vote of the people without the Cope amendment. He was sure that the voters

> will look at this matter of compulsory service on the jury on the part of the housewives, they will look at the old man and the old women and the children will go down and vote against this because they are going to make Ma serve on the jury. That is just as sure and if we want to drive tacks in our coffin lid now this is the best place I know of to drive them. And I have a very deep and abiding faith that if we are going to approve whatever we see fit to send out of here we'd better have these old women and these old men at the cross roads for us and not against us and they're going to be against us if Ma has got to go up there and leave the chickens, got to go up there and leave the cow unmilked and go up there and leave the children unfed. They are going to vote against this and there isn't a shadow of a chance that they won't. I think I know people in Missouri.[93]

This argument—that the new provision would imperil the ratification of the new constitution—was invoked time and time again with respect to many topics, to the point that President Blake said, "Many members of the convention and many listeners became satiated and almost nauseated with the argument[.]"[94] Nevertheless, Blake thought the claim was valid when it came to the issue of women's jury service. Describing his own role in the debate on this issue, including his tie-breaking vote on the women's exemption, Blake later wrote:

> When the president broke a tie vote in favor of an amendment which permitted women on their request to be excused from jury service, he was chided for his vote. And yet, here again the decision was right. A rigid requirement that women must serve on juries

> would have been a potent tool in the hands of the opponents of the new constitution, and would have resulted in many votes against the new constitution.[95]

At the end of that day's debate, the Philips amendment was voted down, 29–38. The women's exemption stayed in the constitution.

In September 1944, the convention was in its final days, and its members were voting for the final passage of the various files. On September 14—nearly five months after the debate on women as jurors had been put to bed—Marr made a motion for the passage of "Engrossed File no. 8," which included the amendments to the bill of rights. He remarked that the file had been "very thoroughly debated" from March 31st through April 26th, and it should be unnecessary to take time for "extended remarks."[96]

Everett Hullverson, a Republican trial attorney from St. Louis, had a different opinion. Hullverson, who had not been present in April when the issue was previously debated, strongly objected to the women's exemption clause. He believed that women should be permitted to serve as jurors, but that they should not be given "any privileges which are not consistent with their duties to serve."[97] In fact, he was concerned that in practice, the women's exemption would result in juries unsympathetic to the plaintiffs he represented in civil suits. He moved for a separate consideration of "Section 26, the section of File 8 that contained the provision for women jurors."

The issue of how women jurors would affect verdicts had been a minor theme running throughout the debate in Missouri and in other states. In New York, for example, property developers and insurance company representatives thought that women jurors would make trials involving their interests more unpredictable and more costly. They thought women were ignorant of the ways of business and might not return the expected verdicts in their favor. Similar concerns were voiced by mining companies in Montana and by business interests in other states.[98] The traditional concern was that women jurors would be overly sympathetic to plaintiffs and influenced by looks, dress, and other irrelevant issues.[99]

During the previous spring, delegates had briefly touched on this issue. Those who had tried cases before women juries in other states had invoked their own experiences to try to reassure the others. Marr said lawyers in Iowa had had positive experiences with women jurors, who were lacking innate prejudices and "not as quickly deceived by a good looking face and a well-rounded figure on the witness stand as men are."[100] Stevens told of his own experiences in Illinois, saying that women were less likely to try to get excused, and that women actually paid attention better than men, and rendered better verdicts.[101] He also read from an article about women jurors in Ohio, to the effect that they were less likely than men to award damages, especially to other women:

> Women jurors, on the other hand, usually can match operation with operation with the litigant, and to recall that it wasn't so bad after all . . .
>
> Women jurors generally are more careful, listen more attentively, think more clearly, and reach more balanced verdicts, say lawyers and judges.
>
> Lawyers and judges alike shuddered at the very thought of representing a woman in a breach of promise action before a woman jury.
>
> Moreover—and this seems to be the final treason of the fair sex against its sisters—women jurors are not apt to favor a woman driver who gets mixed up with the mysteries of driving and the law, in the order named.
>
> And so with an extra pat of their hair and maybe a specially nice show kerchief in their coat pockets, the lawyers these days are making the best of what seems to them to be a better jury situation.[102]

Mayer echoed Stevens's arguments. Based on his experience in Kansas, he argued: "I really believe that women are more conscientious and careful in trying to follow the instructions of the court than men are."[103]

All these remarks, however, had been made before the adoption of the Cope amendment. As Hullverson saw it, the women's exemption turned the traditional concern that women jurors would be overly sympathetic to plaintiffs on its head. He argued:

> This provision gives to any woman the right, upon any whimsical reason, to say, "Well I don't think I'll go down and protect my rights today." It permits those women who have nothing to do to serve on juries and it therefore makes the jury system in my opinion, somewhat of a joke. . . . The result of this section would mean that club women, the wives of executives of corporations, wives of insurance company executives who go down and serve on juries and would not make for a fair proportion of the population.[104]

Hullverson feared these juries would be stacked in favor of corporate defendants. He recalled a similar situation from recent history. "Just before my time in the City of St. Louis the statute provided that in the case any corporation wanted a special jury, all they had to do was put up $75.00 and then the Sheriff would go out and gather a special jury for the corporation. That was resorted to in a great number of cases with the result of course, that the verdict was always for the corporation."[105]

This concern made Hullverson so adamantly opposed to the women's exemption that he proposed jettisoning the entire section of the bill of rights that contained it. Mayer pointed out that if this section were omitted there would be no constitutional provision for jury trial or for a three-fourths verdict. Hullverson disagreed, saying that "the right of trial by jury is so engraved in our thought and in our public policy that we would most certainly have the right of trial by jury and the other matters could be taken care of by the statutes."[106] Another delegate pointed out that if the section were eliminated, there would be no requirement in the constitution that a unanimous verdict was required to convict a person of murder.[107] This argument gave even Hullverson pause.

Crome then tried to divide the section into two parts. She received support from Williams, who viewed the women's exemption clause as "an independent and not a dependent proposition."[108] Hullverson seized on the thought and proposed that this "objectionable feature" be numbered "Number 26 and a half." He later changed that to "Section 26a."[109] This proposal was defeated on a point of order.[110]

Williams then moved that the rules be suspended and section 26 divided into two parts. That motion failed, 13–47, although the two women delegates, Crome and Hargis, voted in favor of it. When a roll call was taken on section 26, Hullverson and Williams voted no, expressly because of the women's exemption language. The vote was 61–3.[111] When the file as a whole was voted on, Tee—diehard in his opposition to women's jury service—cast the only no vote.

The voters approved the new constitution on February 27, 1945. It became known as the "1945 constitution." Although it has since been amended many times, it is still Missouri's governing legal document. Stevens, who had fought so hard for women's jury service during the convention, did not live to see it become law. He died in November 1944, shortly after the convention adjourned.

Many others kept working toward the goal, however. After the general assembly passed the necessary enabling legislation in October 1945, the League of Women Voters turned its efforts to implementation of the new law.[112] Concerned that women should acquit themselves well in this new aspect of citizenship, the league issued press releases urging women to fulfill their duties as citizens to serve and to claim exemptions "at the earliest possible moment" to avoid disruption to jury trials. "It is quite evident that if women wait to assert their claims until the eleventh hour, the success and popularity of jury service for women will suffer."[113] It sponsored "jury schools" for women, using a 1939 model program imported from Illinois, which had adopted jury service for women in that year. Edna Gellhorn was interviewed on the subject on radio station KMOX on December 2, 1945. She lamented the fact that the new provision was permissive rather than mandatory, but she said, "[W]e're going to make the best of it by establishing a precedent to prove that good citizens wish to do their duty."[114]

Jury service for women became a reality on July 1, 1946, the effective date provided by the new constitution. During the summer of 1946, a league committee inspected the jury rooms in St. Louis's Civil Courts building and found them "dirty, dark, and drab." They noted that "the ash trays and waste baskets in some of the rooms were filled with ashes, cigarette and cigar butts and papers, and the toilet rooms in some of the divisions were in a dirty and unkept condition." The committee members met with representatives of the office of superintendent of municipal building, however, and were assured that the rooms would be cleaned and painted, and that appropriate new facilities would be made available.[115]

League members wrote to circuit judges and court clerks with lists of names of women willing to serve. League papers contain copies of a number of such letters, including some written by individual judges to individual prospective jurors, such as one from J. Glennon McKenna, a justice of the peace, to Mrs. Elsa M. Vanderbilt, on October 29, 1946, thanking her for her "kindness in accepting this civic duty[.]"[116] Justice McKenna was particularly excited to observe that the trial in which Mrs. Vanderbilt was to serve as a juror would be the first with a jury composed solely of women.

Despite the league's efforts, not all women eagerly volunteered to fulfill their duties as citizens. In *An Ozark Lawyer's Story,*[117] John K. Hulston told of his own mother's experience. Selected for the first jury panel in Greene County following the constitutional change, she decided she could not vote to send someone to jail. Hulston advised her of her right to be exempted, and she rehearsed how she would explain her choice to the judge. When Myrtle Hulston appeared in Judge F. Hiram McLaughlin's courtroom in Greene County, however, the judge made a stirring speech about the importance of the jury system and the historic occasion of women being on the venire panel. Mrs. Hulston did not ask to be excused.

Others evidently did. The *St. Louis Post-Dispatch* asked what the "earnest women of St. Louis who belong to the League of Women Voters" were going to do about women who claimed the exemption before jury service even went into effect. Leaders of the league wrote an acerbic letter to the editor, pointing out that they had always supported compulsory rather than permissive jury service for women, and stating: "Well, first of all we're going to say, 'We told you so!'" The letter went on:

> You see, we were fearful that women, who are also human beings, might not want to serve on juries if only their personal pleasure were consulted. What do you think 400 men under similar circumstances would have done . . . ?
>
> We gals are not going to take refuge in recriminations, however. We have been conducting Jury Service Schools and we will continue our efforts to have women jurors in Missouri justify all reasonable hopes, in spite of the fact that the permissive provision that the Constitutional Convention tossed us is only a plaything. We'll get around to amending it sooner if you'll continue your helpful spoofing.[118]

They did not "get around to amending it." Thirty-four years would pass before women in Missouri served on juries on the same terms as men—and then, only because of a decision by the United States Supreme Court.

A number of other states enacted "permissive" jury laws in which women were allowed, but not required, to serve. By 1947, some form of permissive jury service was the law in fifteen states and the District of Columbia.[119] These laws were upheld by the courts for many years.[120]

But by the 1960s, the beginning of the end for permissive jury service for women was in sight. What women could not achieve through their legislatures or constitutional conventions, they finally achieved through the courts. The women who had fought so hard for jury service in Missouri in the 1930s and 1940s had based their arguments on the right of women to serve as jurors, to be citizens equal to men. When the Supreme Court finally outlawed the various forms of permissive jury service in the late 1970s, however, it focused on the rights of defendants.

The convoluted legal path that led to the demise of permissive jury service for women is a long and interesting tale in itself and has been the subject of a number of books and law review articles.[121] Various groups successfully challenged jury-exclusion laws as discriminatory.[122] In 1942, in *Glasser v. United States*,[123] the Supreme Court first stated that juries should be composed of a fair cross section of the community. Then, in 1946, the Court overturned a criminal conviction in *Ballard v. United States*,[124] a case in which women had been systematically excluded from the jury pool. Thereafter, women were eligible to serve on federal juries in states that allowed for women jurors.

Despite these developments, when Gwendolyn Holt was convicted in Florida by an all-male jury for killing her husband with a baseball bat, the Supreme Court in 1961 affirmed her conviction, upholding Florida's permissive law in *Hoyt v. Florida.*[125] In rejecting Holt's challenge to Florida's law, the Supreme Court noted that it did not exclude women from jury service but merely gave them "the privilege to serve" rather than imposing it as a duty. The *Hoyt* court reiterated many of the classic arguments for treating women differently—the same ones made by Missouri's constitutional convention delegates in 1944:

> Despite the enlightened emancipation of women from the restrictions and protections of bygone years, and their entry into many parts of community life formerly considered to be reserved to men, woman is still regarded as the center of home and family life. We cannot say that it is constitutionally impermissible for a State, acting in pursuit of the general welfare, to conclude that a woman should be relieved from the civic duty of jury service unless she herself determines that such service is consistent with her own special responsibilities.[126]

But times were changing, and criminal law was evolving. In 1968, the Supreme Court extended the reach of the Sixth Amendment to the United States Constitution, which guarantees a defendant's right to a jury trial, to the states.[127] This set the stage in 1975 for *Taylor v. Louisiana,*[128] in which the Supreme Court struck down Louisiana's permissive jury-service law. Louisiana's law was a true exemption, or "opt-in" law: women were automatically exempt unless they registered for jury service. The court held that the systematic exclusion of women from the jury pools deprived defendants of their right to a fair cross section—a jury of their peers—in violation of the Sixth Amendment.[129]

After *Taylor,* only five states retained such exemption clauses for women: Alabama, Georgia, Tennessee, Rhode Island, and Missouri.[130] In Missouri, the women's exemption had by then been challenged and upheld several times, beginning in 1947. The pattern repeated several times thereafter until the 1970s.[131] The Missouri Supreme Court upheld it for the last time in 1977, in *State v. Duren.*[132]

In *Duren,* the Missouri Supreme Court held that, even after *Taylor,* Missouri's system was sufficiently different from Louisiana's to pass constitutional muster.[133] In a case arising out of Jackson County, the court reviewed evidence that only 15.5 percent of the persons who were summoned and appeared for jury duty at the time of Duren's trial were women.[134] The *Duren* court considered this "well above constitutional standards," although one justice dissented.[135] At this point, Missouri retained the "dubious distinction of being one of only two states in the country which still allows an 'exemption on demand' clause for all women."[136] Not surprisingly, the Supreme Court granted certiorari. Billy Duren's case was the last Ruth Bader Ginsburg argued before the Supreme Court. Thereafter she would hear cases from the bench.[137] She prevailed: the Supreme Court reversed the Missouri Supreme Court's decision.[138]

In 2015, if you pick up a copy of the state constitution and peruse Article I, you will still find the following provision:

> *Section 22(b). No citizen shall be disqualified from jury service because of sex, but the court shall excuse any woman who requests exemption therefrom before being sworn as a juror.*

Seventy years after the constitution was approved by the voters, this example of the quaint sensibility of an earlier time remains enshrined in the document. Since the United States Supreme Court disapproved it in 1978 in *Duren v. Missouri,* it has been a dead letter—a law or ordinance that is no longer enforced but has not been formally repealed. But today, it serves as a reminder of the impassioned debate over women's rights and role in society, a debate that, for a time, dominated Missouri's last constitutional convention, seventy years ago.

NOTES

The author thanks Molly Karcher with her assistance in the researching of this essay.

1. Mark H. Neill, "The Women's Rights in Missouri," *Journal of the Missouri Bar* 67 (March-April 2011): 118, reprinted from the March 1973 issue of the *Journal of the Missouri Bar.*

2. Various chapters of the League of Women Voters were active both in lobbying to obtain jury service for women and in trying to exert influence on the 1944 constitutional convention, particularly the statewide and St. Louis chapters. In this essay, I generally use the term "League of Women Voters" or "league" in a generic sense. Where appropriate, I specify the particular chapter.

3. For example, a recent article notes that the St. Louis League of Women Voters was quite politically active in the early 1920s on behalf of "good government"

causes, briefly becoming involved in partisan and school board elections before focusing more narrowly on civic education and "get out the vote" campaigns. Linda Harris Dobkins, "What Men Expected, What Women Did: The Political Economy of Suffrage in St. Louis, 1920–1928," *Missouri Historical Review* 109 (October 2014): 1–17.

4. Holly J. McCammon, *The U.S. Women's Jury Movements and Strategic Adaptation* (New York: Cambridge University Press, 2012), 38–40.

5. For example, in 1876, members of the National Woman Suffrage Association demanded the right to a "jury of their peers" in a "Declaration of Rights." National Woman Suffrage Association, *Declaration of Rights of the Women of the United States* 4 (1876), microformed on Catharine Gough (Waugh) McCulloch papers, 1862–1945, ser. VI, as cited in Joanna Grossman, "Women's Jury Service: Right of Citizenship or Privilege of Difference?" *Stanford Law Review* 46 (May 1994): 1140.

6. Richard F. Hamm, "Mobilizing Legal Talent for a Cause: The National Woman's Party and the Campaign to Make Jury Service for Women a Federal Right," *American University Journal of Gender, Social Policy and the Law* 9 (Spring 2001), 106–16.

7. Grace H. Harte, "Women Jurors and the American Scene," *Women's Law Journal* 25 (1938–39): 9–10.

8. McCammon, *Jury Movements,* 44 and *passim.*

9. The general assembly enacted a bill allowing women to vote in presidential elections in 1919, and Governor Frederick Gardner signed it on April 5, 1919. The law was never needed because the Nineteenth Amendment became effective on August 26, 1920. Missouri finally adopted its own constitutional amendment allowing women to vote in 1924. On August 2, 1921, the voters adopted the amendment to allow women to hold political offices.

10. McCammon, *Jury Movements,* 38.

11. Judge J. Hugo Grimm and A. V. Lashly, "Judicial Administration," Report to the Missouri Association of Criminal Justice, Central National Bank Building (1927), 23–24. League of Women Voters of St. Louis, Addenda, Folder 822, State Historical Society of Missouri, Columbia, MO (hereafter, STL League papers).

12. E. M. Grossman and George A. McNulty, "Right of Women to Serve on Juries in Missouri," *St. Louis Law Review* 12 (1927): 138.

13. Henry H. Stern to Marie Ames (January 6, 1931), League of Women Voters of Missouri, Papers, 1911–1976, Folder 395, State Historical Society of Missouri, Columbia, MO (hereafter, Missouri League papers).

14. "Report of the Executive Secretary to the State Convention, Missouri League of Women Voters, May 17, 1929, Missouri League papers, Folder 73.

15. "An Inquest on the Body of Bill Jury Service" (May 1929), STL League papers, Folder 822. The characters in the skit were Bill (lately deceased), his

mother, "Mrs. League of Women Voters," and a variety of witnesses such as Indifferent Woman, Mrs. Housekeeper, Old-Fashioned Woman, Old-Fashioned Man, Mr. Lawyer, Mr. Bootlegger, and Mrs. Murderess.

16. McCammon, *Jury Movements,* 159.

17. Missouri League of Women Voters Press Release (December 3, 1942), STL League papers, Folder 822.

18. McCammon, *Jury Movements,* 160–61. The wartime boost to women's effort to win the right to serve on juries was not unique to Missouri; thirteen states made women eligible for jury service during the 1940s. Susan M. Hartmann, *American Women in the 1940s: The Home Front and Beyond* (Boston: Twayne Publishers, 1982), 136. As Hartmann points out, the war was a time of heightened attention to women's status under the law in other areas as well, including equal pay and discussion of an equal rights amendment. Progress in these areas was negligible, however (127–35).

19. Henry J. Schmandt, "The Personnel of the 1943–44 Missouri Constitutional Convention," *Missouri Historical Review* 45 (April 1951): 236–40.

20. Ibid., 244.

21. Ibid., 241–44.

22. Discussion of the provision began in the Committee on Suffrage and Elections, chaired by E. McDonald Stevens (R. University City), but the issue was later transferred to the Bill of Rights Committee, chaired by Phillip M. Marr (D. Milan).

23. George C. Smith to E. McDonald Stevens (December 9, 1943), E. McDonald Stevens, Constitutional Convention papers, 1943–44, State Historical Society of Missouri, Columbia, MO (hereafter, Stevens Papers).

24. Missouri Constitutional Convention (1943–1944), Debates of the 1943–1944 Constitutional Convention of Missouri (hereafter, Debates), http://digital.library.umsystem.edu/ (April 12, 1944), 1635. When citing the debates, dates and speakers are included only if they are not clear in the text. Obvious typographical errors have been corrected.

25. McDonald Stevens to Robert Blake, October 21, 1943, Stevens Papers.

26. Debates (April 11, 1944), 1577.

27. Ibid., 1578.

28. Ibid., 1583.

29. Ibid., 1587.

30. Ibid., 1593–94.

31. Ibid., 1596.

32. Ibid., 1597.

33. Ibid., 1592.

34. Ibid., 1600.

35. The article was evidently "Mothers . . . Our Only Hope," which had appeared in January 1944 in *The Woman's Home Companion,* as cited in Elaine Tyler

May, *Homeward Bound: American Families in the Cold War Era* (New York: Basic Books, 1998), 64, 240.

36. Debates (April 12, 1944), 1601.

37. Technically, Allen's amendment was to the Heege amendment. Cope's amendment, discussed *infra,* was to Allen's amendment to the Heege amendment. For ease of reference in this essay, I call each amendment only by its sponsor's name.

38. Debates (April 12, 1844), 1617.

39. Ibid., 1600.

40. Ibid., 1590.

41. Ibid., 1591.

42. Ibid.

43. Ibid., 1617.

44. Ibid., 1616.

45. Ibid., 1589.

46. Ibid., 1587. And Stevens, the champion of women's right to serve on juries, later tried to assure the delegates that the fear of "a white woman sitting next to a colored man or a colored woman" shouldn't prevail because in the southern part of the state "they are not going to have them on the juries down there anyway" (1808).

47. The "Scottsboro case" was actually a series of cases involving multiple trials, appeals, and new trials arising from the trials of nine young African American defendants alleged to have gang-raped two white women in 1931. After Alabama juries tried and convicted them, and the Alabama Supreme Court upheld their convictions, the United States Supreme Court twice reversed their convictions. In the second such case, *Norris v. State of Alabama,* 294 U.S. 587 (1935), the United States Supreme Court held that the jury selection process for Norris's trial was unconstitutional because all blacks were excluded from the jury.

Much has been written about the Scottsboro cases. A good recent overview, with additional historical perspective, is found in Michael J. Klarman's "Scottsboro," *Marquette Law Review* 93 (Winter 2009): 379–431.

48. Debates (April 12, 1944), 1609–10.

49. Ibid., 1611.

50. Ibid., 1614.

51. Ibid., 1628.

52. Ibid., 1624.

53. At the constitutional convention, the delegates used various terms to describe the exemption, including the "automatic exemption," but as some scholars have pointed out, this type of exemption "is automatic only in the sense that no reason other than the individual's sex must be given to claim the exemption." It was not automatic in operation, as women still had to take some action in order

to be excused. See Martha Craig Daughtrey, "Cross Sectionalism in Jury Selection Procedures after *Taylor v. Louisiana*," *Tennessee Law Review* 43 (Fall 1975): 12. Therefore, I have referred to it as the "women's exemption" in this essay. In a later speech, Daughtrey called it an "opt-out" provision, in which a woman would be included in the venire and subject to the call for jury service unless she took affirmative action to "opt out," as opposed to other states' "opt-in" provisions, in which women were automatically excluded from the venire unless they took affirmative steps to register for jury service, or "opted in." Daughtrey, "Women and the Constitution: Where We Are at the End of the Century," *New York University Law Review* 75 (April 2000): 19 (revised text of 29th annual James Madison Lecture on Constitutional Law, delivered at New York University School of Law on October 6, 1999).

54. Debates (April 18, 1944), 1798.

55. Ibid. (April 12, 1944), 1592.

56. Ibid., 1618.

57. Ibid., 1631.

58. Ibid.

59. Ibid., 1642.

60. Debates (April 18, 1944), 1790.

61. Ibid., 1796.

62. Ibid., 1793.

63. Ibid., 1800.

64. Ibid., 1813.

65. Ibid., 1794.

66. Ibid. (April 12, 1944), 1639–40 (Mayer).

67. Ibid., (April 18, 1944), 1793.

68. Ibid., 1638.

69. Ibid., 1792.

70. Ibid., 1795.

71. Ibid.

72. Ibid., 1806–7.

73. The papers of the St. Louis league contain several responses from convention delegates to letters Gellhorn evidently wrote between April 12 and 19, 1944. William Allen to Gellhorn (April 17, 1944); Israel Smith to Gellhorn (April 17, 1944); William L. Bradshaw to Gellhorn (April 12, 1944), STL League papers, Folder 975.

74. Mrs. Donald C. Bryant, letter to the editor, *St. Louis Star-Times,* April 17, 1944. Indeed, she and Edna Gellhorn wrote to each other in the same vein. Gellhorn wrote that, judging from reports from the convention, women were "to have their cake and eat it too—in other words they may serve if they wish but if they prefer to go out and get a permanent, all that they need to do is to prefer the

permanent," letter, Gellhorn to Mary Bryant, April 19, 1944, STL League papers, Folder 975.

75. Debates (April 18, 1944), 1791.

76. Linda K. Kerber, *No Constitutional Right to Be Ladies* (New York: Hill and Wang, 1998), 134; Grossman, "Women's Jury Service," 1146–50.

77. Debates (April 12, 1944), 1596.

78. David M. Kennedy, *Freedom from Fear: The American People in Depression and War, 1929–1945* (New York: Oxford University Press, 1999), 776–82.

79. Geoffrey Perrett, *Days of Sadness, Years of Triumph: The American People 1939–1945* (Baltimore: Penguin Books, 1974), 343–44.

80. There is a good discussion of the many facets of women's changing roles during the war and society's ambivalence to those changes in May, *Homeward Bound*, especially in chapter 3, "War and Peace: Fanning the Home Fires."

81. Debates (April 12, 1944), 1606.

82. Ibid., 1595.

83. Ibid. (April 18, 1944), 1879.

84. Ibid., 1801.

85. Ibid., 1810–11.

86. Ibid., 1852.

87. Ibid., 1871 (Hemphill).

88. Ibid., 1880 (Richard Nacy, D.-Cole County).

89. Ibid., 1874. When questioned about his survey, Manlove clarified that the respondents were about 2/3 men and 1/3 women, including members of the League of Women Voters and other women's organizations. When pressed further Manlove said he thought that, of the women, a slight majority favored the question.

90. Ibid., 1877.

91. Ibid., 1878.

92. "Tomorrow Last Day for Filing as Public Delegate on Constitution," unidentified newspaper clipping, hand-dated March 5, 1943, Missouri League papers, Folder 38.

93. Ibid., 1869.

94. Robert E. Blake, "Memoirs," 66, unpublished manuscript, Missouri Supreme Court Library.

95. Ibid., 67.

96. Debates (September 14, 1944), 7217.

97. Ibid., 7218.

98. McCammon, *Jury Movements,* 81–83 (New York) and 69 (Montana). McCammon discusses this argument against women's jury service, as well as many other arguments and the measures women took to combat them, in her book.

99. Kerber, *No Constitutional Right,* 144.

100. Ibid., 1588.

101. Debates (April 12, 1944), 1611.

102. Ibid., at 1612. The article had previously appeared in the *St. Louis Daily Record,* March 14, 1944.

103. Ibid., 1639.

104. Ibid. (September 14, 1944), 7218.

105. Ibid., 7232.

106. Ibid., 7219.

107. Ibid., 7220.

108. Ibid., 7227.

109. Ibid., 7233.

110. Ironically, the measure that Hullverson could not divide for ideological reasons in September 1944 was divided in just such a manner for nonideological reasons in 1945. When the legislature's Committee on Legislative Research printed the first edition of the new constitution, an editorial decision was made to separate different paragraphs of sections by letter. In that publication, it was explained that there were "a number of instances where sections were divided into paragraphs but the paragraphs were not similarly identified. In arranging the text here, these paragraphs have been identified by letter." Thus, the women's exemption, formerly the last paragraph of Article I, § 22, became § 22(b). The General Assembly of the State of Missouri, Committee on Legislative Research, *The Constitution of the State of Missouri with Annotations and Index, 1945,* ed. Lester Seacat (Jefferson City, MO: Mid-State Printing Co.), 29, 31.

111. The other no vote belonged to Heege.

112. H.B. 576 *et al.,* A.L. 1945.

113. "Jury Service for Women in Missouri," n.d. (possibly October 1945), STL League papers, Folder 821.

114. Edna Gellhorn, interview transcript, Station KMOX, Sunday, December 2, 1945, STL League papers, Folder 821.

115. Untitled report, July 10, 1946, St. Louis League, STL League papers, Folder 822.

116. McKenna to Vanderbilt, October 29, 1946, STL League papers, Folder 822.

117. Republic, MO: Western Printing Company, Inc., 1976.

118. Mrs. Aaron Fischer, Mrs. George Gellhorn, and Mrs. Virgil Loeb, letter to the editor, *St. Louis Post-Dispatch,* June 4, 1946.

119. Matilda Fenberg, "Jury Service for Women," *Women's Law Journal* 33 (1947): 48.

120. See Joan Hoff, *Law, Gender, and Injustice: A Legal History of U.S. Women* (New York: New York University Press, 1991), 225–27.

121. See, for example, Kerber, *No Constitutional Right,* chapter 4; Hoff, *Law, Gender, and Injustice;* Daughtry, *Cross-Sectionalism;* Grossman, *Women's Jury*

Service; Carole L. Hinchcliffe, "American Women Jurors: a Selected Bibliography," *Georgia Law Review* 20 (1985–86): 299–321; Barbara Allen Babcock; "A Place in the Palladium: Women's Rights and Jury Service," *University of Cincinnati Law Review* 61 (1993): 1139–80; Cristina M. Rodriguez, "Clearing the Smoke-Filled Room: Women Jurors and the Disruption of an Old-Boys' Network in Nineteenth-Century America," *Yale Law Journal* 108 (1998–99): 1805–44.

122. In 1880, in *Strauder v. West Virginia,* 100 U.S. 303 (1880), the Supreme Court struck down a West Virginia law that excluded African Americans from juries. In *Thiel v. Southern Pac. Co.,* 328 U.S. 217, 224 (1946), the Supreme Court called jury service "a duty as well as a privilege of citizenship" when it invalidated a jury selection system that effectively excluded daily wage earners. In *Hernandez v. Texas,* 347 U.S. 475 (1954), the Supreme Court voided the conviction of a Mexican-American by a jury from which Mexican-Americans were systematically excluded, stating, "The exclusion of otherwise eligible persons from jury service solely because of their ancestry or national origin is discrimination prohibited by the Fourteenth Amendment." *Id.* at 479.

123. *Glasser v. United States*, 315 U.S. 60 (1942). Ironically, the argument in *Glasser* was not based on the exclusion of women; the case arose in Illinois, where women had become eligible to serve as jurors mere months before the defendant was indicted. *Id.* at 64. Glasser's jury consisted of six men and six women. *Id.* at 84. Rather, Glasser's challenge was that the only women called for jury duty were members of the Illinois League of Women Voters. *Id.* at 83. Although the court agreed that "the deliberate selection of jurors from the membership of particular private organizations definitely does not conform to the traditional requirements of jury trial," it found the defendant had not made a sufficient showing on this point to reverse his conviction on that ground. *Id.* at 86.

124. 329 U.S. 187.

125. 368 U.S. 57 (1961). A very thoughtful, informative, and readable account of *Hoyt* and its impact on women's exemption laws is found in Kerber, *No Constitutional Right,* chapter 4.

126. 368 U.S at 61–62.

127. *Duncan v. Louisiana,* 391 U.S. 145, 149.

128. 419 U.S. 522 (1975).

129. The fusion of this argument with the argument that exclusion from the jury also violated the rights of the person excluded eventually produced the line of cases that subsequently disallowed peremptory challenges on the basis of race, then gender. Although the Supreme Court had recognized jury service as a right of citizenship for African Americans in the *Strauder* case decided in 1880, it did not do so for women until 1994, in *J. E. B. v. T. B.,* 511 U.S. 127 (1994).

130. Daughtrey, "Cross-Sectionalism," 5.

131. *State v. Taylor,* 205 S.W.2d 734 (Mo. 1947); *State v. Parker* 462 S.W.2d 737 (Mo banc 1971); *State v. Davis* 462 S.W.2d 798 (Mo banc 1971). It is worth

noting, however, that at the same time the Missouri Supreme Court reversed a murder conviction when the defendant established that the jury panel was improperly selected because there was systematic and purposeful exclusion of women from the venire. *State v. Smith,* 467 S.W.2d 6 (Mo. 1971).

132. 556 S.W.2d 11 (Mo banc 1977).

133. Ibid., 17.

134. Ibid., 16.

135. Ibid., 17 (J. Seiler, dissenting).

136. Harriet C. Wright, "The Missouri Supreme Court's Stand against Jury Selection Reform: Note on *State v. Duren*," *University of Missouri—Kansas City Law Review* 47 (1978–79): 246. As Wright noted, the other state was Tennessee. Wright also observed in her note that the United States Supreme Court had granted *certiorari* in *Duren* in 1978, and she warned that Missouri should be prepared to change its jury system "immediately" if *Duren* were reversed (259).

137. "A Conversation with Associate Justice Ruth Bader Ginsberg" (Annual Stevens Lecture at the University of Colorado Law School, September 19, 2012), *University of Colorado Law Review* 84 (Fall 2013): 909.

138. 439 U.S. 357 (1979).

CHAPTER NINE

Shaking the Shackles: Curt Flood's Challenge to Baseball's Reserve Clause

James R. Devine

INTRODUCTION

CURT FLOOD WAS NOT born a Missourian, but when he challenged Major League Baseball's reserve clause—a clause that kept players in highly paid bondage—and fought it all the way to the United States Supreme Court, he became famous as one. Originally from Houston, Texas, Flood was the youngest of six children. The family moved to Oakland, California, when he was young. From early on, Flood "was precociously coordinated." He was able to run, catch, and throw a ball better than much older children. He began playing organized baseball at the age of nine in a police league, and by the time he was a teen, he knew that he might be good enough to make a living at the game. Although he was shorter and lighter than most professional ballplayers, at the age of eighteen, fresh out of high school, in 1956, Flood signed a $4,000 yearly contract with the Cincinnati Reds.[1]

In 1956 and 1957, Reds' management assigned Flood to play minor league baseball, first at Class B High Point-Thomasville in the Carolina League, then Class A at Savannah, Georgia, in the South Atlantic League. Flood faced racial hatred from both his fellow players and the teams' fans, who called him names, and management prohibited him from eating in regular dining rooms and from lodging with the rest of the players. Although this treatment could have made play almost impossible, Flood led the Carolina League in all offensive categories except home runs in 1956 and was named an all-star in the South Atlantic League in 1957. He also received brief call-ups to the Reds at the end of each season.[2]

On December 5, 1957, the Reds traded Flood and Joe Taylor to the St. Louis Cardinals for Marty Kutyna, Ted Wieand, and Willard Schmidt. As the United States Supreme Court would later write in his case: "Flood rose to fame as a center fielder with the Cardinals during the years 1958–1969. He played errorless ball in the field in 1966, and once enjoyed 223 consecutive errorless games." Most commentators consider him one of the best center fielders of his time. Offensively, he led the league in at-bats in 1963 and 1964, in hits in 1964, and in singles in 1963, 1964, and 1968. He played on winning World Series teams in 1964 against the New York Yankees and in 1967 against the Boston Red Sox. He also played on the 1968 Cardinals team that lost the World Series to the Detroit Tigers.[3]

In light of the racism Flood faced as he progressed through the Reds' minor league system, he thought the 1967–1968 Cardinals team was "the most remarkable team in the history of baseball" and not merely because of its performance on the field. The team was, in Flood's view, a culturally enlightened group. "The men of that team were as close to being free of racist poison as a diverse group of twentieth-century Americans could possibly be." Flood, along with Tim McCarver, who was white, captained the team. This biracial leadership united the players without forcing race on any culture. The group was bound together by a shared desire to win so that each team member could make more money. The team believed that it was "the envy of the league," not just because of its members' stellar performance on the field, "but because [they] were the warmest and closest."[4]

High team morale, however, deteriorated in 1969 following negotiations between the Baseball Players Association and team owners over pensions and other issues. In 1966, the association appointed former steelworker's union official Marvin Miller as its executive director. Led by Miller, the association entered into professional sports' first collective bargaining agreement in 1968. One of the labor issues between players and owners was the players' pension fund, which was due to expire just prior to the 1969 season. When Miller learned that owners were not planning on continuing to fund the pension plan, he suggested players not report for spring training in 1969, and only one player showed up on February 13, the reporting date for pitchers and catchers. Player/owner negotiations extended the plan through 1971, and most players showed up for training by February 25th.[5]

Holding out for two days in response to Miller's called-for labor action, Curt Flood garnered a pay raise, going from $72,500 to $90,000. Other players on the team, including Hall of Famers Bob Gibson and Lou Brock, along with Tim McCarver, also received substantial raises. Those raises, however, carried a price. Player holdouts made a number of owners angry, including brewery magnate August A. Busch, Jr., who had purchased the St. Louis Cardinals franchise in 1953 for $3.75 million. Following settlement of the labor dispute, Busch, the owner whose team had appeared in back-to-back World Series, dressed down his players at a meeting held at the Cardinals' St. Petersburg spring training camp. On March 22, 1969, he brought other Cardinal executives and the St. Louis baseball press with him to the meeting and charged that the talk of union activities, not baseball, had dominated the off-season. He complained that players had arrived late for spring training and that some players were not in condition. Busch suggested that baseball was in danger of losing out on entertainment dollars to other sports. He emphasized the sacrifices that he and other city leaders had made in putting up the new Busch Stadium. Finally, Busch told his team that players had the best pension plan anywhere and warned them that if they intended to benefit from that pension plan when they were older, they had better make the fans happy. Apparently referring to some of Marvin Miller's unionist tactics, Busch told the team that he did not "react well to ultimatums." At the end, Busch asked if there were questions. None of the players spoke.[6]

From Curt Flood's perspective, Busch's speech "questioned the integrity of our attitudes." The speech demoralized the team. Regardless of the Cardinals' two World Series appearances, Flood wrote, "[W]e were still livestock." While the players on the team remained close, they no longer believed they were with the best baseball organization. In fact, according to Flood, "The 1969 Cardinals were a sorrowful and embittered group, and showed it on the field." Their enemy was no longer the next team on the schedule; it was their own bosses. The players were left "in a constant state of terrified insecurity." According to some reports, a few days after Busch's speech, the Cardinals traded their most popular player, Orlando "Cha Cha" Cepeda, "underlin[ing] the message" to the players. Management was breaking up the team, and the players knew it. Flood told St. Louis newspapers that team management had given up on the 1969 season, particularly after management put two younger hitters into the batting order behind Flood and Hall of Fame player Lou Brock. Flood protested what he considered injustices, including the questioning of some of his and other team members' outside financial interests. He called 1969 "that horrible season. Each complaint became another nail in my coffin. I was not speaking well of the boss." Flood knew his days in a Cardinal uniform "were numbered."[7]

On October 7, 1969, the Cardinals traded Flood, Tim McCarver, Joe Hoerner, and Byron Browne to the Philadelphia Phillies. In return, the Cardinals received Dick Allen, Cookie Rojas, and Jerry Johnson. Flood learned of the trade the next day when Jim Toomey, assistant to the Cardinals' general manager Bing Devine, called him. "'Good luck, Curt,'" was the reported substance of the conversation.[8]

THE RESERVE RULE'S JUDICIAL CHALLENGE
Curt Flood's "Free" Agency

Before being traded by the Cardinals, Curt Flood had believed in the American dream. Afterward, he "felt unjustly cast out" and considered retirement. Flood was limited in his baseball options because of baseball's long-standing reserve rule. Under that rule, Flood could either play for the team that owned his contract, the Phillies, or he could leave the game. He did not have the right to shop his baseball talents to other teams. As a result, Flood believed that the Cardinals had taken away his rights. A friend suggested he sue. Flood liked St. Louis. It was his home and the locale of his business interests. Flood did, however, meet with Phillies personnel. Following that meeting, Flood was not disturbed so much about moving to Philadelphia as he was about the reserve rule's mandate that he do so if he wanted to continue to play baseball. In a meeting with a lawyer for one of his businesses, the idea of a lawsuit again arose. At that point Flood called Marvin Miller at the Baseball Players Association.[9]

Flood visited with Miller in New York. Flood knew that baseball's reserve rule was a combination of agreements whereby major league teams refused to play any team that signed a player reserved by any other team and which forbade a player from signing with any team other than the team that owned the player's reserve. As a result, the private employers whose teams played one another were engaged in a series of agreements that restrained their employees from moving within the industry. In Flood's view, those agreements violated federal antitrust laws. Flood wanted to sue to overturn the reserve rule. Miller attempted to make Flood aware of the hardship he would face if he sued. Flood likely would be out of baseball, he would never get to be a coach, and his personal life would be an open book and the subject of inquiry. If he wanted to live in St. Louis, his business interests would be subject to disruption by August A. Busch, Jr., whom Flood also would be attacking. Most important, Miller told Flood what he already knew: Flood was making $90,000 playing baseball at age thirty-one. If he did not challenge Major League Baseball, he had a number of years ahead of him in which that salary would increase. Indeed, after Flood met with Miller, the Phillies offered him a salary in excess of $100,000 per year. Miller told him to think about it. Flood returned to St. Louis but called Miller about two weeks later: "Marvin, I'm going ahead with it. Can you help?" Flood appeared before the association's executive committee, and after questioning Flood about his motives, the union agreed unanimously to fund his legal fees. Through Marvin Miller, the association hired

Arthur Goldberg to represent Flood. Goldberg was no ordinary lawyer. He had been a general counsel for Miller's United Steelworkers, a secretary of labor in the Kennedy administration, a United States Supreme Court justice, and an ambassador to the United Nations.[10]

Flood v. Kuhn: *The Supreme Court Revisits the Reserve Rule*

Legal maneuvering in the case began with a letter from Curt Flood to baseball commissioner Bowie Kuhn in which Flood asked that the league declare him a free agent.[11] After the commissioner denied Flood's request, the subsequent lawsuit moved through the courts rapidly. Filed in January 1970, the case was heard in the home of Major League Baseball, New York City, in federal court for the Southern District of New York in May 1970. At trial, Curt Flood testified that he wanted the reserve system struck down. Flood's other witnesses, including former stars Jackie Robinson and Hank Greenberg, however, agreed that some type of modified reserve system was necessary to maintain competitive balance on the field.[12] The press agreed, and at least one reporter indicated that a victory for Flood would destroy baseball.[13] The trial court ruled against Flood in August 1970, finding that a 1922 precedent of the United States Supreme Court had determined that federal antitrust laws did not cover baseball.[14] The Second Circuit Court of Appeals upheld the trial court's decision in April 1971.[15] The United States Supreme Court heard the case on March 20, 1972.[16]

In affirming the opinions of the lower courts, the Supreme Court upheld its own precedent but also acknowledged the modern flaws of the prior cases.[17] Associate Justice Harry Blackmun was an avowed baseball fan. Indeed, in his office were displayed, among other baseball memorabilia, Wheaties cereal boxes to commemorate the two World Series championships of Blackmun's beloved Minnesota Twins.[18] Justice Blackmun wrote the opinion for the Court, and in it, he deferred to the 1922 Supreme Court decision in *Federal Baseball Club of Baltimore, Inc. v. National League of Professional Baseball Clubs*. In *Federal Baseball,* Justice Oliver Wendell Holmes, Jr., had set out his understanding of baseball's relationship to interstate commerce, a necessary element for antitrust law coverage. In analyzing baseball under federal antitrust laws, Justice Holmes recognized that (1) the various Major League Baseball teams were located in different cities; (2) the teams played against one another in games that generated revenue; (3) often, one team crossed a state line to play another; (4) when two teams won the respective championships of their leagues, the teams met in a World Series; (5) the game itself required constant traveling among league cities; and (6) this traveling was controlled and regulated by the game itself. Despite these attributes of interstate commerce, however, Justice Holmes found that the exhibition of baseball itself was not "trade or commerce" under then-existing standards of antitrust analysis. Additionally, the teams' traveling from one league city to another was not interstate commerce because it was incidental to the noncommercial exhibitions the teams gave.[19]

By 1972, however, the restricted definition of interstate commerce the Court had adopted in *Federal Baseball* did not apply to industry generally and certainly not to other professional sports. In a decision dealing with professional boxing in 1955, the Supreme Court began to enlarge its conception of interstate commerce.[20] In subsequent cases, the Court either decided or denied review of cases that placed the following sports under the umbrella of the antitrust laws: professional football, professional basketball, and professional golf.[21]

More to the point, the logic of Justice Blackmun's opinion in *Flood* was inconsistent. The essence of *Federal Baseball* was that conducting professional exhibitions through interlocking agreements between teams and players and between the teams themselves did not constitute interstate commerce. Therefore this set of arrangements, including the rules that empowered teams to maintain a hold on their players, was not subject to the antitrust laws.[22] Justice Blackmun acknowledged that, in a modern world, "[p]rofessional baseball is a business and it is engaged in interstate commerce."[23] He then declared that, by virtue of the court's holding in *Federal Baseball* and another decision in 1953 involving New York Yankee minor-leaguer George Toolson, Major League Baseball was not subject to federal antitrust law. He reaffirmed those decisions with the words "we adhere once again to *Federal Baseball* and *Toolson* and to their application to professional baseball."[24] But *Federal Baseball* held that the sport was exempt from antitrust law in large part because it was not an activity involved in interstate commerce.

Justice Blackmun observed that at various times between *Federal Baseball* and *Flood,* Congress had investigated the status of baseball in the context of the nation's antitrust laws, but at no time had Congress enacted legislation that subjected baseball to those laws. According to Justice Blackmun, Congress's inaction constituted a decision to affirm an exemption for baseball from the antitrust laws.[25]

Flood v. Kuhn's *Internal Inconsistencies and Historical Ignorance*

While Justice Blackmun's theory of an unspoken exemption under federal antitrust law sounds appealing, it missed the point of antitrust law. Under the applicable statute, all "combination[s] . . . in restraint of trade or commerce [are] illegal."[26] Thus, according to the statute, antitrust law covered baseball unless it was exempt. *Federal Baseball* exempted baseball on the theory that baseball was not interstate trade or commerce. The Supreme Court's holding in *Flood* that baseball was an activity in interstate commerce eliminated the exemption. If Congress did nothing, baseball would be subject to the antitrust laws, not the other way around.[27]

The internal inconsistencies in *Flood* were not the only problem in the opinion. There were signs, in other parts of the opinion, that Justice Blackmun had either forgotten or dismissed prior attempts by Major League Baseball players to make the most of their talent and earning power. Part I of *Flood* was labeled "The Game." In this portion of the opinion, Justice Blackmun traced the history of professional baseball. He mentioned, but did not discuss, professional baseball players' prior attempts to enhance their status as "laborers" for baseball's management. He described the Brotherhood of Professional Base Ball Players, the rise of the American League from the former Western Association, and the Federal League.[28] He also alluded to *Metropolitan Exhibition Co. v. Ewing,* a case handed down prior to *Federal Baseball,* but used it only to set out the common understanding of baseball's reserve rule.[29] He did not discuss the specifics of the case or, more important, its holding. Justice Blackmun also mentioned a number of players, reportedly a list of his favorites, with Ty Cobb heading the roster.[30] However, Justice Blackmun did not reference Cobb's attempts, from 1906 through the early 1920s to garner a higher salary from the Detroit Tigers.[31] Justice Blackmun noted the supremacy of the Chicago White Stockings when led by Albert G. Spalding and Adrian "Cap" Anson.[32] He omitted any reference to Spalding's desire to be a "free agent."[33]

The absence of these references is a flaw in Justice Blackmun's opinion. The opinion ignored the historical development of the reserve rule and related legal precedents that would have shown the reasonableness of Curt Flood's request of the court. Given his fondness for baseball's storied history, it is not surprising that Justice Blackmun began the segment of his opinion entitled "Legal Background" with *Federal Baseball.*[34] By doing so, Blackmun rendered the precedents he did not cite more important than those he did. He failed to mention most of the baseball cases prior to *Federal Baseball.*[35] In virtually all of them, players were able to keep or obtain their free agency. Only when one reviews these cases can one appreciate the extent of the missed opportunity that the decision in *Flood* represents.[36]

THE RESERVE RULE'S HISTORICAL CONTEXT

The owners' need to control players' professional services became a prime concern early in the history of professional baseball. In 1871, the amateur National Association gave way to a new organization, the National Association of Professional Baseball Players, a "professional" league. The owners soon saw the futility of relying on mutual good faith to prevent owners from trying to outbid one another for talented players. Indeed, Albert G. Spalding was proof. He and three other players bolted from their Boston team in 1875 and headed for Chicago, along with one of the league's best hitters, Cap Anson, from a Philadelphia team. Fearing repercussions from the free-agent signings of Spalding, his colleagues, and Anson, Chicago owner William Hulbert and Spalding formed a new league, creating the modern National League prior to the 1876 season.[37]

More than other observers at the time, Spalding conceptualized baseball in a way that dictated restraints on players. Spalding took the view that producing a baseball game was no different from producing a baseball bat. He disagreed with the players' contention that the public wanted to see the players, not the owners. He indicated that this logic was not based on "safe or sane business theory." Anticipating the formation of an activist Players Association almost 100 years later, Spalding recognized that the relationship between owners and players in Major League Baseball constituted the traditional labor conflict between management and worker.[38] Later he would expand on his view of this relationship: "Base Ball depends for results upon two interdependent divisions, the one to have absolute control and direction of the system, and the other to engage—always under the executive branch—in the actual work of production."[39] The original owners of the National League, then, saw themselves as monopolists.

Competition among National League owners for premium players generated the earliest policies restricting the players' free agency. Because almost all baseball contracts were for one season, owners, willing to outbid each other to garner a more competitive team, continued to provide pay raises to players who would leave one team for another. This practice, of course, raised baseball's labor costs and led, in 1879, to the first reserve rule.[40]

The National League owners' perception that a reserve rule would resolve problems of free agency was indicative of the extent to which they were able to focus on other problems affecting the popularity of their productions. Owner perception was, in part, reflective of the players' view that a reserve rule was not particularly objectionable because many players were pleased to be designated as the "franchise" players of their era. What created problems for the National

League were morality issues: gambling, Sunday baseball, and alcohol. In 1880, the league adopted a resolution preventing liquor sales at ballparks. When the Cincinnati Red Stockings club protested because it made a substantial portion of its revenue from the sale of beer, the club was ousted from the league.[41]

Other clubs, however, were not as concerned about alcohol sales at baseball games. Indeed, profits from the sale of ardent spirits and beer helped spur the rise of another league that sought to challenge the monopoly enjoyed by the National League owners. German immigrant Christian Friedrich Wilhelm von der Ahe settled in St. Louis and initially worked as a grocery clerk. Eventually, von der Ahe bought the store from his employer and added a tavern to the enterprise. While operating the tavern, he noticed that many of his late-afternoon patrons arrived fresh from watching a baseball game. For $1,800, von der Ahe purchased the American Association St. Louis team, nicknamed the "Browns" after the color of their uniforms. Along with a friend, Alfred H. Spink, von der Ahe put together a corporation to purchase Sportsman's Park as a place for the team to play. Von der Ahe became part of a reorganized American Association, a league that sought to challenge the National League. The association itself was known as the "Beer and Whiskey League" because four team owners had ties to the liquor industry.[42] The American Association's policies, rather than those of the National League, generated the first judicial decision in the United States dealing with the movement of baseball players from team to team. Charles Bennett, called by one of his managers the best catcher to ever live, played with the National League's Detroit team during 1882.[43] In August 1882, however, Bennett signed an option to play with Allegheny of the American Association for the 1883 season, agreeing that he would sign a contract with Allegheny by the end of October 1882. Bennett did not sign that contract. Instead, he threatened to sign again with Detroit. Allegheny sued, seeking to enjoin Bennett from signing with Detroit. The federal court refused to aid Allegheny, denying the team all relief, although the court was not clear on the exact reason for its decision.[44]

The import of *Bennett* was not the legal rationale the court employed to deny relief. Its significance lay in the result of the case; like Curt Flood, Charlie Bennett wanted to play for the team of his choice, and a Pennsylvania federal court affirmed his right to do so a full ninety years before the United States Supreme Court told Flood that he did not have that right.

In February 1883, a "Tripartite Agreement" brought labor stability to baseball. Owners in the American Association, the National League, and the Northwestern League agreed to respect the contract rights of each league. When one league banned a player, the other leagues agreed to do the same. As a result, on issues of "player control, territoriality and outside rivals," the three leagues, though separately operated, were united. With labor peace came financial success. Professional baseball enjoyed its most profitable season in 1883.[45]

The Tripartite Agreement did not, however, change players' desire for free agency. The Union Association, for example, was formed in 1883. A St. Louis team, the Maroons, was the class act of the league. The team won its first twenty games in a row, on its way to amassing a record of 94–19 during the regular season. It won the league championship by twenty-one games. How was it that the St. Louis Maroons became the "New York Yankees of the Union Association"? They did it the same way that the Yankees maintained success in the late twentieth and early twenty-first centuries; St. Louis bought all the best players as free agents. The Union Association did not have, or respect, any reserve of players by league teams.[46]

Following the demise of the Union Association, teams did not compete for players in the major leagues. In 1885, like true monopolists, major league owners imposed a salary cap of $2,000. In response, several New York Giants players, led by Columbia Law School graduate and Giants player John Montgomery Ward, organized the Brotherhood of Professional Base Ball Players. The organization increased its membership as the Giants traveled for games during the 1886 season. At the end of that season, while Ward and other players in the brotherhood were on a team traveling outside the United States, owners increased the restrictions on players by putting each player into one of five salary classifications.[47]

Instead of staging what would have been baseball's first strike, the players responded by organizing the Players' League in 1889. The teams in this league played in eight cities for one season in 1890.[48] The real import of the Players' League was the number of litigated cases it generated. In each of these suits, the player won relief from management. Surprisingly, in *Flood,* the Supreme Court mentioned only one of these cases.[49]

One of the Players' League cases, *Metropolitan Exhibition Co. v. Ward,* stemmed from a suit that the New York Giants filed against organizer John Montgomery Ward.[50] He was under contract with the Giants from April 1, 1889, through October 31, 1889, presumably the length of the 1889 season.[51] Ward's contract with the Giants had the following provisions: First, if Ward attempted to play for any other team during the term of his contract with the Giants, the team could expel him.[52] Second, if Ward attempted to play for any other team, the Giants could bring an action against him seeking damages for Ward's breach or an injunction preventing Ward from playing for another team.[53] Third, the Giants could terminate the contract at any time by giving Ward ten days' notice.[54] If the Giants did so, Ward was entitled to his pay for the ten-day period only if there was no cause for termination.[55] Finally, at the conclusion of the contract, the Giants could "reserve" Ward, at which point he would be obligated to his existing contract for another season.[56]

Ward played for the Giants for the contract year of 1889 but then proposed to play for Brooklyn of the Players' League for the 1890 season.[57] The Giants filed suit seeking to enjoin Ward from playing for another team.[58] The Giants claimed that after they reserved Ward, their prior contract with him renewed under the same terms and conditions.[59] Ward attempted to show the court the absence of logic in the Giants' argument. The court noted that if it enforced the Giants' reading of the agreement, "we have the spectacle presented of a contract which binds one party for a series of years, and the other party for 10 days." The court noted that this situation occurred because when a player signed a contract, he was bound for the current season and, through the reserve clause, bound for the next season. At the conclusion of that next season, the player would then be bound to a new reserve rule by the prior, reserved contract "and so on as long as [the Giants] elect." At the same time, the team could discharge the player at any time, with or without cause, by providing ten days' notice.[60]

In *Metropolitan Exhibition Co. v. Ward,* the New York Supreme Court provided the first detailed discussion of baseball's reserve rule, the same rule that Curt Flood would later challenge. First, the court did not agree with Ward's assumption that his 1890 contract, through the reserve rule, renewed all of the terms of the 1889 contract. But, if the 1890 contract did not contain the same terms as the 1889 contract, the court did not know what terms the new contract would contain and would not, therefore, enforce such an uncertain agreement. On the other hand, if the 1890 contract did incorporate all of the terms of the 1889 contract, then, the court noted, that contract would include the reserve rule. If this reasoning were true, the court agreed with Ward; the Giants would hold the right to his services in perpetuity while the team would have the right to dismiss Ward with ten days' notice.[61] At this point, the contract would lack fairness, each side could not equally enforce it, and, as a result, the Giants could not enforce it. The court thus denied injunctive relief to the Giants and dismissed the case.[62] John M. Ward was able to win what Curt Flood later sought. At the conclusion of his 1889 contract, Ward's obligations to the Giants were completed. He was free to negotiate with another team for the 1890 season. Two other Players' League cases that the Supreme Court did not mention or examine in *Flood* also were resolved in favor of the players' right to free agency.[63]

One of them was *Metropolitan Exhibition Co. v. Ewing.*[64] In *Ewing,* which also involved the New York Giants, the federal court acknowledged that the court in *Ward* had found player contracts so indefinite as to be unenforceable. The court attempted to determine if the totality of the agreements among the parties would provide clarity and express definite contract boundaries. Thus, *Ewing*'s importance comes in unraveling the various agreements that caused a player to be bound to one team under the reserve rule. First, the "National Agreement" among all the major league teams allowed teams to reserve up to fourteen players by October 10 of each year while forbidding any other team from signing a player so reserved. Additionally, the National Agreement required all player contracts to run from April 1 through October 31 of the current year. Finally, the National Agreement prevented a team from making an agreement for the subsequent year with any player until after October 20 of the year. As a result of these agreements, when the Giants elected to reserve Ewing on October 10, 1889, the National Agreement prevented him from negotiating with another team. The "reserve," however, could not set out the terms of Ewing's 1890 contract because, under the National Agreement, teams and players could not enter into new contracts until after October 20. The reserve rule, according to the court, coerced the player into negotiating only with his existing club for the period between October 10 and the end of the contract on October 31. The "reserve" served as no more than an option for that three-week period.[65] If that negotiation failed, and other teams had filled their rosters for the upcoming year, the player could be left without a team.[66] An assumption can be made that the ruling compelled Ewing to negotiate with the Giants under the terms of his contract, a valuable consideration.[67] But if those negotiations failed, the contract would not support injunctive relief against Ewing if he elected to pursue free agency and sign with another team.

After the Player's League ceased operation at the conclusion of the 1890 season, professional baseball at the major league level was free of labor unrest, at least as far as the courts were concerned, for about ten years.[68] But this situation changed when the current American League grew into major league status shortly after the beginning of the twentieth century—the result of an expansion and reorganization of the former minor Western League.[69] A player-jumping dispute involving the Philadelphia Athletics of this new league spurred the legal action. In five seasons, beginning in 1896, Napoleon Lajoie of the Philadelphia National League team never batted below .324 and was in the top three in the National League in slugging percentage in 1897, 1898, and 1900.[70] Following the 1900 season, Philadelphia American League owner Clark Griffith, "under cover of darkness . . . stole into Philadelphia" and signed Lajoie away from Philadelphia of the National League to Philadelphia of the American League. The National League Phillies sought to prevent Lajoie from playing for the cross-town American League A's. The trial court refused to grant injunctive relief prior to the 1901 season.[71]

Because Lajoie played for the A's during 1901, his case was different from those previously decided in which players sought to act as free agents; those cases had been resolved prior to a full baseball season. Part of the difference resulted from Lajoie's 1901 on-the-field performance. During that season, he batted .426 with an on-base percentage of .463 and a slugging percentage of .643. He won the Triple Crown, leading the league in batting average, slugging percentage, runs, hits, total bases, singles, doubles, home runs, runs batted in, runs created, extra base hits, and times on base.[72] When the Pennsylvania Supreme Court heard his appeal from the trial court after the 1901 season, Lajoie's own performance, one that distinguished him among his peers, made it impossible for him to succeed in court. What the National League team sought to do was to hold Lajoie to his existing contract. Under the law at the time, it could do so only if Lajoie was considered "unique." After leading in virtually all offensive statistical categories, Lajoie's 1901 performance prevented him from arguing that he was not a "unique" player.[73]

From a legal perspective, Lajoie's case also differed from previous cases in which players had sought to sever contractual ties to their employers.[74] In earlier cases, the player signed with a team in a new league after the contract with his existing team had ended. In those cases, the only thing binding the player to the team he sought to abandon was the reserve rule. It was this rule, which allowed a team to keep a player indefinitely, coupled with a team's ability to discharge a player on ten days' notice that created the inequity the courts had refused to support. Napoleon Lajoie, however, did not finish his stated contractual obligation with the National League Phillies at the end of 1900. In fact, Lajoie had signed a three-year contract. Without reference to the reserve clause, the Phillies had a right to renew Lajoie's contract for "six months, beginning April 15, 1901, and for a similar period in two successive years thereafter." This feature made the contract different from contracts considered by earlier courts. Lajoie had sold his services for a "stipulated period" of time. Indeed, the court acted equitably when it prevented Lajoie from selling those same services again to another buyer during the term of his existing contract. As a result, the court could and did enjoin Lajoie from playing for the A's during the term of his Phillies' contract.[75]

The National League described the Pennsylvania Supreme Court decision as a "great legal victory" and predicted that Lajoie would land in jail if he played for the rival A's.[76] This victory, however, proved hollow, for two reasons. First, American League Philadelphia owner Connie Mack sold Lajoie to Cleveland. When Lajoie's new Cleveland team came to Philadelphia to play Mack's team, police officers were unable to find Lajoie on the team train and could not, therefore, arrest him for violating the Pennsylvania court order. Apparently, Lajoie vacationed in Atlantic City while his team was in Philadelphia. An attempt to enforce the Pennsylvania order in an Ohio court was unsuccessful. Second, other courts ruled that the decision in *Lajoie* was not binding on them.[77] For example, in *American Base Ball and Athletic Exhibition Co. v. Harper*, a case involving a St. Louis player, the court refused to find pitcher Jack Harper unique and thereby denied injunctive relief.[78]

Ultimately, talks between the National League and the American League led to an agreement between the two early in 1903.[79] With the two leagues unified, player free agency stopped for about ten years. Following the formation of the Federal League in 1914—a league that had started in 1912 as the Columbian League with franchises in St. Louis, Cleveland, and Chicago—players in the league scored another string of reserve-rule legal victories. During its brief three years, the Federal League employed eighty-one players from the American and National leagues, eighteen of whom breached major league reserve rules to play for the Federals.[80] The Federal League produced three cases involving players challenging the rule. These cases generated precedents similar to those produced by earlier leagues. In *Weegham v. Killefer*[81] and *American League Baseball Club of Chicago v. Chase*,[82] the courts refused to enjoin a player from choosing the team for which he wanted to play, thereby allowing him to choose a team willing to pay for his services.

Major League owners, however, ostensibly did win one Federal League case.[83] Armando Marsans began his baseball career with Cincinnati of the National League in 1911. He batted .261, .317, and .297 over the 1911, 1912, and 1913 seasons, primarily playing in the outfield. In 1914, he played thirty-six games with Cincinnati and then jumped to the St. Louis Terriers of the Federal League. He played nine games with the Terriers.[84] At that point, Cincinnati obtained an injunction against further play by Marsans with the Terriers. The court indicated that Marsans had received salary for part of the term of his contract, thereby providing consideration for it. The court found that Marsans's absence would harm Cincinnati, thereby justifying an injunction. Thus the court was willing to enjoin Marsans but required Cincinnati to provide a $13,000 bond as "security to pay any damages that may result to" Marsans as a result of the injunction.[85] While Major League Baseball won the court case, Cincinnati did not keep its outfielder. Records indicate that Marsans played the 1915 season with the St. Louis Federals.[86] Legal records also indicate that the court dismissed the injunction against Marsans in 1915.[87]

By any scorekeeping mechanism, the players were consistent winners before 1915. In all but two cases the courts ruled in favor of the players who sought employment with a new team. Even in the remaining two, however, the owners did not win. In *Marsans,* the court ruled in favor of Cincinnati, but Marsans still was able to play for his chosen team. In *Lajoie,* while the owners won, the case was not about the traditional reserve rule. Rather, it was a very straightforward breach of an ongoing contract case. Even if the reserve rule was involved in the case, Lajoie was able to choose his league when the courts refused to enforce Philadelphia's injunction.

The first suit to claim that the reserve rule violated federal antitrust rather than state contract law arose from the Federal League in 1915, but it did not feature a player as the plaintiff.[88] It followed on the heels of *American League Baseball Club of Chicago v. Chase,* a New York State case in which the court called baseball a common-law monopoly.[89] Perhaps as a result, the Federal League sued the National and American leagues in January 1915. The Federals alleged that the major leagues maintained an illegal monopoly violating federal antitrust law. The case was filed in the Northern District of Illinois and assigned to federal trial judge Kennesaw Mountain Landis. Landis was known for his "trust-busting" decisions, including one in which he had fined Standard Oil $29 million dollars.[90]

The judge was also a baseball fan. At a hearing on January 20, 1915, he asked the parties if they wanted him to prevent the players from going to spring training. He indicated that he did not think that baseball players were laborers. He asserted that any threat to Major League Baseball was, in his opinion, a threat to an American institution. But Landis knew that any decision he rendered would go against the major leagues, and he appears to have been unwilling to do that. He therefore did the next best thing: he did nothing, refusing to render a decision. Teams from the Federal, American, and National leagues all went to spring training, and the 1915 season came and went, with significant financial losses. For example, in 1900, the St. Louis Cardinals drew approximately 380,000 fans, and the team made a profit. The 1914 Cardinals, however, pulled in 600,000 fans and had no profit to show. Throughout the 1915 season, talks continued between the two factions. Ultimately, the owner of the Chicago Federal League team purchased that city's American League team, and in St. Louis, the Federal League team owner purchased the American League Browns. After that, the Federal League collapsed, and by December 1915, it no longer existed. At that point, Judge Landis acted, dismissing the antitrust case.[91]

That case is not the one cited by Justice Blackmun in the *Flood* opinion, however. The decision recalled in *Flood* was from a lawsuit filed after the

Federal League had gone out of business. The Baltimore Federals were excluded from the 1915 settlement.[92] As the sole remaining Federal League team, it stopped operating because there were no teams to play.[93] As a result, approximately a month after Judge Landis dismissed the Federal League's antitrust case, and three months after the Federal League had ceased to exist, the Baltimore Federals filed a second antitrust action. That case was tried and resulted in a verdict in favor of Baltimore's owner for $80,000, which was trebled under the antitrust laws to $240,000.[94]

Reversing the trial court, the District of Columbia Court of Appeals formulated the reasoning that Justice Holmes and the United States Supreme Court would later embrace.[95] First, the court of appeals found that baseball was not trade or commerce as was necessary for protection under the antitrust statute. Trade or commerce required "the transfer of something, whether it be persons, commodities, or intelligence, from one place or person to another." While baseball players and teams moved from one place to another for games, the games themselves all took place in one location and were thus "local," with no transfer of anything to fans who watched, other than enjoyment.[96] Second, even assuming that baseball involved some trade or commerce, the court found that interstate travel was not involved. Under then-existing interpretations of antitrust law, the statute only covered activity that had a "direct" effect on interstate commerce. The court found the reserve rule worked more to "foster the trade and increase the business of those who make and operate" baseball and thus did not directly affect the interstate movement of players or teams. As a result, the court overturned the trial court in a decision published almost five years after the league had collapsed.[97]

When the case reached the United States Supreme Court, Justice Holmes noted that the lower court's decision went "to the root of the case." The Supreme Court then affirmed the court of appeals' judgment.[98]

Flood v. Kuhn

A JUDICIAL SHORTCOMING BUT PRACTICAL SUCCESS

A decision rendered six and one-half years after the demise of the Federal League served as primary precedent in Justice Blackmun's "Legal Background" in *Flood.* In using this focal point, Justice Blackmun omitted any reference to the numerous decisions, stretching back almost ninety years, in which players had been allowed to select their own teams. He glossed over the fact that *Federal Baseball* was not a suit one league brought against other leagues for exercising unlawful monopoly control over their players via the reserve rule—that Judge Landis had dismissed. Instead, one disgruntled owner filed the case after all of the other owners with whom he had enjoyed a contractual relationship had abandoned their common agreement. Finally, Justice Blackmun failed to explore the implications of the fact that *Federal Baseball* was not about the claims of a single player, as was *Flood.*[99] Consequently, any discussion of the reserve rule by the court of appeals, or by Justice Holmes, was only to reference the common agreements among the owners and the teams. Because it involved an owner, *Federal Baseball* could not have had any bearing on the rights of a player within the league. Thus, the facts of *Federal Baseball* were not precedential to *Flood.*

The victory of major league owners in *Flood* might appear to have constituted a complete vindication for the reserve system, then almost one hundred years old. The Supreme Court told both owners and players that they could not challenge the system under federal antitrust laws. The decision, however, did little to solidify the position of the owners. At the time of the decision, there was already a collective bargaining agreement in place between the owners and the players. The players' union was their exclusive bargaining agent. Consequently, any issue related to wages, hours, or working conditions was subject to mandatory collective bargaining between the owners and the union. It is unlikely that Curt Flood or any other player could as an individual take up a dispute over the reserve rule.[100] The owners pointed this fact out in *Flood,* but the Supreme Court ignored the issue because none of the parties had raised it in the courts below—by virtue of an agreement not to do so pending the disposition of the case itself.[101] After the conclusion of *Flood,* a collective bargaining agreement adopted in 1973 once more opened discussion on the issue of the reserve rule.[102]

If Flood lost and if the reserve rule was not even on the table when his case was tried, why, more than thirty-five years after the fact, do we care about one center fielder and his losing battle with Major League Baseball? Flood did not compare himself to Dred Scott, the slave whose demand for freedom was heard in the federal courthouse near Busch Stadium. The comparison nonetheless remains.[103] It was John Montgomery Ward, the Hall of Fame player and lawyer-organizer of the Players' League, who first compared professional baseball players to slaves: "Like a fugitive slave law, the reserve rule denies [the player] a harbor or a livelihood, and carries him back, bound and shackled, to the club from which he attempted to escape."[104] Dissenting in *Flood* years later, Justice Thurgood Marshall also noted the similarity: "To non-athletes it might appear that [Flood] was virtually enslaved by the owners of major league baseball clubs who bartered among themselves for his services."[105]

The aptness of the comparison does not end there. "The Dred Scott decision served as an eye-opener to Northerners who believed that slavery was tolerable."[106] The decision solidified the positions of the North and of the South "to the point where both were willing to fight over the issue."[107] During Curt Flood's trial challenging the reserve rule, no active major league player was willing to testify on his behalf.[108] Flood's case, however, heightened awareness among his fellow players to the point that they too were willing to fight over the issue. As one of Flood's teammates, Tim McCarver expressed it, "there's no doubt in my mind that Curt's action got the ball rolling toward freeing players from the shackles of the ninety-year clause that could tie them to a team against their wills."[109]

The *Flood* decision exposed the antagonism between owners and players that had existed for decades behind the facade of baseball as America's national pastime. Curt Flood's resolve in filing suit thus "raised the consciousness" of fans and players alike and forced not only those in charge of the Players Association, but all players to reassess their complacency about the reserve rule. The lawsuit also forced the hand of owners. The owners wanted baseball's governing structure to appear impartial. When Commissioner Bowie Kuhn denied Flood's request to become a free agent, the owners wished Kuhn to seem a neutral arbitrator. His standing as an employee of the owners made that impossible. As a result, it may have been league lawyers who said to the owners: " [I]f we're going to make this argument that we don't need antitrust law, we've got to at least be able to say we have impartial arbitration of what the contracts mean." Flood's case prompted owners, during negotiations on a 1970 collective bargaining agreement, to agree to neutral grievance arbitration.[110]

From the perspective of the players, neutral grievance arbitration may have been their most important labor victory.[111] After playing out the option year of their respective contracts with the Los Angeles Dodgers and the Baltimore Orioles in 1975, Andy Messersmith and Dave McNally each filed a grievance under the collective bargaining agreement to become free agents.[112] In December of that year, the league's neutral arbitrator declared both players free agents.[113] Messersmith and McNally won the right to choose their own teams—a right denied to Curt Flood but enjoyed by many players who would follow him and make the most of the freedom he had helped to secure for them.[114]

CONCLUSION

From 1958 through the fall of 1969, Curt Flood proved his strength, patrolling center field for the Cardinals.[115] In many seasons during those years, he was the Cardinals lead-off hitter, setting the table for his colleagues.[116] He was a member of three all-star teams and won successive Gold Gloves from 1963 through 1969.[117] When Flood referred to himself as a "slave" in the years after he was traded to the Phillies in the fall of 1969, many commentators criticized him and pointed out that no slave had ever earned the five-figure income that he received that year.[118] Flood responded: "Only the totalitarian-minded will believe that high pay excuses virtual slavery."[119] He knew he likely would lose his lawsuit. "And he went ahead anyway, because he was a very principled man. You could not shake him."[120] Curt Flood did not believe that baseball should be a business exempt from the normal operation of labor law. "After the courts rule that the present reserve system is unlawful, the employers will be obligated to do what they should have done years ago. They will sit down with the players and negotiate reasonable conditions of employment."[121] Flood was right and not just in his own case. Players like Andy Messersmith and Dave McNally would show that what Flood wanted really did make common sense. After a neutral arbitrator told the owners in 1976 that the reserve rule was wrong, the owners had to sit down and meaningfully negotiate with players.[122]

Flood died in 1997, twenty-five years after he lost his suit against Major League Baseball.[123] He did not get to see Congress adopt the Curt Flood Act, which declared that the business of baseball was, indeed, subject to the antitrust laws, at least in the absence of a collective bargaining agreement.[124] But he did get to see the Major League Baseball Players Association rise as the preeminent union in professional sports—thanks in part to his bravery and his insistence on standing up for players' rights.

NOTES

This essay appeared in an earlier iteration as "Curt Flood and the Show-Me Spirit" in the *Missouri Law Review* 77 (Winter 2012), 9–39. The editor thanks the *Law Review's* editor, Jillian Dent, and James Devine's son, Joshua, for their permission to print the essay in its current form.

1. Curt Flood, with Richard Carter, *The Way It Is* (New York: Trident Press, 1971), 19, 21–27, 31–33.

2. Flood, *Way,* 37–40, 44.

3. Quote from "Curt Flood Statistics and History," *Baseball-Reference.com.* http://www.baseball-reference.com/players/f/floodcu01.shtml. Flood believed the Reds did not want to field the all-black outfield of Frank Robinson, Curt Flood, and Vada Pinson; Flood, *Way*, 47, 76–79. His position as center fielder of the St. Louis Cardinals did not stop the racism directed at Flood, even in his own town. Marvin Miller, *A Whole Different Ball Game* (Chicago: Ivan R. Dee, 1991, reprint,

2004), 172; *Flood v. Kuhn,* 407 U.S. 258, 264 (1972) (hereafter, *Flood).* This essay contains citations to the same case as it progressed through lower courts; where those opinions are cited, the court is also identified.

4. Flood, *Way,* 86–90, 94; Peter Golenbock, *The Spirit of St. Louis: A History of the St. Louis Cardinals and Browns* (New York: Spike, 2000), 484–86.

5. Flood, *Way,* 171–74, 181; "History of the Major League Baseball Players Association," Major League Baseball Players Association. http://mlbplayers.mlb.com/pa/info/history.jsp; Miller, *Different Ball Game,* 97, 166–67. The collective bargaining agreement covered both the 1968 and 1969 seasons.

6. Flood, *Way,* 172. At least one source indicated that "[p]rofanity [from Busch] rattled the windows and turned the air blue." Flood's salary by year is set out by the Supreme Court in *Flood* at 265 (quotation, 100).

7. Flood, *Way,* 86, 172–75, 181–84. The text of Mr. Busch's remarks appears in the appendix of *Way,* 228–36; other sources note that Cepeda was traded to the Braves for Joe Torre on March 17, 1969, five days before Busch addressed the team. "Orlando Cepeda Statistics & History," Baseball-Reference.com, http://www.baseball-reference.com/c/cepedor01.shtml.

8. "Curt Flood Statistics," 12; "Dick Allen Statistics & History," Baseball-Reference.com. http://www.baseball-reference.com/a/allendi01.shtml; Flood, *Way,* 184–85. Marvin Miller's account notes that Flood found out in a telephone call from a newspaper reporter, not from the Cardinals, Miller, *Different Ball Game,* 172.

9. Flood, *Way,* 187–93; Flood's parents, despite working multiple jobs, clung to the same American dream, but for their children. "Their goal was to raise children upright and industrious enough to qualify for the good life." The dream was not wealth, but "a decent job, [a] loving family, [and a] nicer home on a nicer street," p. 23.

10. Ibid., 134, 190–95; Miller, *Different Ball Game,* 181, 184–88 "Arthur J. Goldberg: Biographical Note," Pritzker Legal Research Center. http: //goldberg.law.northwestern.edu/mainpages/bio.htm. Flood thought he had "the most famous lawyer in the world." Flood, *Way,* 194.

11. Flood, *Way,* 194–95; Miller, *Different Ball Game,* 190–92, 284–85.

12. *Flood,* 316 F. Supp. 271, 275–276 n.14 (S.D.N.Y. 1970), *aff'd,* 443 F.2d 264 (2d Cir. 1971), *aff'd,* 407 U.S. 258 (1972).

13. Golenbock, *The Spirit of St. Louis,* 508.

14. *Flood,* 316 F. Supp. at 276, 284-85 (citing *Fed. Baseball Club of Balt., Inc. v. Nat'l League of Prof'l Baseball Clubs,* 259 U.S. 200, 209 (1922) 276 n.14, (S.D.N.Y. 1970), *aff'd,* 443 F.2d 264 (2d Cir. 1971), *aff'd,* 407 U.S. 258 (1972).

15. *Flood,* 443 F.2d 264, 266 (2d Cir. 1971), *aff'd,* 407 U.S. 258 (1972). The court of appeals did, however, note that the 1922 ruling in *Federal Baseball* did not constitute a strong precedent in contemporary times. See *id.*

16. *Flood,* 407 U.S. at 258 (1972).

17. *Flood*, 407 U.S. at 269–82.

18. Edward Lazarus, "Blackmun, Baseball, and the Mel Ott Bat: A Justice with a Passion for the Game and the Country That Invented It" *FindLaw* (November 15, 2001), http://writ.news.findlaw.com/lazarus/20011115.html.

19. 259 U.S. at 208–9.

20. *United States v. Int'l Boxing Club of N.Y.*, 348 U.S. 236 (1955). Beginning in 1955 with a non-baseball case, *United States v. Shubert*, 348 U.S. 222 (1955), the Court's rhetoric began to change. The Court held that neither *Federal Baseball* nor *Toolson v. N. Y. Yankees*, 346 U.S. 356 (1953) (per curiam), granted immunity from antitrust to any business that presented local exhibitions. *Id.* at 227. Rather, the Court indicated that the extent of interstate connection had to be considered. *Id.* at 230. The same day the Court decided *Schubert*, it found that individuals promoting professional boxing contests were also subject to the antitrust laws, *Int'l Boxing Club*, 348 U.S. at 244–45. Separating boxing from baseball drew a vigorous dissent by Justice Frankfurter, who noted the incongruity in the Court's apparent separation of baseball from other sports. See *id.* at 248 (Frankfurter, J., dissenting). Justice Blackmun, in *Flood*, makes reference to this dissent. *Flood*, 407 U.S. at 277.

21. *Flood*, 407 U.S. at 282–83; *Haywood v. Nat'l Basketball Ass'n*, 401 U.S. 1204, 1205 (1971) (basketball); *Radovich v. Nat'l Football League*, 352 U.S. 445, 451–52 (1957) (football); *Deesen v. Prof'l Golfers' Ass'n*, 358 F.2d 165 (9th Cir 1966) (golf), *cert. denied*, 385 U.S. 846 (1966).

22. 259 U.S. at 207–9; *Flood*, 407 U.S. at 269–70.

23. *Flood*, 407 U.S. at 282.

24. *Flood*, 407 U.S. at 283–85. In *Toolson*, the Supreme Court simply reaffirmed its *Federal Baseball* precedent, indicating that Congress could change whether antitrust laws applied to baseball. See *id.* at 357. Two justices vigorously dissented, arguing that whatever had been true about "interstate commerce" when *Federal Baseball* was decided, baseball was now an activity in "interstate commerce," *id.* at 357–58 (Burton, J., dissenting).

25. *Id.* at 283–84. Justice Blackmun calls Congress's activity "positive inaction," *id.* Legislative proposals concerning baseball are discussed, *id.* at 280–82.

26. 15 U.S.C. § 1 (2006).

27. As Justice Douglas, dissenting in *Flood*, points out: *Federal Baseball*, in 1922, was decided when "the Court had a narrow, parochial view of commerce." From about 1930 through the 1960s, that view changed. By the time of the decision in *Flood*, with baseball's dependence on radio and television and with national advertisers, baseball could hardly be called a local exhibition. *Id.* at 287. Congress, according to Justice Douglas, has the power to "to reach all phases of the vast operations of our national industrial system," 407 U.S. at 286–87 (Douglas, J., dissenting).

28. *Id.* at 260–64.

29. 42 F. 198 (S.D.N.Y. 1890).

30. *Id.* at 259 n.1, 262–63. Regarding Justice Blackmun's accidental omission of one of his favorites, Hall-of-Famer Mel Ott, see Lazarus, *Blackmun.*

31. See James R. Devine, "The Legacy of Albert Spalding, the Holdouts of Ty Cobb, Joe DiMaggio, and Sandy Koufax/Don Drysdale, and the 1994–95 Strike: Baseball's Labor Disputes are as Linear as the Game" *Akron Law Review* 31, no.1 (1997): 5–14.

32. *Flood*, 407 U.S. at 261.

33. Devine, "Legacy," 41.

34. *Flood*, 407 U.S. at 269. The Legal Background is Part IV of the opinion. Following his discussion of baseball history, Justice Blackmun discusses Curt Flood and his career (Part II) and the litigation leading up to the Supreme Court case (Part III), i*d.* at 264–69.

35. *Id.*

36. Even Marvin Miller was taken in. He thought early cases were all against the players. "[C]ourts have always backed the owners . . . ," Golenbock, *Spirit of St. Louis,* 510.

37. See James R. Devine, "Baseball's Labor Wars in Historical Context: The 1919 Chicago White Sox as a Case-Study in Owner-Player Relations" *Marquette Sports Law Review* 5 (1994), 6–10 and n. 33; see also David Pietruzsa, *Major Leagues: The Formation, Sometimes Absorption and Mostly Inevitable Demise of 18 Professional Baseball Organizations, 1871 to Present* (Jefferson, NC: MacFarland, 1991), 23–25.

38. Devine, "Baseball's Labor Wars," 9–11, nn35, 37.

39. Albert G. Spalding, Samm Coombs, and Robert West, *Base Ball: America's National Game: Historic Facts Concerning the Beginning Evolution, Development and Popularity of* (San Francisco, CA: Halo Books, 1991), 169.

40. Devine, "Baseball's Labor Wars," 12–14. The "reserve rule" was actually a series of agreements by owners: 1) Each team was permitted to "reserve" a certain number of players, originally five and, by 1903, all of the players; 2) No other team would attempt to sign a player "reserved" by one of its competitors; and 3) No team would play a team that signed a previously "reserved" player. *Id.* Eventually, these rules were augmented by another provision, one that prohibited a team from entering into a contract with any player that did not contain a right to reserve that player. See *id.* at 47.

41. Pietrusza, *Major Leagues,* 36–37, 42–46.

42. Devine, "Baseball's Labor Wars," 14; Pietrusza, *Major Leagues,* 67; "Chris von der Ahe," http://www.baseball-reference.com/bullpen/Chris_von_der_Ahe; Golenbock, *Spirit of St. Louis,* 12–13, 15–16. The league was inspired by a former player turned bartender, i*d.* at 62, 67. Additionally, the league was willing to sell alcohol at league games, which was fine with von der Ahe, who saw baseball as a way to increase beer sales.

43. Pietrusza, *Major Leagues,* 73–74.

44. *Allegheny Base-Ball Club v. Bennett,* 14 F. 257, 257–60 (C.C.W.D. Pa. 1882).

45. Pietrusza, *Major Leagues,* 78–80; Devine, "Baseball's Labor Wars," 17.

46. Pietrusza, *Major Leagues,* 81–82, 88; Richard Leech, "The Evolution of Baseball in St. Louis. Sportman's Park." http://www.collectsportsonline.com/earlystl.htm. The source of the statistics is "1884 Union Association Team Statistics and Standings," Baseball-Reference.com. http://www.baseball-reference.com/leagues/UA/1884.shtml. (showing the nearest team in the standings 21 games behind the St. Louis Maroons).

47. Pietrusza, *Major Leagues,* 99–100; Devine, "Baseball's Labor Wars," 19–20.

48. Pietrusza, *Major Leagues,* 104–5, 121.

49. *Flood,* 407 U.S. at 259 n.1. The court mentions *Metropolitan Exhibition Co. v. Ewing* only to show the contents of the reserve rule. There is no mention of the fact that Ewing won his case.

50. 24 Abb. N. Cas. 393, 394–95 (N.Y. Sup. Ct. 1890); Roger I. Abrams, *Legal Bases: Baseball and the Law* (Philadelphia: Temple University Press, 1998), 18–19; Robert M. Jarvis and Phyllis Coleman, "Early Baseball Law," *American Journal of Legal History* 45 (2001), 126 n.58 (The footnote describes a publishing quirk as to the opinion written by Justice Morgan Joseph O'Brien in *Ward.* Due to this quirk, the opinion was not published in West's *New York Supplement,* therefore this Article will cite to the case as found in Diossy's *Abbott's New Cases* on Westlaw).

51. *Ward,* 24 Abb. N. Cas. at 407.

52. *Id.* at 395 n.a1 (detailing the provisions of the contract).

53. *Id.*

54. *Id.* at 415.

55. *Id.*

56. *Id.* at 412.

57. See *id.* at 397–98.

58. Pietruza, *Major Leagues,* 116.

59. Devine, "Baseball's Labor Wars," 22. Ward called the blacklisting of players who violated the reserve rule "tyrannical," *id.* at 19 n.78.

60. *Ward,* 24 Abb. N. Cas. at 414–15.

61. *Id.* at 414–19. In 1970, former Yankee pitcher Jim Bouton pointed out both the severity and the absurdity of this reading of the reserve clause during negotiations toward a Collective Bargaining Agreement. Miller, *Different Ball Game,* 193.

62. *Ward,* 24 Abb. N. Cas. at 419 n.a1; *see* Jarvis & Coleman, *supra* note 196, at 126 n.58.

63. *Id.* The first case involved Bill Hallman, a utility infielder, who signed an agreement in October 1888 with Philadelphia of the National League to play for the 1889 season. *Phila. Ball Club v. Hallman,* 8 Pa. C. C. 57, 58, 61 (Pa. Ct. C.P. 1890). Regardless of the reserve rule, he signed a contract with Philadelphia of the Players' League for the following season. *Id.* at 61–63.

64. 42 F. 198 (S.D.N.Y. 1890). William "Buck" Ewing was considered the premiere catcher of the early twentieth century. See *Buck Ewing Statistics & History, Baseball-Reference.com*, http://www.baseball-reference.com/e/ewingbu01.shtml.

65. *Id.* at 201–5. In legal terms, the option was "merely a contract to make a contract if the parties can agree."

66. *Id.*

67. Pietrusza, *Major Leagues,* 117.

68. Ibid, 124–26.

69. Ibid., 145–65; see also Devine, "Baseball's Labor Wars," 30–33.

70. *Nap Lajoie Statistics & History*, Baseball-Reference.com, http://www.baseball-reference.com/l/lajoina01.shtml.

71. See *id.* Devine, "Baseball's Labor Wars," 34. The court denied relief for the same "mutuality" reasons addressed by earlier courts and because the court found that Lajoie was not so extraordinary as to justify equitable relief. *Phila. Ball Club v. Lajoie,* 51 A. 973, 973 (Pa. 1902).

72. *Lajoie Statistics & History.*

73. *Lajoie*, 51 A. at 973–74. The Pennsylvania Supreme Court found that the trial court had been too restrictive in considering "uniqueness," *id.* Today, all professional athletes are considered unique. See *Cent. N.Y. Basketball, Inc. v. Barnett*, 181 N.E.2d 506, 517 (Ohio Ct. C.P. 1961).

74. See, *e.g., Metro. Exhibition Co. v. Ewing,* 42 F. 198, 200–204 (S.D.N.Y. 1890); *Metro. Exhibition Co. v. Ward,* 24 Abb. N. Cas. 393, *passim.* (N.Y. Sup. Ct. 1890).

75. *Lajoie*, 51 A. at 973–76.

76. Pietrusza, 164 (internal quotation marks omitted).

77. Ibid., 164–65.

78. See *Am. Base Ball & Athletic Exhibition Co. v. Harper,* 54 Cent. L.J. 449 (St. Louis Cir. Ct. 1902). The National League lost another case as well. *Brooklyn Baseball Club v. McGuire,* 116 F. 782, 783 (C.C.E.D. Pa. 1902). James Thomas "Deacon" McGuire was primarily a catcher, who started play with Toledo in the American Association in 1884, later moving to Brooklyn of the National League. See *Deacon McGuire Statistics & History, Baseball-Reference.com,* http://www.baseball-reference.com/m/mcguide01.shtml. McGuire then "jumped . . . to the Detroit Tigers" prior to the 1902 season, *id.* Brooklyn sought an injunction to prevent McGuire from playing for Detroit. See *McGuire*, 116 F. at 782–83; *Deacon McGuire Statistics & History, supra*. Because the team could terminate the contract with ten days' notice, specific performance was unavailable to McGuire. See *McGuire*, 116 F. at 782–83. The court therefore rendered it unavailable to the team and denied an injunction, *id.* at 783.

79. Pietruza, *Major Leagues,* 178–81.

80. Devine, "Baseball's Labor Wars," 41–49 and n.185. The Federal League declared itself a major league in 1914, *id.* at 42. It then competed directly with major league teams in Brooklyn, Pittsburgh, Chicago, and St. Louis, *id.*

81. 215 F. 168 (W.D. Mich. 1914). Bill Killefer, a catcher, played the 1913 season with Philadelphia of the National League. *Bill Killefer Statistics & History*, Baseball-Reference.com, http://www.baseball-reference.com/players/k/killebi01. shtml. At the end of the contract, Philadelphia sought to reserve Killefer for the 1914 season. *Killefer* 215 F. at 170. Instead, Killefer signed with the Chicago Federal League team for the three seasons of 1914, 1915, and 1916 for a salary of $5,833.33 per year. *Id.* Apparently using this salary as leverage, Killefer then again signed with Philadelphia for the same three years for $6,500 per year, *id.* The court refused injunctive relief to all of the parties, thereby allowing Killefer to select his team, *id.* at 173.

82. 149 N.Y.S. 6 (N.Y. Special Term 1914). Known as "Prince Hal," Chase was regarded as one of the preeminent first basemen of his era. *Id.* at 8; see *Hal Chase Statistics & History*, Baseball-Reference.com, http://www.baseball-reference.com/players/c/chaseha01.shtml. Already under contract with Chicago of the American League in June, 1914, Chase gave his team ten days' written notice that he was leaving. *Chase*, 149 N.Y.S. at 7–8. So happy was Buffalo of the Federal League to have Chase that they sponsored "Hal Chase Day" upon his arrival. Devine, "Baseball's Labor Wars," 44–45. The New York court refused Chicago's request for an injunction to prevent Chase from playing for Buffalo, thereby allowing Chase to be a free agent. *Chase*, 149 N.Y.S. at 20. For the first time the court in *Chase* raised a new issue: whether equity could be used to enforce "an agreement which is a part of a general plan having for its object the maintenance of a monopoly," *id.* The court said that it would "not extend its aid to further the purposes and practices of an unlawful combination." *id.* at 17.

83. *Cincinnati Exhibition Co. v. Marsans*, 216 F. 269, 270 (E.D. Mo. 1914).

84. *Armando Marsans Statistics & History*," Baseball-Reference.Com. http://www.baseball-reference.com/m/marsaar01.shtml.

85. *Marsans*, 216 F. at 269–70. This injunction was issued on July 1, 1914, obviously in the middle of the baseball season, *id.* at 269. Thus, this is consistent with the actions of Hal Chase in giving Chicago notice in mid-season. See *supra* note 268.

86. *A Marsans Statistics & History*.

87. Devine, "Baseball's Labor Wars," 48; see *also* Eric Enders, Armando Marsans, *The Baseball Biography Project*, http://bioproj.sabr.org/bioproj.cfm?a=v&v=1&pid=8838&bid=971.

88. Devine, "Baseball's Labor Wars," 48–49.

89. 149 N.Y.S. 6 (N.Y. Special Term 1914). In the lawsuit by Chicago, Chase was represented by Federal League lawyers. See "Baseball's Labor Wars," *supra* note 138, at 44.

90. Pietrusza, *Major Leagues*, 235.

91. Ibid., 235–36; Devine, "Baseball's Labor Wars," 49.

92. Pietrusza, *Major Leagues*, 248–49.

93. *Nat'l League of Prof'l Baseball Clubs v. Fed. Baseball Club of Balt., Inc.*, 269 F. 681, 682 (D.C. Cir. 1921), *aff'd*, 259 U.S. 200.

94. Devine, "Baseball's Labor Wars," 49 & n. 229; *Nat'l League of Prof'l Baseball Clubs*, 269 F. at 682.

95. *Compare Nat'l League of Prof'l Baseball Clubs* with *Fed. Baseball Club of Balt., Inc.*, 259 U.S. at 208–9.

96. *Nat'l League of Prof'l Baseball Clubs*, 269 F. at 684–85. Further, the travel of the players from one venue to another, even across state lines, was merely incidental to the otherwise local game. See *id.* This was consistent with the opinion of the court in *Chase*. See *id.* at 686 (citing *Am. League Baseball Club of Chi. v. Chase*, 149 N.Y.S. 6 (N.Y. Special Term 1914)). In *Chase*, the court reviewed the status of baseball under the antitrust laws, finding that baseball players were not commodities but rather offered a service. *Id.*; *Chase*, 149 N.Y.S. at 16. The court also found that interstate "commerce" required the sale of a commodity: "Baseball is an amusement, a sport, a game . . . and it is not a commodity or an article of merchandise subject to the regulation of Congress on the theory that it is interstate commerce," *Chase*, 149 N.Y.S. at 1617. The court also noted, however, that baseball was clearly a common-law combination in restraint of trade. See *id.*

97. *Id.* at 684–88.

98. *Fed. Baseball Club of Balt., Inc. v. Nat'l League of Prof'l Baseball Clubs*, 259 U.S. 200, 208–9 (1922).

99. *Flood*, 407 U.S. at 269–70.

100. Abrams, *Legal Bases*, 81–83; Miller, *Different Ball Game*, 94–98 (describing the first collective bargaining agreement that covered the 1968–69 Major League Baseball seasons and the 1970 agreement that was in place when Flood brought his case), 214.

101. *Flood*, 407 U.S. at 295 (Marshall, J., dissenting). This is not quite true. The issue of the reserve clause being a mandatory subject of collective bargaining was initially raised as a defense to Flood's antitrust claim, but, by agreement between owners and players, the issue was removed from the suit. See *Kansas City Royals Baseball Corp. v. Major League Baseball Players Ass'n*, 532 F.2d 615, 624–26 (8th Cir. 1976); Miller, *Different Ball Game*, 97–98.

102. *Kansas City Royals Baseball Corp.*, 532 F.2d at 618–19.

103. Flood, *Way*, 14 (mentioning that the St. Louis Arch is not far from where Dred Scott's case was tried).

104. Pietrusza, *Major Leagues*, 102.

105. See *Flood*, 407 U.S. at 289 (Marshall, J., dissenting).

106. *Impact of Dred Scott*, Watson.org, http://www.watson.org/~lisa/black history/scott/impact.html (last updated Oct. 31, 1999).

107. Ibid.; *The Dred Scott Decision*, *History Place*, http://www.historyplace. com/lincoln/dred.htm.

108. *Flood*, 407 U.S. at 275–76.

109. Golenbock, *Spirit of St. Louis*, 508–11.

110. Miller, *Different Ball Game*, 214; Golenbock, *Spirit of St. Louis*, 510–12.

111. Miller, *Different Ball Game,* 215.

112. See *Kansas City Royals Baseball Corp. v. Major League Baseball Players Ass'n,* 532 F.2d 615, 618 (8th Cir. 1976); Miller, *Different Ball Game,* 243. The reason these two players were the ones to make the challenge is detailed in the chapter bearing their name in Miller, 238–53.

113. *Nat'l & Am. League Prof'l Baseball Clubs v. Major League Baseball Players Ass'n,* 66 Lab. Arb. Rep. (BNA) 101, 118 (1976).

114. Miller, *Different Ball Game,* 214.

115. "All Star Game Player Index," *Baseball Almanac.* http://www.baseball-almanac.com/asgbox/asgpl-f.shtml.

116. "Curt Flood – A Hero for the Ages," *Baseball's Black Heritage.* http:// www.baseballsblackheritage.com

117. "All Star Game Player Index," 351; "Curt Flood Statistics and History."

118. Flood, *Way,* 139.

119. *Id.*

120. Golenbock, *Spirit of St. Louis,* 510.

121. Flood, *Way,* 206.

122. Miller, *Different Ball Game,* 267.

123. "Curt Flood Statistics and History,"; Flood's baseball career ended in 1971. He was traded by the Phillies to the Washington Senators in November, 1970 and played 13 games in 1971 for the Senators.

124. Adopted in 1998, "The Curt Flood Act" is set forth in 15 U.S.C. § 27a-c (2000); see *also Brown v. Prof'l Football, Inc.,* 518 U.S. 231, 231 (1996). The Curt Flood Act provides that "the conduct, acts, practices, or agreements of . . . major league baseball . . . are subject to the antitrust laws . . . ." 15 U.S.C. § 27a(a). It gives only major league baseball players standing to sue for a violation of the Act. *Id.* § 27a(c). Under Federal labor law, however, even in an action by a player, antitrust law is inapplicable whenever there exists a collective bargaining agreement relationship between the baseball owners and players. See, *e.g.*, *Brown*, 518 U.S. at 237. As a result, the only time a player could actually sue under the Curt Flood Act would be when a union does not exist as the exclusive bargaining agent for the players, either because the collective bargaining relationship has truly ended or because there is no union. See *id.*

CHAPTER TEN

In the Midst of All Such Excitement
The Nancy Cruzan Case

Edward "Chip" Robertson, Jr.

But, in the midst of all such excitement, it is proper that the judicial mind, calm and self-balanced, should adhere to principles established when there was no feeling to disturb the view of the legal question upon which the rights of parties depend.
Scott v. Emerson, 15 Mo. 576, 589–90 (M0. 1852) (Gamble, J. dissenting)

ON JANUARY 11, 1983, at 12:50 a.m., twenty-five-year-old Nancy Beth Cruzan's 1962 Rambler failed to negotiate a turn on Krummel Nursery Road in Jasper County, south of Carthage, Missouri.[1] The wreck that followed left the car upside down, and Nancy, who was ejected, facedown in a ditch. When Sergeant Dale Penn of the Missouri Highway Patrol arrived, he checked Nancy for a pulse and found none. "She's dead," he announced.[2] But she was not.[3]

The Missouri Supreme Court is used to dealing with death. The state's constitution gives the court original appellate jurisdiction over cases in which the death sentence follows a conviction for first-degree murder. The court regularly considers wrongful death cases and matters involving decedents' estates in probate court. Thus, consideration of death and its legal consequences is a frequent topic of the legal work within the Supreme Court building. But all of the court's familiarity with the subject of death had not prepared its members for Nancy Beth Cruzan's case when it arrived for oral argument on September 29, 1988, more than half a decade after Nancy's accident.

What follows is perhaps best described as an historical reflection on the events and judicial proceedings in the *Cruzan* case. It is a reflection because the author of this chapter was an actor in the courthouse drama and offers insights into the court's functioning, generally, and in the *Cruzan* case, specifically. An effort, however feeble, has been made to remain neutral, but that is certainly not wholly accomplished. The reader will know when recounting gives way to reflection.

NANCY'S CONDITION

After her initial release from the hospital, Nancy had lived first at a private home. When that proved too difficult, she came under the State's care at the Missouri Rehabilitation Center in Mount Vernon, a former tuberculosis hospital. By 1988, Nancy had lapsed into what physicians had come to describe as a persistent vegetative state. She no longer ate orally but was fed through a gastrostomy feeding tube. She hovered somewhere between life and death, her body keeping her alive without the aid of any mechanical devices, but her higher cognitive functions appeared lost.

Her father and mother, as her court-appointed legal guardians, had kept a faithful vigil by her bedside for those many years. They, as well as other family members, would visit several times each week. Finally, the family's hope exhausted, her father asked the staff at the Mount Vernon facility to stop feeding her, to stop providing her with the hydration she would need to survive. The facility required a court order to accommodate the family's wishes. The family turned to William H. Colby, an associate at Shook, Hardy and Bacon of Kansas City, who agreed to handle on a pro bono basis the potentially touchy legal issues surrounding the ending of Nancy Cruzan's life.[4]

Colby, a former law clerk at the U.S. Court of Appeals for the District of Columbia, brought a bright mind and a level of commitment to the Cruzans' case that made him the ideal choice. At the outset, many believed that the case would be almost routine, a matter of a court permitting the family to carry out its wishes for Nancy, whose best interests they were required to pursue as her lawful guardians.

Colby met with Judge Charles Teel, the probate judge who had appointed Nancy's parents as her guardians and with whom Joe Cruzan had discussed the family's wishes informally. Judge Teel had told Mr. Cruzan that he needed to move carefully; taking his daughter home and stopping food and water might be murder under Missouri law.[5] When Colby and the judge met, the judge indicated that a court order would be necessary to allow the guardians to proceed. He laid out the procedural path and told Colby that the State of Missouri and the hospital would need to be defendants in the case.[6] In late October 1987, Colby filed the case in Jasper County Circuit Court. He raised constitutional issues, including the right to privacy, as a basis for the trial court deciding in his clients' favor.

Judge Teel appointed Thad McCanse and David Mouton, both Carthage attorneys, as guardians *ad litem,* to speak as independent voices for Nancy Cruzan in the proceedings. The firm in which they practiced, Flanigan, McCanse and Lasley, traced its roots to 1877 and boasted that one of its prior partners, George Flanigan, had become a judge of the Missouri Court of Appeals, Southern District. McCanse, the senior of the two, was an accomplished trial lawyer, well regarded throughout the state; Mouton, who would, coincidentally, ultimately take Judge Teel's place on the bench, had been a lawyer only slightly more than a year when he accepted the appointment.

Robert Presson, an experienced and well-regarded litigator with the Missouri Attorney General's Office, and Robert Northcutt, the general counsel for the Missouri Department of Health, represented the State of Missouri and the hospital.

The trial that ensued brought the usual parade of competing experts and fact witnesses, all of whom viewed Nancy through the lens of their own understandings of her condition. The trial lasted a week, was closely followed by the national media, including the PBS news program *Frontline,* which had earlier aired a story on Nancy and her family's wishes to terminate the nutrition and hydration given to her,[7] and saw Joe Cruzan interviewed live by Ted Koppel for ABC's *Nightline*[8] program during the trial. The national, public clamor made it plain that this was not the usual case.

Judge Teel issued his judgment on July 27, 1988. He found as facts that Nancy's respiration, blood pressure, and pulse were all within normal ranges for a thirty-year-old woman, despite the fact that none of those functions were artificially maintained.[9] He also found that "her highest cognitive brain function is exhibited by her grimacing perhaps in recognition of ordinarily painful stimuli, indicating the experience of pain and her apparent response to sound"; that "she is a spastic quadriplegic"; and that "she has no cognitive or reflexive ability to swallow food or water to maintain her daily essential needs. That she will never recover her ability to swallow sufficient to satisfy her needs."[10]

These facts supported several conclusions of law from Judge Teel. The first was that clear and convincing evidence is required to permit a guardian to withdraw nutrition and hydration. Judge Teel found that the evidence supporting that conclusion was a conversation Nancy Cruzan had had several years before with a "housemate friend that if sick or injured she would not wish to continue her life unless she could live at least halfway normally. . . ."[11] The judge also found as a matter of law that "the maintenance of nutrition and hydration through a gastrostomy tube was medical treatment because the tube was surgically implanted."[12] Judge Teel further concluded that Nancy's "right to liberty," which permits a person to refuse medical treatment, remained with her, and to the extent that she could not exercise her right, it could be exercised by her guardians. To deny her guardians that right would be to deny Nancy equal protection of the law.[13]

Judge Teel added two rhetorical flourishes to support his points. The first went to Divine Will:

> Nancy's present unresponsive and hopeless existence is not the will of the Supreme Ruler but of man's will to forcefully feed her when she herself cannot swallow thus fueling respiratory and circulatory pumps [her heart and lungs] to no cognitive purpose for her except sound and pain.[14]

Later in his order, the rhetoric grew more choral.

> To decide . . . that medical treatment once undertaken must be continued irrespective of it's [*sic*] lack of success or benefit to the patient in effect gives one's body to medical science without their consent. We could then sing, less fervently of the land of the free, but as medical science advances to new horizons, much more fervently of the land of the brave. If we are the victim we might not be cognizant of our bravery.[15]

The judge's order cited a single case, *Addington v. Texas,*[16] three statutes, and two state and two federal constitutional provisions to support his order, all in four footnotes.

THE NATIONAL LEGAL SCENE

Despite the paucity of legal authority in Judge Teel's order, Nancy Cruzan's case was not the first presenting the difficult issues surrounding profoundly brain-injured persons with no hope of recovery. In 1987, the best-known of these cases was the first that had reached a decision in a state's highest court.

Twenty-one-year-old Karen Ann Quinlan was found unconscious and not breathing after she returned home from a party. Her roommates revived her but too late to avoid anoxia, a condition brought about by the absence of oxygen to vital organs. Severe brain damage occurred; medical experts diagnosed her "as terminally ill and in a persistent vegetative state."[17] She received nutrition through a feeding tube; a respirator assisted her breathing.[18] The medical experts believed that she could not survive without the respirator.[19] The trial court found that there was no reasonable possibility that she would return to a "cognitive or sapient life."[20] Her father became her guardian. He asked the hospital to remove the respirator, an act that would lead to her death, according to the medical experts. When the hospital refused, Karen's father turned to the courts.

The trial court denied her father the authority to order removal of the respirator. Karen's father appealed. The New Jersey Supreme Court concluded that the right to privacy found by the United States Supreme Court lurking in the shadow of the Bill of Rights,[21] included the right to refuse extraordinary medical treatment.[22] The court concluded that Karen had a still-viable right to privacy despite her lack of cognitive function.

Thus, even though she was "grossly incompetent and we cannot discern her supposed choice . . . we have concluded that Karen's right of privacy may be asserted on her behalf by her guardian under the peculiar circumstances here present."[23] The New Jersey court thus permitted Karen's father to authorize the withdrawal of the respirator, provided Karen's physicians, the hospital ethics committee, and the rest of the family agreed.[24] When those constituencies agreed, the hospital removed the respirator. Karen died nine years later of pneumonia.

Quinlan relied on the New Jersey guardianship statute that required a guardian to seek the ward's best interests in caring for the ward's person and property. Thus, the privacy foundation for *Quinlan*'s decision necessarily assumed that a decision by the guardian to remove the respirator was a decision Karen herself would have made had she been able to pursue her own best interests:

> We have no doubt, in these unhappy circumstances, that if Karen were herself miraculously lucid for an interval (not altering the existing prognosis of the condition to which she would soon return) and perceptive of her irreversible condition, she would effectively decide upon discontinuance of the life-support apparatus even if it meant the prospect of natural death.[25]

Another case came to the Massachusetts Supreme Court the following year, in 1977. Joseph Saikewicz, then sixty-seven years old, was a profoundly mentally retarded man and suffered from acute myeloblastic monocytic leukemia. Since Saikewicz could not, and could never have made an informed decision about his health given his mental retardation, the institution in which he lived, the Belchertown State School, sought the appointment of a guardian to make healthcare decisions for him. Given Saikewicz's medical challenges, his court-appointed guardian recommended that he receive no treatment for his leukemia.

The Massachusetts Supreme Court concluded that the exercise of the right of privacy that formed the basis for the decision in *Quinlan,* "may be asserted by that person's guardian."[26] But the decision would be reviewed by a court employing a "substituted judgment" standard. First, the Massachusetts court concluded that only a court could bring to bear the necessary experience and neutrality to make the proper judgment.

> We take a dim view of any attempt to shift the ultimate decision-making responsibility away from the duly established courts of proper jurisdiction. . . . Such questions of life and death seem to us to require the process of detached but passionate investigation and decision that forms the ideal on which the judicial branch of government was created. Achieving this ideal is our responsibility and that of the lower court, and is not to be entrusted to any other group purporting to represent the "morality or conscience of our society," no matter how highly motivated or impressively constituted.[27]

Thus, *Quinlan*'s insistence on agreement among a community of interested groups—family, legal guardian, and the medical community—would not apply in Massachusetts. There, a court would be the sole arbiter and would place itself in the position of the person unable to decide and make the decision from that perspective.

And how would the court decide? The learned justices would become, in Mr. Saikewicz's case, temporarily incompetent, but with the ability to reason competently.

> The decision in cases such as this should be that which would be made by the incompetent person, if that person were competent, but taking into account the present and future incompetency of the individual as one of the factors which would necessarily enter into the decision-making process of the competent person.[28]

The Massachusetts Supreme Judicial Court affirmed the trial court's decision to forgo treatment for Mr. Saikewicz.

In 1985, New Jersey took another turn at the issue. Claire Conroy, an incompetent nursing home patient, faced a decision by her guardian to terminate feeding her through a nasogastric feeding tube. Despite opposition of the guardian *ad litem,* the trial court approved the termination of nutrition. On appeal, the New Jersey Supreme Court reversed the decision, despite Conroy's death during the pendency of the appeal. The court used the case to establish criteria that, if followed, would permit the guardian to make a decision to terminate nutrition and hydration with minimal court involvement. Because that criteria was not met in *Conroy*, the court found that the guardian had acted without the proper authority.[29]

Then, in 1986, the Massachusetts court decided *Brophy v. New England Sinai Hospital, Inc.*[30] Paul Brophy suffered the rupture of an aneurysm located at the apex of the basilar artery. Brophy, a robust man until the moment of the rupture, never regained consciousness and was diagnosed as in a persistent vegetative state. He was unable to chew or swallow and was maintained by a gastrostomy tube. The Massachusetts Supreme Judicial Court affirmed the lower court's decision to permit cessation of feeding and hydration, noting that Massachusetts has shifted "emphasis away from a paternalistic view of what is 'best' for a patient toward a reaffirmation that the basic question is what decision will comport with the will of the person involved, whether that person be competent or incompetent."[31]

In 1981, the New York Court of Appeals advanced a different theoretical approach to refusal-of-treatment decisions. In the *Storar/Eichner cases,*[32] the court found the common-law right to refuse treatment sufficient to warrant termination of treatment (a) where a Catholic theologian on a respirator had, while teaching other Catholics about the *Quinlan* case, spoken concerning his intent should he become disabled (*Eichner*) and (b) rejected the substituted-judgment analysis in matters relating to persons who experienced lifetime incompetency (*Storar*). The court found a discussion of constitutional rights unnecessary to its decisions.

In re Jobes[33] presented facts similar to Nancy Cruzan's case. Nancy Jobes was pregnant and in excellent health. She was in an automobile accident, and afterward, doctors had to operate to remove the child killed in her womb. During surgery, she lost oxygen flow to her brain. Irreversible brain damage followed; she needed assistance breathing and received nourishment through a tube inserted into the jejunum of her small intestine. Her husband sought permission to remove her feeding tube. The court found that Mrs. Jobes's previous statements about refusing life support under conditions like Karen Quinlan's were "remote, general, spontaneous, and made in casual circumstances. Indeed, they closely track the examples of evidence that we have explicitly characterized as unreliable."[34] See *Conroy* . . . 486 A.2d at 1238 (negating probative value of "an offhand remark about not wanting to live under certain circumstances made by a person when young and in the peak of health"). Assuming again that a persistently vegetative patient would choose to have all life support terminated if able, the court determined that Ms. Jobes's family could make the determination to remove her life support. As in a number of previous cases, the court was able to discount entirely the State's interest in the preservation of life, finding it "difficult to conceive of a case in which the State could have an interest strong enough to subordinate a *patient's right to choose* not to be sustained in a persistent vegetative state."[35]

These precedents, which had been followed by a number of other courts, did not find their way into Judge Teel's decision. But there seemed a fairly consistent pattern developing in the various state laws prior to the Cruzans' case making its way to the Missouri Supreme Court.

THE UNHAPPY COURT

The court to which the Cruzan case journeyed was not a happy one—nor was it a very collegial one. Supreme courts are often populated with persons of strong will and large ego. In highest courts in states where the judges are elected, jurists are chosen more for their popularity, capacity to raise money, and a promised issue neutrality, sometimes delivered with a wink to the policy ends of their campaign supporters. By contrast, judges chosen by a merit selection plan can, in moments of weakness, come to believe that they actually deserve their appointments. More, the work of being the final arbiter of a state's laws lends itself to a simmering self-assurance that can, if not checked, boil over into feuding petulance. And no place had that petulance become more prominent than the Missouri Supreme Court in 1987. By then, the court's internal dissensions had emerged in public bickering, tarnishing the court's image and casting doubt on the court's decisions.

Judge Andrew Jackson Higgins had been a trial judge in Platte County before becoming a commissioner for the court. Commissioners, who were phased out under the 1979 amendment to the state constitution's judicial article, were the common laborers for the judges of the court. The commissioners wrote hundreds of opinions, often sat with the judges on the bench, but served at the pleasure of the court, which took credit for their work but denied the commissioners themselves any public acclaim. In 1979, Higgins had finally become a judge of the Missouri Supreme Court at the hand of Governor Joseph Teasdale. Steady and loyal to the court from years of habit, Higgins did not change once he became a full member of the court. He did, however, insist that his name remain on his parking place when security concerns dictated that parking spaces be numbered rather than assigned by name. Higgins enjoyed being a judge, worked hard at it, was a fixture in the Jefferson City Orchestra, and ate lunch daily with a collection of town gadflies at a round table reserved for them at the Governor Hotel. They offered opinions about the failings of state government, the folly of the state's current leadership, and whatever news items occupied the pages of the Jefferson City *News Tribune*. But Higgins returned to work each afternoon, putting in a full day plowing the fields of the law, his furrows straight and the crops harvested exactly on time.

Albert Rendlen made his way to the court from a family law firm in Hannibal. The Rendlen firm enjoyed a sterling reputation in that part of the state. But Rendlen no longer spoke with its members as a result of some grievance that arose when Rendlen left after he secured an appointment to the Missouri Court of Appeals Eastern District. From there, his reputation grew until he made a panel for the Supreme Court and Governor Kit Bond appointed him in 1977. Rendlen had dabbled in Republican politics, rising to the position of state chairman before becoming a judge.

Warren Dee Welliver, a former president of the Missouri Bar, had secured election as a Democratic senator representing Boone County. From that position, and reportedly using his ability to constipate the legislative process as a bargaining tool, he had convinced Governor Teasdale to appoint him to the Supreme Court when the Missouri Appellate Judicial Commission placed his name among the three from whom Teasdale could choose in filling the vacancy created by the retirement of James A. Finch. Welliver kept a baby scorpion encased in Lucite on his desk—a nod to his nickname within the court, the "Scorpion."[36] The judges elected one of their peers on a rotating basis every two years to serve as chief justice, a largely ceremonial role. Welliver had suffered the ignominy of being the only member of the court ever passed over by his colleagues for the position.[37] For Welliver, that wound still festered; his dissents became personal, often hyperbolic, and tended to obscure his first-rate legal mind.[38]

Charles Blakey Blackmar began his legal career in his father's law firm in Kansas City. Possessed of a reputation as a brilliant legal scholar, and several medals for valor during World War II, Blackmar had made public comments regarding the court's decision concerning Kit Bond's legal residency litigation that permitted Bond to run for governor.[39] In the process he had alienated Bob Donnelly, who dissented in the case. The two barely tolerated each other's presence. Perhaps too brilliant for the everyday demands of private law practice, Blackmar had become a tenured professor at the St. Louis University School of Law, had coauthored an acclaimed federal jury instruction treatise, and seemed at ease with every subject in the law. Blackmar wrote his opinions quickly with little need for assistance from his clerks.

William Howard Billings, Jr., first donned the judicial robes as an elected circuit judge in Dunklin County, a seat once held by his father. Indeed, his father had run for a seat on the Missouri Supreme Court in 1938, the chosen candidate of Boss Tom Pendergast. That Democratic primary election, which the senior Billings lost, had taken such a nasty turn that the newspapers and the out-of-power Republicans in the legislature had spearheaded a drive that led to the adoption of the state's nonpartisan plan, by which judges were selected on merit. Bill Billings had driven his father around during the 1938 election and had gone on to become a Marine fighter pilot in the Pacific World War II. After the war he had befriended Warren Hearnes in law school at the University of Missouri, and had helped the Democrat Hearnes get elected governor in 1964, when the Democratic machine had wanted Hilary Bush. Billings had become a judge on the Missouri Court of Appeals Southern District and earned a reputation as a tough-on-crime jurist. Republican Kit Bond appointed him to the state supreme court.

Edward D. Robertson, Jr., came to the court in 1985. Controversy surrounded his appointment because of his age (thirty-three), his lack of judicial experience, and his relationship with Governor John Ashcroft, whom he had served as both deputy attorney general and as chief of staff in the governor's office.

The *St. Louis Post-Dispatch* had questioned the wisdom of the appointment. Thomas Engelhart, the *Post's* editorial cartoonist, informed Robertson that he would not give him the original of the satirical editorial cartoon that appeared at the time because Robertson's appointment was "the worst in the history of the state."[40] Given that several known drunks and future felons had received gubernatorial appointments in the past, the accolade placed Robertson at an inverted pinnacle few could reach.

But in fact, Robertson's appointment was a response to the turmoil on the court. Several members of the Missouri Bar had asked the governor to do something to fix its contentiousness. Governor Ashcroft knew that over the course of the next eight years, mandatory retirements would give him a chance to appoint judges to the court who might serve more collegially. Years later when Robertson was awarded the Statesman of the Year Award by the Jefferson City *New Tribune* as an outstanding public servant to the state (the only supreme court judge to ever receive the award), Ashcroft had generously described Robertson as his best appointment as governor. But whatever judicial reputation Robertson would ultimately develop was both unknown and largely unformed in 1988.

The court's longest-serving member, Robert True Donnelly, had announced in September that he would retire, after twenty-three years on the court, on January 1, 1989. No replacement had been named in the fall of 1988 because the vacancy did not technically yet exist. In order to finish his caseload and vote on the cases he had heard, Donnelly decided he would hear no more cases. His retirement, then, was really a recusal for purposes of the *Cruzan* case. Recusals invoked a procedure the court had long employed in the interests of judicial economy and to avoid delay: the sitting chief justice simply appointed a qualified judge to fill the case-specific, temporary vacancy without consulting the other members of the court. In a given year, this would occur in several cases without comment.[41]

Chief Justice Billings appointed James Reinhard, who had served on the U.S. Court of Appeals, Eastern District, since 1977, to sit on the *Cruzan* case. Reinhard had also served as a judge in the Tenth Circuit (Monroe, Marion, and Ralls Counties). A prolific writer for the Eastern District, Reinhard had a reputation for fairness and integrity. No one had questioned Reinhard's willingness to make independent judgments on appellate cases . . . until Judge Welliver later implied otherwise in this case.

Chief Justice Billings had taken some unusual steps to move the Cruzans' case to the Missouri Supreme Court on an expedited basis. Unbeknownst to the other members of the court, Billings had called Judge Teel. The chief justice asked his former law school classmate whether he could complete his judgment by the end of July.[42] When Teel indicated that he could, Billings also asked Teel to arrange for an immediate appeal of the decision to the supreme court, bypassing the court of appeals. Teel had passed that request along to Thad McCanse, Nancy Cruzan's guardian *ad litem*.

Billings's unusual communications with Teel likely proceeded from a desire for the Missouri Supreme Court to speak authoritatively on issues that suddenly seemed to need clarity under the law because of the pendency of Phillip Rader's case. Billings had long understood that some issues ought not to percolate up through intermediate courts of appeals, with the potential for an inconsistent hodgepodge to infect the law on important issues until the supreme court could speak if the courts of appeals reached different conclusions. The divergence in the legal theories New Jersey and Massachusetts had developed invited such an inconsistency, if not in result at least in the controlling legal prescription. Phillip Rader's case raised that possibility in Missouri.

Rader was a seventeen-year-old who had undergone a third surgery to correct a cleft palate in November 1987. Following the surgery, while apparently recovering, he stopped breathing. Doctors resuscitated him, but his heart stopped a few hours later. Again, medical staff revived him. But a respirator kept him alive, and ultimately, a feeding tube supplied his nutrition and hydration. Doctors abandoned hope of recovery and recommended removal of the respirator. His parents refused. After a year, the doctors sought a court order. The trial court agreed, but gave the Raders time to appeal. The trial court requested that the Missouri Supreme Court take the case on July 18. Billings's call to Teel followed.

It was serendipitous that these two cases could arrive at once, and Billings's request was consistent with the court's sense of its important role in harmonizing and making consistent the laws of Missouri. And given the issues—one set of parents, told their son was dead, did not give up hope and opposed the medical profession's desire to terminate care and another set of parents, told their daughter was alive but would never recover, who sought to bring about her death by withdrawal of nutrition and hydration—the court would have the chance for a full spectrum of arguments and concerns as it announced the law of Missouri.

THE ORAL ARGUMENT

The case came up for oral argument on September 29, 1988. By then, Phillip Rader had died. His case was no longer before the court.

In the usual case, the supreme court's room is a literal echo chamber, with few extra bodies there to prevent the sound from bouncing back and forth between the walls. The portraits of the judges' brooding ancestors do little to soften the sound. The nine gilded frames each surrounded a white male, with a brooding countenance that spoke of the seriousness of all that happened in the room and the popularity of facial hair in years past. On nice days, the janitorial staff cracked the window blinds to permit a wandering judicial mind to contemplate life outside the building when an advocate became convinced that the number of words uttered, rather than their quality, had some influence on the court's decision.

But Nancy Cruzan's case was different in nearly every respect. The gallery chairs filled early that day until there was no longer any room for spectators by the time the marshal gaveled the crowd to silence. The marshal directed the spectators and lawyers to rise, and informed the crowd that it was in the Missouri Supreme Court (as though any had doubts). The judges filed in from the conference room and took their seats, arranged papers and scanned the crowd for familiar faces. The crowd underscored what each judge already knew—that while all cases are important or they would not be at the court, this one might have more than the usual public interest and would speak to the public about the court's processes and role in ways that many cases did not.

Chief Justice Billings called the case. Assistant Attorney General Robert Presson, who lost the case at the trial court, made his way to the podium and began arguing on behalf of the State, which had refused to withdraw food and water from Nancy despite her family's request. He sought a decision of the court that would require the caregivers at the Mount Vernon hospital to continue feeding Nancy. He was followed by Thad McCanse, who informed the court that the guardian *ad litem* recommended that Nancy's parents' wishes to terminate food and nutrition be honored. Bill Colby came next, representing the parents and asserting, at the critical point of the argument, that Nancy's right to liberty continued despite her personal inability to exercise it. In her stead, he argued, the guardian must exercise it for her. Presson returned to make a few points in reply. The argument lasted nearly an hour—so much at stake in so little time.

According to Colby, a question at oral argument by Robertson seemed to have been the critical one. Robertson asked,

> This woman can't make a decision. I want you to give me some legal basis that would allow me to consider the judge's order as being legal. So far, you've said an individual has the right to make a decision about their body. That may or may not be the case, but assuming it is for the moment, how can this person make a decision?[43]

Years later Colby noted that, "Judge Robertson had gone straight to the fundamental issue in our case, and all cases like it: How can a patient in a hospital bed, with no ability to think or speak, exercise rights at all?"[44]

The oral argument for any appellate court draws a line of demarcation between the public and private aspects of the case. Until the argument, matters lie with the lawyers, who provide the court with all manner of written efforts to persuade. But once the argument is completed, the case slides into the monastery, where the judges toil in silence so far as the lawyers and parties are concerned.

But first, the judges gather immediately after the argument to vote tentatively. The vote is tentative because any judge can change his (and now, her) vote. The tentative vote simply permits the court to assign the case to a judge to write an opinion. But there is no assignment by the chief justice. Provided a judge votes in the majority and is next up, that judge gets every seventh opinion.

Prior to the oral argument, Chief Justice Billings had done the math and determined that the case would likely fall to Judge Robertson. So had Judge Robertson. Billings, who occupied the lone judge's office on the second floor of the Supreme Court Building, came up to Robertson's office on the third—a rare face-to-face meeting between judges on matters of business, three weeks before the argument. "Looks like you might draw *Cruzan*," he noted, his voice serious, his face unsmiling. "Think you are ready for it?"

"Guess it depends how the votes go," Robertson replied. "I might vote myself out. But if I get it, of course I'm not ready. Who would be?"

Billings smiled. "You'll do fine." With that, he left.

At the post-argument conference following the Cruzan argument, the discussion was fairly terse and unusually tense. The judges had formed fairly hard opinions and if there was to be any persuasion it would take place after the conference, when the written proposed opinions were circulated.

At the conference, the judges voted in reverse seniority order by tradition. There was some idea that the more senior judges ought not to influence the more junior members or visiting judges. Judge Reinhard voted first, and voted to reverse, without much explanation, beyond expressing grave concern for both the family and for the law. It was clear that he was torn and touched by the family's plight, but had tentatively sided with a strict application of the law. Judge Rendlen voted next and, too, would reverse. He offered no explanation. Judge Higgins voted to affirm, he talked briefly about the standard of review and the deference due the trial court. He also reminded everyone of the importance of the case and the plight of the family. It was a useful, if short, explanation of his vote. Judge Welliver, ever waiting to express himself in writing, voted to affirm without explanation. Judge Robertson, voted to reverse uttering only that single word without looking up. Judge Blackmar, the next in line for chief justice, voted to affirm, expressing his concern for the family and shaking his head as he voted, as though he could not understand any contrary vote. That left the assignment in Chief Justice Billings's hands. If he voted to affirm, Judge Blackmar would get the case. If he voted to reverse, the opinion would fall to Judge Robertson. Billings did not hesitate. "Reverse," he said. And then, "The case is assigned to Judge Robertson."

It is a bit hypocritical for the rules to impose on lawyers severely limited times to file their briefs, while allowing a judge as much time as the judge wants to write the opinion. Whatever time it takes, the opinion, when written, must be circulated to the other judges at least ten days before the court's regular monthly conference, which is usually held on a Thursday. The court hands down its opinions the following Tuesday at 1 p.m. Within this ten-day period the other judges determine whether to join the opinion, seek amendments to the proposed draft, or dissent, either in writing or simply by noting that disagreement in the final vote.

In the interim, Bob Presson sent a letter informing the court that New York's highest court had decided the case of Mary O'Connor on October 14, 1988. That court had reversed a trial court's decision denying a hospital's request to insert a G-tube into a mentally incompetent patient to sustain her life because there was no clear and convincing evidence of Mary's commitment to decline assistance under her circumstances.[45] The *O'Connor* case seemed consistent with the tentative vote in *Cruzan*.

Robertson circulated an opinion just after Thanksgiving, giving the other judges a few extra days to consider their vote before the December 8 conference. Almost immediately, word came to Judge Robertson's office that Judge Blackmar would dissent. Judge Higgins also had begun working on a dissenting opinion. The chief justice and Judge Rendlen sent notes expressing their concurrence. The court waited on Judge Reinhard and Judge Welliver, both of whom remained silent, waiting for the separate opinion cutoff on the Monday before conference to let the other judges know their positions officially. Judge Reinhard indicated he would wait to read the dissenting opinions to decide. Everyone knew that Judge Welliver was sharpening his knife.

The opinion Judge Robertson circulated concluded that Nancy Cruzan's right to decide her medical fate was hers. It could not be exercised by someone else absent strict formalities. He wrote:

> This is not a case in which we are asked to let someone die. Nancy is not dead. Nor is she terminally ill. This is a case in which we are asked to allow the medical profession to make Nancy die by starvation and dehydration. The debate here is thus not between life and death; it is between quality of life and death. We are asked to hold that the cost of maintaining Nancy's present life is too great when weighed against the benefit that life conveys both to Nancy and her loved ones and that she must die.[46]

He noted that the majority of the other state courts that had decided the issue had decided to permit the guardians' wishes to remove a respirator or cease the provision of nutrition and hydration. Indeed, the debate among the circulating opinions in the court was a debate between two constructions of the law: one that adhered to traditional interpretation of the best interests standard, and one that believed that the law should be adjusted to reach an end that most agreed was the more compassionate one, and certainly the more popular one, given the other court decisions and the popular press.

In some ways, the *Cruzan* case asked the Missouri Supreme Court to answer a perplexing question it had previously confronted—one that history judged it got wrong in 1852. The question centered on the rights that attach to a person—indeed, whether that person was a person at all, subject to the control of another, or possessed of rights exercisable without any reference to wishes of others.

The court's first effort at answering that question in a much different context contributed to a Civil War. In *Scott v. Emerson,* the issue was whether Dred Scott, a slave who had left proslavery Missouri, and been taken by his master to the free state of Illinois, became a slave again when he returned to Missouri. Scott's status depended on the acts and intent of his master. The court had concluded:

> In all ages, and in all countries in which slavery has existed, the slave has been regarded not merely as property, but also as a being capable of acquiring and holding certain rights, *by the act of the master.* He could acquire and enforce his right to freedom in modes recognized by the law of the country in which he dwelt.[47]

But Judge Gamble dissented, suggesting that well-settled principles of law ought to control, rather than the political or emotional preferences of the individual judge or the political storms in which the country found itself.

> There is with me, nothing in the law relating to slavery, which distinguishes it from the law on any other subject, or allows any more accommodation to the temporary public excitements which are gathered around it. . . .
>
> But, in the midst of all such excitement, it is proper that the judicial mind, calm and self-balanced, should adhere to principles established when there was no feeling to disturb the view of the legal question upon which the rights of parties depend.[48]

At bottom, Judge Robertson's opinion agreed that Nancy had rights, but that they were hers and hers alone. The law had developed historically to protect persons who were helpless, not to serve as a tool to permit others to terminate their lives. Those protections could be removed only through the exercise of personal rights by the person whose protection the law was intended to guarantee. Thus, unless Nancy had expressed how she would exercise those rights under this circumstance prior to her arrival at this horrific state, the law should not assume that those who bore the burden of caring for her could speak for her to terminate her protection.

Votes on opinions are cast orally at the court's monthly conference. It is the first order of business and is usually perfunctory, the judges letting their written efforts speak for themselves.

It was particularly unusual with the 1988 court for there to be much discussion during the vote, as the judges' minds had been occupied with the consideration of circulating drafts, their own independent research and whatever muses whispered to them as they determined how to vote. And besides, the tension between the members of the court had made conversation between them unusual on a number of fronts.

The December 1988 conference proved different. At nine a.m. the judges gathered in the Division Two courtroom. The janitors had arranged the several tables together in a "T" with the long part running east-west so that three judges could sit on each side with plenty of room for files and papers, with the chief sitting at the head. The judges sat in the same spot for two years, and even then only the next chief and the outgoing chief changed places. As the most recent former chief justice in the every-two-year rotation, Judge Higgins voted first. There were several other cases on which opinions were ready, and a few of those were called first, with the voting proceeding as normal. Each judge would vote with a stock phrase, either "concur," "concur in separate opinion filed," "dissent," or "dissent in separate opinion filed." And if the voting judge agreed with a separate opinion authored by another judge, the vote would be "concur in separate concurring (or dissenting) opinion of (name), J." This odd way of speaking reflected what would be communicated in writing at the end of each opinion as published, down to the addition of the "J."

Chief Justice Billings called the *Cruzan* case. He announced that Judge Reinhard had concurred in the proposed majority opinion in a letter he sent Billings. The traditional oral voting would follow, but with the news of Reinhard's vote, all the judges knew the vote would be 4–3 favoring Robertson's opinion.

"Judge Higgins?" the chief justice inquired. Judge Higgins said, "Dissent in separate opinion filed." Then, unusually, he pushed his chair back and turned to his left directly to face Judge Robertson, from whom he was separated on the same side of the long conference table by Judge Rendlen. "Chip," he said, his voice angry, "your opinion ignores the standard of review and the evidence in the case. We don't treat trial court judgments this way. You're just wrong."

Robertson interrupted him, his own voice rising to join the confrontation. "Jack, I kept the legal file in my office near the door and waited for your office to send for it. How do you know what the evidence at the hearing was? You never came and got the transcript or the rest of the file."

The chief pointed at Judge Higgins. "Gut shot, Andy," he said. "You've been gut shot."[49] Judge Higgins said nothing.

This testy exchange, which ended nearly as quickly as it began, served to terminate further discussion during the voting. But the judges' strong views and personal discord had found their way into the written opinions.

Judge Higgins, a normally gentlemanly dissenter, described the proposed majority opinion as "an inexcusable exercise for this Court."[50] He continued in this vein, accusing the majority of having an agenda:

> Should not a reader ask the majority why it projects the irony of recognizing yet rejecting this abundance of dispositive case law in favor of its non-supported assertion of "erroneous declaration of law?" Is it because of its "public policy" bootstrapped from a statute that

> all parties in this case, the trial judge and the majority agree has no application in this case; or is it because the majority would have this Court abdicate its responsibilities to Nancy Cruzan under the Constitution and the common law and deny her rights in deference to some yet unspecified and unconsidered legislation; or is it because of the majority's unarticulated "concerns of medicine, ethics, morality, philosophy, theology and law"; or is it simply because the majority elects to ignore the facts and law of this case and "choose(s) to err" on the side of life of incompetent persons who may wish to live, a case not before the Court at this time?[51]

The Robertson opinion for the court took the bait and was less than charitable in its response to Judge Higgins and those who joined him. After citing the more than fifty cases that had "[n]early unanimously . . . found a way to allow persons wishing to die, or those who seek the death of a ward, to meet the end sought,"[52] Judge Robertson had added a footnote accusing the dissenters of adopting a "me too" jurisprudence "without burdening themselves with any analysis of the legal reasoning upon which *Quinlan* and cases following it rely." Then, the opinion implied that the dissenters had eaten of "'the insane root which takes the reason prisoner.'"[53]

Judge Blackmar's tone, while more collegial, seemed to reflect the pain of his experience associated with his first wife's death. His theme was that the family ought to decide without the state's interference and if the matter came to a court, the court's job was simply to ratify the family's choices.

> Nor would I accept the thought that decisions of relatives as guardians about life sustaining measures necessarily require judicial confirmation. I agree with those courts which hold that relatives may ordinarily make important decisions of this kind without going to court, unless there is a challenge."[54]

And later, "I believe that decisions about Nancy's future should be made by those near and dear to her, and that no state policy requires the state to intervene in these decisions."[55]

Blackmar's disagreement with the result identified the fundamental divide between the views expressed in the majority opinion and the dissenters, essentially the same controversy that had divided the court in the Dred Scott case so many years before—the difference between judges who would focus on the more popular outcome, this time clothed not in political expediency but in a horrific human tragedy, and those who attempt to establish rules that would have a more general application:

> Many other judges have struggled with problems similar to the ones before us. Their opinions demonstrate this struggle. It is often difficult to find the proper words to express a conclusion, and it is easy to criticize the struggles of others. Our task, however, is to decide cases. . . . The principal opinion attempts to establish absolutes, but does so at the expense of human factors. In so doing it unnecessarily subjects Nancy and those close to her to continuous torture which no family should be forced to endure. I am grasping for words which elude me, and so will not say more.[56]

Judge Welliver's dissent first attacked the constitutionality of the Living Will Statute and the majority opinion's reference to it.

> The opinion unnecessarily and by dictum seeks to place a mantle of constitutionality on the Missouri Living Will Statute, which statute in my opinion has been a fraud on the people of Missouri from the beginning and which statute, if directly attacked, must, in my opinion, be held to be unconstitutional.[57]

The rhetoric was strong, but not unusual for Judge Welliver in his later years on the court. That all agreed that the constitutionality of the Living Will Statute was not at issue at all made no difference.

Then Judge Welliver unsheathed his knife. He turned his attention to Judge Reinhard's role in the case. Judge Reinhard was sitting because Judge Donnelly's resignation had created a vacancy on the court. At the time of the oral argument in September, the Appellate Judicial Commission had not met to name a panel from which the governor could select a new judge. By the time the court handed down the decision, the governor had a panel before him but had not yet named a judge.[58]

Judge Welliver's dissent also attempted to lay the groundwork for a motion for rehearing: "It has always been my belief that as a matter of court policy cases of great magnitude, cases that directly affect all of the people of the State, should never be heard or decided by other than the duly appointed regular members of the Supreme Court."[59] Judge Welliver went so far as to suggest that prior to the hearing he had raised concerns about the special judge casting the deciding vote. Because that had come to pass, "[i]t is deeply regrettable to me that an issue of this magnitude and importance to every citizen of the State is decided by the single vote of any special judge while the *sitting* members of the regular Court are evenly divided on this issue."[60]

This latter argument was unusual given the court's consistent practice of making sure that an odd number of judges hear a case so that the case could be decided on a single argument. This long-standing policy served in the usual case to relieve the parties of the delay and expense of a second argument in the event that the sitting members of the court were evenly divided on the outcome. Judge Welliver cited examples of affirmance by the Supreme Court of the United States when the justices were evenly divided. But no one can replace a sitting justice of the United States Supreme Court. The Missouri Supreme Court's judges can be replaced upon recusal or when a vacancy exists on the court. The court's policy made individual judges irrelevant to the progress of the law and assumed, as the judicial system must, that a judge is a judge is a judge. Perhaps this is a naïve view, but the system, and the public's perception of it, simply cannot operate on a different assumption.

Judge Welliver's argument was unusual for another reason. Judge Donnelly was technically a sitting member of the court during the time the case was argued and decided. Though he had announced his intentions months earlier, he did not officially retire until January 1, 1989. Thus, there was no vacancy on the court; Donnelly had simply recused. The court had followed its usual practice in handling recusals with the appointment of Judge Reinhard. Judge Welliver's assertion that there was a vacancy on the court was incorrect, though his point that the court could have waited to hear the case in January 1989 rather than hearing it in September 1988, was accurate.

Perhaps Judge Welliver's legislative experience colored his views. Changes in the general assembly often alter outcomes, such as when one party replaces another. But if one looks at the votes based on the former political affiliations of the sitting judges, it is clear that partisan considerations did not play a role in the outcome of the Cruzan case. Two former Democrats (Higgins and Welliver) voted to affirm. One former Democrat (Billings) voted to reverse. Two former Republicans voted to reverse (Rendlen and Robertson) and one voted to affirm (Blackmar). Judge Reinhard was a former Democrat. John Ashcroft, a Republican, would appoint Judge Donnelly's replacement. If Judge Welliver had played the odds, he should have liked them better with Judge Reinhard, a former Democrat.

But more curious was Judge Welliver's concern with Judge Reinhard. The panel to replace Judge Donnelly under consideration by Governor Ashcroft included Ann K. Covington, of the Missouri Court of Appeals Western District; David Steelman, a private practitioner who had served as a Republican member of the general assembly and yes, James Reinhard, the very same judge who sat on the case. Governor Ashcroft did not appoint Ann Covington until December 20, 1988. At the time Judge Welliver filed his dissent, Judge Reinhard was a genuine if unlikely possibility to become a sitting member of the Supreme Court. Judge Welliver had no way of knowing who would be appointed; he risked greatly offending a potential colleague with his dissent—a risk he undoubtedly discounted to zero given his current colleagues' decision to by-pass him for chief justice.

Whatever his intent, Judge Welliver's dissent raised an issue the Cruzans seized upon in their motion for rehearing. While these motions were the usual practice in most cases, raising the issue Judge Welliver had mentioned was very unusual. In addition to the usual arguments on rehearing that the Court had overlooked facts or misinterpreted law in its opinion, the Cruzans asserted that the court should not have permitted Judge Reinhard to hear the case. And now that Judge Covington had received the appointment, they wanted her to sit on the court that decided their case.

The court denied the Cruzans' motion for rehearing, but Judge Welliver decided to double down on his argument. He took the highly unusual step of filing a dissent to the denial of the motion for rehearing. In it, he cited two authorities for his view that the case should be reheard. The first was the court's own rule 84.15, which suggested that the court ought to hear the case first and appoint a special judge to hear it only if necessary to break the tie. As noted, the court had long since truncated that process in the interest of judicial economy and to avoid unnecessary delay by filling recusals on the first hearing. But more important, the rehearing would have taken place well before December—the tie would have been known on September 29, 1988. Given the court's previous expedited review of the case, the court would likely have rescheduled the argument almost immediately given the circumstances and the court's decision to expedite. Judge Reinhard would have sat anyway.

Second, Welliver cited a statute directing the court how to handle vacancies. Section 477.020, RSMo, was first passed in 1939 and last amended in 1973. The statute permitted counsel for the parties to agree on a replacement judge when the court reached a tie vote and only if counsel could not agree would the court appoint the special judge. Reliance on this statute was likewise remarkable. In 1976, the voters had adopted a wholesale revision of the judicial article of the Missouri constitution. Effective January 1, 1979, the supreme court acquired constitutional authority to adopt procedural rules; those rules superseded previous statutory procedural rules and could be amended by the legislature only by the passage of a bill that expressly referenced the Supreme Court rule it intended to amend and addressed no other subject. The court's rule and the statute were at loggerheads. Indeed, the court had jealously guarded its authority under the new constitutional provision. Yet Welliver, adept at making mischief by now, would sacrifice the court's constitutional prerogatives to make his point.

In Welliver's defense, the rule itself required two steps—a hearing with a tie vote then a rehearing. But the court had, as previously discussed, adopted a settled process by naming a substitute judge for the first hearing. No one had complained until now, including Welliver.

Judge Higgins also filed an opinion dissenting from the court's decision not to rehear the case. This time he read the transcript and picked snippets from the facts that supported his view that the court had, to use the court's internal code, "put short pants" on the trial court's fact-finding. Indeed, it was Judge Higgins oft-repeated mantra that a written dissent is permanent proof of an inability to persuade. In any event, Judge Higgins new effort swayed no one and the vote for rehearing matched the vote on the majority opinion.

That both Judges Higgins and Welliver demanded that their dissents on rehearing be published further revealed the intensity of the rift between the sides on this case. That rift was made more publicly apparent when, at the Jefferson City Country Club Christmas Party in 1988, Judge Higgins walked by the table at which Judge Robertson was seated with nine others in a crowded dining room and very publicly raised the middle finger of his left hand to Judge Robertson and shook it. As one of Robertson's tablemates commented, "That must be a fun place to work."

BUT THERE WAS MORE

Even the most vociferous disagreements become muted over time in a court with an important caseload. The usual alliances fell apart for the court in *Cruzan*. Judges Blackmar, Higgins, and Welliver seldom saw eye-to-eye on cases, but they had formed an alliance founded on common views that seemed to begin a healing in the court. The possibilities of new alliances on subsequent cases and the addition of Judge Ann Covington to the court seemed to improve the working relationships among the judges. With Judge Donnelly's departure, Judge Welliver was more isolated than ever, as only Judge Donnelly had joined Judge Welliver in voting to give Welliver the Chief Justiceship. Indeed, Judge Welliver would soon determine that he had had enough. He resigned less than nine months later.

Surprisingly, the United States Supreme Court granted certiorari in *Cruzan* on July 3, 1989.[61] And, nearly a year to the day after the Missouri Supreme Court had issued its opinion, the nine justices heard oral argument in the case.

The U.S. Supreme Court affirmed—holding that the clear and convincing evidence standard adopted by the Missouri Supreme Court complied with constitutional standards: "We believe Missouri may legitimately seek to safeguard the personal element of this choice through the imposition of heightened evidentiary requirements . . . [because] [n]ot all incompetent patients will have loved ones available to serve as surrogate decision-makers."[62] Moreover, "we do not think the Due Process Clause requires the State to repose judgment on these matters with anyone but the patient herself."[63] The law cannot assume that there is an "automatic assurance that the view of close family members will necessarily be the same as the patient's would have been had she been confronted with the prospect of her situation while competent."[64]

Four justices dissented, with Justice Stevens writing praise of Judge Blackmar's dissent, which he called "persuasive."[65] It was not, however, persuasive to a majority of the justices. Nancy Cruzan's case would make its way back to the Jasper County Probate Court.

REMAND TO STATE COURT

Despite his initial dejection at the court's decision, Bill Colby seized on a single phrase in Chief Justice Rehnquist's majority opinion.[66] The chief justice had written that the preservation of the status quo resulting from Missouri's clear and convincing standard allowed the possibility of "discovery of new evidence regarding the patient's intent."[67]

Colby had received a letter from a former employer of Nancy's who recalled a conversation he and Nancy had had about the Karen Quinlan case. And another witness came forward to describe Nancy's reaction to feeding a person Nancy described as a "vegetable."[68] At that time Nancy had indicated that she would not want to live like that.[69] Attorney General William Webster withdrew the State from the case. Thus, when Colby returned the case to Judge Teel's courtroom, the judge heard the evidence, found it met the clear and convincing standard, and ordered the hospital to withdraw nutrition and hydration. No one appealed.

Doctors removed the G-tube on December 14. On December 26, 1990, shortly after midnight, Nancy died.

FINAL COMMENTS

Cases like *Cruzan* are rare, and thankfully so. In response to the decisions in this case, former Missouri Attorney General and then-United States Senator John Danforth, among others, introduced the Patient Self-Determination Act which, when passed in 1990, required providers to inform all adult patients about their rights to accept or refuse medical or surgical treatment and the right to execute an "advance directive"—a written instruction relating to the provision of health care when the individual is incapacitated.[70] Yet, as the Terry Schiavo case in 2005 revealed, legislation cannot predict all events and in the event of legislation's inability to cover all possible eventualities, courts are often thrust into the middle of these difficult issues. Justice Scalia's concurring opinion in *Cruzan* spoke with unusual candor about the judiciary's ability to reach the right decision in these cases:

> the point at which life becomes "worthless," and the point at which the means necessary to preserve it become "extraordinary" or "inappropriate," are neither set forth in the Constitution nor known to the nine Justices of this Court any better than they are known to nine people picked at random from the Kansas City telephone directory.[71]

After the Missouri Supreme Court decision and before the United States Supreme Court issued its decision, Judge Robertson was asked to give a speech at the University of Missouri-Kansas City concerning right-to-die issues generally. When he arrived at the speech venue, he found himself surrounded by Kansas City policemen, who informed him that someone had called and threatened to assassinate Robertson during the speech that night.

The hall was crowded with several hundred people, including two or three national news reporters. After he was introduced, Robertson informed the crowd of the threat and moved out from behind the podium to expose himself fully to the crowd. "I am going to stand here as still as I can for the next little bit," he said. "If someone is going to shoot me, I want him to have a good, clean shot. I don't want to end up like Nancy Cruzan." When no one took a shot, he returned to the podium and finished his remarks. Few lost the point: no one wants to find themselves or a loved one hovering between life and death, where hope and hopelessness daily cross paths and medicine has given up.

For reasons unknown, but which only compounded the tragedy, Joe Cruzan hanged himself on August 17, 1996.[72] The final line of his suicide note read, "I love Nancy and am sorry about what happened."[73]

And last, and perhaps most telling of all, Judge Bill Billings grew gravely ill before his planned-for retirement from the court. As Billings neared the end of his final illness, Judge Robertson visited him at his home in Jefferson City. Billings sat wheelchair-bound, weak and having difficulty speaking. Still, he and Robertson managed to spend some time reminiscing about their time together on the court. As Robertson said his final good-bye, Billings said. "You know, Chip, I'm not sure we got that *Cruzan* case right."

"Judge," Robertson replied, "all we could do was what we thought was right."

Billings nodded. "I guess it worked out in the end."

Robertson patted his shoulder and left. Billings died two days later.

Justice Scalia surely had it right. On matters like this, judges who are sure they got it right either misunderstand the issues or have lost sight of the limitations imposed by the human condition.

NOTES

1. *Cruzan by Cruzan v. Harmon,* Judgment Circuit Court of Jasper County, July 27, 1988.
2. William H. Colby, *Long Goodbye: The Deaths of Nancy Cruzan* (Carlsbad, CA: Hay House, 2002), 9.
3. Paramedics arrived and by 1:12 a.m., they had restored respiration and heart function.
4. Colby, *Long Goodbye,* 55.
5. Ibid., 61.
6. Ibid., 64.
7. "Let My Daughter Die," *Frontline,* episode 1988-6, aired on PBS, March 1, 1988.
8. Ted Koppel, *Nightline,* aired on ABC, March 10, 1988.
9. *Cruzan by Cruzan v. Harmon,* 4.
10. Ibid.
11. Ibid., 6.
12. Ibid.
13. Ibid., 7.
14. Ibid.
15. Ibid.
16. *Addington v. Texas,* 441 U.S. 418 (1979). *Addington* interpreted the due process clause to require clear and convincing evidence to support involuntary mental health commitments, a subject with which a probate judge would be familiar.
17. *Matter of Quinlan,* 137 N.J. Super. 227, 246, 348 A.2d 801, 812 (Ch. Div. 1975).
18. Ibid.
19. Ibid., 655.
20. Ibid., 663.
21. *Griswold v. Connecticut,* 381 U.S. 479 (1965).
22. *Matter of Quinlan,* 70 N.J. 10, 40, 355 A.2d 647, 663 (1976)
23. Ibid., 664.
24. Ibid., 672.

25. Ibid., 663–64

26. *Superintendent of Belchertown State Sch. v. Saikewicz*, 373 Mass. 728, 739-40, 370 N.E.2d 417, 424 (1977)

27. Ibid., 434–35.

28. Ibid., 431.

29. *Matter of Conroy*, 486 A.2d 1209 (1985)

30. *Brophy v. New England Sinai Hosp., Inc.*, 497 N.E.2d 626, 627 (1986)

31. Ibid., 633.

32. *In the Matter of John Storar et al v. Dillon,* 52 N.Y.2d 363, 420 N.E.2d 64, 438 N.Y.S.2d 266 (1981)

33. *In the Matter of Jobes,* 108 N.J. 394, 529 A.2d 434 (1987),

34. Ibid., 443.

35. Ibid., 444, *quoting In re Peter,* 108 N.J. 365, 529 A.2d 419, 427 (1987) (emphasis added).

36. The fable goes something like this: A scorpion seeks passage across a river from a turtle. The turtle, upon hearing the scorpion's request, refused, informing the scorpion, "I will not let you ride on my back, you will just sting me." To which the scorpion replied, "If I sting you, we will both drown." The turtle relented, reasoning that the scorpion's own best interests would prevent the scorpion from stinging him. The scorpion climbed on the turtle's back, edged his way toward the turtle's exposed neck and settled in for the ride across the river. Halfway across, as the turtle swam, the scorpion stung the turtle. The turtle began to sink, unable to swim. Bewildered, the turtle asked, "Why did you sting me? Now we will both die." The scorpion replied, "It's just my nature."

37. Allison Retka, "Ex-Missouri Supreme Court Judge Warren Welliver dies at 87." *St. Louis Daily Record*, November 1, 2007.

38. See, for example, *Associated Indus. of Missouri v. State Tax Comm'n of Missouri*, 722 S.W.2d 916, 926 (Mo. 1987) (Welliver, J. dissenting) and *Lippard v. Houdaille Indus., Inc.,* 715 S.W.2d 491, 504 (Mo. 1986) (Welliver, J., dissenting).

39. *State ex rel. King v. Walsh*, 484 S.W.2d 641, 642 (Mo. 1972)

40. Telephone call between author and Thomas Engelhardt, June 28, 1985, in which Engelhardt refused to give the author the original artwork, despite his usual practice in doing so if requested.

41. For instance, *State ex rel. King v. Walsh*, 484 S.W.2d 641, 642 (Mo. 1972), the Bond residency case, Judge J. P. Morgan had not participated, though he had been a member of the court since 1969. Judge Jensen sat in his place.

42. Colby, *Long Goodbye,* 236.

43. *Cruzan by Cruzan v. Harmon,* Audio Recording (available at the Missouri State Archives).

44. Colby, *Long Goodbye,* 251.

45. *Matter of Westchester Cnty. Med. Ctr. on Behalf of O'Connor*, 72 N.Y.2d 517, 531 N.E.2d 607 (1988)

46. *Cruzan by Cruzan v. Harmon*, 706 S.W.2d 408, 412 (Mo. 1988)

47. *Scott v. Emerson*, 15 Mo. 576, 587 (1852)(emphasis added).

48. Ibid., 589–90 (Gamble, J., dissenting)

49. The judges variously called Andrew Jackson Higgins either "Jack" or "Andy."

50. *Cruzan by Cruzan v. Harmon,* 760 S.W.2d at 435 (Higgins, J., dissenting).

51. Ibid., 440–41 (Higgins, J., dissenting) (footnotes omitted).

52. Ibid., 413.

53. Ibid.

54. 760 S.W.2d at 428 (Blackmar, J., dissenting).

55. Ibid.

56. Ibid., 430 (Blackmar, J., dissenting).

57. Ibid., 441 (Welliver, J., dissenting).

58. Governor John Ashcroft ultimately chose Ann K. Covington to replace Judge Donnelly's replacement. Covington became the first woman to serve on both the court of appeals and the supreme court.

59. Ibid., 442 (Welliver, J., dissenting).

60. Ibid.

61. *Cruzan by Cruzan v. Dir., Missouri Dep't of Health*, 492 U.S. 917 (1989)

62. Ibid., 281, 110 S. Ct. 2841, 2852–53, 111 L. Ed. 2d 224 (1990).

63. Ibid.

64. Ibid.

65. Ibid., 336 (Stevens, J., dissenting).

66. Colby, *Long Goodbye,* 322.

67. Ibid., 283.

68. Ibid., 345.

69. Ibid.

70. Public Law No. 101-508 (November 5, 1990).

71. *Cruzan by Cruzan v. Dir., Missouri Dep't of Health*, 492 U.S. 917 at 293 (Scalia, J, concurring).

72. Colby, *Long Goodbye,* 393.

73. Ibid.

Contributors

Douglas E. Abrams, Associate Professor of Law at the University of Missouri–Columbia, serves on the Advisory Boards of the Missouri Division of Youth Services and the University of Missouri Children's Hospital, and on the Board of Directors of the Missouri Juvenile Justice Association. Among his publications is *A Very Special Place in Life: The History of Juvenile Justice in Missouri.* He is a past recipient of the Meritorious Service to the Children of America Award, presented by the National Council of Juvenile and Family Court Judges. The U.S. Supreme Court has cited his law review articles in four opinions.

Dennis W. Belcher has written or edited four books on the Civil War: *The 10th Kentucky Volunteer Infantry in the Civil War, The 11th Missouri Volunteer Infantry in the Civil War, This Terrible Struggle for Life: The Civil War Letters of a Union Regimental Surgeon,* and *General David S. Stanley, USA: A Civil War Biography.*

James R. Devine was Associate Dean for Academic Affairs and David Ross Hardy Professor of Law and Trial Practice at the University of Missouri–Columbia School of Law at the time of his passing on May 12, 2010. An avid fan of professional baseball, including the Brooklyn Dodgers, the New York Mets, and the St. Louis Cardinals, he wrote many scholarly articles about the sport.

Paul Finkelman is the Ariel F. Sallows Visiting Professor of Human Rights Law at the University of Saskatchewan College of Law and a Senior Fellow at the Program on Democracy, Citizenship, and Constitutionalism at the University of Pennsylvania. He is the author or editor of more than 40 books and more than 200 scholarly articles. In 2014 he was ranked as the fifth most cited legal historian among law professors. The U.S. Supreme Court has cited his scholarship in four opinions.

William E. Foley is Professor Emeritus of History at the University of Central Missouri. He served as General Editor of the Missouri Biography Series and has written or edited numerous books, including *Wilderness Journey: The Life of William Clark* and *The Genesis of Missouri: From Frontier Outpost to Statehood.*

Edward "Chip" Robertson, Jr., served as a Justice of the Missouri Supreme Court from 1985 to 1998, serving as Chief Justice from 1991 to 1993. He authored approximately 200 majority opinions during his service, including the one for *Cruzan by Cruzan v. Harmon.* He is also a former special consultant to the U.S. Attorney General. He is currently a partner at Bartimus, Frickelton, Robertson & Goza.

Bonnie Stepenoff, Professor Emerita of History at Southeast Missouri State University, has authored five books, including *Working the Mississippi: Two Centuries of Life on the River* and *Thad Snow: A Life of Social Reform in the Missouri Bootheel.*

Karen Anderson Winn is a member of the Missouri Administrative Hearing Commission, a tribunal that decides disputes between citizens and state agencies. She served in various positions as an attorney for the state, including as General Counsel for the Office of Administration and General Counsel for the Department of Economic Development. Prior to that, she was in private practice. She received her J.D. and an M.A. in history from Washington University in St. Louis.

Kenneth H. Winn served as the State Archivist of Missouri and as the Director of the Library and Public Services for the Missouri Supreme Court. As State Archivist he directed a statewide project initiative that made millions of pages of Missouri legal records publically accessible for the first time. He is the author or editor of a number of books and articles on political and cultural history and has taught history at Washington University in St. Louis and the University of Missouri–Columbia.

Index